Microsoft® Windows® 8

Step by Step

Ciprian Adrian Rusen
Joli Ballew

Published with the authorization of Microsoft Corporation by:
O'Reilly Media, Inc.
1005 Gravenstein Highway North
Sebastopol, California 95472

ISBN: 978-0-7356-6402-9

3 4 5 6 7 8 9 10 11   QG   7 6 5 4 3 2

Printed and bound in the United States of America.

Microsoft Press books are available through booksellers and distributors worldwide. If you need support related to this book, email Microsoft Press Book Support at *mspinput@microsoft.com*. Please tell us what you think of this book at *http://www.microsoft.com/learning/booksurvey*.

Microsoft and the trademarks listed at *http://www.microsoft.com/about/legal/en/us/IntellectualProperty/ Trademarks/EN-US.aspx* are trademarks of the Microsoft group of companies. All other marks are property of their respective owners.

The example companies, organizations, products, domain names, email addresses, logos, people, places, and events depicted herein are fictitious. No association with any real company, organization, product, domain name, email address, logo, person, place, or event is intended or should be inferred.

Acquisitions and Developmental Editor: Kenyon Brown
Production Editor: Melanie Yarbrough
Editorial Production: nSight, Inc.
Technical Reviewer: Todd Meister
Cover Composition: Girvin
Illustrator: Rebecca Demarest

[2012-12-21]

Contents

1   Introducing Windows 8   1

2   Making Windows Look and Sound the Way You Want   47

3   Using Apps on the Start Screen   75

4 Saving, Browsing, and Organizing Files and Folders 107

5 Using Internet Explorer 10 153

6   Using SkyDrive   179

7   Using the Social Apps   197

8   Shopping in the Windows Store   233

9 Having Fun with Multimedia   249

10 Playing Games   267

11 Connecting to a Network and the Internet   279

12   Allowing Others to Use the Computer   305

13   Sharing Files and Folders with My Network   351

14 Keeping Windows 8 Safe and Secure 391

15 Preventing Problems 425

Introducing Windows 8

Windows 8 is the latest operating system from Microsoft, launched three years after the successful Windows 7. Unlike recent versions, Windows 8 brings many important changes to the world of Windows operating systems.

If Windows 7 was made to run on more traditional computers such as laptops, desktops, or netbooks, Windows 8 was made to run on a wider variety of devices. It can also be used successfully on tablets, computers with touch screens, and hybrids that combine the versatility of a laptop with the mobility of a tablet.

If Windows 7 was an incremental update to Windows Vista, Windows 8 is a re-imagination of the Windows experience. It brings to the table many new features and improvements and, most of all, a new user interface inspired by the work Microsoft did on the Windows Phone platform. The new interface is designed with touch-compatible devices in mind, but it also runs perfectly on computers with traditional mouse and keyboard input.

Windows 8 also adds support for ARM processors, used in today's smartphones and tablets. It is the first time Windows can be used on processors other than those made by Intel or AMD (x86 architecture).

If you have read about Windows 8 or you have seen it in action, you know that there are many new things to learn, even if you are familiar with Windows 7. In this book, you'll learn not only which are the most important changes Windows 8 introduces but also how to use the most important tools and features so that you are productive and feel at ease as soon as possible.

Windows 8 Features by Edition

There are three main editions of Windows 8: Windows 8, Windows 8 Pro, and Windows RT. Consumers can purchase the first two from stores selling Windows 8. Windows RT is available only pre-installed on PCs and tablets powered by ARM processors such as those used in today's smartphones and tablets; as a consumer, you can't purchase Windows RT separately and install it on your own computer or device. A Windows 8 Enterprise edition is available only to large businesses.

Windows 8, Windows 8 Pro, and Windows 8 Enterprise are available in both 32-bit and 64-bit editions.

The key features of each edition of Windows 8 are included in the following table.

Feature name	Windows 8	Windows 8 Pro	Windows RT
Upgrades from Windows 7 Starter, Home Basic, Home Premium	x	x	
Upgrades from Windows 7 Professional, Ultimate		x	
Start screen, Semantic Zoom, live tiles	x	x	x
Windows Store	x	x	x
Apps (Mail, Calendar, People, Messaging, Photos, SkyDrive, Reader, Music, Video, etc.)	x	x	x
Microsoft Office (Word, Excel, PowerPoint, OneNote)			x
Internet Explorer 10	x	x	x
Device encryption			x
Connected standby	x	x	x
Microsoft account	x	x	x
Desktop	x	x	x
Installation of x86/64 and desktop software	x	x	
File Explorer	x	x	x
Windows Defender	x	x	x
SmartScreen	x	x	x
Windows Update	x	x	x
Enhanced Task Manager	x	x	x
Switch languages on the fly (Language Packs)	x	x	x
Better multiple monitor support	x	x	x
Storage Spaces	x	x	
Windows Media Player	x	x	
Exchange ActiveSync	x	x	x
File history	x	x	x
ISO / VHD mount	x	x	x
Mobile broadband features	x	x	x
Picture password	x	x	x
Play To	x	x	x
Remote Desktop (client)	x	x	x
Reset and refresh your computer or device	x	x	x
Snap	x	x	x

Touch and Thumb keyboard	x	x	x
Trusted boot	x	x	x
VPN client	x	x	x
BitLocker and BitLocker To Go		x	
Boot from VHD		x	
Client Hyper-V		x	
Domain Join		x	
Encrypting File System		x	
Group Policy		x	
Remote Desktop (host)		x	

Windows 8 Enterprise provides all the features in Windows 8 Pro and additional features to assist with IT organization (Windows To Go, AppLocker, App Deployment, and so on). This edition is available only to Software Assurance customers.

Minimum System Requirements

To run Windows 8, Microsoft recommends using a computer or device that has at least:

- 1 GHz or faster processor

- 1 GB RAM (32-bit) or 2 GB RAM (64-bit)

- 16 GB available hard disk space (32-bit) or 20 GB (64-bit)

- DirectX 9 graphics device with WDDM 10 or higher driver

However, this is the bare minimum required for Windows 8 to run, and there are a few caveats you need to be aware of:

- Windows 8 apps have a minimum 1024 × 768 screen resolution. If you attempt to run the new Windows 8 apps with less than this resolution (e.g., 800 × 600, 1024 × 600), you'll receive an error message.

- To use the snap feature with the new Windows 8 apps, you must have a minimum resolution of 1366 × 768. Therefore, it is best to use Windows 8 on a display that has at least this level of resolution. The higher the maximum supported resolution, the better.

- Using Windows 8 on a single-core processor running at 1 GHz is possible but won't be a great experience. Using at least a dual-core processor running at 1 GHz (processors that were sold from 2006 onward) is recommended. Windows 8 is optimized to work better than Windows 7 with modern processors. Therefore, the newer the processor, the smoother the experience.

- Using the 32-bit version of Windows 8 on a system with 1 GB of RAM will work, but the experience won't be great. For a smooth experience, using at least 2 GB of RAM, regardless of the Windows 8 version you are using, is recommended.

- The 16 GB or 20 GB (depending on the version) of space you must have available on your hard disk is the bare minimum for installing and using Windows 8. If you plan to install many apps and games, having at least 25 GB or more for the partition on which Windows 8 is installed is recommended.

- Using Windows 8 on solid state disks (SSDs) instead of traditional hard drives will provide a huge performance increase. You will enjoy the fastest start procedure ever experienced with a Windows operating system. Also, the apps and games will launch much faster than with traditional hard disk drives.

If you plan to install Windows 8 by yourself, read Appendix C, "Installing and Upgrading to Windows 8." It provides clear, step-by-step instructions for installing and upgrading to Windows 8.

What's Different from Windows 7?

The list of differences is long and starts with many differences that are not visible at first.

First of all, Windows 8 was designed to be slimmer and lighter than Windows 7. Its aim is to work on a multitude of devices, including desktops, laptops, hybrids such as the Microsoft Surface (half-laptop and half-tablet), or tablets. That's why the core of Windows 8 is lighter than that of Windows 7. This means faster start and shutdown times—incredibly fast when using SSDs. A start in five seconds is very feasible with Windows 8 on a fast computer. A shutdown in three seconds is also possible.

Windows 8 also runs better on newer hardware components. For example, it is able to deliver better performance on newer processors than Windows 7 can.

It supports touch displays, implemented at a level never seen before on Windows operating systems. Windows 8 can run on touch-compatible devices as small as 10.6 inches wide or on huge 82-inch touch displays, and it provides better support for using multiple displays.

There are also many visible changes when compared to Windows 7. This book covers only the ones the authors consider most important.

- **A NEW LOCK SCREEN AND NEW LOGON PROCEDURE** Windows 8 can be set to display useful data on the Lock screen, and you can log on using new methods (PIN or picture password), not just with your user account password.

- **THE START MENU HAS BEEN REPLACED BY THE START SCREEN** Unlike the Start menu, the Start screen uses all the available screen space to display shortcuts to installed apps. It can also be set to display live data from your most used apps. Search works faster than from the Start menu, and it can be used very easily with touch-compatible displays.

- **WINDOWS STORE** This a new feature that provides a one-stop shop for finding, purchasing, and installing apps and games.

- **NEW WINDOWS 8 APPS** These are delivered only with Windows 8. They provide easy access to your mail, calendar, social networks, photos, music, videos, and so on.

- **INTERNET EXPLORER 10** This version of Internet Explorer has received many enhancements. It is the fastest, safest, and most standards-compliant version of Internet Explorer ever made.

- **LOG ON WITH YOUR MICROSOFT ACCOUNT** You can use Windows 8 with your Microsoft account and synchronize your data and settings automatically across Windows 8 computers and devices.

- **A NEW FILE EXPLORER** This much improved version of Windows Explorer (as named in Windows 7) includes a ribbon-based interface for easy access to all the important functions, and file copying has been improved from Windows 7.

- **ENHANCED WINDOWS DEFENDER** This version now provides complete antivirus and antispyware protection.

- **A NEW TASK MANAGER** Task Manager has been dramatically improved. It is not only easier to use but provides more useful functions for managing your system, apps, and available resources.

- **SWITCH LANGUAGES ON THE FLY** Unlike Windows 7, with Windows 8 you don't need to purchase a special version to install a new display language. You can switch between them on the fly in all versions of Windows 8.

- **WINDOWS MEDIA CENTER** It's been removed in Windows 8 and is available as an additional purchase.

- **FILE HISTORY** This is a new feature that provides an easy way to make automated backups of your data.

- **ENHANCED PARENTAL CONTROLS** The parental controls in Windows 8 offer many improvements from their Windows 7 counterparts.

This list is by no means complete. To discover all the new features in Windows 8, read this book and experiment with all the new things Windows 8 has to offer.

Which Edition of Windows 8 Should I Buy?

The answer depends on how you plan to use Windows 8. If you are a casual user who needs to browse the web, use productivity applications, play games, watch movies, and view pictures, then the basic Windows 8 edition will work just fine.

If you are a more knowledgeable user who wants to use more advanced features such as BitLocker encryption or make Remote Desktop connections to your computer, Windows 8 Pro is a good choice. For small businesses that don't need an expensive enterprise version, the Windows 8 Pro edition is a very good choice.

The next question worth clarifying is: 32-bit or 64-bit? If you plan to use Windows 8 on an older computer with less than 4 GB of RAM, the 32-bit edition works just fine.

However, on newer computers, you should always use the 64-bit edition. You get a bit more performance and security, but most importantly, you get support for large amounts of RAM. The 32-bit version cannot manage more than 4 GB of RAM memory. If you plan to use more than that (such as for playing games), you should use the 64-bit edition.

Let's Get Started

Welcome to *Windows 8 Step by Step*. After reading this book, the authors hope you will agree that this book is the best guide for learning how to use Windows 8.

Who This Book Is For

This book is for people new to Windows 8 and Windows 8 apps as well as for those upgrading from previous versions of Windows to Windows 8.

It's assumed that this book's readers are familiar with earlier Windows operating systems. Although the readers are new to Windows 8, they are not new computer users. They are familiar with the basics of using a computer, using a mouse and keyboard, opening, viewing, and saving files, switching between windows, finding content, and so forth.

What This Book Is About

This book is about Windows 8. It covers all the important things you need to learn about this operating system so that you can be productive when using it.

It starts with setting up Windows 8 for the first time and exploring the new Start screen. Each chapter covers more advanced information and considerations such as how to purchase Windows 8 apps, use the new Windows 8 apps, browse the web with Internet Explorer 10, connect to a network, share files and folders, and prevent problems with your Windows 8 computer or device. This list is by no means complete; many other topics are also covered.

The book ends with a list of 20 useful tips and tricks that will improve the experience of Windows 8 and a few appendixes useful to people who like to do things by themselves such as installing or upgrading to Windows 8.

Acknowledgments

We would both like to thank Kenyon Brown and the team at Microsoft Press for making this book possible. It was a lengthy project with lots of work, but the result was worth it. We are proud of this book, and we hope all our readers will enjoy it and find it useful.

Ciprian would like to thank his teammate at 7 Tutorials—Marte Brengle—for patiently double-checking all his writing and pointing out mistakes he would not have noticed otherwise.

Joli would like to thank her agent, Neil Salkind, for all his hard work over the years, along with her family, Jennifer, Andrew, Allison, Dad, and Cosmo.

Modifying the Display of the Ribbon in File Explorer

The goal of the Windows 8 File Explorer environment, available on the desktop, is to make finding, sharing, organizing, and working with Word documents, music files, pictures, videos, and other data as intuitive as possible. In addition, from File Explorer, you can easily access data stored in your homegroup, data on other drives connected to or part of your computer, and any data available to you on your network.

You access data in File Explorer by selecting the desired folder or location in the Navigation pane, on the left side of the File Explorer window, and then selecting the desired file(s) in the content area on the right. With a folder or file selected, you can then use the ribbon to manage that data. The ribbon contains tabs and groups to help you perform tasks on the data you select.

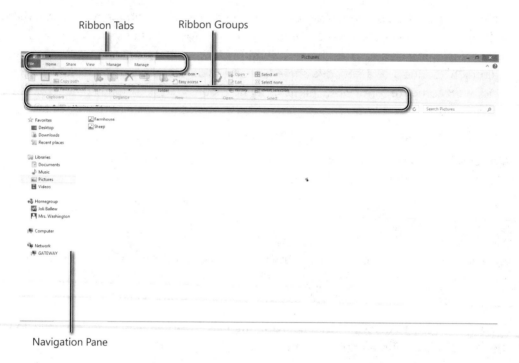

Navigation Pane

Commands are organized on task-specific tabs of the ribbon and in feature-specific groups on each tab. Commands generally take the form of buttons and lists. Some appear in galleries. Some groups have related dialog boxes or task panes that contain additional commands.

Throughout this book, we discuss the commands and ribbon elements associated with the program feature being discussed. In this topic, we discuss the general appearance of the ribbon, things that affect its appearance, and ways of locating commands that aren't visible on compact views of the ribbon.

TIP Some older commands no longer appear on the ribbon but are still available in the program. You can make these commands available by adding them to the Quick Access toolbar, located just above the tabs on the ribbon by default, although it can be moved.

Dynamic Ribbon Elements

The ribbon is dynamic, meaning that the appearance of commands on the ribbon changes as the width of the ribbon changes. A command might be displayed on the ribbon in the form of a large button, a small button, a small labeled button, or a list entry. As the width of the ribbon decreases, the size, shape, and presence of buttons on the ribbon adapt to the available space.

For example, when sufficient horizontal space is available, the buttons on the View tab of the File Explorer window are spread out, and you can see all the commands available in each group.

If you decrease the width of the ribbon, small button labels disappear and entire groups of buttons hide under one button that represents the group. Click the group button to display a list of the commands available in that group. Depending on the content of the ribbon you're working with, you might also see small unlabeled buttons or a scroll arrow.

Changing the Width of the Ribbon

The width of the ribbon depends on the horizontal space available to it, which depends on these three factors.

- **THE WIDTH OF THE PROGRAM WINDOW** Maximizing the program window provides the most space for ribbon elements. You can resize the program window by clicking the button in its upper-right corner or by dragging the border of a window that isn't maximized.

  TIP On a computer running Windows 8, you can maximize the program window by dragging its title bar to the top of the screen.

- **YOUR SCREEN RESOLUTION** Screen resolution is the size of your screen display expressed as pixels wide by pixels high. The greater the screen resolution, the greater the amount of information that will fit on one screen. Your screen resolution options depend on your monitor. At the time of writing, the lowest possible screen resolution was 800 × 600. The highest resolution depends on your monitor and your computer's display capabilities. In the case of the ribbon, the greater the number of pixels wide (the first number), the greater the number of buttons that can be shown on the ribbon and the larger those buttons can be.

  On a computer running Windows 8, you can change your screen resolution from the Screen Resolution window of Control Panel. You set the resolution by dragging the pointer on the slider.

- **THE DENSITY OF YOUR SCREEN DISPLAY** You might not be aware that you can change the magnification of everything that appears on your screen by changing the screen magnification setting in Windows. Setting your screen magnification to 125 percent makes text and user interface elements larger on screen. This increases the legibility of information, but less fits on each screen.

On a computer running Windows 8, you can change the screen magnification from the Display window of Control Panel. You can choose one of the standard display magnification options or create another by setting a custom text size.

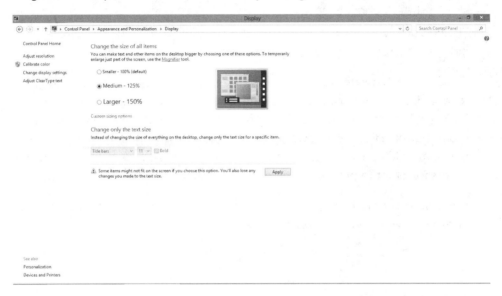

The screen magnification is directly related to the density of the text elements on screen, which is expressed in dots per inch (dpi) or points per inch (ppi). (The terms are interchangeable and, in fact, are both used in the Windows dialog box in which you change the setting.) The greater the dpi, the larger the text and user interface elements appear on screen. By default, Windows displays text and screen elements at 96 dpi. Choosing the Medium—125 percent—display setting changes the dpi of text and screen elements to 120. Likewise, choosing Larger increases the dpi even more.

Adapting Exercise Steps

The screen images shown in the exercises in this book were captured at a screen resolution of 1280 × 768, at 100 percent magnification, and in the default text size (96 dpi). If any of your settings are different, the ribbon on your screen might not look the same as the one shown in the book. For example, you might see more or fewer buttons in each of the groups, the buttons you see might be represented by larger or smaller icons than those shown, or the group might be represented by a button that you click to display the group's commands.

Instructions to give a command from the ribbon in an exercise appear in this format:

- On the **View** tab, in the **Layout** group, click the **Large icons** button.

  If the command is in a list, the instruction appears in this format.

- On the **Home** tab, in the **Organize** group, click the **Copy to** button and then, in the list, click **Choose location**.

The first time you are instructed to click a specific button in each exercise, an image of the button is displayed in the page margin to the left of the exercise step.

If differences between your display settings and the book's cause a button on your screen to look different, you can easily adapt the steps to locate the command. First, click the specified tab. Then locate the specified group. If a group has been collapsed into a group list or group button, click the list or button to display the group's commands. Finally, look for a button that features the same icon in a larger or smaller size than that shown in the book. If necessary, point to buttons in the group to display their names in ScreenTips.

If you prefer not to have to adapt the steps, set up your screen to match the one in the book while you read and work through the exercises.

Conventions and Features in This Book

This book has been designed to lead you, step by step, through all the tasks you're most likely to want to perform in Windows 8. If you start at the beginning and work your way through all the exercises, you'll gain enough proficiency to use Windows. However, each topic is self-contained. If you have worked with a previous version of Windows, or if you completed all the exercises and later need help remembering how to perform a procedure, the following features of this book will help you locate specific information.

- **Detailed table of contents** Search the listing of the topics and sidebars within each chapter.
- **Chapter thumb tabs** Easily locate the beginning of the chapter you want.
- **Topic-specific running footers** Within a chapter, quickly locate the topic you want by looking at the running footers at the bottom of odd-numbered pages.
- **Glossary** Look up the meaning of a word or the definition of a concept.
- **Keyboard shortcuts** If you prefer to work from the keyboard rather than with a mouse, find all the shortcuts in one place.
- **Detailed index** Look up specific tasks and features in the index, which has been carefully crafted with the reader in mind.

You can save time when reading this book by understanding how the *Step by Step* series shows exercise instructions, keys to press, buttons to click, and other information.

Convention	Meaning
1	Numbered steps guide you through hands-on exercises in each topic.
➜	The Set Up icon precedes a step-by-step exercise and indicates the practice files that you will use when working through the exercise. It also indicates any requirements you should attend to or actions you should take before beginning the exercise.
✖	The Clean Up icon follows a step-by-step exercise and provides instructions for saving and closing open files or programs before moving on to another topic. It also suggests ways to reverse any changes you made to your computer while working through the exercise.

Convention	Meaning
TIP	This section provides a helpful hint or shortcut that makes working through a task easier.
IMPORTANT	This section points out information that you need to know to complete the procedure.
TROUBLESHOOTING	This section shows you how to fix a common problem.
NOTE	These paragraphs provide a helpful hint or shortcut that makes working through a task easier.
Ctrl+C	A plus sign (+) between two key names means that you must press those keys at the same time. For example, "Press **Alt+Tab**" means that you hold down the Alt key while you press Tab.
Boldface type	Program features that you click or press are shown in boldface type.
Blue italic type	Terms that are explained in the glossary at the end of the book are shown in italic type within the chapter.
Blue boldface type	Text that you are supposed to type appears in color and bold in the procedures.
Italic type	Folder paths, URLs, and emphasized words appear in italic type.

Downloading and Using the Practice Files

Before you can complete the exercises in this book, you need to copy the book's practice files to your computer. These practice files, and other information, can be downloaded from here:

http://go.microsoft.com/FWLink/?Linkid=263546

Display the detail page in your web browser and follow the instructions for downloading the files.

IMPORTANT The Windows 8 software is not available from this website. You should purchase and install that software before using this book.

The following table lists the practice files for this book.

Chapter	File
Chapter 1: Introducing Windows 8	Notepad.txt
Chapter 2: Making Windows Look and Sound the Way You Want	Sheep.jpg
Chapter 3: Using Apps on the Start Screen	Carriage.jpg
	Farmhouse.jpg
	Sheep.JPG
	Trees.jpg
	Flying over the Hoover Dam.3GP
Chapter 4: Saving, Browsing, and Organizing Files and Folders	Notepad Text Document.txt
	Sheep.jpg
	Take Off.3GP
Chapter 5: Using Internet Explorer 10	None
Chapter 6: Using SkyDrive	Document1.docx
Chapter 7: Using the Social Apps	None
Chapter 8: Shopping in the Windows Store	None
Chapter 9: Having Fun with Multimedia	None
Chapter 10: Playing Games	None
Chapter 11: Connecting to a Network and the Internet	None

Chapter	File
Chapter 12: Allowing Others to Use the Computer	PictureA.jpg
	PictureB.jpg
Chapter 13: Sharing Files and Folders with My Network	None
Chapter 14: Keeping Windows 8 Safe and Secure	None
Chapter 15: Preventing Problems	None
Chapter 16: Supervising a Child's Computer Use	None
Chapter 17: Making My Computer Accessible	None
Chapter 18: Using Windows 8 at Work	None
Chapter 19: Using Windows 8 on Touch-Compatible Devices	None
Chapter 20: 20 Tips for Improving Your Windows 8 Computing Experience	Show Start.exe
	Lock - Switch User
	Recycle Bin
	Restart
	Shut Down
	Sign out
	Sleep
	Stop Shut Down
Chapter 21: Troubleshooting Problems	None

Getting Support and Giving Feedback

The following sections provide information on errata, book support, feedback, and contact information.

Errata

Every effort has been made to ensure the accuracy of this book and its companion content. If you do find an error, please report it on the Microsoft Press site at oreilly.com.

1   Go to *http://microsoftpress.oreilly.com*.

2   In the Search box, enter the book's ISBN or title.

3   Select your book from the search results.

4   On your book's catalog page, under the cover image, you'll see a list of links.

5   Click View/Submit Errata.

You'll find additional information and services for your book on its catalog page. If you need additional support, please send an email to Microsoft Press Book Support at *mspinput@microsoft.com*. Please note that product support for Microsoft software is not offered through the preceding addresses.

We Want to Hear from You

At Microsoft Press, your satisfaction is our top priority and your feedback is our most valuable asset. Please tell us what you think of this book at:

http://www.microsoft.com/learning/booksurvey

The survey is short, and we read *every one* of your comments and ideas. Thanks in advance for your input!

Stay in Touch

Let's keep the conversation going! We're on Twitter at:

http://twitter.com/MicrosoftPress

Chapter at a Glance

Explore

Explore the Start screen, page 5

View

View live thumbnails, page 10

Use

Use charms, page 13

Multitask

Multitask between open desktop windows, page 26

Introducing Windows 8

IN THIS CHAPTER, YOU WILL LEARN HOW TO

- Set up Windows 8.

- Explore and customize the Start screen.

- Customize live tiles.

- Access the traditional desktop.

- Work with windows and apps.

- Work with PC Settings and Control Panel.

- End a computing session.

The first time you press the power button on a new computer, laptop, or tablet running Windows 8, you are prompted to perform a few setup tasks. After those tasks are complete, each time you press the power button or wake the computer from sleep, the Windows 8 Lock screen appears. Use this screen to unlock the computer and gain access to the Windows 8 Start screen. The Start screen is the starting point for everything you do with Windows 8, including accessing apps, the Internet, the desktop and shortcuts you've placed there, and applications you've installed, such as Microsoft Office.

In this chapter, you'll learn how to work through the primary set up tasks, and then you'll learn to use the Start screen, open windows on the traditional desktop, access Control Panel, and safely end a computing session. Along the way, you'll begin to personalize the computer so that it's uniquely yours.

TIP Do you need a quick refresher on the topics in a chapter? See the key points at the end of each chapter.

PRACTICE FILES Before you can complete the exercises in this chapter, you need to copy the book's practice files to your computer. The practice files you'll use to complete the exercises in this chapter are in the Chapter01 practice files folder. A complete list of practice files is provided in "Using the Practice Files" at the beginning of this book.

Setting Up Windows 8

The first time you turn on a new computer running Windows 8, you are prompted to personalize the background color of the Start screen, name your computer, and choose how you sign in to your computer, among other things. If a network is available, you can opt to connect to that, too. You might have already done this. However, if you have not, here is a list of the options you will likely see.

TIP If you have already set up your computer running Windows 8, it is possible to make changes to your choices using Control Panel and PC Settings if you aren't pleased. You'll learn how to access Control Panel later in this chapter, and you'll learn about the PC Settings hub throughout this book.

The Windows 8 setup process prompts you to configure or input the following information.

- **BACKGROUND COLOR** You choose the background color by using a slider provided for that purpose.

- **COMPUTER NAME** Your computer must have a name that is unique on your local area network. You can't have spaces or special characters in the name, such as !, @, +, and so on, but you are prompted if you try to input a character that is prohibited.

- **NETWORK** If your computer running Windows 8 detects a network, you are prompted to join it. If you want to join, and if it is a protected network, you must also input the passcode. You should connect to your local area network during setup. If you aren't prompted to join a network during the setup process, but you know one is available, make sure after setup completes that you've either connected an Ethernet cable or enabled the Wi-Fi feature on your computer.

- **SETTINGS** These settings relate to how and when the computer installs updates; how Windows 8 protects the computer from unsafe content; whether apps can personalize the information offered through them based on your location, name, and account picture; how to share your data; and which keyboard settings to use. You can customize the available settings or use Express Settings. Often Express Settings is fine; you can always change the options later.

- **MICROSOFT ACCOUNT OR LOCAL USER ACCOUNT** You choose how you want to log on to your computer. If you have a Microsoft account and you want to access the data already associated with it, such as apps you've acquired from the Windows Store or photos you've saved to SkyDrive, or you want to sync settings (such as for Microsoft Internet Explorer Favorites and desktop backgrounds) across other computers running Windows 8, you should configure your Microsoft account during this step. You must have a Microsoft account to access and make purchases from the Store. If you do not have an account or do not want to sync with your existing Microsoft account, choose a local account instead.

  TIP If you configured a local user account during setup and now want to use a Microsoft account, you can make the change in PC Settings, from the Users tab.

- **PASSWORD** This is the password you enter to unlock your computer. If you input a Microsoft account during setup, input the password already associated with that account. If you created a local account during setup, you can create a password for that account now. Although creating a password for a local user account is not mandatory, you should input one. Later, you can create other ways to unlock the computer, including using a picture password or a four-digit PIN (personal identification number).

- **PASSWORD HINT** This comprises a few words that you type to remind you of your password if you ever forget it.

Using the Lock Screen

Windows 8 offers a new Lock screen, which is much more functional than any Lock screen you might have encountered in previous Microsoft operating systems. It offers quite a bit of information. It offers the time and date, and it shows whether you're connected to a network. If you are using a laptop, it also shows the status of the battery. You can also add thumbnails for your favorite apps here so you can see the status of those apps without leaving the Lock screen, and some apps show information here by default. (As an example, you might see a Mail glyph with a number by it, announcing that new, unread mail is available.)

12:42
Wednesday, August 8

The Lock screen offers different ways to unlock the computer. You can slide the picture up and off the screen, click or tap it one time, or tap any key on the keyboard. Once you bypass this screen, you input your password.

How you unlock the Lock screen depends on the type of computer you're using.

- **TRADITIONAL DESKTOP COMPUTER** Tap any key on the keyboard or click with the mouse anywhere on the screen, or click near the bottom of the screen and drag upward. If applicable, type your password when prompted.

- **TRADITIONAL LAPTOP COMPUTER** Hold down the left track pad button while moving the cursor upward, or perform a similar movement. Alternatively, tap any key on the keyboard or click with the mouse (or appropriate track pad button) anywhere on the screen. If applicable, type your password when prompted.

- **TOUCH-COMPATIBLE COMPUTER OR TABLET** Place your finger anywhere near the middle or bottom of the screen and flick upward. If applicable, type your password when prompted.

  SEE ALSO Chapter 13, "Sharing Files and Folders with My Network."

Exploring the Start Screen

After you've unlocked the computer, the Start screen appears; it holds tiles. If there are more tiles than there is space on the screen, you'll see a scroll bar across the bottom of the screen (which doesn't appear in the figure).

Tiles can serve many purposes. Many of the tiles open apps such as Mail, People, and Messaging. Some of these tiles also offer up-to-date information for the application they represent and are considered live tiles. You do not need to open the app to view basic data it offers. For example, the Weather app, after it is configured, can show up-to-date weather information for your city, and the Calendar app can show upcoming appointments and birthdays. This data appears on the Start screen so you have access to it without opening the app. The information is dynamic and changes as the information it represents does. If you need to see more than a preview of the information, you can click the tile, and the app opens in a new screen from which you can access all its features. Messaging, People, Calendar, Photos, Mail, and similar apps all do this. You can get more apps from the Store.

SEE ALSO Chapter 8, "Shopping in the Windows Store."

Beyond offering access to the default apps that come with Windows 8 (and any you acquire from the Store), the Start screen can also offer tiles for many of the programs and applications you install yourself. You might see tiles for Microsoft Word, Outlook, or PowerPoint, Adobe Photoshop, or other programs. These are not apps. They're called desktop apps, and they are the traditional applications with which you're familiar. Often you obtain these by downloading them from a website or by installing them from a CD or DVD. (In contrast, you can get apps only from the Windows Store.)

To open an application, whether it's an app or a desktop app, you click or touch the tile on the Start screen. What you see after this depends on the type of app or application you've opened. It's important to note that you can remove apps from the Start screen if you don't plan on using them. Just right-click the unwanted tile and choose Unpin From Start. (If you do not have a keyboard, mouse, or track pad and can use your finger only, tap, hold, and drag downward to display the option to remove it. You'll know you've done this correctly when a check mark appears on the selected app.) When you unpin an app from the Start screen, note that this only removes the tile and does not uninstall the related app. As you'll learn later, it's easy to access all your apps from a single screen if you want to use the app again.

Beyond opening apps and desktop apps, some tiles offer access to familiar parts of the computer such as the desktop. From the desktop, you can open File Explorer by clicking the folder icon located on the taskbar.

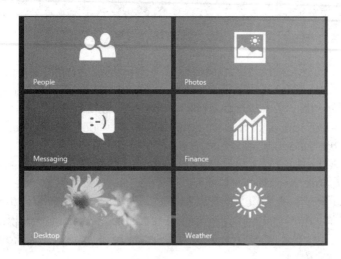

If you leave the Start screen and want to go back, tap the Windows key on your keyboard. Tablets often have a physical Windows button. Alternatively, you can position the cursor in the bottom-left corner and click when the thumbnail of the Start screen appears.

Finally, you can add tiles. You can pin your favorite folder (perhaps My Documents or Public Documents) to the Start screen, and you can do the same with your favorite website (perhaps Facebook). You can pin almost anything. Pinning items to the Start screen is a great way to personalize Windows 8 and makes the Start screen much more useful. If you've already pinned a few items, you'll see them. If not, wait; you'll learn to pin items in Chapter 2.

Moving Around in the Start Screen

If you have more tiles than can appear on the Start screen, and you know that other tiles are available to the right or left of what you can see, you need to know some techniques for getting to those tiles. To move around in the Start screen, you can use your mouse, keyboard, track pad, or appropriate touch gesture. The method you choose depends on what kind of computer you have. Listed here are a few ways to move around in the Start screen (and there are others not listed here).

- **SCROLL BAR** Left-click, hold, and drag the scroll bar. On a laptop with a track pad, hold down the left mouse button while you drag across the track pad. On a tablet, you will see the scroll bar across the bottom when you flick left and right, but you don't need to have your finger on it to use it.

- **FLICK** Place your finger on an empty area of the screen and flick from left to right or right to left. You can also drag your finger slowly in lieu of flicking quickly. You must have touch-compatible hardware for this to work.

- **AUTO SCROLL** Use your mouse's scroll wheel (in an up-and-down motion) to move through apps from left to right.

- **RIGHT-CLICK** You can right-click an empty area of the Start screen and then click or touch All Apps to access all the apps and programs on your computer. On a tablet, flick upward from the bottom.

- **PINCH** Using touch, position two or more fingers apart from each other on the screen. Pinch inward to make all the tiles smaller, which will enable you to see more tiles on the screen, as you can see here.

TIP To make everything smaller on the Start screen without using the pinch technique, position your mouse in the bottom-right corner and click the - sign that appears on the right end of the scroll bar. Click anywhere to return the tiles to their original size.

As you might expect, if you click or touch any tile, the app, program, or window opens, and the Start screen disappears. What you see when you move away from the Start screen depends on what you've selected. If you open an app, it opens in its own screen and might offer configuration options, often in the form of *charms*. You'll see an example of this later in this chapter when you open and configure the Weather app. If you open a program (such as Microsoft Word or Paint), a traditional window appears on the desktop. You'll experience this later in the chapter when you open a file in Notepad. What you see with desktop applications will look familiar.

Moving Tiles on the Start Screen

You'll use some tiles more than others, so you might want to reposition the tiles on the Start screen to make your most-used tiles easily accessible. For instance, if you use the Music app often, you might put that app in the first position on the Start screen.

In this exercise, you'll move a tile from its current position on the Start screen to the first position. Repeat with other tiles as desired to personalize your Start screen.

→ SET UP **Start your computer and unlock the Lock screen. You need access to the Start screen.**

TIP When an instruction requires you to click something with a mouse, note that you can generally touch the item (if applicable) to achieve the same result.

1 From the **Start** screen, click (or touch) and hold **Music**.

2 Drag the **Music** tile to the first position in the far-left side of the screen and drop it there.

✖ CLEAN UP **The app is repositioned.**

TIP If you move too many tiles now, what you see on your Start screen will be different from what you see in this chapter.

Customizing the Start Screen with Live Tiles

You know you can move tiles on the Start screen to another area of the screen to make those tiles more accessible. You can also personalize a few select tiles independently so that the information available from them suits your personal needs. For example, you can tell the Weather app where you live (or give it permission to determine your location), and the app will supply current weather information from the Start screen (provided it can get that information from the Internet). If you want to know more about the weather, you just click the app to open it. These interactive and customizable tiles are live tiles, which means that they are often updated with new information.

Customizing any interactive tile generally only requires you to open the app, access the customizable tools and features (called charms) that enable you to change the settings, and input the desired information or make the desired choices.

In this exercise, you'll personalize the interactive Weather app located on the Start screen.

 SET UP **If you aren't on the Start screen, position your mouse in the bottom-left corner of the screen and click the Start screen thumbnail that appears. On a tablet, press the Windows button if available. You do not need any practice files to complete this exercise.**

1 From the Start screen, click or touch **Weather**. If prompted, click **Allow** to let this app learn your location.

2 Right-click the screen to access the available settings or use touch gestures to flick from the bottom of the screen upward.

TIP Charms often appear after right-clicking inside an app.

3 Click or touch **Places**.

4   Click the + sign (not shown) and then type your city and state as applicable; if your
    city appears in a list, click it. Otherwise, click **Add**. Repeat as desired.

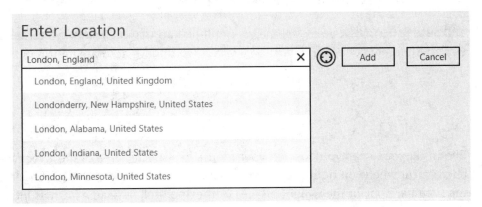

5   Click or tap any city to access full weather information for it.

CLEAN UP To leave this app and return to the Start screen, position your cursor in the bottom-left corner of the screen and click Start.

TROUBLESHOOTING Live tiles and apps get their information from the Internet; thus, a working Internet connection must be available to retrieve accurate information.

Using Charms

Charms appear when you position your mouse in a specific area of the screen. Charms can also appear when you right-click inside an app or flick upward with your finger (such as for the Weather app), or they might be part of the app itself, available from its interface all the time. Charms can be customized by software and hardware manufacturers, so you won't always see the same charms for every app. In the previous section, you saw the charms available from the Weather app.

Windows 8 has some default charms that appear when you call on them, and they do not change. To see these charms, position your mouse in the bottom-right corner of any screen. This is called a hot corner. When you position your cursor here, the charms fly out from the right side. Alternatively, you can use the Windows+C keyboard command. Charms include Settings, Devices, Start, Share, and Search.

TROUBLESHOOTING If you are using a device without a physical keyboard or mouse, swipe with your finger or thumb from the middle of the right side of the screen to the left (inward) to see the default charms.

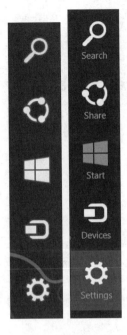

After the charms appear, their titles appear next to them as you move your cursor toward them. This technique works on the Start screen, on the desktop, in apps, and in other windows and views. What you see when you click any charm depends on what is currently open when you access the charms.

These aren't the only charms you'll see as you work with Windows 8. You'll see charms in other places as you work through this book. Charms can appear on the side or across the top or bottom of the screen. Often they appear when you position the cursor on a preconfigured hotspot. Other times, a right-click or an upward flick makes hidden charms available. In still other instances, charms are available all the time without positioning the cursor in a particular area of the screen or right-clicking anywhere.

After a charm is available, just click (or touch) it to use it. When you select a charm, a new pane opens and configuration options (or search or share options) appear. What you see depends on the charm you click.

The following list describes the five default charms available in Windows 8, from any screen, from the bottom-right hot corner.

- **SETTINGS** Use this charm from the Start screen to access the PC Settings hub, to get information about your network, to change sound levels, to set screen brightness, to turn notifications on or off, to choose a power option, and more. You click Settings to power off your computer completely. If you access this charm while in an app (perhaps Calendar), you'll see additional options.

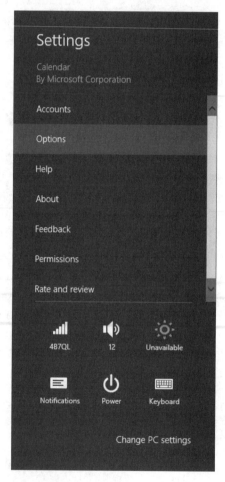

- **DEVICES** Choose this charm to access settings related to the devices that are available for use with the current app, screen, or window. For instance, you can use a second monitor if such a device is available.

- **START** Use this charm to access the Start screen.

- **SHARE** Choose this charm to access share options applicable to the current activity or open application. What you see here will differ depending on the application that's open. Sharing photos with others is a common way to use the Share charm.

- **SEARCH** Use this charm to open the Search pane and to access all the available tiles. You can use this option to search for anything on your computer, including things you find in Control Panel, but understand that there are other ways to search, too.

  TIP Try to get used to using the Windows+C keyboard shortcut to access these charms. Note that Windows+Q brings up a list of all the applications installed on your computer. Put these two keyboard shortcuts into your long-term memory! They make navigating Windows 8 much easier.

TIP While in the Search window, you can type a few letters, a word, or a file or folder name and then choose where to search by clicking one of the options under it (perhaps Apps, Settings, or Files) to cull the results.

Searching for Data, Programs, Files, and Settings

As you now know, Search is one of the default charms available when you position your mouse in the bottom-right corner of the screen. To get to it you must first make the charms accessible. After that, you have to click Search and type what you're looking for in the Search window. You might even have to click an option underneath to find the results you want. That's a lot of clicking and tapping. This is not generally the fastest or most effective way to search.

In most cases, the Windows 8 Start screen is the best place to start a search. You just start typing. You don't have to press a specific key on the keyboard, and you don't have to access any charms or toolbars (unless you need to bring up the onscreen keyboard on a tablet). You just type the file or folder name, app name or program name, or a few keywords that detail what you're looking for, and Windows 8 does the rest. Results appear automatically as you type, and the more information you provide, the shorter the list of results will be. You might see what you're looking for right away, as is the case if you type the name of an app, or you might have to make another choice to tell Windows the type of item you're looking for.

If you don't see what you're looking for in the resulting list, select another category from the Search pane. You can look under Files, for instance. If you see a number next to a category, compatible information is there.

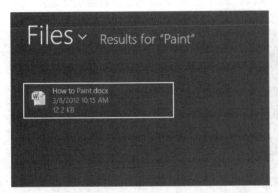

TIP You can use keyboard shortcuts while searching. After typing your keywords, click Windows+W to search Windows Settings. After typing the name of any file, click Windows+F to access files.

In this exercise, you'll search for the Notepad.txt file you've already saved to the Documents folder on your computer and open it, and you'll search directly from the Start screen.

➡ SET UP You need to have copied the Notepad.txt file located in the Chapter01 practice file folder to your computer's Documents library to complete this exercise.

1 Using any method, access the **Start** screen. One way is to click the Windows key on the keyboard.

2 Type **Note**.

The Search screen appears, and Note is in the Search window.

3   Click or touch **Files**.

The Notepad.txt file appears.

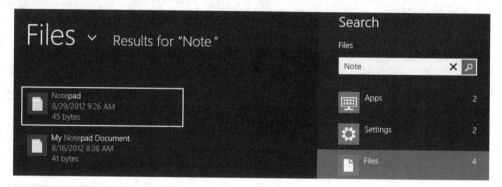

4   From the results, click the **notepad** document.

The document opens on the desktop.

5   Click the **red x** in the top-right corner to close the Notepad file.

❌ CLEAN UP To leave the desktop and return to the Start screen, position your cursor in the bottom-left corner of the screen and click the Start screen thumbnail or press the Windows key on the keyboard.

TROUBLESHOOTING Files open in a specific program that you configure. Thus, the Notepad. txt file in this exercise might open in Notepad, WordPad, Microsoft Office Word, or another program you have installed.

Accessing the Traditional Desktop

If you've ever used a Windows-based computer, you are familiar with the traditional desktop. That's the screen where the Recycle Bin and the taskbar are, and it is where you've always accessed your personal folders, opened and worked with files, and used Windows Explorer, now renamed and referred to as File Explorer. The traditional desktop is still available, it's still called Desktop, and it's still where you'll do quite a bit of your work. You access the desktop from the Start screen.

TIP The first difference you'll notice between the Windows 8 desktop and previous desktops is that the Start button is missing. The desktop still has a taskbar, you can still personalize the background, you can still right-click to create folders and shortcuts, and you still open File Explorer from it.

You can open the desktop from the Start screen by clicking the Desktop tile. You can also use the Windows+D shortcut. In addition, if you click a desktop application's icon or a related shortcut on the Start screen (one you may have saved there), perhaps for Microsoft Word or File Explorer, the desktop will open on its own to house the application and make it available to you. After the desktop is open, you'll see familiar elements. Look for the taskbar, the Notification area, the Recycle Bin, and other recognizable essentials.

TIP The three icons in the top-right corner of most windows enable you to manipulate the window. The small - minimizes a window to the taskbar; the rectangle (or two rectangles if applicable) enables you to resize the window; the red x closes a window.

Seeing the time-honored desktop is often a welcome relief to traditionalists!

IMPORTANT Try not to slip into old habits and use the desktop for everything just because you're used to it. Give the Start screen a chance. For a couple of months, initiate your work from the Start screen and always use apps instead of desktop apps when possible. If you do, you'll be better positioned to quickly adopt future technology because apps will become the norm, especially on phones and tablets, and you'll be able to use those devices seamlessly.

Using the Taskbar and Start Button

Yes, you still need the desktop; it hasn't gone away. Applications such as Paint, WordPad, Notepad, Adobe Reader, and others still open there. These aren't apps; they are desktop apps and thus need the desktop to work. These and other common applications might become apps in the future, but that is another conversation.

When you find yourself at the desktop, by choice or necessity, you'll see features with which you are likely already familiar. The taskbar is one of them. The taskbar is the blue bar that runs across the bottom of the screen when the desktop is active. (Apps don't open on the desktop and thus don't have a taskbar.) The taskbar is where you access running programs, your open windows, and an available touch keyboard, among other things. As with previous Windows editions, a Notification area on the far right offers access to various system settings, including those that correspond with available networks, system sounds, the current state of the system, and the time and date. The bottom-right corner is a hot corner that brings up the five default charms when you require them.

TROUBLESHOOTING If you don't see the taskbar, make sure you're at the desktop and not in an app. If you're sure you are on the desktop, position the cursor at the bottom of the screen; it could be that the taskbar is hidden and will appear when you position your cursor there.

You can personalize the taskbar by pinning icons for programs you access often to it. You'll learn to do this in an exercise later in this chapter. You can also move the taskbar by dragging it to another area of the screen (if it's unlocked), change the size of the icons that appear on it, and rearrange the icons by dragging them to different positions. You can right-click the taskbar to add or hide toolbars, too; the touch keyboard and the Address bar might prove helpful. Toolbars appear next to the Notification center when added.

SEE ALSO The "Customizing the Taskbar" section in Chapter 2.

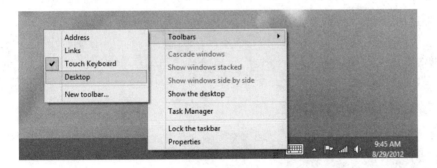

The main purposes of the taskbar, beyond any of the personalization options, are to offer immediate access to previously opened programs, files, folders, and windows; to make it easy to minimize, restore, and switch between open programs; and to navigate quickly to other areas of the computer through toolbars you add. You can click any icon on the taskbar to access the program, file, or folder it represents. For example, you can click the Internet Explorer icon to open the desktop version of Internet Explorer. You can click the Folder icon to open File Explorer.

TIP Some applications offer both an app version and a desktop version. Internet Explorer is one of these applications. When both options exist, use the app. If you decide later that app doesn't offer what you need, try the desktop version. (The desktop version is the same app but in a different skin, with a different graphical user interface and more features.)

Because you might not yet have much experience with files, folders, windows, and programs from which to draw, review some taskbar basics. The following list details what the icons on the taskbar do.

- **TOUCH KEYBOARD** You can show or hide the touch keyboard. Just right-click the task-bar, point to Toolbars, and click Touch keyboard.

- **ACTION CENTER FLAG** Click the Action Center icon (a flag) to see whether your computer requires your attention.

- **NETWORK** Click the Network icon to show the Network pane. Click anywhere outside the pane to hide it. The Network icon sits to the right of the Action Center icon (a flag).

- **SOUND** Click the sound icon and move the slider to raise or lower the volume.

- **TIME AND DATE** Click the time and date to show the calendar and to access the date and time settings.

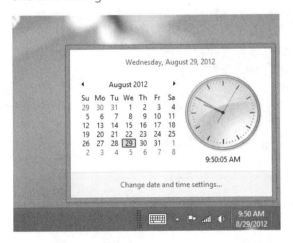

You can reposition icons on the taskbar and click them to open folders and programs available on your computer.

- **REPOSITION AN ICON** Click and drag any icon to a new position.

- **OPEN FILE EXPLORER** Click or touch the folder icon to open File Explorer. From there, you can navigate to any area of your computer's hard drive.

SEE ALSO Refer to "Browsing for Files and Folders" in Chapter 5, "Using Internet Explorer 10."

As you know, you can personalize the taskbar. You'll learn quite a bit about that later in Chapter 2, but you can sample a taste of what's to come here.

In this exercise, you'll pin the Calculator application to the taskbar to personalize it.

SET UP There is no setup for this exercise. You do not need any practice files to complete this exercise. If you are not on the Start screen, click the Windows key or position the cursor in the bottom-left corner of the screen and click or tap the Start screen thumbnail.

1   While on the Start screen, type **Calc**. The results appear.

2   Right-click **Calculator**. The related touch gesture is to tap, hold, and drag downward until a check mark appears on the Calculator entry.

3   Click **Pin to taskbar**.

TIP The option next to Pin To Taskbar is Pin To Start. If you choose this option, a tile appears on the Start menu that offers access to the application.

CLEAN UP To return to the desktop, use the Windows+D shortcut. You can also use the mouse to click in the top-left corner. Using touch gestures, position the cursor in the top-left corner and touch there to return to the previous screen or flick inward from the left side with your thumb. If you do not have a keyboard or mouse, flick inward from the left side of the screen until the desktop appears.

TIP If you work at the desktop regularly, pin your favorite desktop apps to the taskbar. To unpin something from the taskbar, right-click its icon on the taskbar and choose Unpin This Program From Taskbar. You can also unpin an item from the Start screen. To do so, right-click its tile and then click Unpin from Start.

Working with Multiple Windows and Apps

As you saw earlier, when you open a file such as a text document, the desktop appears, and a program opens to make the file available. It might be Microsoft Word, WordPad, Notepad, or something else. That program and the file are contained in a single window, and the program's features and data are available from it. You'll often have more than one window open at a time, though, and you need to know ways to move among the windows effectively. You might have a document, a web browser, and File Explorer open, all of which are available from the desktop.

Likewise, you might also have opened several apps from the Start screen. You might have opened Maps, Mail, Weather, Music, and others. These apps aren't all available from one area such as the desktop; instead, you must switch among them by using keyboard and touch techniques. By default, only one app appears on the screen at any given time, although a technique is available to show two.

In this section, you'll learn the traditional ways of managing multiple open windows on the desktop and then how to manage multiple open desktop applications and apps.

Let's start with the desktop. One way to manage multiple open windows on the desktop is to size them so that you can see all of them at one time. When positioned this way, you need to click only once in the window you want to use. The window you choose appears in the foreground and becomes the active window. This view isn't always effective, though, and you'll often need to maximize a window so that it takes up the entire screen.

TROUBLESHOOTING If you can't access all the features in a window, maximize it.

The problem with maximizing a window so that it takes up the entire screen is that you no longer have easy access to the other open windows. They are now behind the active window in which you're working. To get to those other windows requires knowing a few tricks.

Here are the most common ways to manage multiple open windows:

- **MINIMIZE TO THE TASKBAR** You can minimize any maximized window to the taskbar. Doing so removes it from the desktop. After it is removed (minimized), you can see the windows that were previously underneath it. One way to minimize a window is to click the respective icon on the taskbar; a more familiar way is to click the dash in the top-right corner of the window. To restore the window, click its icon on the taskbar.

- **SHAKE THE WINDOW TO KEEP** To remove all but one window from the desktop and minimize the others to the taskbar, click, hold, and then shake the top of the window you'd like to keep. The other windows will fall to the taskbar.

- **RESIZE A WINDOW** You can resize a maximized window by dragging the window downward by the top-center part of the topmost toolbar. When it's in restore mode, you can drag from the corners of the window to further manipulate its size.

    TROUBLESHOOTING You can't drag from a window's corner if the window is maximized. All desktop corners are hot corners, so when you position your cursor there, charms, the Start thumbnail, the last-used app, and so on appear.

- **SNAP A WINDOW TO TAKE UP HALF THE SCREEN** You can drag from the top part of most windows to the left or right of the screen to snap it into place so that it takes up half the screen. You can also double-click when you have the double arrow at the top of a window to have the window fill to the height of the screen without changing the width.

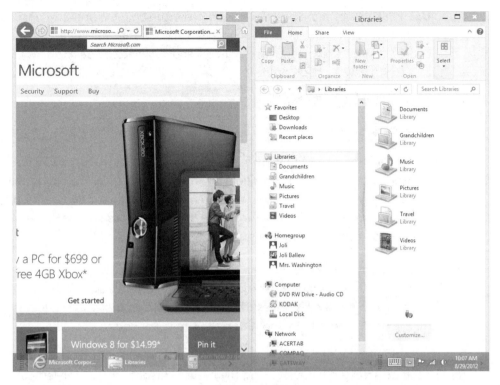

- **USE FLIP** The Alt+Tab keyboard shortcut offers thumbnails of open applications in the center of the screen. To use this shortcut, keep the Alt key depressed and tap the Tab key to flip through the available programs, which are represented as thumbnails. When the desired thumbnail is displayed, let go to make that application active. As you'll see, you can also flip to apps by using this method.

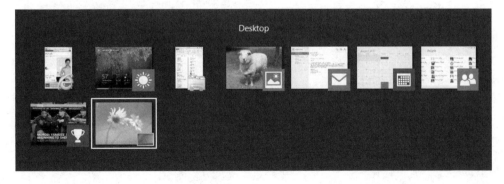

- **USE PEEK** While at the desktop, position your cursor in the bottom-right corner of the taskbar. The open windows will become transparent, enabling you to see the desktop underneath. If nothing happens, right-click and click **Peek at desktop**. (You want Peek At Desktop to have a check beside it.)

These are all traditional ways to work with the desktop. Many are probably not new to you, such as resizing a window or minimizing a window to the taskbar. You might have even used Flip before. There are new, novel ways to move among apps and desktop applications, though. These involve positioning your mouse in a specific area of the screen and using touch gestures on compatible devices.

TIP It's okay to leave lots of apps open if you want. You don't have to open and close them continually. After they are in the background (not in use), they become inactive and use very few (if any) computer resources. They are designed so that you can leave them open and available without worrying about using too many of your computer's resources.

One way to move among the multiple open apps and the desktop is to use the Switch list. This list can be accessed by positioning the mouse cursor in the upper-left corner of your computer screen and then slowly moving the cursor downward. You can also use the keyboard shortcut, Windows+Tab. After you have access to the list, you can left-click, right-click, drag, touch, or navigate to the app you want to use (for example, by repeating the Windows+Tab keyboard shortcut).

If you simply click (or touch) a thumbnail in the Switch list, it opens in full-screen view (or, in the case of desktop applications, the way you last left it). You have other options. With a mouse, you can right-click to access options to close the app or to snap it to the left side or right side of the screen. When you do this, you can show two things on the screen at one time; one can be an app and the other a desktop app, for instance. You can also drag items from the list to a specific area of the screen.

TROUBLESHOOTING If you don't see the option to Snap Left or Snap Right when you right-click an app thumbnail, or if you can't drag and drop an app to snap it to the side of the screen when another app is open, change the resolution of your computer screen to 1366 × 768 or higher.

In this exercise, you'll open three apps from the Start screen and switch among them by using various techniques involving a keyboard and mouse. You will then close one app and position another to take up a third of the screen.

 SET UP There is no setup for this exercise. You do not need any practice files to complete this exercise.

1   Position your cursor in the bottom-left corner of the screen and, when the Start screen thumbnail appears, click it.

2   Click **Weather**.

3   Repeat to open **Music** and then **Maps**. If prompted to allow an app to use your location, choose Allow.

4   With Maps active, on the keyboard, hold down the **Windows** key.

5   While holding down **Windows**, press **Tab** several times.

     Different thumbnails are selected.

6   Let go of both keys when the **Music** thumbnail is selected.

     The Music app opens.

7   Press and hold the **Windows** key, and tap the **Tab** key one time.

8   On the Switch list, right-click the **Maps** app. Click **Close**.

9   With the **Music** app still active and the Switch list open, drag the **Weather** app inward from the right side.

     It snaps into place.

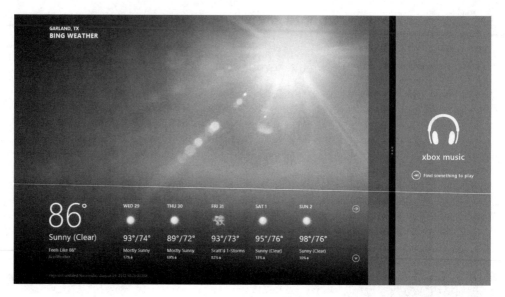

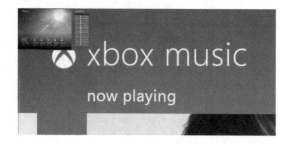

CLEAN UP To return to the Start screen, press the Windows key on the keyboard.

TIP After an app is snapped to one side of the screen, you can use the black bar that separates from the rest of the screen to hide or move it. Just click and drag.

If you'd rather not use a keyboard shortcut, you can access the Switch list by using the mouse only, but this is a little trickier. To access the Switch list by using only a mouse, you first position the cursor in the top-left corner. You'll see the last app used. You can click that to access it, or you can move the cursor down the left side, slowly, to show the entire Switch list shown earlier.

TROUBLESHOOTING If you have so many windows and apps open that Flip is encumbered, close windows and apps you don't use.

If you have the option to use touch gestures, all of this is a little more intuitive. You can just swipe your finger to move from app to app. You'll learn more about using touch in Chapter 19, "Using Windows 8 on Touch-Compatible Devices."

Working with PC Settings and Control Panel

Control Panel is still part of Windows 8. It's where you make changes to how Windows 8 looks and functions; where you add, manage, and remove users; and where you manage networks, configure Internet options, and more. It looks like the Control Panel you're already used to; it's virtually the same Control Panel as was included with Windows Vista and Windows 7. Control Panel is a desktop application. You can open it by searching for it from the Start screen.

There's a more user-friendly way to make changes to your system, which is by using PC Settings. The most common settings that can be changed, such as your account picture or Lock screen image, can be configured here. Although there are several ways to access PC Settings, one way is to opt to change your account picture from the Start screen. In fact, many options by which to make a personal change to the computer cause PC Settings to open.

From the PC Settings screen, you have access to two panes. The left pane offers a listing of available categories, including but not limited to Personalize, Users, Notifications, General, and HomeGroup. You see a scroll bar if the categories run off the screen, provided you position your mouse between the two panes.

When you click a category in the left pane, the options for it appear in the right. You click in the right pane to make changes. You apply many of these changes with a single click or touch; you apply others by selecting from additional options that appear. For example, you can apply a new Lock screen image with only two or three clicks, provided you select an image from the options shown. If you click Browse instead, you must perform additional tasks, including finding the picture to use.

PC settings

Personalize

Users

Notifications

Search

Share

General

Privacy

Devices

Ease of Access

Sync your settings

HomeGroup

Windows Update

Lock screen   Start screen   Account picture

Browse

Lock screen apps

Choose apps to run in the background and show quick status and notifications, even when your screen is locked

In this exercise, you'll open PC Settings from the Start screen and use the PC Settings hub to change the picture on the Lock screen.

 SET UP There is no setup for this exercise. You don't need any practice files to complete this exercise.

1   Access the **Start** screen. Type **Lock**.

2   Click **Settings** in the right pane.

3   In the left pane, click **Customize your lock screen and notifications**.

4 Click one of the available pictures.

The picture on the Lock screen is changed.

✖ CLEAN UP Leave this window open.

With a feel for how the panes work, you can now explore the categories on the left side of the PC Settings hub. It's not important right now for you to understand every option; you'll return to these settings many times as you work through this book. What's important now is to explore PC Settings and get an idea of what's available.

Here are a few category options to explore. (This is not a complete list, but you are encouraged to explore all of them.)

- **PERSONALIZE** Use this setting to change the Lock screen background and the picture associated with your User tile and to choose apps that appear on the Lock screen with detailed status information. You can change the color of the Start screen's background and design here, too.

- **USERS** Use this setting to apply a password to your user account or to change or remove a password. This is where you switch from using a local account to using your Microsoft account. You can also add new users here, if you are logged on as an administrator.

Your account

 Joli Ballew
Joli_ballew@hotmail.com

You can switch to a local account, but your settings won't sync between the PCs you use.

Switch to a local account

More account settings online

Sign-in options

Change your password

Create a picture password

Create a PIN

Any user who has a password must enter it when waking this PC.

Change

Other users

There are no other users on this PC.

■ **NOTIFICATIONS** Use this setting to choose how and when to be notified of updated information from apps such as Calendar, Mail, Messaging, and so on.

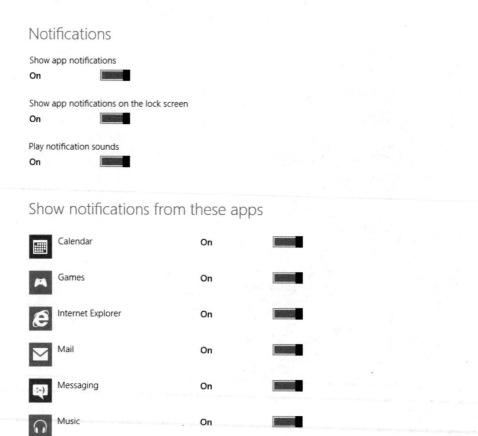

40   Chapter 1 Introducing Windows 8

- **HOMEGROUP** Use this setting to set up and configure your network homegroup. A homegroup makes it easy to share files and folders over a trusted home network.

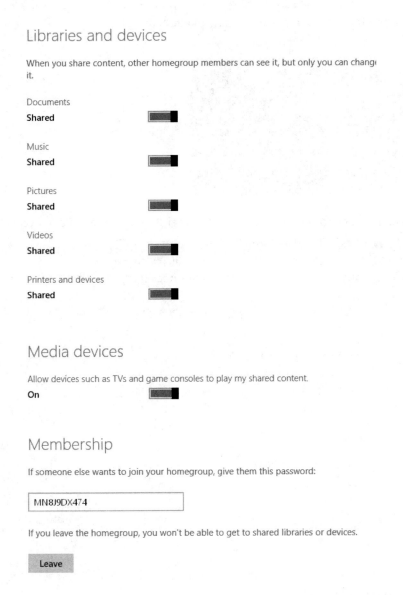

Libraries and devices

When you share content, other homegroup members can see it, but only you can change it.

Documents
Shared

Music
Shared

Pictures
Shared

Videos
Shared

Printers and devices
Shared

Media devices

Allow devices such as TVs and game consoles to play my shared content.
On

Membership

If someone else wants to join your homegroup, give them this password:

MN8J9DX474

If you leave the homegroup, you won't be able to get to shared libraries or devices.

Leave

TIP Click every category in the left pane of PC Settings now to see what's available, but don't make any changes beyond personalizing the Lock screen, your User tile, and other nonessential areas.

If you need access to more configuration options than those available in PC Settings, you can use Control Panel. Control Panel is just a different presentation of PC Settings with more options. You use the same technique to open Control Panel as you used to open PC Settings. From the Start screen, type Control Panel and then select it from the list of Apps available.

Control Panel opens to the familiar Control Panel. To use Control Panel, you choose the desired entry, access the areas you want to change, and make changes by selecting from the choices offered. As with PC Settings, you'll access these options often throughout this book when the required or desired options are necessary for instruction.

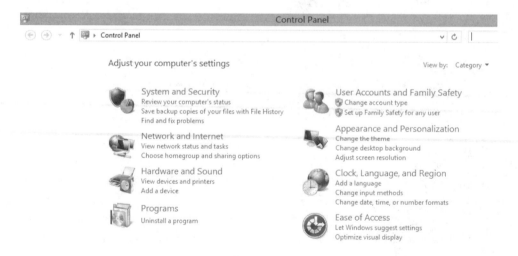

TIP If time allows, explore the options in both PC Settings and Control Panel, but don't make any major changes to the system yet.

Ending a Computing Session

When you are ready to end a computing session, you should, at the very least, secure your computer so that others can't access it. You can do this by locking the computer. You can access the Lock option from the Start screen, or you can use the Windows+L combination. If you use the Start screen, click your User tile in the top-right corner. When you lock your computer, your open files, programs, apps, and windows remain open so that when you unlock your computer you can continue working where you left off. Lock your computer when you want to leave it unattended for a short period of time. You should lock your computer when you go to lunch, run an errand, or go for coffee.

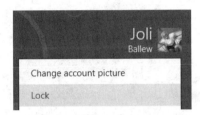

IMPORTANT If you lock your computer but don't have a password configured to unlock it, locking it doesn't do much good. Anyone can flick the Lock screen upward and gain access.

You can also sign out of your computer. When you do this, you are closing your computing session. When you return, you must sign back in and start a new computing session, which means reopening apps, programs, and previously opened windows. Sign off to secure your computer if you'll be away from it for a long period of time.

Your computer is likely configured to go to sleep after a specific period of time. While your computer is sleeping, it uses very little electricity. The hard drive(s) and monitor(s) power down and are quiet and dim. It's best to let your computer go to sleep when you can rather than turning it off. It causes less wear and tear, and the computer can be awakened much more quickly than it can be restarted. When a computer sleeps, your programs and windows remain open and ready. Your computer will go to sleep after a specific period of inactivity. In the default power scheme, Balanced, the monitor will sleep after 10 minutes and the computer after 30.

Finally, you can completely shut down your computer. Because other options are encouraged, the option to turn off the computer is more difficult to access. The option to turn off your computer is available from the Settings charm, from the Power options. Although you can access that setting from there, it's much easier to use the Windows+I keyboard shortcut.

TIP Shut down your computer when you want to move it, transport it, or know you won't be using it for at least two days.

In this exercise, you'll shut down your computer.

SET UP There is no setup for this exercise. You do not need any practice files to complete this exercise.

1   Position your cursor in the bottom-right corner of the screen and, when the charms appear, click **Settings**.

2   Click **Power**.

3   Click **Shut down**.

CLEAN UP Leave the computer turned off until you are ready to use it again.

TROUBLESHOOTING If you see other options that prompt you to install updates before shutting down, choose that option.

Key Points

- When you set up Windows 8, you have to input some information, including your user name, computer name, a password, and more.

- You click or flick upward to bypass the Lock screen.

- The Start screen contains tiles that represent apps and programs and offers access to various parts of the computer, including the desktop and Control Panel.

- Charms offer access to additional, embedded settings, features, and configuration options.

- Some tiles on the Start screen are configurable and will offer up-to-date information obtained from the Internet.

- The traditional desktop is available from the Start screen and is still where you will do most of your work.

- There are many ways to work with multiple open windows, including Flip, the Switch list, and hot corners.

- Control Panel offers access to configuration options you can apply, including adding users and configuring networks.

- You can end a computing session by locking the screen, logging off, letting the computer go to sleep, or shutting it down.

1

Chapter at a Glance

Pin

Pin apps to the Start screen, page 51

Use

Use a Microsoft account, page 56

Your account

Joli Ballew
BallewWin8@hotmail.com

You can switch to a local account, but your settings won't sync

Switch to a local account

More account settings online

Personalize

Personalize the taskbar, page 63

Switch

Switch between power plans, page 70

Power Options

nel ▸ All Control Panel Items ▸ Power Options

Choose or customize a power plan

A power plan is a collection of hardware and system settings (like display brigh how your computer uses power. Tell me more about power plans

Preferred plans

◉ **Balanced (recommended)**
Automatically balances performance with energy consumption on capal

○ Power saver
Saves energy by reducing your computer's performance where possible.

Show additional plans

Making Windows Look and Sound the Way You Want

2

IN THIS CHAPTER, YOU WILL LEARN HOW TO

- Personalize your Start screen.
- Personalize your Lock screen.
- Personalize the desktop and taskbar.
- Change the sound scheme.
- Access and explore advanced settings.
- Create your own power plan.

Now that you have Windows 8 set up and know your way around the Lock screen, Start screen, and desktop, it's time to personalize the computer further so that it suits your exact wants and needs. In this chapter, you'll learn how to configure the Start screen to hold only tiles you use regularly and how to personalize the Lock screen with the desired live information. You'll also learn to personalize the desktop and associated elements, change some of the advanced settings for resolution and sound, and even switch to a new power plan. After you've worked through this chapter, your computer will be distinctively yours.

PRACTICE FILES Before you can complete the exercises in this chapter, you need to copy the book's practice files to your computer. The practice files you'll use to complete the exercises in this chapter are in the Chapter02 practice files folder. A complete list of practice files is provided in the "Using the Practice Files" section at the beginning of this book.

Personalizing the Start Screen

You learned quite a bit about the Start screen in Chapter 1, "Introducing Windows 8." You learned how to move tiles around and configure the Weather app to show up-to-date information. There's probably quite a bit you'd still like to change, though. You want to remove tiles for apps you don't use and add tiles for those you do, configure how large or small a tile appears on the screen, and change the background, to name a few. You might also want to disable some of the live tiles.

TIP Before you start, think about the apps and desktop apps you use most often, the websites you visit most often, and the configuration options you access the most often. Start by adding those to your Start screen. Then consider removing tiles for apps you rarely use.

In this exercise, you'll personalize the Start screen with a new background color.

→ SET UP **Start your computer and unlock the Lock screen. You need to have access to the Start screen. You do not need any practice files for this exercise.**

1   On the **Start** screen, type **Start screen**.

2   Under **Settings**, click or touch **Settings** and then choose **Customize your start screen**.

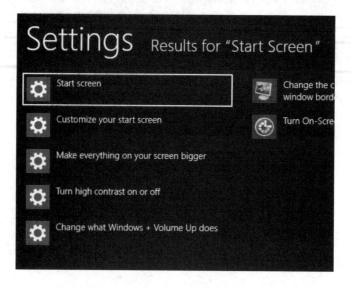

3 In the **PC settings** window:

Lock screen   Start screen   Account picture

a.   **Choose a background** You choose the background for the Start screen by click-
      ing or touching any thumbnail.

b.   **Choose a background color** You choose the background color by using a slider
      provided for that purpose.

TIP If you are using a local user account, you should switch to a Microsoft account if you
want the changes you make on the Start screen and throughout this chapter to follow you
from computer to computer. This is possible only if those other computers can access the
Internet to download your profile information, and only if you sign in on those computers
by using your Microsoft account.

⊗ CLEAN UP **Return to the Start screen when ready.**

Now you can personalize your Start screen to hold only the tiles you use often. The command to remove a tile is Unpin From Start. You access this command by right-clicking the unwanted app tile. This displays a toolbar that runs across the bottom of the screen and holds the charms you need to perform this task and others. What you see when you right-click an app depends on the tile. You might see Smaller, Larger, or Turn Live Tile Off. If you right-click multiple tiles, you also see Clear Selection. (You can also tap, hold, and pull the tile downward slightly to view this toolbar if you prefer to use touch gestures.)

TIP Uninstall is an option from the toolbar that appears when you right-click a tile. Don't uninstall anything yet, though; you might decide later that you want to use the app.

A live tile has information that changes often. You might have noticed that the News app scrolls through the latest headlines or that Mail scrolls through received emails. This information is live; thus the name *live tile*. You might want to disable the live feature of some of those tiles if the constant flipping bothers you or if you don't want to be distracted by new information about Facebook updates, tweets, email, or other data every time you access the Start screen. You might not want onlookers to see data you're acquiring, either. You can disable a live tile by using the same technique you learned earlier to remove tiles you don't want. Right-click the live tile to change it and then click Turn Live Tile Off. The tile will remain, but updates won't appear.

TIP You might want to make a tile live, too. For instance, when Calendar is configured as live, appointments and events appear there as the day and time draws near.

Finally, you'll want to add tiles for programs, features, and even web pages you visit often. This requires a few more steps than removing a tile or repositioning one, but it's still easy.

TROUBLESHOOTING If you uninstall an app and decide you want it back, check the Store. You just might find it there.

In this exercise, you'll add a tile to the Start screen for Windows Media Player, Control Panel, and your favorite Windows desktop application.

SET UP Start your computer and unlock the Lock screen. You need to have access to the Start screen. You do not need any practice files to complete this exercise.

TIP When an instruction requires you to click something with a mouse, note that you can generally touch the item to achieve the same result. When a right-click is needed, try a long touch and short drag downward or an upward swipe from the bottom of the screen. In some instances, a simple, single, long touch will suffice.

1 Right-click an empty area of the **Start** screen; click **All Apps**.

2 Right-click **Windows Media Player** (located under **Windows Accessories**). Click **Pin to Start**.

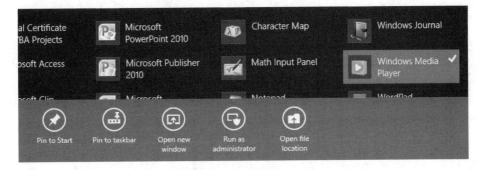

3 Right-click **Control Panel** (located under **Windows System**) and click **Pin to Start**.

4 If you've installed programs on your own, right-click your favorite desktop program (located somewhere on the All Apps screen) and click **Pin to Start**.

CLEAN UP If applicable, return to the Start screen.

Personalizing the Lock Screen

You learned a little about the Lock screen in Chapter 1, including that it's more functional than any Lock screen you might have encountered in previous Microsoft operating systems. You learned in Chapter 1 how to choose a new background, and you learned that the Lock screen offers the time and has tiles that represent apps on it. You probably know that you can't click and engage those tiles, but you can get a quick glance at what's been updated since you last used your computer. For example, after you've set up Mail, you'll see the Mail tile there with a number beside it to notify you of how many new email messages are unread. You might also see a Calendar tiles, a People or Messaging tile, and others, depending on how Windows 8 is currently configured.

In this section, you'll learn how to customize the Lock screen. You'll learn how to personalize it with a picture of your own, how to add and remove tiles for apps, and more.

In this exercise, you'll make changes to the Lock screen to personalize it.

 SET UP Start your computer and unlock the Lock screen. You need to have access to the Start screen.

1   On the **Start** screen, type **Lock**.

2   In the results, click **Settings**.

3   Click **Customize your lock screen and notifications**.

    The PC settings screen appears.

Browse

Lock screen apps

Choose apps to run in the background and show quick status and notifications, even when your screen is locked

Choose an app to display detailed status

4   Click one of the plus (+) signs.

5   Click the app you'd like to appear in the selected position.

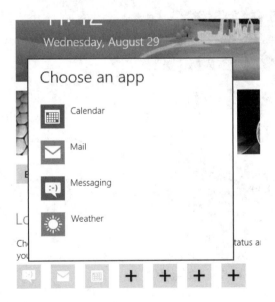

6   To view detailed information for an app on the Lock screen, click the icon under **Choose an app to display detailed status** and select the desired app.

TIP If you select an app to appear that is already showing on the Lock screen, its placement on the screen will be altered.

7   Press **Windows key+L** to access the Lock screen and review your changes.

✖ CLEAN UP Unlock the computer and return to the Start screen.

In this exercise, you'll browse for a picture you've saved to your computer and use it as your Lock screen picture.

→ SET UP You need to have copied the Sheep.jpg file located in the Chapter02 practice file folder to your computer's My Pictures folder to complete this exercise. Using any method, access the Start screen. One way is to press the Windows key on the keyboard.

1   Type Lock, click **Settings**, and click **Customize your lock screen and notifications**.

2   To the right of Change Your Picture, click **Browse**.

3   In the **Pictures** folder, which opens by default, click the image of the sheep. Click **Choose Picture**.

TROUBLESHOOTING If you don't see this picture and you're sure you've copied it to the Pictures folder, click or tap Go Up. You might not be in the proper folder.

4   Press **Windows+L** to see your changes.

5   Unlock the computer and log on.

❌ CLEAN UP Return to the PC Settings screen where you configured the Lock screen changes and tap Users to segue nicely into the next section.

Changing Your User Account Type

A user account is what defines you when you log on to your computer and is associated with your specific user profile. You have three options for your user account. You can use a local user account, a domain account, or a global Microsoft account.

A local user account is an account that's available only from your own, personal computer. The settings you configure for your applications, apps, desktop and taskbar, backgrounds, Internet Explorer Favorites, app configuration on your Start screen, and other customizations are applied to and available from only your local computer. Your user profile is stored on your local computer and available only from there. If you use only one computer, this should be fine. However, if you use multiple Windows 8–based computers (one at work, one at home, and perhaps a laptop when you're on the back porch) or use a Windows 8 tablet or a Windows phone, you will want to consider using a Microsoft account instead.

A Microsoft account is a roaming user account (as opposed to a local one). Your profile is stored on the Internet in the cloud, and your user profile is accessible from the other computers, tablets, and devices running Windows 8. This means that all your settings, preferences, and configurations are available from any computer to which you can log on by using this account, provided that that computer is connected to the Internet and can access that profile. The purpose of storing your user profile on the Internet is so you can move from computer to computer or device to device and have the same experience on one as you do on the other. In this scenario, any changes you make while logged on are saved to your profile, too, so if you make a change to your laptop's Start screen, that change will be applied when you log on to your desktop computer next time, provided you've logged on to those devices with your Microsoft account. (You might notice a slight delay in loading your profile after logging on to a computer with your Microsoft account.)

TROUBLESHOOTING A Microsoft account syncs only your personal settings and preferences. It's a roaming user profile. You can't access programs you've installed on another computer running Windows 8, print to a remote computer's local printer, or use your home computer's webcam from another computer, for instance. You're not accessing your computer remotely with this feature; you're accessing only your *user profile*, which is stored on a server on the Internet.

You switch from a local account to a Microsoft account (or vice versa) on the PC Settings screen from the Users category. (You saw this screen earlier.) A Microsoft account is an email address such as your_name@hotmail.com or yourname@live.com, but it does not have to be from either of these domains. You might already have a Microsoft account. A Windows Live ID, a Live email address, or a Hotmail email address are Microsoft accounts. A Microsoft account is preferred over a local user account in most instances. You can sign up for an account at www.live.com if you don't have one.

Your account

Joli Ballew
joli_ballew@hotmail.com

You can switch to a local account, but your settings won't sync between the PCs you use.

Switch to a local account

Depending on how your computer is currently set up, click the appropriate switch option and follow the prompts. What you see will depend on the account to which you are switching and whether you have the required accounts in place. If you are already using a Microsoft account, you don't need to do anything here unless you'd rather not use it.

TIP In PC settings, click Sync Your Settings in the left pane and turn on or off the sync settings desired. You can sync colors, background, Lock screen, and account pictures, for instance, but not themes, taskbar, and high-contrast settings. By default, your profile won't sync over metered connections, which charge you based on your data usage, but you can enable the feature if you'd like.

Customizing Your User Account Settings

After you've decided what type of account to use and applied the change if applicable, and note that a Microsoft account is preferred in most instances, you can make other changes to your user account to customize it further. The changes will be saved to your user profile. One item to change is your user account picture.

TIP From Users in PC Settings, you can choose to trust your home or work PC. When you do, sign-in information for some apps, websites, and networks syncs with your user profile.

In this exercise, you'll change the picture associated with your user account.

 SET UP **Start your computer and unlock the Lock screen. You need to have access to the Start screen.**

1   From the **Start** screen, click your **User name** in the top-right corner.

2   Click **Change account picture**.

3   Click **Browse**.

Lock screen   Start screen   Account picture

Browse

Create an account picture

 Camera

4   If you don't see the picture you want to use, click the **Files down arrow**; choose
      Pictures and the desired folder or subfolder.

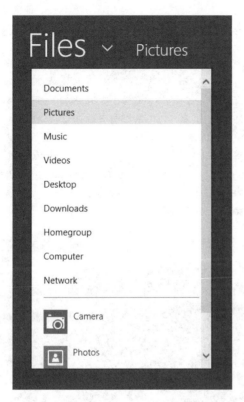

Files ⌄   Pictures

Documents
Pictures
Music
Videos
Desktop
Downloads
Homegroup
Computer
Network
_____

📷 Camera

🖼 Photos

5   Click the image to use and select **Choose image**.

✕ CLEAN UP No clean up is required.

TIP Explore other PC Settings options now. You can, for instance, make changes to the password you use to log on. You can create a PIN. This is a personal identification number, and it can be used on your computer in place of the complex password you've been using until now. (Click Users to get started.)

Personalizing the Desktop

You learned about the desktop in Chapter 1. There you discovered that the desktop still exists in a form very similar to what you're likely already used to if you've spent any time with other Windows-based computers. You can personalize the desktop in the same ways, too. You can apply a new background, personalize sounds, set a screen saver, and more. You can have the background switch to show a slide show of pictures you select. You can also choose a theme, a group of settings that, combined, provide a motif. One theme, Nature, combines backgrounds, screensavers, window colors, and sounds and is available from the Windows 8 Desktop Personalization options. You can just choose a new background; there are many beautiful pictures from which you can choose.

In this section, you won't learn how to personalize every aspect of the desktop; that could fill an entire chapter if not more! You'll learn how to select a new background and apply a theme, and from there you can surmise how to make additional changes.

In this exercise, you'll apply the Nature theme and customize which backgrounds you want to appear.

→ SET UP Access the Desktop. If you are on the Start screen, use the Windows+D keyboard shortcut.

1   Right-click the **desktop**. Click **Personalize**. The Personalization window opens.

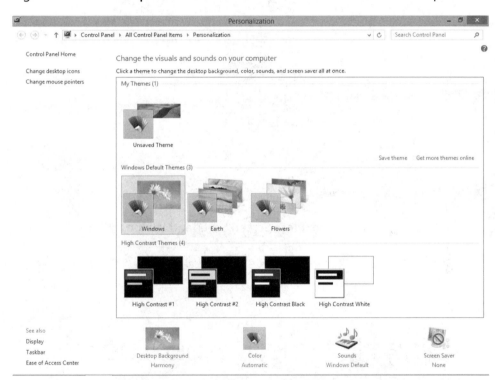

2   Click **Earth**. The theme is immediately applied, and new colors are associated with windows and the taskbar.

3   Click **Desktop Background**.

4   Clear a few images.

5   Use **Change picture every** to select an option.

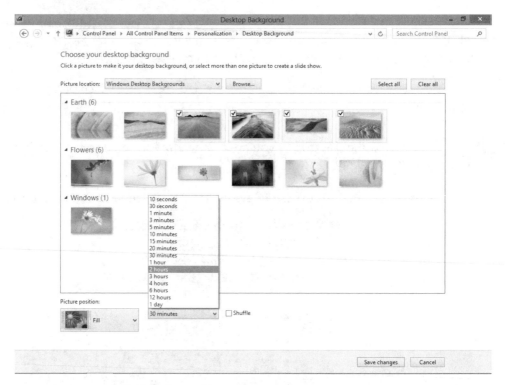

6   Click **Save Changes**.

❌ CLEAN UP If desired, explore Screen Saver and Window Color.

SEE ALSO "Change the Sound Scheme" and "Customize Advanced Settings" later in this chapter.

Changing How the Taskbar Looks

The taskbar is the blue bar that runs across the bottom of the screen when you're using the desktop. It might be a different color if you've applied a theme. By default, it's locked and can't be moved. If you unlock it, you can drag it to a different area on the screen. You might prefer the taskbar on the left side of the desktop, for instance (or across the top).

Beyond unlocking and then dragging the Taskbar to a new place on the screen, you can:

- **REPOSITION BUTTONS** Click and drag icons from one area of the taskbar to another.

- **PIN ICONS** Pin things to the taskbar, including icons for desktop apps, documents, folders, and more.

- **AUTO-HIDE THE TASKBAR** Auto-hide the taskbar to keep it off the screen when it's not needed.

- **CHANGE TASKBAR BUTTON SIZE AND GROUPING** Use small or large taskbar buttons and choose to group or not group like icons when the taskbar is full.

- **USE DIVIDERS** Hide and show elements added to the taskbar, including a shortcut to Libraries.

- **ENABLE PEEK** Enable or disable Peek, a feature outlined in Chapter 1 that enables you to look at the desktop by temporarily making all open windows transparent. You use Peek by positioning your mouse in the bottom-right corner of the screen.

- **CUSTOMIZE THE NOTIFICATION AREA** Select which icons and notifications appear on the taskbar.

- **USE JUMP LISTS** Enable or disable jump lists and configure how they work. Jump lists can show recently opened programs or recent items you've opened in a program.

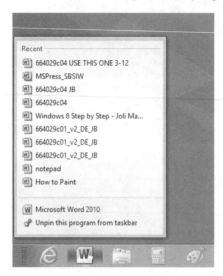

- **SHOW OR HIDE TOOLBARS** Show or hide toolbars, including the Address, Links, Touch Keyboard, and Desktop toolbars.

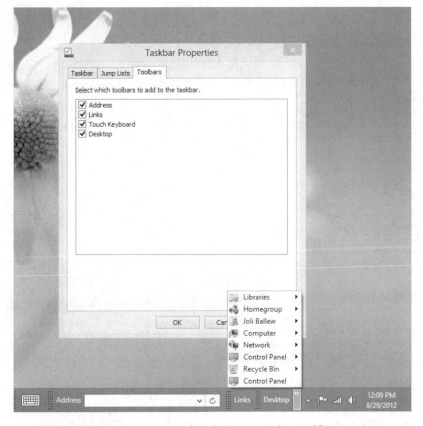

Try some of these features now. On the desktop at the taskbar:

- **REPOSITION THE TASKBAR** Right-click the taskbar and, in the resulting menu, clear the check by Lock The Taskbar if applicable. Drag the taskbar to the left side of the screen.

- **SHOW HIDDEN BUTTONS** Drag any slider, if possible, to view hidden taskbar buttons.

- **TEST PEEK** Open any window or multiple windows. Position your mouse in the bottom-right corner of the screen. If the windows turn transparent, Peek is enabled. If they do not, Peek is disabled.

In this exercise, you'll configure the taskbar by using the Taskbar Properties dialog box.

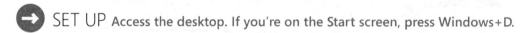 SET UP **Access the desktop. If you're on the Start screen, press Windows+D.**

1 Right-click an empty area of the taskbar and click **Properties**. (To use gestures, use a long touch, then tap **Properties.**)

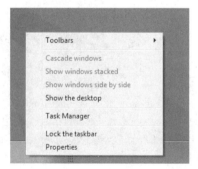

2 In the **Taskbar Properties** dialog box, on the **Taskbar** tab, select or clear the desired choices. Click **Apply**.

TIP From the Taskbar Properties Taskbar tab, next to the Notification area, click Customize to change how you are notified of system events and to hide or show icons there. Refer to Chapter 14, "Keeping Windows 8 Safe and Secure," to learn more about this.

3   Click the **Jump Lists** tab and make the desired choices. Click **Apply**.

4   Click the **Toolbars** tab; make the desired choices. Click **OK**.

❌ CLEAN UP No cleanup is required.

Changing the Sound Scheme

The sounds your computer makes when system events occur are part of the Windows Default sound scheme. Some of the system sounds with which you might be familiar include Critical Stop, New Mail Notification, and Windows Change Theme (if you changed the theme earlier). You can change the Windows Default sound scheme to one of several others, all with names that are representative of the sound scheme they offer. One of the schemes is No Sounds.

You can change the sound scheme from the Personalization window you learned about earlier. Click Sounds and, from the Sounds tab, select a new scheme. (Right-click an empty area of the desktop and choose Personalize to access the Sounds option.)

Accessing and Exploring Advanced Settings

There just isn't enough space in a single chapter to cover all the personalization options available in Windows 8. However, you can access all the options from a single window, Control Panel, and you can certainly explore and configure these settings to the extent you'd like. You can't harm your computer by changing these options, but you might make it look quite a bit different from what you'll see in this book.

In this exercise, you'll first view all the Appearance and Personalization options and then change the screen resolution.

 SET UP Start your computer and unlock the Lock screen. You need to have access to the Start screen.

1 From the **Start** screen, type Control.

2 In the results, click **Control Panel**.

3   Verify that the view is **Category** and then choose **Appearance and Personalization**.
     All the personalization options appear.

4   Under **Display**, click **Adjust screen resolution**.

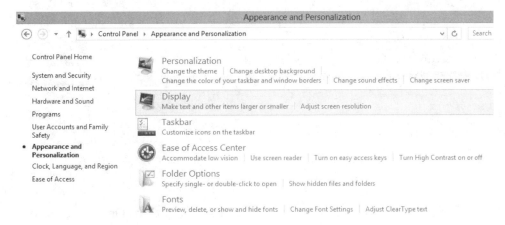

5   Configure settings as desired and click **Apply**.

❌ CLEAN UP Continue to explore the options as time allows.

As you explore Control Panel, you'll see that clicking some options, such as Change The
Theme or Change Desktop Background, open windows that you've already explored in this
chapter. You'll also notice that you have access to the available fonts and to folder options
that enable you to view hidden files or state how you'd like to open icons. If you've used a
Windows operating system before, these will look familiar. You'll also see a Back arrow and
an Up arrow so you can return quickly to the previous screen as you explore.

TIP In the Appearance And Personalize window, tapping a heading such as Taskbar results
in a different dialog box than tapping an item under it, such as Customize icons, on the
taskbar.

Switching to a Different Power Plan

A power plan is a group of settings that defines when your monitor goes to sleep and when the computer goes to sleep. This occurs after a specific amount of idle time. In the case of laptops and tablets, there are two sets of settings, one for when the computer is plugged in and one for when it's running on battery power. You change the power plan from Control Panel, under Hardware And Sound, in Power Options. To select a plan and apply it, select the desired plan by clicking the option button beside the plan name.

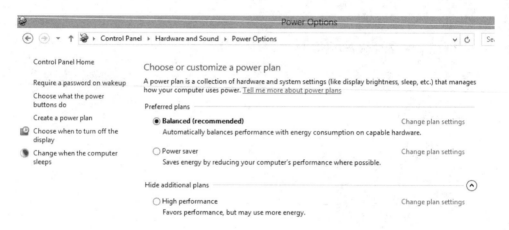

There are three power plans (but you can create your own). On a desktop computer, the settings are as listed here. (Laptops have a second set of settings for when the laptop is running on battery power.)

- **BALANCED** This is the default plan. The display turns off after 10 minutes; the computer goes to sleep after 30 minutes.

- **POWER SAVER** This plan is the best for minimizing power usage. The display turns off after five minutes; the computer goes to sleep after 15 minutes.

- **HIGH PERFORMANCE** This plan is best when you need all the computing power you can obtain. The display turns off after 15 minutes; the computer never goes to sleep. To access this plan, you must click the arrow by Show Additional Plans.

From this window, you can perform other power-related tasks. You can choose what the power buttons do, for instance. If you have a laptop, you might want the computer to shut down when you close its lid. You might just want it to sleep. Likewise, you might want to press the Power button on a desktop computer to cause it to sleep, shut down, hibernate, or, perhaps, do nothing.

You can change aspects of a plan. For instance, if you like the Balanced plan but would rather the display and computer go to sleep after 30 minutes, you can easily make the change. You can restore the defaults for a plan with a single click, too. You can create your own power plan from scratch. However, the three default plans will likely suffice with a little tweaking.

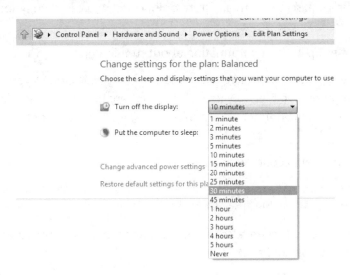

In this exercise, you'll choose a power plan.

SET UP No setup is required for this exercise.

1   Using any method, access the **Start** screen. One way is to press the Windows key on the keyboard.

2   Type **Power**. Click **Settings**.

3   Click **Change power-saving settings**.

4   Select a plan to use.

5   Close the **Power Options** window.

CLEAN UP Close the Power Options window and return to the Start screen.

Key Points

- When you personalize the Start screen, you remove tiles you won't use, add tiles you will use, and reposition them as desired.

- You can personalize the Lock screen with a picture or PIN, and you can then unlock your computer with either.

- The Lock screen can offer up-to-date information about running apps.

- You can use a local user account or a Microsoft account when you log on to your Windows 8–based computer or tablet. A Microsoft account enables you to sync information among your devices, including backgrounds, Internet Explorer Favorites, and preferences.

- You can personalize your user account with a picture.

- Personalization options enable you to easily change the desktop, taskbar, and notification areas when working on the desktop.

- It's possible to pick a new sound scheme, set a new resolution, and perform other personalization tasks from Control Panel.

- Power plans are configurations that determine when your computer sleeps and when the display dims.

Chapter at a Glance

Explore

Explore the Photos app, page 76

Play

Play music, page 84

Get

Get directions, page 90

Learn

Learn more about each app, page 93

Using Apps on the Start Screen

3

IN THIS CHAPTER, YOU WILL LEARN HOW TO

- View and manage photos with the Photos app.

- View and manage music with the Music app.

- View and manage video with the Video app.

- Find a location with the Maps app.

- Explore other default apps.

- Uninstall, remove, and edit apps.

- Explore accessories and tools.

You know about the apps available on the Start screen, and you've explored a few of them already. You've moved them, hidden them, and changed their sizes, and you know how to move among them when multiple apps are open. Now you're ready to learn a little about what each of the most popular default apps offers.

In this chapter, you'll learn how to use the Photos, Music, Video, and Maps apps effectively (because these are the ones you'll likely use the most from the start), and then you'll learn what the other apps offer and where to learn more about them in this book.

PRACTICE FILES Before you can complete the exercises in this chapter, you need to copy the book's practice files to your computer. The practice files you'll use to complete the exercises in this chapter are in the Chapter03 practice files folder. Copy the entire Windows8Pictures folder to the Pictures library. A complete list of practice files is provided in "Using the Practice Files" section at the beginning of this book.

Using the Photos App

By using the Photos app, available from the Start screen, you can browse the Pictures library on your computer and pictures you've stored on the Internet in places such as SkyDrive, Facebook, and Flickr. You can also access pictures stored on connected devices.

When you open the Photos app, what you see depends on your presence on the Internet, how you've previously set up the Photos app, and what online accounts you've already associated with your Windows 8 computer. For example, if you've used SkyDrive and have pictures stored there, you'll see and have access to your SkyDrive folder. If you've associated your Windows 8–based computer with your Facebook account in any app, you'll see your Facebook photos here, too. However, you might only see pictures from your Pictures library, or you might be prompted to tell Windows where your pictures are stored.

When you're in the Photos app, you can use your mouse's wheel to scroll through the photo folders (or the photos in a folder you've opened). Scrolling with a mouse wheel moves the images and folders left and right. You can also use the scroll bar that appears at the bottom of the Photos app, or you can use your finger to navigate photo folders by swiping and flicking using touch gestures. You must click or tap a folder to manage your photos and to view them. When you enter a folder, you're in Preview mode.

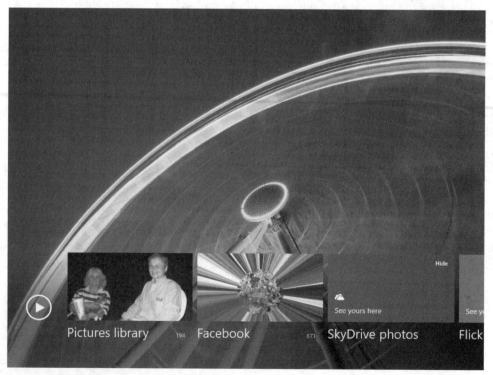

After you've opened a folder, whether it's the Pictures library, SkyDrive, Facebook, or another library, you can view and manage the photos available in it. For now, however, click or tap any photo in any folder to view it in fullscreen mode. Note the back arrow that appears to help you navigate the app. As you continue to use the app, you'll see more back and forward options. Finally, position your mouse near the bottom-right corner of the screen. There you'll find a + and - sign to enable you to zoom in and out.

TROUBLESHOOTING If you don't see any icons on the screen, move the mouse or tap the screen one time. The icons disappear after a second or two when they aren't needed.

If you don't yet have any photos on your computer, you can copy the files provided in the Practice Files folder for this book. If you'd like to add your own pictures, you can do so by placing your pictures in the Pictures library. Although there are several ways to do this, the easiest is to browse to the files to include (whether they are on a CD or DVD, on a network drive, or on a USB key or Secure Digital [SD] card), select the desired files, copy those files, and then paste them into the Pictures folder. If you're unsure how to browse to, copy, and paste files, refer to Chapter 4, "Saving, Browsing, and Organizing Files and Folders."

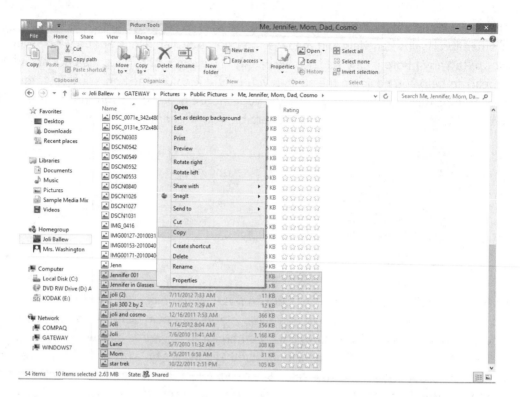

After you have photos in your Pictures library and can view them, you'll find that Photos also offers charms, just like all other apps. Using touch gestures, you can swipe upward from the bottom to view the charms; otherwise, right-click with the mouse. The charms you see depend on which folder you're in or what picture you're viewing. For example, right-clicking a photo in the Facebook folder while it's in full screen mode offers the option to view the photo on Facebook, but right-clicking a photo in the Pictures library does not.

In this exercise, you'll use the Photos app to browse to a folder that contains pictures and to scroll through them. You'll also review the available options in both Preview and fullscreen mode.

SET UP You need to have saved the Windows8Pictures folder to the My Pictures folder on your computer to complete this exercise. This folder is located in the Chapter03 practice file folder.

1   From the **Start screen**, click (or touch) **Photos**.

2   If you've used the Photos app before, it might open with a photo or folder already selected. If so, click the **Back** arrow until you are at the main screen. (You might have to click to see the Back arrow.)

3   Click **Pictures library** and then click or touch the **Windows8Pictures** folder**.**

Pictures libra

Windows8Pictures

4   Click or tap any picture in the folder to open it in fullscreen mode. Move the mouse
    around to see the **Back** and any **Forward** arrows that appear and then click the
    screen to access the applicable Back button.

5   Click the top-most **Back** button to return to the **Windows8Pictures** folder. You may
     have to click the screen to see it.

6   Right-click the Sheep picture to select it and view the available charms.

⊗ CLEAN UP Leave the Photos app open to this screen.

Now that you've seen some of the charms, at least those that specifically apply when you
are viewing pictures stored on your computer, you can see how you could easily delete a
single picture or view a slideshow of the images in a folder. You can also see that the picture
you right-clicked was automatically selected (which means you can quickly delete it). You
can select additional photos by right-clicking them, too. (If you're using touch, tap, hold,
and drag downward to select additional photos.)

The options you can access by right-clicking a photo while in the Pictures library include:

- **CLEAR SELECTION** Click this to clear the files you've previously selected. You can
  select files from only one folder at a time.

- **___ SELECTED** View this to see how many photos are currently selected.

- **DELETE** Click this to delete the selected photo(s).

- **SLIDE SHOW** Click this to watch a slide show of the pictures in the selected folder.

- **SELECT ALL** Click this to select all the pictures in a folder. It does not appear that you can do anything with the selected files yet except delete them, but you might be able to copy or cut those files in the future.

- **IMPORT** Click to choose a device from which to import photos.

Using the Music App

The Music app offers access to your personal music collection and to music available from the Xbox Music Store (which is often referred to simply as the marketplace). You can easily view information about what's currently hot and trending in music, including a list of new releases. From the marketplace, you can browse, preview, and purchase music and related media.

SEE ALSO In Chapter 9, "Having Fun with Multimedia," learn how to burn your CD collection.

There are multiple areas in the Music app:

- **MY MUSIC** To view music to which you have access from your computer. Click My Music to access all your music files and to sort them by albums, artists, songs, and playlists, and to sort what you see by the date you added them, alphabetically, and other options.

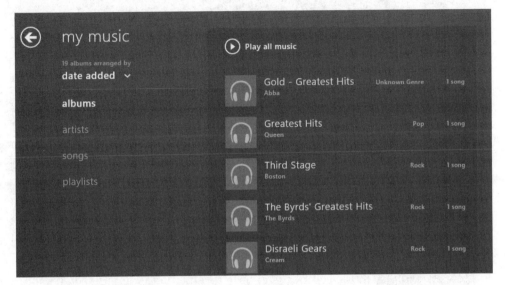

TIP Like the Photos app, you right-click a song or album in any folder or category to view the charms related to it (such as Add To Playlist, Play Selected, Shuffle, Repeat, Previous, Play or Pause, and Next).

- **NOW PLAYING** To see what's currently playing, access the playback controls, skip to the next song in the playlist or on the album, restart the song, and more. Click and right-click to access the options.

- **XBOX MUSIC STORE** To browse, preview, and buy music. You can browse by genre, featured, what's new, and what's popular.

- **MOST POPULAR** To access the most popular music at the moment and to preview that music. You can also make purchases from here.

TIP As with other apps, click the Back arrow to return to the previous screen.

To view and play music you own and have saved to your computer, you choose the desired music under the My Music area of the Music app. If what you want to play isn't on the screen, click the My Music heading. After you select a song, album, or playlist and opt to play it, you can obtain information about the music from the Now Playing area. Once on that page, right-click to see the available charms. You can also right-click the details page for the song or album to access playback controls.

In this exercise, you'll play a song in your music library and view the track list for the album and then pause the music.

➜ SET UP From the Start screen, open the Music app. You do not need any practice files for this exercise; instead, you will play music you own or the sample music provided with Windows 8 (assuming there will be sample music).

1 From the **Start screen**, click or tap **Music**.

2 Under **Music**, click **my music**.

3 Click any album thumbnail and, from the resulting dialog box, select a song and click **Play**.

4 Click the graphic located at the bottom of the screen that represents the album. (If you don't see this, right-click.) A visualization screen opens and offers access to the Track List view and various controls.

5 Click the Track List icon located in the bottom-left corner under the artist name. (Click the screen if you don't see this.)

6 Click the **X** to close the Track list; click the **Back** button to return to the previous screen.

7 Right-click the screen and click **Pause**. (If you don't see the option to Pause, click or touch the screen one time.)

❌ CLEAN UP Leave this screen open.

TIP While a song is playing, continue to browse your music and click Add To Now Playing to play songs you'd like to hear next.

As you would suspect, while playing a song or album you can use media controls to manage what's playing. You can shuffle the songs, too, which means playing the songs in the playlist or on the album in random order. From the available charms, you can easily skip to the previous and next songs, and you can pause and play songs. The Back arrow takes you to the previous screen. To access the controls, right-click any music file.

TIP There are many features to explore in Music. You can sort the music in various ways, you can play music on a networked Xbox, you can create playlists, and more. There isn't enough room here to detail everything you can do, so spend some time exploring the Music app before moving on.

If you don't have any music of your own and you'd like to acquire some, or if you're ready to enhance your current music library, you can purchase music from the marketplace. To get started, open the Music app and click Xbox Music Store access the store.

In this exercise, you'll access the music marketplace and preview a song.

→ SET UP From the Start screen, open the Music app. You do not need any practice files for this exercise, but you will need access to the Internet.

1   From the **Start screen**, click (or touch) **Music**.

2   Scroll right and click **Most Popular**.

3   Click any genre in the left pane.

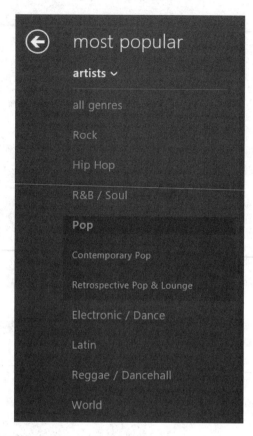

4   Click any subcategory, if applicable.

5   Browse to locate a song to preview; click the album or song. Click **Preview**.

6   Charms will appear that enable you to pause the song or wait for the preview to finish.

⊗ CLEAN UP Click the Back arrow as many times as required to access the main Music screen.

TIP If you want to make a purchase, click the appropriate buy option. You'll be prompted to buy Microsoft Points that you can use to make that purchase.

Using the Video App

If you've become familiar with the Music app, the Video app will be very easy to use. You'll see an area named My Videos that offers access to videos stored in the Videos library on your computer. (Compare that to the Music app's My Music area.) Next to that is Spotlight, where featured videos appear, and that is followed by the Movies Store and the Television Store. As with the music marketplace, you can obtain media here and browse to media using specific categories. Much of the time, you can either buy or rent the media, and you can watch it on your Xbox if you have one.

If you don't own any compatible home videos or have professionally made movies or TV shows available, you can still browse and shop the marketplace, but the area under My Videos won't have any entries. If you have these kinds of media, however, you can browse to them and play them, just as you would with the music app. When you locate and play a video, you have access to media controls that are already likely familiar to you.

TIP If you have a Windows 7–based computer, you can copy Wildlife In HD from the Sample Videos folder there to your Windows 8–based computer to view it.

When playing a video, you have access to media controls that are similar to controls in other apps. If you copied the practice files, and if you copied the "Flying over the Hoover Dam" video to the Videos folder, you can play the "Flying over the Hoover Dam" video now.

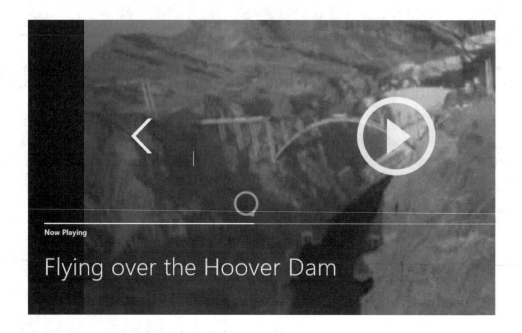

Now Playing

Flying over the Hoover Dam

Using the Maps App

The last app you'll explore in depth is Maps. As with any other app, you click its tile on the Start screen to open it. If you are prompted, make sure to enable location services so that Maps can determine your location. When it's open, right-click the screen to see the available charms.

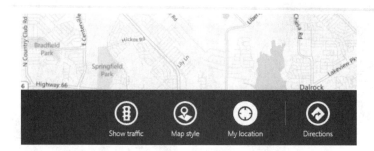

The features available in Maps are:

- **SHOW TRAFFIC** Click this to show the traffic in your area or on a route you've mapped. Traffic is represented by red, yellow, and green. Traffic information won't be available in all areas.

- **MAP STYLE** Click this to change the style of the map from Road View to Aerial View.

- **MY LOCATION** Click this to pinpoint your location. The diamond represents your location. Maps cannot detect your current location if you did not enable the required location services when you first opened Maps or if you are not connected to the Internet.

  TIP Click the diamond that represents your location for more information about it.

- **DIRECTIONS** Click this to get directions from one place to another. By default, your current location will be used as one of the entries (provided location services is enabled). Type an address and tap the right-facing arrow to get directions.

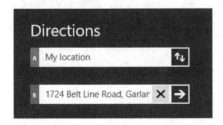

- **REVERSE ROUTE** Click the two arrows located between the two points when Directions is selected to reverse the route offered.

- **GO ARROW** Click Go after inputting the required information to get directions to a place.

In this exercise, you'll get directions from your current location to New York City.

 SET UP From the Start screen, open Maps.

1   From **Maps**, right-click and then click **Directions.**

2   If you don't see **My location** in one of the boxes, type your current address.

3   In the empty box, type **New York City** and click the **Go arrow**.

The route appears with turn-by-turn directions.

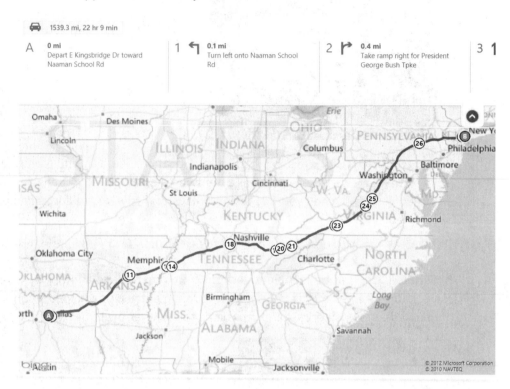

4   Click the + and - buttons to zoom in and out on the map. Position your mouse in the middle of the left edge if you don't see the + and - buttons.

TIP You can zoom in and out by using the scroll wheel of your mouse or the icons on the screen or by pinching in and out with your fingers if you have a compatible touch screen.

5   To hide the directions or start over, right-click and then click **Clear map**.

❌ CLEAN UP **Return to the Start screen.**

Exploring the Other Apps

There are many other apps on the Start screen besides Photos, Music, Video, and Maps, but they all open similarly, most offer right-click options or upward swipe options, you can scroll and touch when there's more data than will fit on the screen, and you can often click screen elements to cause something to happen or a new app page to open. In this section, you'll learn a little about those other apps and where to learn more about them in this book.

3

Additional apps available from the Home screen include:

- **MAIL** To set up, obtain, and manage email. You'll learn about the Mail app in Chapter 7, "Using the Social Apps."

- **PEOPLE** To access information about your contacts. Here, you link the app to your Microsoft account, Facebook, Twitter, and others. This enables you to see what your contacts are up to from a single app. You'll learn about the People app in Chapter 7.

- **MESSAGING** To send messages to others by using the Internet. You'll learn about the Messaging app in Chapter 7.

- **WEATHER** To obtain up-to-date weather information from your current location and other locations you configure. You learned about the Weather app in Chapter 1, "Introducing Windows 8."

- **NEWS** To get the latest news from msnbc.com. News is an easy app to use; just scroll through the headlines and click to read more.

- **DESKTOP** To open the desktop from which you run desktop apps such as Paint and use system tools such as Control Panel.

- **CALENDAR** To access your calendar, on which you can input appointments, events, birthdays, and other data. As with other apps, you can click to change the view, input information, and more. You'll learn about Calendar in Chapter 7.

- **TRAVEL** To open Bing Travel, where you can view featured destinations and panoramas, read articles, and more.

- **SPORTS** To open Bing Sports, where you can read top sports stories, sports news, schedules, and more.

- **GAMES** To access, manage, and view your games and game activity. You can also access the marketplace, where you can purchase new games. If you have an Xbox and have configured an avatar, you'll see it here. You'll learn about games in Chapter 10, "Playing Games."

- **INTERNET EXPLORER** To access the Internet by using Internet Explorer. You'll learn about this app in Chapter 5, "Using Internet Explorer 10."

- **FINANCE** To follow stock prices and access stock report information. You can personalize this app with your own information or just browse the latest financial news.

- **STORE** To access the Windows store, where you can get apps (classified in many categories, including Travel, Productivity, Games, and the like), obtain music and video, access books and reference materials, and more. You'll learn about the store in various chapters, including Chapter 8, "Shopping in the Windows Store."

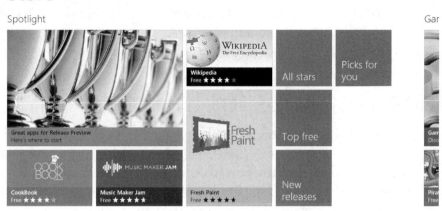

- **SKYDRIVE** To access your personal SkyDrive folders, where you can store pictures, documents, music, and other data on Internet servers. You can then access your SkyDrive data from anywhere. You'll learn about SkyDrive in Chapter 6, "Using SkyDrive."

- **CAMERA** To access the camera available on your computer as applicable and to view camera options. You'll use your camera, if you have one, to hold video chats.

- **BING** To access the Bing search engine. This is an easy way to find something on the web quickly.

    TIP There are other apps available from the All apps screen, including Reader and apps you've obtained from the Store.

Managing Apps for the Long Term

You learned quite a bit about apps in Chapter 1 and Chapter 2, "Making Windows 8 Look and Sound the Way You Want," including how to move apps, use live tiles, and customize those tiles. You learned here how to use many of the apps, including Photos, Music, Video, and Maps, and where to learn more about the rest of the apps on the Start screen. There are a few more things to know, including how to manage apps for the long term.

Here are a few things you can do with apps to make the Start screen more user friendly, to hide apps you won't use, to make app tiles larger or smaller on the Start screen, and more.

- **SHOW ALL APPS AND ACCESSORIES** Right-click an empty area of the Start screen and then click All Apps to see the apps and programs available from your computer. From the resulting screen, you'll see categories that enable you to access the default apps, apps you've installed, desktop apps, suites of applications such as Microsoft Office, and programs such as QuickTime, Skype, and others. You'll also be able to access all the Windows accessories, such as Calculator and Notepad.

- **UNPIN AN APP FROM THE START SCREEN** Right-click any app and click Unpin From Start to remove it from the Start screen.

- **UNINSTALL AN APP** Right-click any app and click Uninstall to remove it completely from your computer.

  TIP Remember, a tap, hold, and downward pull equals a right-click on the Start screen.

- **MAKE AN APP TILE LARGER OR SMALLER** Right-click a rectangular tile and click Smaller to make the app appear smaller on the screen. Right-click again to access Larger. You cannot make a natively square tile larger.

- **MAKE AN APP TILE STOP FLIPPING THROUGH INFORMATION OR SHOWING PERSONAL INFORMATION ON THE START SCREEN (OR TO ALLOW IT TO DO THIS)** Right-click an app with a live tile and choose Turn Live Tile Off (or Turn Live Tile On).

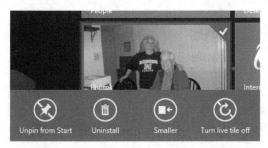

- **CLEAR MULTIPLE SELECTIONS** Click Clear Selection. (You can select multiple apps on the Start screen by right-clicking them.)

- **RUN AS AN ADMINISTRATOR** Right-click any compatible desktop application to run it with administrator privileges. You can also open the file location, uninstall the application, and more.

Exploring Accessories and Tools

Finally, the Start screen offers access to the Windows 8 accessories and system tools. There are quite a few of each and too many to detail here. However, most of the accessory names are intuitive, as are the Windows system tools names. To access the available accessories and system tools, right-click the Start screen, click All Apps, and scroll right. To open one of these, just click it one time or tap it with your finger if applicable.

Not every accessory or tool is covered in this book; there are too many. However, a few are worth noting and exploring here.

- **PAINT** Use to draw your own artwork by using paint brushes and tools such as the Pencil, Paint Bucket, and Text. You can use this program to create a flyer, for example.

3

- **SNIPPING TOOL** Use the snipping tool and drag the cursor (or your finger) around an area of the screen to capture it.

- **CONTROL PANEL** Use this to open Control Panel, which opens on the Desktop and offers access to more personalization, networking, and security options.

In this exercise, you'll access the Help and Support option from the Windows System category when viewing All Apps on the Start screen.

SET UP Start your computer and unlock the Lock screen. You need to have access to the Start screen.

1   At the **Start screen**, type Help and Support.

2   Click **Help and Support** from the results.

3   Maximize the window if applicable.

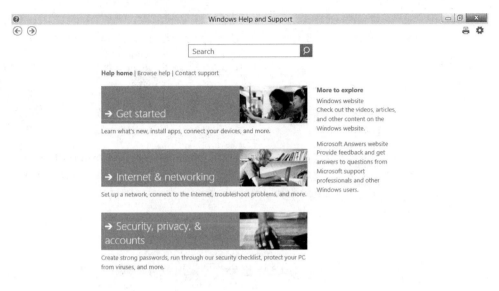

4   Browse the **Help And Support** pages as you would any web page.

CLEAN UP No cleanup is required.

Key Points

- Windows 8 comes with many default apps that are available from the Start screen.

- You use the Photos app to manage and view photos stored on your hard drive, shared networked drives, and social networking sites.

- You use the Music app to access and play your own music and to buy music from the music marketplace.

- You use the Videos app to access movies, TV shows, and compatible videos that are stored on your computer and shared networked drives and to buy movies and TV shows from the video marketplace.

- You use the Maps app to find places and businesses, to get directions, and to get turn-by-turn directions to places you've mapped.

- There are lots of other apps to explore, including People, Calendar, Messaging, and others, many of which are outlined in this book in various chapters.

- The All Apps screen offers access to apps that don't appear on the Start screen, accessories, and system tools. You can also access third-party programs and apps you've acquired from the marketplace.

Chapter at a Glance

Navigate
Navigate files, folders, and libraries, page 109

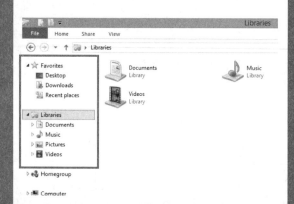

Understand
Understand the File Explorer ribbon, page 113

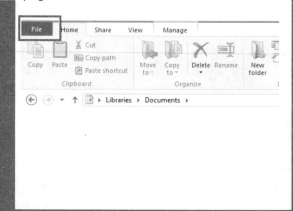

Rename
Rename files and folders, page 135

Create
Create your own library, page 143

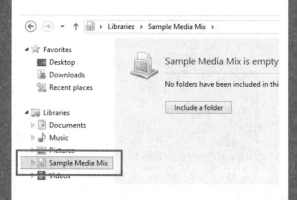

Saving, Browsing, and Organizing Files and Folders

4

IN THIS CHAPTER, YOU WILL LEARN HOW TO

- Understand files, folders, and libraries.

- Describe the most common file types.

- Access your User folders and save files effectively.

- Navigate the File Explorer ribbon interface.

- Organize and share files and folders.

- Customize and search File Explorer.

- Customize libraries.

You acquire all kinds of data files, including but not limited to documents, spreadsheets, pictures, presentations, videos, and executable programs. You save those files with recognizable file names inside appropriate folders. For instance, you save the personal documents you create inside the My Documents folder and documents you want to share with others inside the Public Documents folder. There are other folders beyond those related to documents, including My Pictures and Public Pictures, My Music and Public Music, My Videos and Public Videos, and so on. As you acquire more data, you can create subfolders inside these to expand this built-in folder system.

TIP Always store data in related default folders, at least for now. When you run most backup programs, the default folders and the subfolders in them will be included automatically.

Windows 8 also offers libraries. A library is a place to access data that's been saved to either your personal folders or public ones. Like folders, libraries have names that represent what you should save there: Documents, Pictures, Music, and Video. Libraries offer more flexibility than folders and simplify the process of grouping and accessing data.

Although there are multiple ways to access the data you acquire, File Explorer is the most comprehensive, and you can add a tile for it on the Start screen if you find you use it often. By using File Explorer, you can access your data, view it in various ways, search for files and folders, and even burn files to CDs and DVDs, all from a single window.

IMPORTANT

PRACTICE FILES Before you can complete the exercises in this chapter, you need to copy the book's practice files to your computer. The practice files you'll use to complete the exercises in this chapter are in the Chapter04 folder. A complete list of practice files is provided in "Using the Practice Files" at the beginning of this book.

Understanding Files, Folders, and Libraries

The first step to understanding how best to save, browse to, and organize data is to learn the differences among files, folders, and libraries. With that knowledge, you can save data better and use File Explorer more effectively to locate and manage your data in the future.

TIP File Explorer offers a ribbon for performing common tasks and a Navigation page for locating files, folders, and libraries.

The main differences among files, folders, and libraries are as follows.

- **FILE** Any unique, stand-alone piece of data such as a single document, spreadsheet, or presentation; an executable file; a picture or video; a screen shot of a map; or an itinerary. You save files in folders.

- **FOLDER** A mechanism for grouping data, generally data that is alike in some way. Windows 8 has several preinstalled folders you can use, including My Documents, Public Documents, My Pictures, Public Pictures, My Music, Public Music, and so on. You can create your own folders, too.

- **LIBRARY** A more flexible mechanism for accessing and grouping data. The Documents library, for instance, offers access to two folders by default: My Documents and Public Documents. This access is virtual. The files available here aren't actually stored here; they are stored in their respective folders on the computer's hard drive. You can configure access to other folders here, too. You can also create your own libraries and configure which of your existing folders to make accessible from them. Because libraries are indexed by Windows, searches for data stored in libraries are very fast.

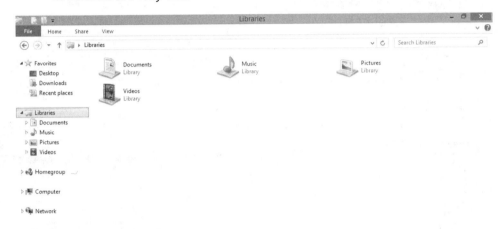

In this exercise, you'll explore the files, folders, and libraries on your own computer by using File Explorer. What you see when you click a library in the Navigation pane (the left pane in the File Explorer window) includes two areas by default: the data that you've saved in your personal folders and the data in the related Public folders. You might see only the practice files that you've copied in these folders, or you might see those and data of your own, depending on how you've used your computer thus far.

 SET UP Copy the practice files that are located in the Chapter04 folder to your computer as outlined in the "Using the Practice Files" section at the beginning of this book. Specifically, copy Notepad Text Document.txt to the Documents library; Sheep.jpg to the Pictures library; and Take Off.3GP to the Videos library.

SEE ALSO To learn how to install the practice files, refer to "Using the Practice Files" located in the introduction of this book.

1   From the **Start** screen, type Explorer. In the results, click **File Explorer**.

> **TIP** Try the Windows key+E keyboard shortcut to open File Explorer from anywhere, even from the Start screen.

2   Under **Libraries** in the Navigation pane, click **Documents**.

The list of documents saved in the Documents library appears.

> **TROUBLESHOOTING** If you do not see the Navigation pane, click View, choose Navigation Pane, and select Navigation Pane to show it.

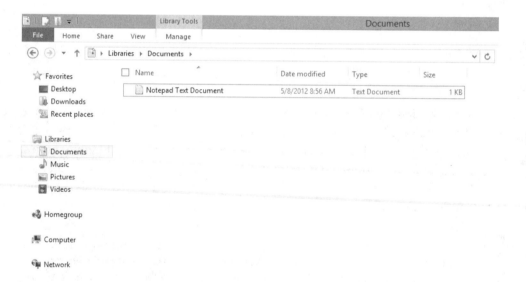

> **TIP** The Documents library might contain only the practice files you copied from the Chapter04 folder, or it might contain your personal documents and other data.

3   Under **Documents**, click **Music**.

The Music library appears.

4   Under **Music**, click **Pictures**.

The Pictures library appears.

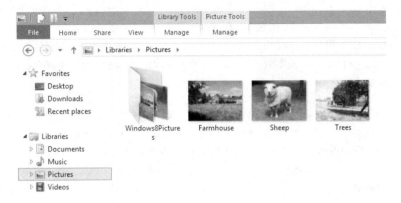

TIP The Pictures Library might contain more data than the files you copied from the Chapter04 folder; it might also contain your personal pictures, folders you've created, and other data.

5   Under **Pictures**, click **Videos**.

The Videos library appears.

CLEAN UP Return to the Start screen by pressing the Windows key or by any other method.

TIP Although you'll learn more about libraries later in this chapter, if you'd like to separate the personal data from the public data available in a library before then, position the mouse over the library name in the Navigation pane and click the arrow that appears. You can then click one of the two folders that appear underneath.

Explaining the Most Common File Types

You can open and view hundreds of kinds of files on your Windows 8–based computer. The most common sorts of files are documents, spreadsheets, presentations, music, pictures, videos, and executable files. You might occasionally work with recorded TV or specialized files from third-party programs, but for the most part the types of files you encounter will be common ones.

You save each of these files as a specific *file type*. You choose the file type during the save process. (If you copy a file from another source, it already has a file type.) For example, when you save a document you've created by using Microsoft Word, you name the file, choose a place to save it, and select the desired file type from a list. The file type gives the file a specific extension, generally three or four letters that appear at the end of the file name (but don't generally appear in the list of options). The name, place, and file type you select defines the file so that Windows 8 can distinguish it from other files, locate it, and offer it for viewing.

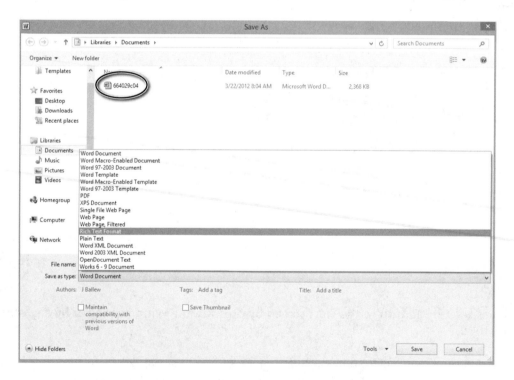

To save files effectively, you need to know a little about the choices available in programs you'll use to create them. Here are the types of files you'll encounter most often and their file name extensions.

TIP To show file extensions in File Explorer, click the View tab and select File Name Extensions.

- Microsoft Office files

  - Microsoft Word (.doc and .docx)

  - Microsoft Excel (.xls and .xlsx)

  - Microsoft PowerPoint (.ppt and .pptx)

  - Microsoft Publisher (.pub and .pubx)

- Music files

  - Windows Media audio files (.asx, .wm, .wma, and .wmx)

  - Windows audio files (.wav)

  - MP3 audio files (.mp3 and .m3u)

  - AAC files (.aac)

- Picture files

  - JPEG files (.jpg and .jpeg)

  - TIFF files (.tif and .tiff)

  - RAW files (.raw)

  - GIF files (.gif)

  - Bitmap files (.bmp)

  - PNG files (.png)

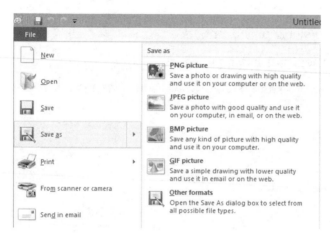

- Video files

  - Windows Media files (.wm, .wmv, and .asf)

  - Apple QuickTime files (.mov and .qt)

  - AVI files (.avi)

  - Windows Recorded TV Show files (.wtv and .dvr-ms)

  - MPEG Movie files (.mp4, .mov, .m4v, .mpeg, .mpg, .mpe, .m1v, .mp2, .mpv2, .mod, .vob, and .m1v)

  - Motion JPEG files (.avi and .mov)

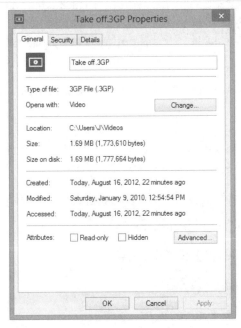

1.69 MB   Library includes: 2 locations

TIP If you can't determine the file type from the file name, you can determine it from the file's Properties page, as detailed in the next set of steps.

- Miscellaneous
  - Executable files (.exe)
  - Microsoft Notepad (.txt)
  - Adobe Reader (.pdf)
  - OpenOffice and LibreOffice (.odt, .ott, .oth, and .odm)

File Explorer (about which you'll learn quite a bit in this chapter), in its default configuration, offers the names of the files in the Open window but not the types of the files. If you are interested in knowing the file type, you can do this by viewing the Properties page. The Properties page for any file offers its file extension and other information. You can open the Properties page by right-clicking the file and choosing Properties. The Properties page for any file also offers the name of the program with which the file is configured to open, the option to open the folder that contains the file, and other data and options.

TIP The list of options you see when you right-click a file will depend on the type of file you've chosen. For example, if you right-click a compatible image, the option to Set As Desktop Background is available. This option is not available when you right-click a text document or a video.

In this exercise you'll open the Properties page for a file on your own computer and learn its file type.

→ SET UP You need to have the Notepad Text Document.txt file saved to the My Documents folder to complete this exercise. This file is located in the Chapter04 folder.

1   Open the **File Explorer** window by using the **Windows+E** keyboard shortcut.

2   Under **Libraries**, click Documents.

3   Right-click **Notepad Text Document**.

A contextual menu appears.

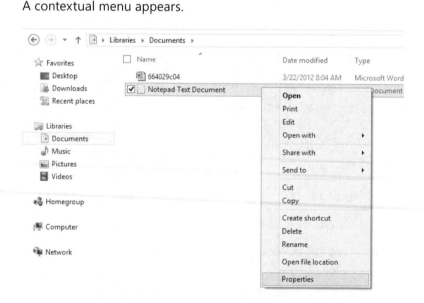

4   Click **Properties**.

The Properties dialog box appears.

TIP By default, extensions for files aren't shown.

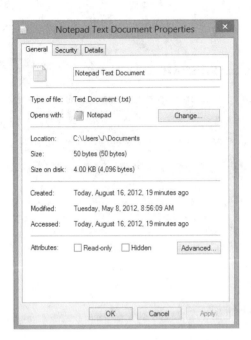

5   On the **General** tab, note what's listed beside **Type of file**.

In this example, Text Document (.txt) is the type.

TIP To change how a specific type of file will open by default, from the Properties page and the General tab, click Change and select a new program.

⊗ CLEAN UP **Click Cancel on the Properties page to close the dialog box. Close the Documents window.**

Accessing Your User Folders

Often, using File Explorer is all you need to access the data you want. In most cases, using the available libraries suits your purposes. There are other personal folders, though, including Downloads, Saved Games, and Searches, among others. Those user folders are a little more difficult to find. In fact, if you never browse to them specifically, you might never know where they are or that they even exist.

In this exercise, you'll explore your Windows 8 User folder and pin that folder to the Start screen for easy access in the future.

SET UP No setup is required.

1   Open **File Explorer**. You can use the **Windows+E** keyboard shortcut.

2   In the Navigation pane, click **Computer** and, in the **Content** pane, double-click **Local Disk**.

This is likely drive C, but it could be something else.

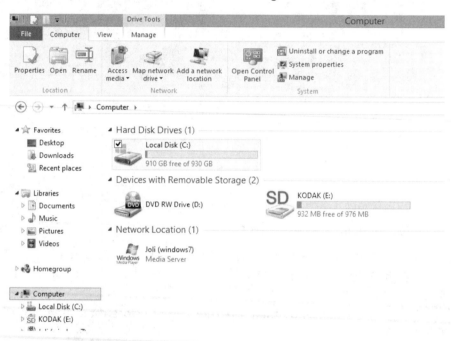

3   In the right pane, double-click **Users**.

4   Right-click your **user name** and choose **Pin to Start**.

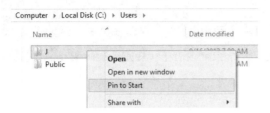

TIP Notice that the Public folders are available under C:\Users. If you think you'll use the Public folders often, pin them to the Start screen, too.

5   Double-click your **User folder** to see what's inside.

6   Click the **X** in the top-right corner of **File Explorer** to close it.

✖ CLEAN UP   Return to the Start screen to see your new pinned folder. It will be listed in the far-right position.

SEE ALSO "Understanding User Folders," next.

Beyond your libraries and your User folder, you'll find other areas of Windows 8 where you can access data. For instance, from File Explorer you can click Network in the Navigation pane and have access to shared User folders, including those that share data from media devices. These types of shared media folders often contain playlists, pictures, videos, and music, although you may use them to hold work-related data as well. You'll learn more about networks in Chapter 11, "Connecting to a Network and the Internet"; Chapter 12, "Allowing Others to Use the Computer"; and Chapter 13, "Sharing Files and Folders with My Network"; and learn more about media in Chapter 9, "Having Fun with Multimedia."

Understanding User Folders

In the previous section, you pinned your User folder to the Start screen for easier access. If you opened that folder, you saw that inside your User folder are subfolders for storing and organizing your personal data, including but not limited to Contacts, Downloads, My Documents, My Pictures, and Saved Games. If you share your computer with other people, and they have their own user accounts on the computer, they have unique User folders, too.

TIP The items in the My Documents subfolder of your User folder are the same documents available from the My Documents folder available from File Explorer (in the Documents library).

In this exercise, you'll explore your personal User folder and its subfolders.

SET UP Verify that you have copied the files located in the Chapter04 folder to your computer as outlined in the "Using the Practice Files" section at the beginning of this book.

1   Click your **User** folder from the **Start** screen.

Earlier, you pinned it there. Your User folder opens.

TIP To change how the folders appear in your User folder, click the View tab. Then click any layout. Try Small Icons or Large Icons.

2   In your User folder, double-click **My Documents**.

Your documents are available.

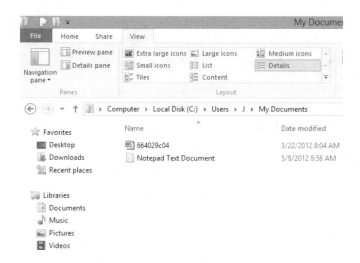

3   Click the **Back** button or the **Up arrow**.

The Back button is a gray, back-facing arrow that turns blue when you position your mouse over it.

Double-click **Links**.

Links appear, and you can create more if desired.

4   Click the **Back** button.

5   Repeat these steps to explore the other subfolders as time allows.

❌ CLEAN UP Click the red X in the top-right corner of File Explorer to close it, or leave it open for the next exercise.

Inside any folder, for the most part, you can double-click to open any file (or any sub-folder that contains files). This is a common way to locate files you want to access; how-ever, it's a little outdated. In fact, searching from the Start screen, as detailed in Chapter 1, "Introducing Windows 8," might be better in most instances. You start typing while on the screen, and results appear in a list. No matter which option you choose to open your files, it's still important to understand how files and folders are organized on your computer.

Another way to access data is to use the Start screen to navigate to and open the program you use to work with a file and locate the file from the program interface. Microsoft Word, like many other programs, offers a list of recent documents from the File tab. What you see and have access to depends on the program you've used.

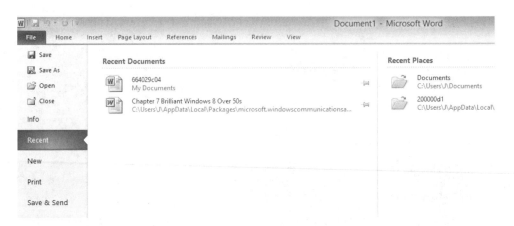

Saving Files Effectively

When you save a file, you name the file, choose a place to save it, and select a file type. It's important to save files with descriptive names so that later, perhaps even a year from now, you can tell what the file is without opening it. Additionally, at least at first, you should strive to save data files in their respective default folders. Save personal documents to the My Documents folder, personal pictures the My Pictures folder, personal audio files to the My Music folder, and so on. Windows 8 makes it easy to do this.

Similarly, you should opt to save data you'd like to share with others or access from net-worked devices (such as media centers) to their Public folder counterparts. For instance, you should consider saving your music files to the Public Music folder, your vacation videos to the Public Videos folder, and your favorite pictures to the Public Pictures folder because, when you do, you make those files easily accessible from any device on your network. You have to choose this option specifically, though; no data is saved to the Public folders by default.

TIP When you save a file by using a Save As dialog box, and when you click a library in the Navigation pane (Documents, Pictures, Music, or Videos), the data will be saved to the related personal folder. Data is never saved to the Public folders unless you specifically state to do so.

In this exercise, you'll create a file in Notepad and save it to your personal Documents folder.

→ SET UP **Return to the Start screen. No other setup is required for this exercise.**

1   At the **Start** screen, start typing **Notepad**.

2   Click or tap **Notepad**.

3   Type **I will save this file as a Text Document**.

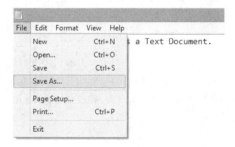

4   Click **File** and choose **Save As**.

5   In the File name window, type **My Notepad Document**.

6   Under **Libraries**, click **Documents**.

7   Click **Save**.

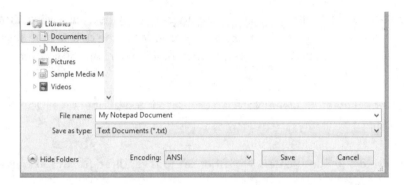

TIP When you choose Documents under Libraries, the file is saved to your personal My Documents folder. It is not saved to the Public Documents folder.

CLEAN UP **Click the red X in Notepad to close it.**

SEE ALSO To learn how to save a file to the Public folders, refer to the next section, "Understanding Libraries."

It is important to understand that the options you see in the Save As Type drop-down list depend on the program you're using to save the file. In Notepad, if you click the arrow by Save As Type: Text Documents (*txt), you can see that you have only one option, Text Documents (*.txt). As you saw earlier, though, there are many more options in programs such as Microsoft Word, including .doc and .docx. Likewise, art or photo-editing programs offer many different file type options, including .jpg, .bmp, and .gif. You'll see additional options as you gain experience with different software applications.

TROUBLESHOOTING If you have the option of saving a file as a type already called out in this chapter (such as a .doc, .jpeg, or .gif) versus something you've never heard of (such as .ged), save the file by using the most universal format. That way you'll be able to open the file in other programs, not just in the program in which you created or saved it.

Understanding Libraries

Libraries are organizational units that appear to be folders but are more flexible than folders. When you click a library name, you actually have access to two distinct folders: your related personal folder and the related Public folder. While in a library, the data in both folders appears to be in the same place on the computer, even though it is not. Windows

8 helps you get started with libraries by offering four: Documents, Music, Pictures, and Videos.

For the most part, when using libraries to *access* data, you won't care where the data is stored; you'll just be concerned about quickly getting to the data you want. Sometimes, though, you might want to see what data is in your personal folder and what is in the Public one, perhaps to see how your data is organized and to understand what you've already made public. In this case, you can separate the data and view the content independently. This separation technique is also necessary when you need to save data to a Public folder because, as you know, by default data is saved to your personal folders. If you want to save data to a Public folder, you have to select it specifically.

In this exercise, you'll view your personal folders in the default libraries separately.

 SET UP No setup is required.

1   Open **File Explorer**.

2   In **File Explorer**, from the Navigation pane, under **Libraries**, click **Documents**.

TROUBLESHOOTING If you see only Libraries in the Navigation pane of File Explorer and nothing underneath it, click Libraries and then click the right-facing arrow to expand what's in that folder.

3   Click the **right-facing arrow** to the left of Documents.

It changes to a down-facing arrow.

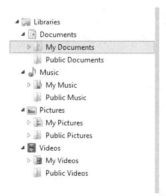

A library holds two folders by default.

4   Click **My Documents** and then click **Public Documents**.

5   Repeat steps 3 and 4, accessing **My Music**, **Public Music**, **My Pictures**, **Public Pictures**, **My Videos**, and **Public Videos**.

✖ CLEAN UP Leave this window open for the next exercise.

SEE ALSO "Customizing Libraries," later in this chapter.

When you want to save a file to any of the Public folders, you use this process to separate the library into its two distinct parts, and you choose the proper Public folder to which to save.

Navigating the File Explorer Ribbon Interface

File Explorer has a type of graphical user interface that is becoming more common. It has a *ribbon*. The ribbon runs across the top of the window and offers tabs. You click any tab to access the groups, options, and tools available from it. Each time you click a new tab, what's shown on the ribbon changes. The names of the tabs are mostly intuitive and share attributes with other ribbon-enabled windows and programs.

The ribbon is a highly contextual interface. The tabs and options on the ribbon change depending on what you have selected in the Navigation pane. For example, if you click Libraries in the Navigation pane, you see a specific set of tabs on the ribbon that includes File, Home, Share, and View. Library Tools (Manage) also appears. You can see what's under each tab by clicking the tab. If you click a specific item in a library, the tabs change again. If you open a library, for instance the Videos library, you see File, Home, Share View, Library Tools (Manage), and Video Tools (Play).

TIP If you click an option under Favorites you'll see only File, Home, Share, and View.

To understand how to use the ribbon, you must know which tabs will appear most often and what is available under these tabs. When working with libraries and folders, the following are the most common tabs you'll encounter.

- **FILE** Enables you to open a new File Explorer window or a command prompt, to clear history, to get help, or to access your favorite places for storing data. For the most part, what you see under the File menu is the same no matter what you have selected in the Navigation pane.

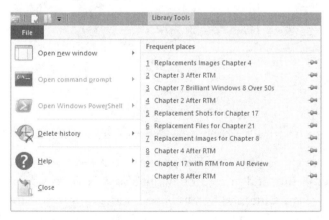

- **HOME** Enables you to cut, copy, and paste compatible data available in the window. You can also copy the file path, move or copy data, delete data, rename data, create a new folder, and select data, among other things. Options you see here will change depending on what's selected in the folder window.

  TROUBLESHOOTING If you don't see a ribbon, but instead see only menu titles, click the arrow located to the left of the Help button and below the red X in the top-right corner of the window.

- **SHARE** Enables you to send files in an email message, compress (zip) files, burn selected files to a CD or DVD, print, fax, and share with users in your homegroup, among other things and as applicable. (You can't print a video you've selected, for instance, so Print will be dimmed in that case.)

  TIP Additional tabs might appear, such as Picture Tools, if you select an item in the open folder or library.

Use the Share tab to choose with whom to share the data, among other things.

- **VIEW** Enables you to change how the files appear in the window (Extra Large Icons, Large Icons, Medium Icons, and so on). You might also be able to hide or show the Navigation pane, Preview pane, and Details pane, choose how to sort the data in the window, and show or hide file name extensions, among other things.

TROUBLESHOOTING If you can't see all the tabs, or if the items on the tabs seem condensed, maximize the File Explorer window. If you don't see the ribbon, but instead see only tab names, click the arrow on the Quick Access toolbar at the top of the window and clear Minimize Ribbon.

■ **MANAGE** When you select a library in the Navigation pane, the Manage tab enables you to manage your libraries and the data in them in various ways, including adding access to additional folders.

TIP Rarely, an unexpected tab will appear or a common tab will be missing. For instance, if you click Computer in the Navigation pane, you'll see only three tabs: File, Computer, and View.

In this exercise, you'll explore various tabs on the File Explorer ribbon and use the ribbon to delete the Notepad Text Document file. Later, you'll learn how to use more of the commands you see on these tabs.

→ SET UP You need the practice files located in the Chapter04 folder as outlined in the "Using the Practice Files" section at the beginning of this book.

1 Open **File Explorer** by using any method desired.

2 In the Navigation pane, under **Libraries**, click **Documents**.

3 Click the **Home** tab (if applicable).

4 Click one time (do not double-click) the **Notepad Text Document** file.

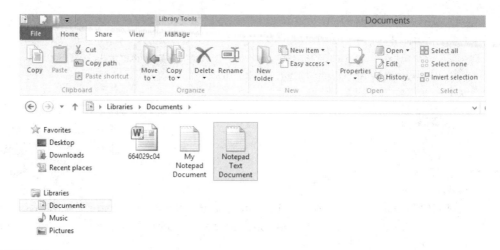

5   On the **Home** tab, click **Delete**.

SEE ALSO "Working with Deleted Files and the Recycle Bin," later in this chapter.

❌ CLEAN UP **Leave this window open.**

When you select a library or folder from the Navigation pane, you'll have access to its contents in the contents pane. As you saw in the previous exercise, you can select an item in the folder and perform tasks on it such as deleting a selected file. Sometimes when you select data in the contents pane additional tabs appear. Here, a picture is selected, and a new tab, Picture Tools, is available. From this new tab, you can rotate the picture, set the selected picture as the desktop background, and play a slide show.

SEE ALSO "Setting Up Media Libraries," in Chapter 12, "Having Fun with Multimedia."

Here, a video is selected. The new tab, Video Tools, offers various Play options, including the option to add the video to a playlist. You'll learn more about multimedia files in Chapter 12.

To summarize, the ribbon offers the tools you need to perform tasks when working with files, folders, and libraries, and the tabs are named so that you can tell what should be available from them. For instance, if you want to *share* a file by printing it, emailing it, burning it to a CD, or even faxing it, the Share tab offers this functionality. If you want to change how you view files in File Explorer or if you'd like to sort your files, group them, or hide or view specific parts of File Explorer, the View tab offers this functionality. Don't worry if this is all new to you; it's pretty intuitive, and you'll catch on quickly.

TIP In the next few sections you'll learn how to use the tools available under other tabs, including Share and View.

Organizing Files and Folders

There are many ways to organize your files and folders beyond saving them in their proper folders and with recognizable names. One way to organize your files for the long term is to create subfolders inside the existing default folders and move data into them. By using subfolders, you can easily expand the existing file system. This becomes necessary when you have acquired enough data that a folder is difficult to navigate. Windows 8 makes it easy to create a subfolder, and you'll learn how in the next exercise.

TIP The best way to keep your data organized is to create folders with descriptive names and move corresponding data into them. Consider creating folders named Travel, Taxes, Health, Pets, and so on.

Either before or after you create subfolders and begin to move data into them, you can give those folders more recognizable names than they have now. Names such as Tax Summary 2012, Jennifer's Wedding, or My Las Vegas Vacation 2011 are certainly decipherable and better than something less descriptive (such as Taxes, Pictures, or Vacation). You can delete files you no longer need, too. Finally, if you decide to archive data you no longer want to store on your computer, you can burn those files to a CD or DVD.

In this exercise, you'll create a subfolder inside the My Pictures folder.

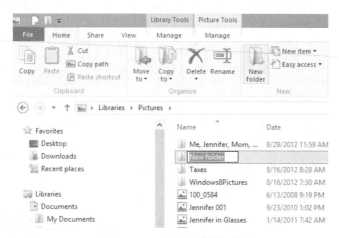 SET UP **You do not need any practice files for this exercise.**

1 Open **File Explorer** by using any method desired.

2 In the Navigation pane, under **Libraries**, click **Pictures**.

3 From the **Home** tab, click the **New Folder** icon.

A new folder appears, waiting to be renamed.

4 Type a name for the folder and press the **Enter** key.

TROUBLESHOOTING If something happens and the folder gets named New Folder, click it once and, from the ribbon, click Rename. Alternatively, you can right-click the folder and click Rename.

CLEAN UP **Leave File Explorer open for the next exercise.**

After you create a subfolder, it's easy to move data there. You can just drag and drop files from the window into the newly created folder. This works great if the new folder in which you created it is in the same window as the data you'd like to move there. However, if dragging and dropping isn't so straightforward, you can use the Move To command on the Home tab of the ribbon.

TIP You can select multiple noncontiguous files by holding down the Ctrl key while you select them. To select all the files in a window or contiguous files, hold down the Shift key and click the first and then the last of the files to include.

In this exercise, you'll move two files at one time from one folder to another by using the Move To command in File Explorer.

SET UP You need the practice files located in the Chapter04 folder as outlined in the "Using the Practice Files" section at the beginning of this book. Specifically, copy Sheep.jpg and Farmhouse.jpg.

1   Open **File Explorer** by using any method desired.

2   In the Navigation pane, under **Libraries**, click **Pictures**.

3   Click the **Farmhouse** file one time (do not double-click).

4   Hold down **Ctrl** and click **Sheep** once.

> **TIP** Remember, if you are using a tablet you'll have to tap, hold, and drag downward until a check mark appears.

5   From the **Home** tab, click **Move to**.

6   Click **Choose location**.

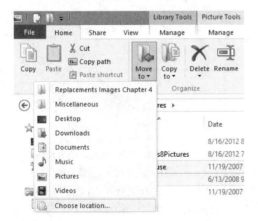

> **TIP** If you see the folder to which you'd like to move the files, you can select it. If you do not see the folder, click Choose Folder and browse to it.

7   In the **Move Items** dialog box, expand **Libraries** and **Pictures** and then click **Public Pictures**.

8   Click **Move**.

After you click Move, the dialog box closes, and the two files you selected are now available from the Public Pictures folder.

✖ CLEAN UP Leave File Explorer open for the next exercise.

TIP Use Copy To if you want to copy the files instead of move them. The process is the same.

Renaming Files

When you import pictures from a digital camera by using the built-in tools in Windows 8, your camera software, or a photo-editing program, those imported pictures are given names. Every file has to have its own name. The names given aren't very descriptive, though. The file names applied might be a cryptic form of the date on which the photos were imported, or they might be partial names created by using tags you applied during the process, but usually they are not the names you'd apply to them, given the opportunity.

TIP You will learn how to import pictures from a digital camera in Chapter 12.

Other types of files are also often named inappropriately, generally because you're in a hurry to save them. File names such as Dad, Summary, Presentation, Taxes, and so on don't give much information about their contents. If you have to open the file to figure out what it is, the name is not descriptive enough.

TIP The File Explorer ribbon, specifically the Home tab, offers the Rename icon, which becomes available only after you select a file.

In this exercise, you'll rename a file by using the Rename command in File Explorer.

 **SET UP** You need the practice files located in the Chapter04 folder as outlined in the "Using the Practice Files" section at the beginning of this book. Specifically, copy the Take off file to the Videos library.

1   Open **File Explorer** by using any method desired.

2   In the Navigation pane, under **Libraries**, click **Videos**.

3   Click the **Take off** file once (do not double-click).

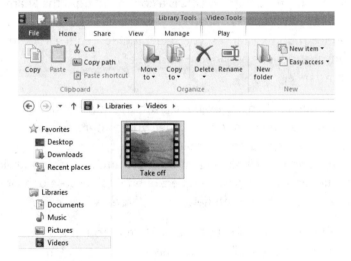

4   From the **Home** tab, click **Rename**.

5   Type **Helicopter Ride**.

6   Press **Enter**.

CLEAN UP Leave File Explorer open for the next exercise.

SEE ALSO Learn how to download files safely in the "Exploring the SmartScreen Filter" section in Chapter 5, "Using Internet Explorer 10."

Sharing Files with the Share Tab

Now that you have some experience with File Explorer, the ribbon, and working with files, you can use that knowledge to explore other tools available on the ribbon and to use those tools with less guidance. For instance, you can likely figure out how to burn the Helicopter Ride.3GP file to a CD or DVD because Burn To Disc is a command from the Share tab. Likewise, you can deduce how to print the Sheep.jpg photo by using the Print command located from that same tab. In both instances, you select the desired file, click the desired command, and follow any instructions provided. You might have to insert a disc or put paper in the printer, for instance.

Some commands are less intuitive than, for example, Print. The Zip command is one of those. When you zip something, you compress it. When you compress a group of files or a single large file, it takes up less space on your hard drive. People often zip large files or groups of files before they send them in email to reduce the amount of time it will take the files to arrive at their destination. In the past, people zipped files because of a lack of hard drive space. That is not often a problem with newer computers.

Fax is another intuitive but odd command. It's a little different from the others because you need access to a fax server or telephone line to actually send a fax, and most home users don't have that access. If you already have something in place that enables you to send faxes from your computer, though, the process is intuitive. If you'd like to be able to send faxes from your computer, you'll have to perform the setup tasks that appear when you click the Fax command.

There are some tools you can now explore on your own from the Share tab. (Remember that not all options appear for all data.)

- **EMAIL** Select any file (or multiple files) in a File Explorer window to activate this option. Click Email. If you've chosen a picture (or multiple pictures) to send in email, you'll be prompted to choose a picture size first. After you click Email, your default email program will open, and the file(s) will be attached.

  TROUBLESHOOTING If you do not have a dedicated email client installed and configured on your computer this command won't work and will be grayed out.

- **ZIP** Select multiple files to compress them. After they are compressed, you can send the compressed folder (which contains the files) in email. To decompress, double-click the compressed files. You can tell a file is zipped because a zipper appears on it.

- **BURN TO DISC** Select the file or files to burn (copy) to a CD or DVD. Click Burn To Disc. Insert a disc when prompted and follow any prompts to complete the copy process.

- **PRINT** Select the file or files to print and click Print. You might be prompted to choose a printer, set printer properties, or perform other tasks, depending on your printer and current computer setup. The document might just begin to print with no other input from you. The Print command will be dimmed if you have selected something, such as a song in the Music library, that can't be printed.

- **FAX** Select a file to fax. Click the Fax command. Follow any prompts to complete the fax process.

SEE ALSO To share data with others on your network, which can involve using the various homegroup and share commands on the Share tab of File Explorer, refer to Chapter 13.

Customizing File Explorer with the View Tab

From the View tab in File Explorer, you can change how the window appears on the screen. You can hide or show the Navigation pane, change how the files appear (for example, as a detailed list or as icons), and hide files and folders you don't use very often. You can show panes that do not currently appear, including the Preview pane and the Details pane. You can also group files in various ways, show file name extensions, and more. The best way to learn your way around these options is to show and hide these panes, show and hide files, and change how the files and folders appear in the File Explorer window.

TIP You might not want to customize File Explorer too much right now, especially anything having to do with hiding files, folders, or the Navigation pane. If you change it too much, it won't look like what you see in the screen shots of this book.

Here are the options you can safely explore from the View tab.

- **NAVIGATION PANE** The Navigation pane is the left pane that contains the folder and libraries lists. To hide this pane, click Navigation Pane and, in the resulting drop-down list, click Navigation Pane again. This hides the pane. Repeat to show the pane.

- **PREVIEW PANE** The Preview pane offers a preview of the selected file, so you don't have to open it. Click Preview Pane to show this pane and click again to hide it.

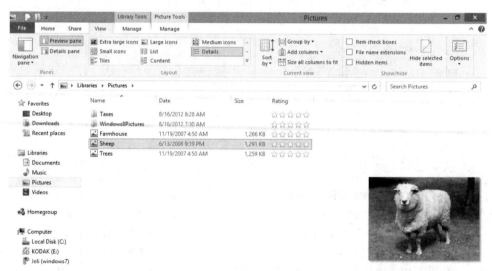

- **DETAILS PANE** The Details pane offers detailed information about a file. The information offered is similar to what you'd see if you viewed the file's Properties page. Click Details Pane to show this pane and click again to hide it.

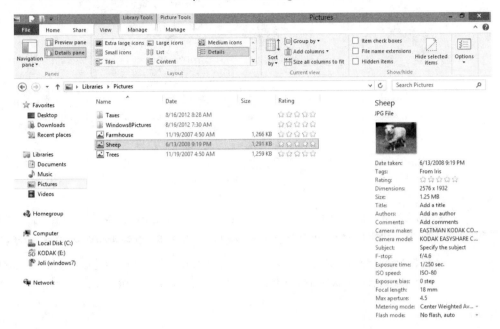

- **LAYOUT GROUP OPTIONS** The options in the Layout group include Extra Large Icons, Large Icons, Medium Icons, Small Icons, List, Details, Tiles, and Content. Click each to view it.

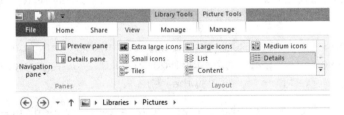

- **GROUP BY** Files and folders are listed alphabetically and in ascending order in File Explorer by default, but you can change that with the Group By options. Click Group By and select any option to group by that criterion.

- **SORT BY** You use the Sort By option to sort data by Date, Size, Rating, and other attributes. Click Sort By and select an option, such as Date Taken, to group data differently.

- **ITEM CHECK BOXES** Place a check by Item check boxes to show the check mark when items are selected. Clear the check marks to hide these marks.

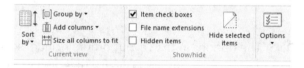

- **FILE NAME EXTENSIONS** Place a check by File Name Extensions to see the extension after the file name.

- **HIDDEN ITEMS** Place a check beside this to show the data you've previously hidden. The data you'll see (that is currently hidden) will appear in grayscale, and you can use Hide Selected Items to display the items.

- **HIDE SELECTED ITEMS** With this option, you hide items you don't need to access regularly while leaving those items available on your computer. To hide any item, select it and then click Hide Selected Items. The items will be hidden. To reveal them, check Hidden Items (detailed in the previous bullet), select the item to reveal, and click Hide Selected Items to display the item.

Searching in File Explorer

You know how to share files by using File Explorer and how to change how you view files there. As you acquire more data, however, it will become more difficult to sift through it to find what you want. One way to deal with lots of data is to customize what's shown in a File Explorer window by searching for the files you want. When you do this, only the files that match criteria you set appear in the window. This is a good way to cull information when you've stored a lot of data.

In this exercise, you'll search for a specific file in File Explorer.

SET UP You need the practice files located in the Chapter04 folder as outlined in the "Using the Practice Files" section at the beginning of this book.

1   Open **File Explorer** by using any method desired.

2   In the Navigation pane, click **Libraries**.

3   In the **Search Libraries** window, type **Farmhouse**.

Farmhouse

CLEAN UP Leave File Explorer open for the next exercise.

TIP If you have so many files that you have to use this method to find them, do some housecleaning. Create subfolders and move data into them and delete files you no longer need.

Customizing Libraries

You know quite a bit about libraries, including what kind of data is accessible from them. You have learned that the Documents library, for instance, offers access to the data in both the My Documents folder and the Public Documents folder. If you've done a good job of saving, organizing, and managing your data as we've suggested so far, what you have in the Documents library is only documents and perhaps a few related presentations, invoices, tax summaries, or databases. Likewise, you have only pictures in the Pictures library, Music in the Music library, and Videos in the Videos library.

Not all data can be grouped in such a way, though. Consider a scenario in which you're trying to group data for a trip you're planning. You might have a scanned itinerary from a travel agent; pictures, videos, and audio files for learning a new language; airplane tickets received by email; and other travel documents such as immunization records you've acquired from various sources. If you stored that data in folders in a traditional way, you'd have the documents stored in the My Documents folder, the audio files in the My Music folder, pictures of your destination in the My Pictures folder, and so on. This is certainly unwieldy and inefficient. However, if you try to group all of this, for example, in a subfolder of My Documents, it wouldn't really be organized properly. It would be much better to create a new *library* named Travel and make all the data related to your trip available there.

In the following exercises, you'll create a new library, name it, and include access to some of the existing folders stored in different places on your computer's hard drive. For this to work on a personal level, you'll have to create your own folders, perhaps named Travel Plans, Language Tutorials, Itineraries, and Health Records, and put related data into them. Then, you'll follow the steps here to create a new library named Travel and include those folders (and their data) in it.

In this exercise, you'll create a new library and name it Sample Media Mix, and then you'll add access to three folders: My Pictures, My Music, and Public Videos.

SET UP **You do not need to perform any setup tasks for this exercise.**

1   Open **File Explorer** by using any method desired.

2   In the Navigation pane, right-click **Libraries**.

3   Point to **New** and click **Library**.

4   Type **Sample Media Mix** and press **Enter**; click **Sample Media Mix** in the Navigation pane.

5   Click **Include a folder**.

A new window opens.

TIP It's important to understand that libraries only point to, or make access available to, data. Data is not moved to libraries. Thus, you can create, add, remove, and personalize libraries however you like. You won't actually be moving any data.

6   Click **My Pictures** and choose **Include folder**.

7   Right-click **Sample Media Mix** in the Navigation pane and choose **Properties**.

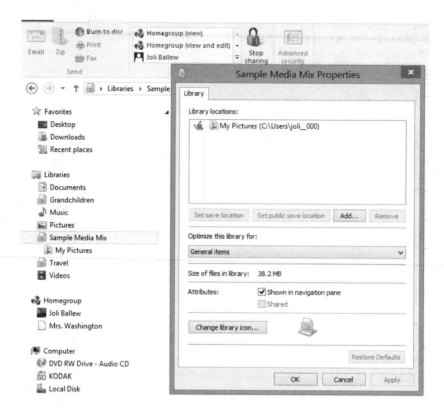

8   Click **Add**.

9   In the Navigation pane, expand the Music library, click **My Music**; choose **Include folder**.

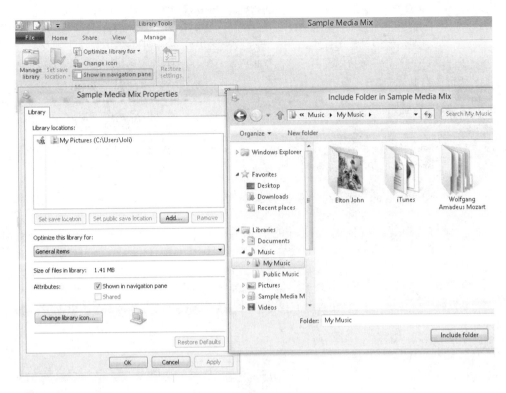

My Music is added to the Sample Media Mix library.

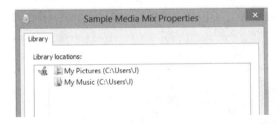

10   Click **Add** and repeat step 9 to add the Public Videos folder.

11   Click **OK**.

✖ CLEAN UP Leave File Explorer open for the next exercise.

TIP After you've created a library, you can add more folders to it from the library's Library Tools, Manage tab. Click Manage Library to get started.

After you have created a library, you can further personalize it. You can select the new library and, from the Manage tab, add access to additional folders (click Manage Library), for instance. You can also remove folders. You can delete a library, too. Although you might be apprehensive about deleting a library, it's important to understand that a library only points to data, making it accessible. Data isn't actually stored in a library, it is stored in folders, so when you delete a library, you delete only the library itself and not the data.

TIP To delete data from your computer, delete it from the folder in which it's saved (My Documents, My Pictures, and so on).

To work with a library, you select it in the Navigation pane. From there you can:

- Prevent a folder from being included in a library. From the Library Tools, Manage tab, click Manage Library. Then select the folder to remove and click Remove (and then OK).

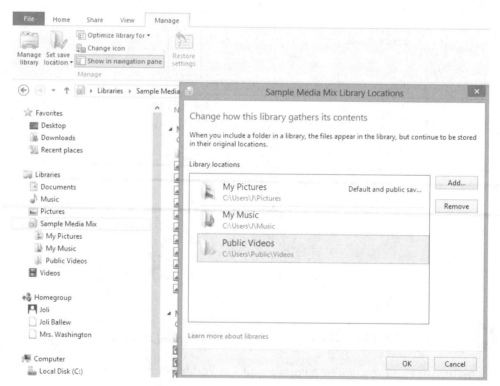

- Delete a library. Right-click the library in the Navigation pane and click Delete. (Don't do this yet.)

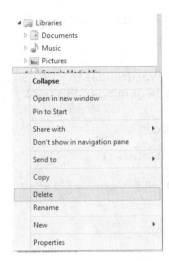

■ Set a save location. With a file or folder selected in a library, from the Manage tab, click Set A Save Location. Then you can select the default save location. When you add new files or folders to the library, Windows will store them in this location.

■ Optimize a library for a specific type of data. From the Manage tab, click Optimize A Library. From this menu, select the type of content contained in the library. This makes File Explorer show relevant tags and sorting fields to the content of the library. It also changes the icon of the library to match its content.

■ Change the icon used to represent the library. To set an icon to represent the library, from the Manage tab, click Change Icon. Select an icon and click OK.

■ Show or hide the library in the Navigation pane. Right-click the library to see options to hide or show the library in the Navigation pane.

Working with Deleted Files and the Recycle Bin

You learned earlier in this chapter how to delete a file (or other item) in File Explorer; you just select the item and click Delete on the ribbon's Home tab. You can select multiple items by holding down Shift or Ctrl. You might know other ways to delete a file, including right-clicking the item and then choosing Delete from the resulting contextual menu or pressing the Delete key. However you do it, files and folders you delete are sent to the Recycle Bin and are removed from their current positions in the folder. The Recycle Bin holds deleted files and data until you manually empty it.

In this last exercise, you'll delete a file (if you haven't already deleted it) and restore it by using the Recycle Bin.

SET UP You need to have copied the Chapter 04 Practice files to your computer as outlined in the "Using Practice Files" section at the beginning of this book.

1   Open **File Explorer** by using any method desired.

2   In the Navigation pane, under **Libraries**, click **Documents**.

3   If you deleted Notepad Text Document earlier, skip to step 6. Otherwise, select **Notepad Text Document**.

4   Click **Delete** from the **Home** tab.

5   Click the **dash** in the top-right corner of File Explorer to minimize it.

6   On the **desktop**, double-click the **Recycle Bin**.

7   Right-click **Notepad Text Document**.

8   Click **Restore**.

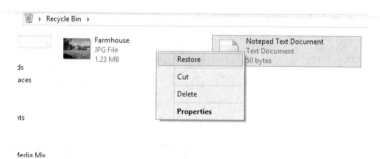

There are a few other things you can do while in the Recycle Bin, including emptying it. You can also restore every item that's in there. You should make it a habit to empty the Recycle Bin two or three times a year. You do this from the Manage tab. To access this screen, from the desktop, double-click the Recycle Bin.

The Recycle Bin has other tabs to explore, too. When you explore them, you'll find similar tools under each. For instance, from the Recycle Bin Home tab, you can delete specific files permanently, move files somewhere else, and even view the properties for a file. Likewise, from the Share tab, you can send email and burn files to a disc. From the View tab, you can change how items in the Recycle Bin appear in the window.

Key Points

- You save data as files, save files in folders and subfolders, and access folders from libraries.

- Windows 8 comes with its own file system that includes various default folders to which you should save data, including but not limited to My Documents, Public Documents, My Pictures, Public Pictures, My Music, Public Music, My Videos, Public Videos, Contacts, Downloads, and others.

- Libraries offer access to data stored in folders. Four libraries exist: Documents, Pictures, Music, and Videos. Each offers access to two folders by default, the related personal folder and the Public folder.

- It's very important to save files to their respective folders and to create subfolders when data starts to amass.

- File Explorer is the best way to navigate to the data you keep and offers the ribbon to help you navigate it.

- The most-often-used tabs on the File Explore ribbon are Home, Share, and View. You use these tabs to work with the data you collect, including renaming, deleting, sending email, printing, moving, and so on.

- It's possible to customize File Explorer by hiding and showing data or culling data by searching for something specific.

- You can create your own libraries to hold data that should be grouped together but does not fit the limited standards of a single folder. After you create a library, you choose which folders to make accessible from it.

Chapter at a Glance

Learn

Learn about the new full-screen interface of Internet Explorer, page 159

Active tab   Tabs opened in the backgro

Pin

Pin websites to the Start screen, page 166

Browse

Browse the web privately, page 167

InPrivate is turned on

InPrivate Browsing helps prevent Internet Explorer from storing c
your browsing session. This includes cookies, temporary Internet
and other data.

To turn off InPrivate Browsing, close this browser tab.

Read the Internet Explorer privacy statement online

Choose

Choose the Internet Explorer version you want as the default, page 171

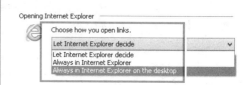

Using Internet Explorer 10 | 5

IN THIS CHAPTER, YOU WILL LEARN HOW TO

- Launch the different versions of Internet Explorer.
- Use the new Internet Explorer 10 interface.
- Pin websites to the Start screen.
- Browse the web using the InPrivate mode.
- Manage the files you download from the web.
- Set the default Internet Explorer version you want to use regularly.

One of the major changes introduced in Windows 8 is the way you browse the web by using Internet Explorer. This operating system includes the new Internet Explorer 10, which has two incarnations that can be used to browse the web: a minimalistic full-screen version and the desktop version you know from earlier Windows operating systems. The browsing experiences are very different, and this chapter focuses on the new full-screen way of using the browser.

You'll first learn the important changes brought by Internet Explorer 10. Then, you'll review the new interface and learn how to use it to browse the web. Next, you'll see how to create shortcuts or pins to websites on the Start screen, how to browse the web without leaving any traces in your browser, and how to download files. You'll understand one of the most important security features in Internet Explorer and Windows 8—SmartScreen Filter—and its role in securing your system. In addition, you'll learn how to set either of the two Internet Explorer versions as the default.

PRACTICE FILES You don't need any practice files to complete the exercises in this chapter. For more information about practice file requirements, see "Using the Practice Files" at the beginning of this book.

What Is New about Internet Explorer 10

Internet Explorer 10 in Windows 8 incorporates two important changes from Internet Explorer 9 and Windows 7 or Windows Vista.

The first and most important change is that in Windows 8 there are two versions of Internet Explorer 10. One is available directly from the Start screen, with which it shares the same full-screen interface. It is referred to as the Internet Explorer Windows 8 app. The other version is available from the desktop and uses the traditional desktop look to which you are accustomed from Internet Explorer 9 and previous versions of Windows. It is referred to as the desktop Internet Explorer.

They are the same application, and the same engine is used for browsing the web. However, their looks are very different and so is the experience of browsing the web.

The Internet Explorer Windows 8 app runs in full-screen mode, giving all the screen space you need for viewing webpages and browsing the web. Its interface elements are minimalistic and optimized for touch. This mode of browsing the web doesn't offer any support for add-ons or plug-ins except Adobe Flash Player, which is built into the browser. According to benchmarks published by different sources, the Internet Explorer app offers slightly less performance than its desktop counterpart does. However, the performance differences are very small (up to a maximum of five percent in some tests), and most people will not notice the difference when browsing the web. It is great for people who are using tablets or computers with touch and for those who want a web-browsing experience without clutter, toolbars, and add-ons. Even though it is optimized for touch, the Internet Explorer app can be used just as easily with a mouse and keyboard. It might seem scary at first because it is new and different, but if you read the rest of this chapter, you should have no problem getting acquainted with it and using it comfortably.

The Internet Explorer desktop version uses an interface with which you are familiar, optimized for use on desktop computers or laptops with a mouse and keyboard. The web-browsing performance it offers is slightly better than the Internet Explorer app. It also offers full support for add-ons and plug-ins.

The second important change you will find in Internet Explorer 10 is its noticeably better web-browsing performance. First, it has excellent support for open web standards such HTML 5 or Cascading Style Sheet (CSS3), and the speed with which it loads websites has improved considerably. This means that, compared with earlier versions of Internet Explorer, you get a much better browsing experience. Also, you get longer battery life on a laptop or tablet when browsing the web with the new Internet Explorer than with other browsers. This is because it includes power-saving features that balance the resources used while browsing the web and the amount of energy required for them. Last but not least, Internet Explorer 10 sends the Do Not Track signal to websites to help protect your privacy. Therefore, websites that provide support for this signal will not track your visits and cannot store detailed information about the pages you visited.

Launching Internet Explorer

You can launch Internet Explorer by using the default shortcuts Windows 8 provides. However, which of the two versions you launch depends on where the shortcut is placed.

On the Start screen is a tile named Internet Explorer. If you click or tap it, it opens the Internet Explorer app.

If you want to start the Internet Explorer desktop application, you must go to the Desktop. Click the Internet Explorer icon on the bottom-left side of the taskbar.

The Desktop
Internet Explorer

5

You can launch Internet Explorer by using the search function on the Start screen. Just type the word *Internet*, and its shortcut appears instantly. This shortcut launches the version of Internet Explorer that is set as default. If you have made no configuration changes to Windows 8, it will open the Internet Explorer app.

Using the Internet Explorer App

The new Internet Explorer app, even though simple in structure, can be confusing at first, especially to those who have not used mobile browsers such as the one found on smartphones powered by Windows Phone.

When you open it, you see the homepage that is set (if not changed, the homepage is the Microsoft Bing search engine) and a small toolbar at the bottom of the window with a few buttons and options. The toolbar is minimized as soon as you click or tap where websites are loaded.

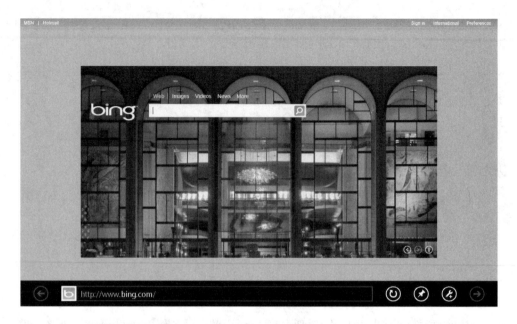

If you want to bring the toolbar back, swipe from the bottom edge of the window toward the middle. You can also right-click with a mouse.

Let's look at the buttons one by one, from left to right, and see what they do:

- The Back button takes you to the previous page you visited. The button is active after you visit more than one web page. Click or tap it, and it will take you back. The same effect can be achieved by flicking right if you are using a touch-enabled screen. A transparent version of this button is shown if you move the mouse to the left side of the browsing window.

- Next to the Back button is an icon that always changes. It just loads the icon of the website you are currently viewing. If no icon is detected for that website, the default Internet Explorer icon appears.

- The Address bar is where you type the address of the website you want to visit. This bar can also be used as a search box. You can type a search term and press the Enter key or click (tap) the Go button that appears near it. Internet Explorer displays the search results relevant to your search term by using the default search engine you have set. If you have not changed its default configuration, search results will be displayed by using Bing, the search engine owned by Microsoft.

- The button near the Address bar is called Refresh and can reload the web page you are viewing so that you can see the updates that have been made to it, if any, since the last time you viewed it.

- The Pin To Start button can pin the web page you are viewing as a shortcut on your Start screen.

- The Page Tools button gives access to a small contextual menu that can be used to search on the current web page, view the same page on the Internet Explorer desktop application, or access the app for the loaded website when one is available.

- The Forward button takes you to the next page if you used the Back button. Click or tap it, and it will take you forward. The same effect can be achieved by flicking left if you are using a touch-enabled screen. A transparent version of this button appears if you move the mouse to the right side of the browsing window.

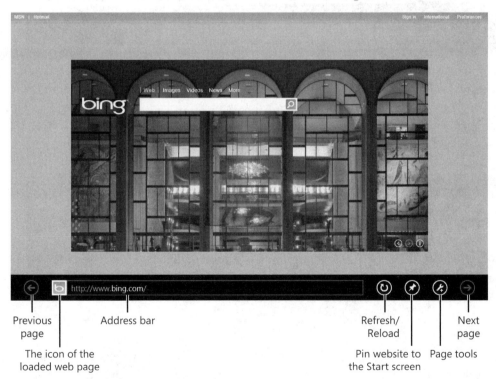

Previous page | Address bar | Refresh/ Reload | Next page

The icon of the loaded web page | Pin website to the Start screen | Page tools

When using the Address bar, the Internet Explorer window changes to help you find what you want as quickly as possible. First, it displays the websites you visit frequently and those that you have pinned.

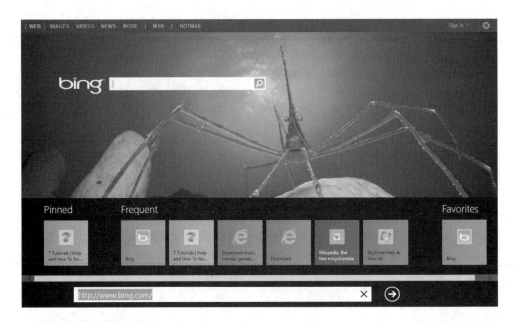

As you start typing (it doesn't matter whether it is the address of a website, the name of a website, or a search term), Internet Explorer starts searching your most frequently visited websites, the websites you pinned to the Start screen, and your browsing history. If it finds entries that match what you have typed so far, it will display the appropriate results. Then you can just click or tap the result that matches where you want to go.

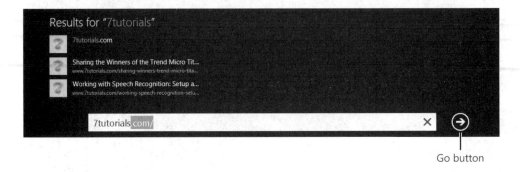

Go button

If you want to search the web for something that you have not visited so far, finish typing the search term and click or tap the Go button that appears near the Address bar. This triggers a web search, using the search engine set as default.

If you right-click somewhere in the middle of the Internet Explorer window or swipe down from the top of the window toward the middle, you will see an additional menu at the top. Again, a right-click brings up the menu.

This menu first shows the tabs you opened and the websites loaded in each tab. The active tab has blue margins, whereas the tabs open in the background have no visible margins. Each tab has an X button that closes that tab.

To switch between tabs, click or tap the one you want to view. If you want to create a new tab, click or tap the + button found at the top right of the window.

Beneath the new tab button is a button with three dots. This button offers two options: start a new InPrivate tab and clean up (close) the tabs that are not active.

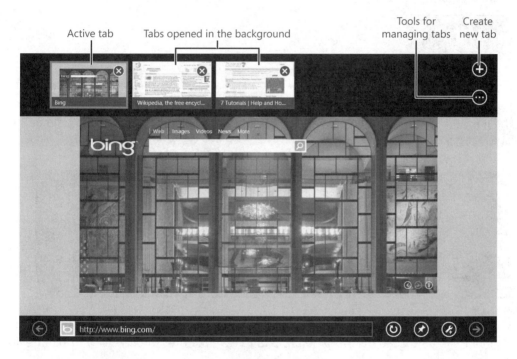

When browsing the web, notice that the Page Tools button on the bottom toolbar can have a slightly different icon, depending on the websites you are visiting. On most websites, it will show a wrench-like icon.

On some websites, however (Wikipedia, for example), it will also show a small plus sign.

 No app available

 App available

When this sign is displayed, it means the website you are visiting has an Internet Explorer app available in the Store. If you click or tap it, the Page Tools menu appears. This time, the menu will have an option named Get App For This Site. A click or tap takes you to the Store, from which you can install the app specific to that website.

If you have copied a link to a web page, you can paste it into the Address bar to view that page. Many users will appreciate the Paste And Go option, which automatically pastes the link and loads it into the browser. To bring it up, right-click or press and hold in the Address bar.

When used on web pages, the right-click menu enables you to copy content and links and open links in a new tab or the same tab and to save pictures directly to your picture library.

To make navigation easier for desktop users, the Internet Explorer app enables you to navigate backward and forward without having to bring up the toolbar on the bottom of the app window. Hovering the mouse on the left or right side of the window displays a transparent Back or Forward button, depending on where you placed the button. Clicking it takes you to the previous or next web page you visited in the active tab.

The Internet Explorer app includes a new Flip Ahead feature so you can navigate your favorite sites like you read a magazine. It replaces the need to click or tap links with a more natural forward swipe gesture on touch-centric devices (and forward button with the mouse).

As you can see from this section, the new Internet Explorer app is not very difficult to use. If you take some time to experiment, visit a few websites, and do searches on the web, you'll become comfortable using it and start to enjoy this new way of browsing the web. That's true both for readers who use a classic desktop computer and for those who use a computer with touch or a tablet.

Using the Internet Explorer Desktop Application

The Internet Explorer desktop application has a more complex interface than its Windows 8 full-screen counterpart. At the top of its window are several buttons and fields for managing the way you navigate the web. At the top right are three buttons that give you access to different configuration menus.

On the bottom and right side are scroll bars that can be used to scroll through the content of a web page that is bigger than your Internet Explorer window.

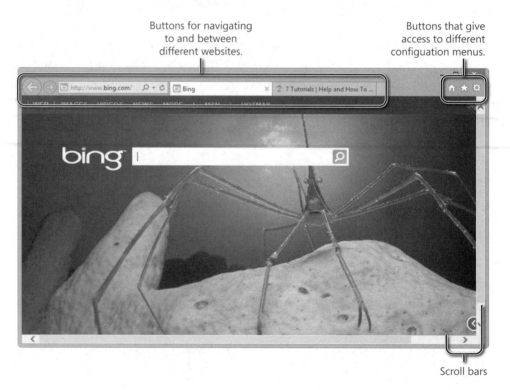

Buttons for navigating to and between different websites.

Buttons that give access to different configuation menus.

Scroll bars

The middle of the window, taking up most of the space, is where websites are loaded and viewed.

Let's see in more detail what each button does. Moving from left to right are the following buttons:

- The Back and Forward buttons. They become active as soon as you browse to more than one page on the Internet. You can use them to navigate back and forth between the different pages you opened.

- The Address bar, where you type the address of the website you want to visit. This bar can also be used as a search box. You can type a search term and press Enter or click the Search button in the Address bar. Internet Explorer displays the search results relevant to your search term by using the default search engine you have set. If you have not changed its default configuration, search results will be displayed by using Bing, the search engine owned by Microsoft.

- A button in the Address bar that looks like a piece of paper torn in half. It reloads a web page in compatibility mode and is useful when browsing dated web pages that were created with earlier technologies. If a web page simply doesn't look right, click this button, and the page reloads in compatibility mode. Chances are the webpage will then be generated correctly.

- The Refresh button. Use it to reload the web page you are viewing so that you can see the updates that have been made to it, if any, since the last time you viewed it.

- Next to the Address bar are the tabs you have opened. The tab that is active always has a lighter color, whereas those in the background have a slightly darker tone. When you open a web page, its name becomes the title of the tab. To change between tabs, just click them. If you want to close the active tab, click the little X button near its name.

- Next to the opened tabs is a square button with no name. Use this button to open a new tab. Click it, type the address of the website you want to visit in the Address bar, and press Enter. The website is now loaded in its own tab.

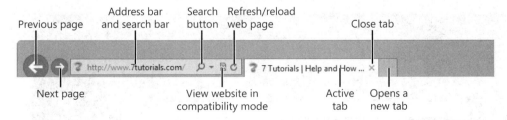

On the top-right side of the Internet Explorer window are three buttons. Let's see what they do:

- The first, in the shape of a house, takes you to the homepage you have set for Internet Explorer on the desktop. By default, this is the MSN.com website, and it can be changed to something else.

- The second button, in the shape of a star, opens a menu for managing your favorite websites, the feeds to which you have subscribed, and the history of your browsing.

- The third button, in the shape of a gear, opens the Tools menu that is used to configure many aspects of how Internet Explorer works.

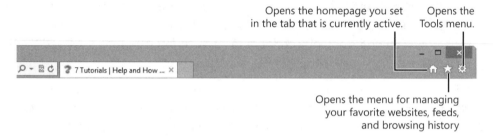

Opens the homepage you set in the tab that is currently active.

Opens the Tools menu.

Opens the menu for managing your favorite websites, feeds, and browsing history

If you are familiar with Internet Explorer 9, which was available in Windows 7 and Windows Vista, you'll notice that not much has changed in terms of the interface. If you are comfortable using Internet Explorer 9, you will have no problems using the Internet Explorer 10 desktop application.

Pinning Websites to the Start Screen

In the Internet Explorer app, you won't find any menus and lists of Favorites, as you might be used to seeing in previous versions of Internet Explorer. When you open a new tab, you get a list of the websites you frequently visit and the websites you pinned to the Start screen. In a way, pinned websites are the new Favorites.

Pinned websites appear as shortcuts on the Start screen. Each shortcut includes the icon of the website (if any) plus the name of the website. Websites that provide specific support for this feature can display custom icons, backgrounds, and the latest updates. When you click or tap the shortcut, the website opens in Internet Explorer.

In this exercise, you'll learn how to pin a website to the Start screen.

 SET UP Go to the Start screen and start Internet Explorer. Navigate to the Facebook website (www.facebook.com). If you don't use Facebook, you can go to any other website you use frequently.

1   Click or tap the **Pin to Start** button to open the Pin To Start dialog box.

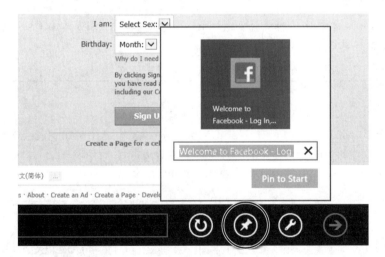

2   Type **My Facebook Account** in the available text field.

3   Click or tap the **Pin to Start** button.

❌ CLEAN UP Close Internet Explorer.

Facebook is now pinned to the Start screen, and you can use the shortcut that was created to quickly access this social network whenever you want.

Where Can I Set My Homepage?

Internet Explorer 10 will open either the homepage you have set (the Bing search engine is the default) or the tabs opened in the last browsing session. You can change this behavior from the desktop Internet Explorer only, in the Internet Options menu.

Browsing the Web Using the InPrivate Mode

InPrivate mode is a way of browsing the web without leaving traces in the browser. When you open an InPrivate tab, all the websites you visit in that tab, the passwords you enter, the cookies that are created, and the temporary files that are downloaded are deleted as soon as you close the tab or you close Internet Explorer. An InPrivate tab is marked by the blue InPrivate icon. This icon does not appear on a normal tab.

InPrivate is turned on

InPrivate Browsing helps prevent Internet Explorer from storing data about
your browsing session. This includes cookies, temporary Internet files, history,
and other data.

To turn off InPrivate Browsing, close this browser tab.

Read the Internet Explorer privacy statement online

This way of browsing is useful when you don't want to be tracked or when you're using
someone else's computer and you don't want to leave traces of what you visited. This
browsing mode is highly recommended when using public computers to browse the web.

In this exercise, you'll learn how to visit a website by using the InPrivate mode.

➡ SET UP **From the Start screen, start Internet Explorer.**

1   Right-click somewhere in the middle of the Internet Explorer window or swipe down
    from the top of the window toward the middle, to view the menu with options for
    opening new tabs.

2   Click or tap the **button with three dots** on the top-right side of the window.

3   Click or tap the **New InPrivate** tab so that a new tab is opened in the InPrivate mode.

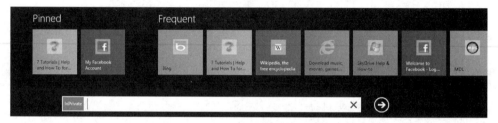

4   Type the address of the website you want to visit and click or tap the **Go** button.

❌ CLEAN UP **Close Internet Explorer when you have finished browsing the web.**

The website is now loaded in InPrivate mode. As soon as you close this tab, any traces of your visit to this website are deleted.

Downloading Files from the Internet

The process for downloading files is similar to other browsers to which you are accustomed. You are first asked whether you want to run or open the file you are about to download (depending on its type) or to save it on your computer.

When you click Save, the file is automatically downloaded to the Downloads folder. You are not asked whether you want to save the file to another location.

A progress bar appears. If you are downloading multiple files at the same time, the information is aggregated, and you are shown how many downloads are in progress and how much time remains until all of them are finished. You can close this notification or cancel the download altogether.

After a file is downloaded, you are given options relevant to its file type. You can run executable files, whereas you can open other files.

Understanding SmartScreen Filter in Internet Explorer

Sometimes when you try to download files, Internet Explorer doesn't allow you to do so and says that the file has been reported as unsafe by SmartScreen Filter and cannot be downloaded. The same can happen when trying to view certain websites to which your access is blocked, and you get a similar message.

SmartScreen Filter, mentioned in this message, is a security feature Microsoft introduced after Internet Explorer 8. It tracks what Internet Explorer users visit and, when an infected file or website has been detected, it blocks access to it to protect you. Files that are reported and confirmed as malware won't download to your computer due to this security feature. Also, websites that are reported and confirmed as distributing malware or trying to steal personal information from their visitors are automatically blocked. Therefore, don't worry! You just have avoided harm to you or to your system.

> ## This website has been reported as unsafe
>
> www.iloveflappybam.com
>
> We recommend that you do not continue to this website.
> This website has been reported to Microsoft for containing threats to your computer that might reveal personal or financial information.
>
> More information

SmartScreen Filter also looks at how commonly files are downloaded. If you are trying to download a file that is rarely downloaded by other Internet Explorer users, you are warned that the file "is not commonly downloaded and could harm your computer."

If you know what that file is supposed to do and you trust the source from which you download it, you can go ahead and run it. If not, it is best either to delete it or to scan it for malware by using Windows Defender or any other security solution before trying to run it. This way, you make sure that you stay away from viruses and other forms of malware.

File Explorer uses the same technology, and you are warned before running files that are marked as infected by SmartScreen Filter.

Setting the Default Internet Explorer Version

In Windows 8, you can set one of two versions of Internet Explorer as your default. Having both available and starting in different scenarios can be confusing. It is best to give both a try, decide which you like best, and set that one as your default.

Set your default version on the Programs tab in the Internet Options window. There, you are asked to choose how you open links. The default is to let Internet Explorer decide. If you choose Always In Internet Explorer, the Internet Explorer app will always be used to open links on your Start screen or in the applications you use.

Opening Internet Explorer

Choose how you open links.

Let Internet Explorer decide ▾

Let Internet Explorer decide
Always in Internet Explorer
Always in Internet Explorer on the desktop

However, the Internet Explorer shortcut on the Desktop will continue to open the Internet Explorer desktop application. All the other shortcuts and links will open the Internet Explorer app.

Setting the Internet Explorer desktop application as your default involves a bit more configuration. That's why, in this exercise, you'll learn the steps for setting up this option.

➔ SET UP Go to the Desktop and start Internet Explorer.

1 Click the **Tools** menu icon in the upper-right corner of the Internet Explorer window.

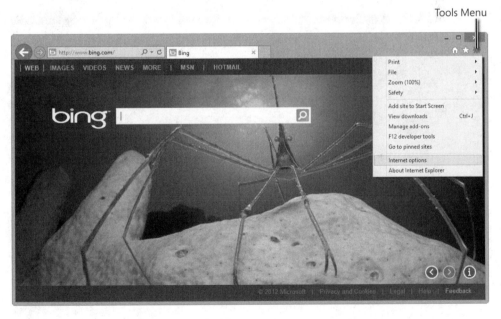

Tools Menu

2 In the **Tools** menu, click **Internet options** to open the Internet Options window.

3   Click the **Programs** tab to find the options for configuring how Internet Explorer is
     opened.

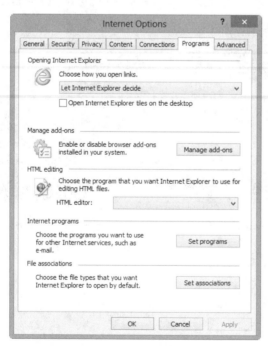

4   In **Opening Internet Explorer**, in the **Choose how you open links** list, select **Always in Internet Explorer on the desktop**.

5   Beneath the list box, select **Open Internet Explorer tiles on the desktop**.

6   Click **OK**.

✕ CLEAN UP Close Internet Explorer.

Now all the Internet Explorer shortcuts in Windows 8 will open only the desktop Internet Explorer version. Also, when you click a link to a website in any application or on the Start screen, it will be opened by using the same version.

TIP If you want the Internet Explorer app to be used as the default, follow the same procedure but select Always In Internet Explorer at step 4 and clear the **Open Internet Explorer tiles on the desktop** check box.

Key Points

- The new Internet Explorer brings many changes and improvements to the browsing experience.

- Pinning websites is a way of storing your favorite websites on the Start screen and accessing them from there.

- When browsing the web from a public computer, it is best to browse by using the InPrivate mode. This way, you leave no traces, and Internet Explorer does not store your personal data.

- SmartScreen Filter is a Microsoft technology that protects you from downloading and running infected files and from accessing malicious websites.

- After you decide which Internet Explorer version you like best, it is good to set it as your default.

Chapter at a Glance

Browse

Browse SkyDrive from the SkyDrive app, page 179

Upload

Upload files to SkyDrive, page 183

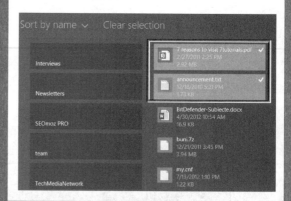

Download

Download files from SkyDrive, page 187

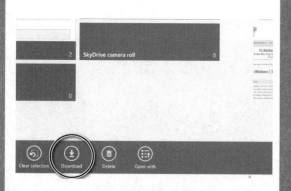

Synchronize

Synchronize your Windows 8 settings, page 190

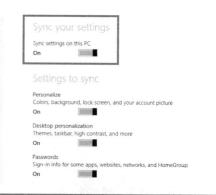

Using SkyDrive

6

IN THIS CHAPTER, YOU WILL LEARN HOW TO

- Work with SkyDrive and learn about its features and limitations.

- Upload files to SkyDrive.

- Download files from SkyDrive.

- Synchronize your Windows 8 settings.

SkyDrive is a service by which you can store your files on the Microsoft servers. You can upload documents, pictures, and other types of files and access them from anywhere: your web browser (Internet Explorer 10, for instance), your Windows Phone, or Windows 8–based computers and devices. By using SkyDrive, you can synchronize files among multiple devices or share some of your stored files and folders with other people. It's useful for sharing big files with friends and family and for doing collaborative work on Microsoft Office documents. Further, synchronizing important files across devices frees you to use them whenever you need them from almost any device or computer with an Internet connection.

Windows 8 can also use SkyDrive to synchronize your settings across the computers and devices with which you log on to your Microsoft account, so you can configure your Windows 8 settings on one computer and have them replicate automatically on all others that use the same Microsoft account.

The basic SkyDrive service is free to all users with a Microsoft account and includes 7 GB of space. However, paid plans are also available for people who want more storage space. The features are the same in all plans, and so is the functionality.

In this chapter, you'll learn how to access SkyDrive, upload files to it, download files from it, access it from a web browser, and synchronize your Windows 8 settings across multiple computers and devices.

Using SkyDrive

To use SkyDrive in Windows 8, you need a Microsoft account instead of a local account so you can log on to Windows. If you try to access SkyDrive from a local account, Windows 8 will ask you to change your account settings.

Sign in to use SkyDrive

To access your SkyDrive, sign in with your Microsoft account.

Close

SEE ALSO If you want to learn more about user accounts in Windows 8 and how to use a Microsoft account, read Chapter 12, "Allowing Others to Use the Computer."

To access SkyDrive, upload, download, or sync files and settings, you must have a working Internet connection.

We can't display the folder

Check your Internet connection, and then tap or click to refresh the page.

SEE ALSO If you want to learn more about connecting to a network and the Internet, read Chapter 11, "Connecting to a Network and the Internet."

Browsing SkyDrive from the SkyDrive App

You open the SkyDrive app from the Start screen by clicking or tapping its icon.

You can also search for the word *SkyDrive* and click or tap the appropriate search result.

When you open SkyDrive, the application takes a few seconds to load information about the folders and files you have uploaded. It will always show your last accessed folder. If you haven't used it before, it will show your SkyDrive home location.

For each folder, you see its name and the number of files found inside. For each file, you see an icon representative of its type and the name of the file. For pictures, you see a preview of the file.

If you right-click a file, a contextual menu opens at the bottom of the SkyDrive app window, the file is selected, and a check mark appears on its icon's upper-right corner. The same result can be achieved with a press and hold on the file and a slight downward movement with your finger.

To open a folder or a file, click or tap it. When you open a file, SkyDrive opens it with the application that is set as the default on your computer for opening that file type. For example, PDF documents are opened by default with Reader.

If you want to browse through different areas of SkyDrive, click or tap the name of your SkyDrive to open a menu with the standard locations defined for your SkyDrive: your SkyDrive, Recent Documents, and Shared.

The Recent Documents area displays the files you recently opened. If no files were accessed, the list will be empty. The Shared area displays folders and files others have shared with you. If none are shared, the list will be empty.

On the left side of the name of your SkyDrive is the Back button, which you use to go back to the previous location. This button is visible only after you have opened folders found on your SkyDrive. When accessing your SkyDrive start location, it is not visible.

The contextual menu shown at the bottom of the SkyDrive window displays useful buttons, depending on where you are in SkyDrive and what was selected.

Let's look at each option:

- **CLEAR SELECTION** Shown only if at least one file or folder was selected. Its purpose is to clear the current selection of files or folders.

- **DOWNLOAD** Displayed only when one or more files were selected. This button is used to download the selected file(s) to your computer.

- **DELETE** Shown only if at least one file or folder was selected. A click or tap deletes the item(s) you have selected.

- **OPEN WITH** Allows you to select the app with which to open the selected item.

- **REFRESH** Refreshes the list of items displayed on your SkyDrive.

- **NEW FOLDER** Allows you to create a new folder on the SkyDrive at the current location.

- **UPLOAD** Uploads new items to SkyDrive.

- **DETAILS (OR THUMBNAILS)** Changes the way items are displayed. The default view is Thumbnails. Clicking Details shows items using this view, and the button is changed to Thumbnails.

- **SELECT ALL** Selects all the items displayed in the current location.

Using your mouse or finger to point to an item from SkyDrive reveals more information about it, including its name, the date when it was last modified, its size, and the people with whom it is shared.

You can see that SkyDrive is relatively easy to use. To be productive when using it, don't hesitate to go through the next sections and exercises.

Uploading a File with the SkyDrive App

Uploading files to SkyDrive is a simple task. You can upload one or more files at one time. With the SkyDrive app, you can browse through multiple folders and select only the ones you want uploaded. When selected, the files are displayed on the bottom half of the window, in the SkyDrive list. To remove a file from that list, click or tap it.

After you select the files, click or tap Add To SkyDrive and wait for the upload to finish.

On SkyDrive, you can upload any type of files. However, official support is only provided for the following file types.

- Documents saved as Portable Document Format (PDF) files, text files, Microsoft Office files of any kind, and files saved with the Open Document Format (ODF) such as those created by using LibreOffice or OpenOffice

- Photos saved as the JPG, JPEG, GIF, BMP, PNG, TIF, and TIFF file types

- Videos saved as AVI or WMV file types
- Audio files saved as WAV or MP3 file types

During the upload process, progress information is shown in the upper-right corner of the SkyDrive app window.

2 items in progress...

If you click or tap it, more information about the process appears. When the upload is complete, the word *Done* appears.

In this exercise, you'll learn how to upload a file to SkyDrive by using the SkyDrive app.

SET UP To complete this exercise, you need the Document1.docx file in the Chapter06 folder in your practice files. When this file is available, open the SkyDrive app and browse to the folder to which you want to upload the file.

1   Right-click somewhere in the empty space of the **SkyDrive** app window or swipe from the bottom edge of the window to open the contextual menu.

2   Click or tap the **Upload** button to open the Files window.

3   Click or tap **Files** and browse to where you saved the Document1.docx practice file.

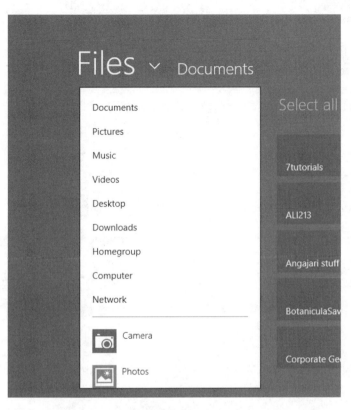

4 Click or tap the **Document1.docx file** to select it.

5   Click or tap the **Add to SkyDrive** button to start the upload procedure.

6   Wait for the upload procedure to end.

     It should not take more than a few seconds.

✖ CLEAN UP When the upload is complete, close the SkyDrive app.

The Documment1.docx file is now uploaded to your SkyDrive.

Downloading a File with the SkyDrive App

Downloading files with the SkyDrive app is just as easy as uploading them. Browse to the file you want to download, select it, and click the Download button. During the download process, progress is shown on the upper-right side of the SkyDrive app window.

1 item in progress...

If you click or tap the progress line, more information about the process appears. When the download is complete, the word *Done* appears.

Like the upload process, you can download one file at a time or select multiple files and download them to the same location on your computer. However, folders cannot be downloaded.

In this exercise, you'll learn how to download a file from SkyDrive by using the SkyDrive app.

➡ SET UP Open the SkyDrive app and browse to the folder that contains the file you want to download.

1   Right-click the file you want to download or press and hold on it while moving slightly downwards.

     This opens the contextual menu at the bottom of the SkyDrive app window.

2   Click or tap **Download** to open the Files window.

3   Browse to where you want to save the file and click or tap the **Choose this folder** button.

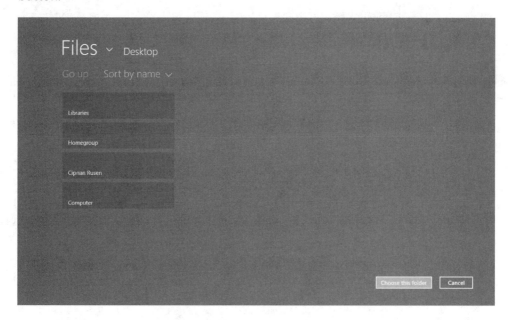

4   Make sure the location where you want to save the file is the one you selected and click **OK**.

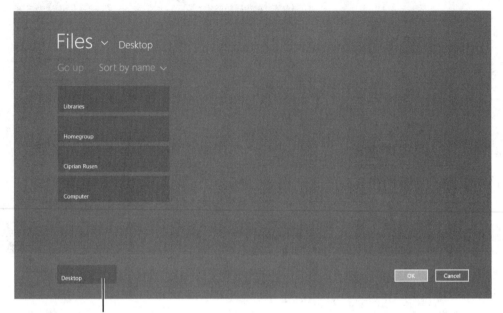

The location where the selected file will be downloaded.

5   Wait for the download to finish.

❌ CLEAN UP **When the download is complete, close the SkyDrive app.**

The file you selected is now saved on your computer at the location you specified.

Accessing SkyDrive from a Web Browser

You can access SkyDrive from a web browser at any time. Go to https://skydrive.live.com and log on with your Microsoft account details. You now have complete access to all your files and folders stored on SkyDrive. If you have logged on with your Microsoft account in Windows 8, and you're using Internet Explorer as your browser, you won't need to log on to the SkyDrive service. You are automatically logged on by Windows.

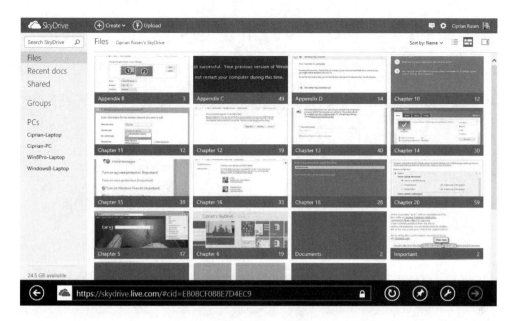

With the help of your web browser, you can download files from SkyDrive, organize them in folders and subfolders, or add new files. You can also share files and folders with others.

Last, you can view the pictures uploaded to SkyDrive and edit Microsoft Office documents by using the Microsoft Office Web apps. They are simplified versions of Microsoft Office that allow document viewing and basic editing.

Synchronizing Your Windows 8 Settings

One of the greatest features of SkyDrive is that Windows 8 can use it to synchronize your user account settings across the computers on which your Microsoft account is used. If you make a change on one computer, it will be reflected on other computers the next time you log on.

However, not all Windows 8 settings are synchronized, even though most of them will be. The settings that are synchronized, if you set them to be, are the following.

- Your desktop background, desktop colors, the Lock screen, and your user account picture
- The active desktop theme, high contrast, and taskbar settings
- Ease of access settings: the narrator and the magnifier
- Your language preferences: keyboard, input methods, and the display language
- User settings and purchases for apps that support the synchronization feature
- Your mouse and mouse cursor settings and those of File Explorer
- The sign-in information for the HomeGroup, network access, some of your apps, and websites (if you are using Internet Explorer 10 as your browser)

Another great aspect of the synchronization feature is that the SkyDrive space used for storing your settings is not counted against your SkyDrive space allocation. That space is reserved for uploading the files you want.

As with other SkyDrive features, you need a Microsoft account to sync your settings. SkyDrive doesn't work on local user accounts.

Also, after you log on to your computer or device by using your Microsoft account, you need to set it as trusted for your passwords to be synchronized. If you haven't done this, you can do so from the Sync Your Settings area found in PC Settings. Just click or tap the Trust This PC link and follow the instructions.

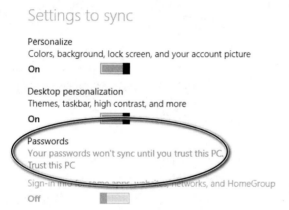

In this exercise, you'll learn how to turn on the synchronization of your Windows 8 settings and select what is being synced.

➡ SET UP Open PC Settings.

1   Click or tap the **Sync your settings** area to open the synchronization settings.

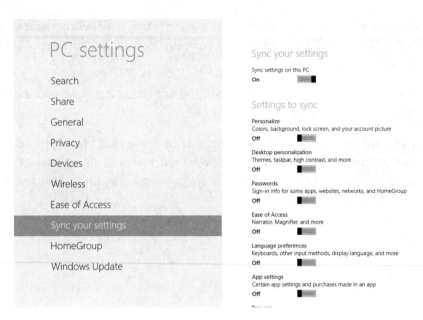

2   Change the position of the switch for Sync Settings On This PC from Off to **On**.

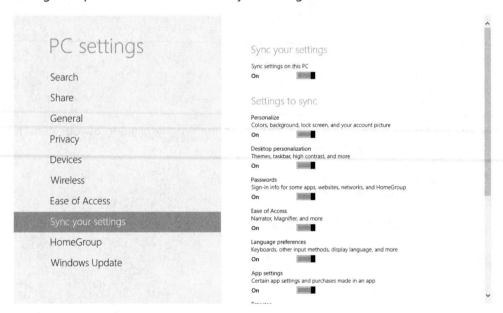

3   In the **Settings To Sync** area, change the switch for the things you want to sync from Off to **On**.

⊗ CLEAN UP   Close PC Settings and then repeat this procedure on all the computers that use the same Microsoft account and on which you want settings to be synchronized.

From now on, each change you make in the Windows 8 settings will be synchronized on all the computers on which sync was set up.

Key Points

- Using SkyDrive requires a Microsoft account and an Internet connection.

- Use the SkyDrive app to browse the content of your SkyDrive and to upload, download, and view files.

- You can upload or download multiple files at once to and from SkyDrive.

- SkyDrive can also synchronize your settings across computers and devices with Windows 8.

6

Chapter at a Glance

Add
Add a Hotmail account to the Mail app, page 200

> **Add your Hotmail account**
>
> Enter the information below to connect to your Hotmail accour
>
> Email address
> seventutorials@live.com
>
> Password
> •••••••••

Connect
Connect to your Facebook account using the People app, page 210

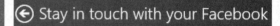
> ← Stay in touch with your Facebook
>
> Chat with your Facebook friends and see their updates here, a
> websites where you use this Microsoft account. Just connect F
> ciprianrusen@gmail.com
>
> What else happens when I connect? ⌄

Manage
Manage your schedule with the Calendar app, page 215

Chat
Chat with your friends, using the Messaging app, page 222

People you are chatting with.

Using the Social Apps

IN THIS CHAPTER, YOU WILL LEARN HOW TO

- Use the Mail app and send an email with a SkyDrive attachment.

- Use the People app and add your Facebook account.

- Use the Calendar app.

- Use the Messaging app.

- Use the Camera app.

Being social is a key component of anyone's computing life. Windows 8 tries to meet the need for interaction with our friends, family, and coworkers by offering a few well-integrated apps: Mail, Calendar, People, and Messaging. Their tiles on the Start screen are very visible, and they are placed in the same group. When you start using the apps, their tiles automatically display live data such as updates from your friend on Facebook whose birthday is today or the schedule of your next meeting.

These apps are integrated and, after you add an account on one of them, it can be accessed from all the others. For example, you can add your Google mail account to the Mail app and your Facebook account to the People app. Then, you can view your Google calendar in the Calendar app, and you can chat with your Facebook friends by using the Messaging app.

In this chapter, you'll learn the basics about using all these apps, and you'll learn how to use the Camera app.

PRACTICE FILES You don't need any practice files to complete the exercises in this chapter. For more information about practice file requirements, see "Using the Practice Files" at the beginning of this book.

Using the Mail App

The Mail app runs in full-screen mode, just like all Windows 8 apps. Its interface is minimalistic and focuses on browsing and reading your email messages. Unfortunately for users who are accustomed to the Desktop, it might not be easy to find your way at first, so learning the basics for navigating this app is the place to start. As you'll see in this section and the ones that follow it, Mail is a simple app that is easy to learn.

When you open the Mail app for the first time and no email accounts have been added to it, there's nothing to see. It's just an empty window with no displayed information.

As soon as you have added email accounts, things change. The application window is then split into three columns.

- On the left is the Mail column, where you can see the email accounts that have been added so far. Listed above the list of accounts are the folders for the selected email account. A click or tap on a folder reveals its content.

- In the middle is the Inbox column, displaying the inbox folder for the selected email account. The following summary information is displayed for each message: sender name, when it was received and its subject. This column can also display messages from folders other than those in your Inbox (Sent Items, for instance). On smaller displays and lower resolutions (such as 1024 × 768 pixels), this column is merged with the first column. For example, when you select an email account or folder, the Mail column is replaced by the Inbox column. To get back to the Mail column, click or tap the Back button at the top of the column.

- On the right, the messages you select are displayed in their entirety.

To display the menu with contextual options, right-click or swipe from the bottom edge. This menu includes the following buttons:

- **SYNC** Use this button to start the synchronization procedure that downloads any new email messages you've received since the last time you checked the email account and sends the messages that are in the send queue, if any.

- **PIN TO START** Use this button to pin the selected inbox to the Start screen.

- **MOVE** Use this button to move the selected email message to another folder.

- **MARK UNREAD** Use this button to mark the email message that is currently open as unread.

The three buttons on the top-right side of the window are for:

- Creating a new email message.

- Opening a small menu with options to reply to the message or forward it to other people.

- Deleting the email message.

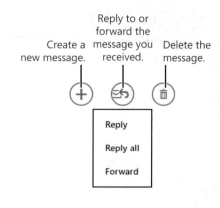

Create a
new message.

Reply to or
forward the
message you
received.

Delete the
message.

Reply

Reply all

Forward

Ciprian Rusen
August 29, 2012 7:26 PM
To: Ciprian Rusen

Hello!

Hi are you today?

Sent from Windows Mail

After you start using the Mail app, it remembers the last email account and folder you accessed, so each time you start the app, it opens the last accessed folder for the last accessed email account.

Adding a Hotmail Account to the Mail App

You can add any number of email accounts from different email services to the Mail app. By default, it is well integrated with the popular Hotmail and Outlook services from Microsoft and Google mail from Google. You can also add business email accounts, which use the Microsoft Exchange email service.

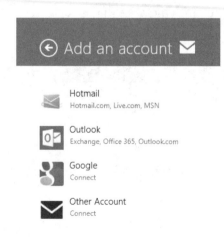

(←) Add an account ✉

Hotmail
Hotmail.com, Live.com, MSN

Outlook
Exchange, Office 365, Outlook.com

Google
Connect

Other Account
Connect

The integration with Hotmail is very good, considering that both Windows 8 and Hotmail are created by Microsoft. You can add multiple Hotmail email accounts to the Mail app.

In this exercise, you'll learn how to add a Hotmail account to the Mail app.

SET UP Make sure your Windows 8 device is connected to the Internet. Then, open the Mail app and have your account details at hand: the correct email address and password. If you have already added other email accounts, open the Accounts column, as shown in the previous section.

1   Press **Windows+C** or swipe from the right side of the screen and select the **Settings** charm.

2   Click or tap **Accounts** to open the list of accounts already added to the Mail app.

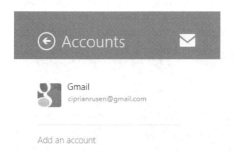

3   Click or tap **Add an account** to open the list of types of accounts you can add.

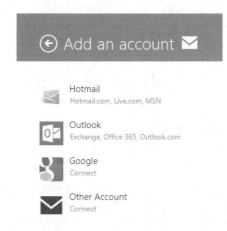

4   Click or tap **Hotmail** to open the Add Your Hotmail Account window.

5   Type the email address and password in the appropriate fields.

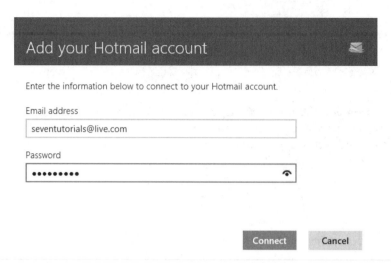

Add your Hotmail account

Enter the information below to connect to your Hotmail account.

Email address

seventutorials@live.com

Password

•••••••••

Connect   Cancel

6   Click or tap **Connect.** Wait a few seconds for the Mail app to connect to your email account and display the messages in your inbox.

CLEAN UP Close the Mail app.

The email account you specified is now added to the Mail app and can be accessed each time you use the app. You can add other email accounts, including a Google account, by following the same procedure. However, before you do so, it is best to read the next section about adding a Google mail account.

Adding a Google mail Account to the Mail App

You add a Google mail email account to the Mail app the same way you add a Hotmail account except that you click or tap Google instead of Hotmail.

Unlike Hotmail users, Google mail users can use a two-step verification process that enhances the security of their email accounts and lowers the chances of unwanted people gaining access to the accounts. If this process is enabled for your Google mail account, you cannot use your standard Google mail password to add your account to the Mail app. First, you need to generate a new application-specific password just for the Mail app and use that instead of your password at step 5 in the preceding exercise.

You can generate application-specific passwords by going to your Google account, choosing Security, and then selecting Authorizing Applications & Sites. Choose an appropriate name for the new application-specific password and then click or tap Generate Password.

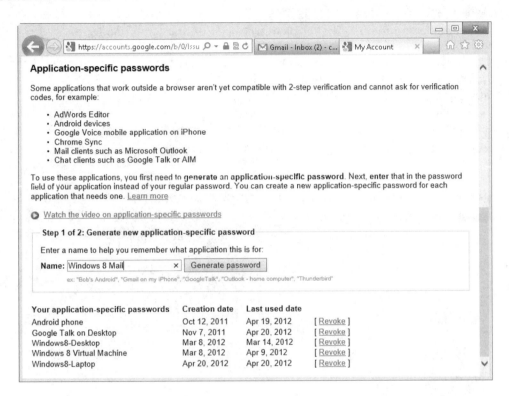

Google generates a random password that you can type in the Mail app instead of your Google mail password to access the messages in your Google mail inbox.

Sending an Email with a SkyDrive Attachment

When sending files as email attachments, you use both inbox space and some bandwidth when uploading the file. The recipient will also use space and bandwidth.

By using the SkyDrive app, you upload a file once to your SkyDrive and then share it by email, using the Mail app, with as many people as you want. You don't need to upload the file each time you want to send it to someone.

The people to whom you send the file can access it through a direct link that is automatically included in the message. It doesn't fill up their inbox space, and they can download the file if and when they want.

Files can be shared with anyone; it doesn't matter whether the person uses the SkyDrive service. Also, you can type the email address of the people to whom you want to send it or select them from your list of contacts stored in the People app.

In this exercise, you'll learn how to send an email message that shares a file uploaded to your SkyDrive. For illustration purposes, use the same practice file that you used in Chapter 6. You can use the same file or any other file you have uploaded to your SkyDrive.

SET UP Make sure your Windows 8 device is connected to the Internet. Open the Sky-Drive app and browse to the folder that contains the file you want to share.

1   Right-click the file you want to share or press and hold until a check mark appears on the top-right corner of its icon.

2   Press **Windows+C** or swipe from the right side of the screen and select **Share**.

3   Click or tap **Mail** to display the Mail app on the right side of the screen.

4   In the **To** field, type the email address of the person to whom you want to send the message.

Mail

Ciprian Rusen
ciprianrusen@gmail.com

To

Ciprian Rusen

Document1

Add a message

Sent from Windows Mail

Document1.docx
https://skydrive.live.com/redir?resid=EB0BCF088E...
Store photos and docs online. Access them from
any PC, Mac or phone. Create and work together
on Word, Excel or PowerPoint documents.

5   In the body of the message, type the message you want to send.

6   Click or tap the **Send** button on the top-right side of the Mail app window.

✖ CLEAN UP   Close the SkyDrive app.

The email message has been sent, and the recipient can access the SkyDrive file from the
direct link included in the message.

Using the People App

The People app displays all the contacts you have for all the email accounts and services you have added in the Mail app and, through your Microsoft account (also known as Windows Live ID), it can access social networking services such as Facebook, Twitter, and LinkedIn after you authorize your Microsoft account to access these services. The People app will download all your friends and contacts and share their latest updates.

When you open the People app, you are presented with a lot of information. A column on the left is for accessing your own updates, viewing notifications, and accessing what is new. On the right, your contacts are listed in alphabetical order. The top-right corner displays Connected To, followed by a list of icons that represent the accounts to which the People app is connected.

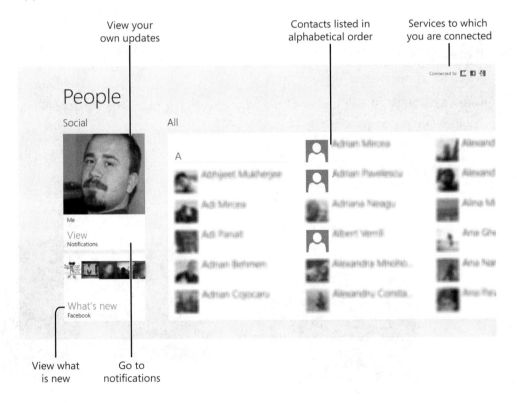

View your own updates   Contacts listed in alphabetical order   Services to which you are connected

View what is new   Go to notifications

In the left column are three sections:

- **ME** Shows your updates and notifications on the social networks to which you're connected

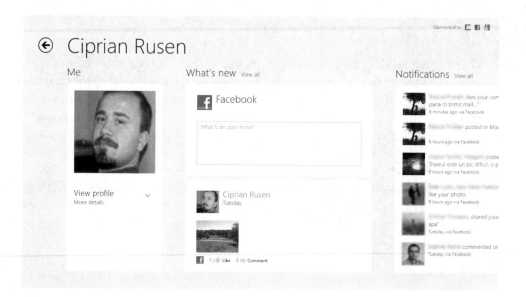

- **VIEW NOTIFICATIONS** View the latest notifications available on the social networks you are connected to

- **WHAT'S NEW** Shows updates from all your contacts on all the social networks to which you're connected

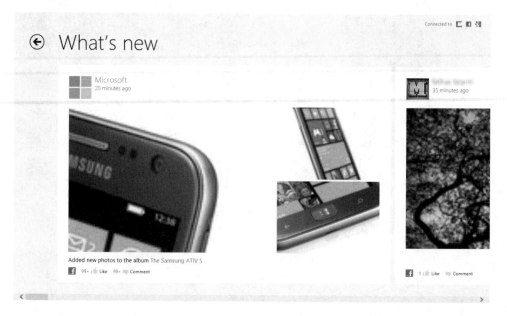

Access a contact by clicking or tapping the name. The People app shows the contact details that have been stored and, if available, any updates from that person on the social networks to which you are connected.

To show the menu with contextual options, right-click or swipe from the bottom edge to display the following buttons:

- **Home** Returns you to the People area. It serves as a shortcut that takes you to the home screen of the People app.

- **Online Only** Filters the list of people to show only those who are listed as online at that moment. Another click or tap reverts this setting and displays all your contacts.

- **New** Enables you to create a new contact.

As you can see, using the People app is relatively easy. If you integrate it with the social networks you are using, it can be a great tool for managing your connections with other people.

Connecting to Your Facebook Account Using the People App

The People app can be easily integrated with Facebook. After you add your Facebook account, your Microsoft account is also connected to it, so your Hotmail contacts will be synchronized with Facebook, and the Messaging app and Windows Live Messenger (if you use it) will be integrated with your Facebook account.

If your Microsoft account (Windows Live ID) is already connected to your Facebook account, your Facebook friends will show up in the People app, and you won't need to add the Facebook account again.

When you connect the People app to your Facebook account, Facebook asks you to enter a name for the device from which the connection is made. Make this name meaningful so that you aren't confused when Facebook sends you the appropriate notifications through email. This name will then be visible in your Facebook account settings.

In this exercise, you'll learn how to add your Facebook account to the People app.

SET UP Make sure your Windows 8 device is connected to the Internet and then open the People app.

1 Press **Windows+C** or swipe from the right side of the screen and select **Settings**.

2   Click or tap **Accounts**.

3   Click or tap **Add an account**.

4   Click or tap **Facebook** and then wait for a few seconds.

The Stay In Touch With Your Facebook Friends window appears.

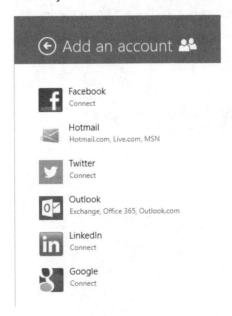

5   Click or tap **Connect**. At the prompt, type your Facebook login details.

Chat with your Facebook friends and see their updates here, and in other apps and websites where you use this Microsoft account. Just connect **Facebook** to ciprianrusen@gmail.com

What else happens when I connect? ∨

Connect   Cancel

6   Type your email address and your password and select **Keep me logged in**.

7   Click or tap **Log in**. When prompted, name the device from which you are connecting.

8   Type an appropriate name for the device and click or tap **Save Device**.

After a few seconds, you receive the announcement that you're ready to go.

9   Click or tap **Done** and wait for the People app to sync with Facebook.

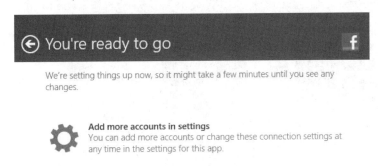

 CLEAN UP Close the People app.

The People app needs some time to sync with your Facebook account. Don't be surprised if it takes minutes instead of seconds, especially if you have a slow Internet connection or many friends and updates that need to be synchronized.

Adding a New Contact to the People App

You can add new contacts from the People app to all your email accounts. However, the People app cannot add contacts to the social networks to which you are connected. You have to do that by accessing the social networks themselves in a web browser such as Internet Explorer.

In this exercise, you'll learn how to add a new contact to the People app.

 SET UP Make sure your Windows 8 device is connected to the Internet. Then, open the People app.

1   Right-click or swipe from the bottom edge to open a contextual menu at the bottom of the window.

2   Click or tap **New** to open the New Contact window.

3   In the **Account** box, select the account in which you want to store this contact.

4   Complete the contact details you want to store.

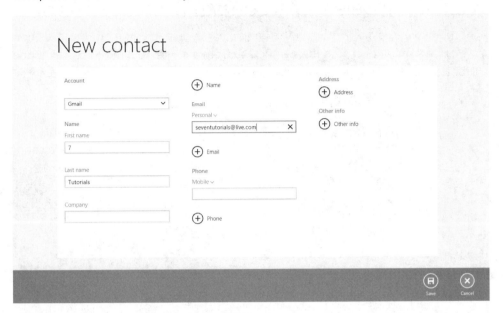

5   Click or tap **Save**.

CLEAN UP Close the People app.

The contact you created is saved and automatically synchronized with the account you selected.

7

Editing or Deleting a Contact from the People App

When you access a contact in the People app, you can edit it, add to it, remove information from it, or delete the contact, all from a contextual menu that you open at the bottom of the People app window by right-clicking or swiping from the bottom edge.

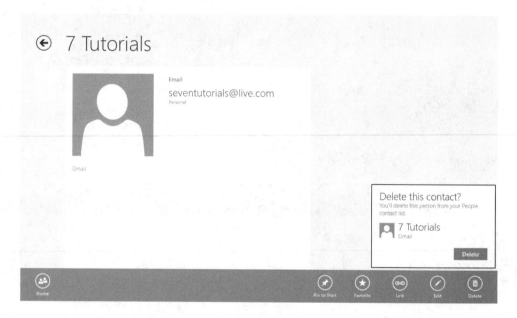

You can delete only contacts that are stored with your email accounts. Contacts from the social networks to which you are connected can be deleted only by accessing those social networks in a web browser.

Using the Calendar App

The Calendar app is very simple. It automatically takes your calendar data from all the email accounts you added in the Mail app and shows all events from all accounts. The events are shown in different colors, depending on the account to which they were added.

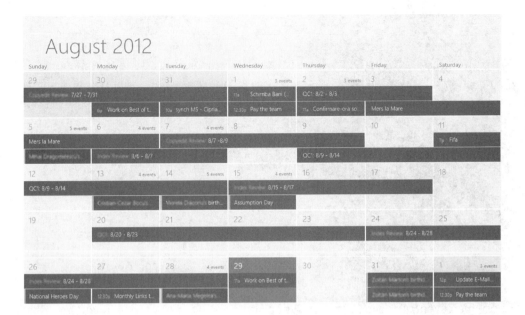

August 2012

Sunday	Monday	Tuesday	Wednesday	Thursday	Friday	Saturday
29	30	31	1 3 events	2 3 events	3	4
Copyedit Review 7/27 - 7/31			11a Schimba Bani (	QC1: 8/2 - 8/3		
	6p Work on Best of t...	10a synch MS - Cipria...	12.30p Pay the team	11a Confirmare-ora so...	Mers la Mare	
5 3 events	6 4 events	7 4 events	8	9	10	11
Mers la Mare		Copyedit Review 8/7 -8/9				7p Fifa
Mihai Dragomirescu's	Index Review 8/6 - 8/7			QC1: 8/9 - 8/14		
12	13 4 events	14 5 events	15 4 events	16	17	18
QC1: 8/9 - 8/14			Index Review 8/15 - 8/17			
	Cristian Cezar Bocus	Monela Diaconus birth...	Assumption Day			
19	20	21	22	23	24	25
	QC1 8/20 - 8/23				Index Review 8/24 - 8/28	
26	27	28 4 events	29	30	31	1 3 events
Index Review 8/24 - 8/28		11a Work on Best of t...			Zoltan Marton's birthd...	12p Update E-Mail...
National Heroes Day	12.30p Monthly Links t...	Ana-Maria Megetean's			Zoltan Marton's birthd...	12.30p Pay the team

To change how you view the calendar, right-click or swipe from the bottom edge. A contextual menu appears with a few options. On the left are buttons for changing how you view your calendar: by day, by week, or by month. The Today button shows only today's events in your calendar. The New button adds events to your calendar.

You can add new accounts or edit the permissions and different options for the Calendar app by using the Settings charm.

To open an event, just click or tap it. When you open a recurring event, you are asked whether you want to Open One or Open Series. If you click or tap Open One, only the current event opens, and any changes you make will be saved to it. If you click or tap Open Series, you open the series of recurring events, and any changes you make will be saved for the whole series.

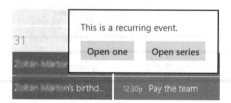

When you open the event, you can add details to or remove details from it. To save your changes, press the Save button in the top-right corner. To close the event without saving the changes you made, press the button with an X in the middle, near the Save button.

To delete an event, click or tap the Delete button.

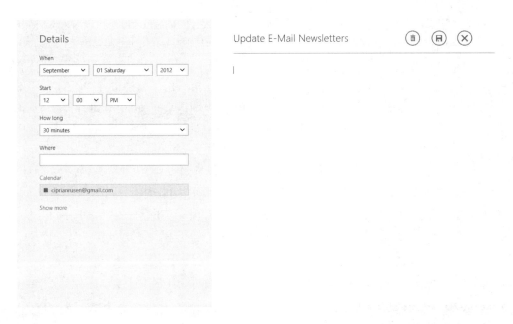

The Calendar app is not very complex, and you should easily become familiar with the way it works.

Adding an Event to Your Calendar

Adding an event to any of your calendars is an easy task, too. However, you need to complete some information for the event to be created and saved. The Calendar app asks you to complete the following fields:

- **WHEN** You must fill in when the event is taking place.

- **START** You must fill in when the event starts.

- **HOW LONG** Fill in the duration of the event. The default value is one hour, but if your event doesn't last for an hour, it is best to change the duration to the length of time you expect it to last.

- **WHERE** In this field, you specify information about where the event takes place, but you do not have to fill in this field.

- **CALENDAR** Select the calendar on which you want this event to be saved.

- **HOW OFTEN** You can set the frequency of the event. It can be set to once, every day, every weekday, every week, every month, or every year.

- **REMINDER** Set this for when you want to receive a reminder and for how long in advance of the event you want to be reminded. You can choose one of the following values: none, 5 minutes, 15 minutes, 30 minutes, 1 hour, 1 day, 18 hours, or 1 week.

- **STATUS** This field is for setting your status during the event and is shown to others who have access to your calendar data or in the Messaging app during the duration of the event. The default value is Busy. Other possible choices include Free, Tentative, Out of Office, or Working Elsewhere.

- **WHO** Use this field to invite others to the event and share the event details. You can type the email addresses of the people you want to invite.

- **PRIVATE** This option is useful when your calendar is shared with others. If you set the event as private, other people can't view the details of this event.

- **ADD A TITLE** This field is for adding a name for the event. This field is at the top of the empty white space on the right side of the app window.

- **ADD A MESSAGE** Use this field to add a message to share with the people you will invite or to add any information that is useful to you or others. This field is just beneath the title.

To save the event, click the Save button on the top-right side of the window.

If you have invited other people to the event, the Save button will change to a Send Invite button. Clicking it saves the event in your calendar and sends invitations to the people you specified in the Who field.

In this exercise, you'll learn how to add a new event to your calendar.

SET UP **Open the Calendar app.**

1   Right-click or swipe from the bottom edge to open a contextual menu at the bottom of the window.

2   Click or tap the **New** button to open the event Details window.

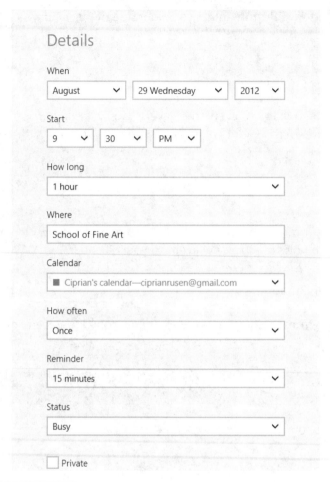

Details

When

| August ∨ | 29 Wednesday ∨ | 2012 ∨ |

Start

| 9 ∨ | 30 ∨ | PM ∨ |

How long

| 1 hour ∨ |

Where

| School of Fine Art |

Calendar

| ■ Ciprian's calendar—ciprianrusen@gmail.com ∨ |

How often

| Once ∨ |

Reminder

| 15 minutes ∨ |

Status

| Busy ∨ |

☐ Private

3   In the **Details** column, complete all the important fields with the relevant information: Where, When, Start, How Long, and then click or tap Show More to reveal the fields with other additional details to complete.

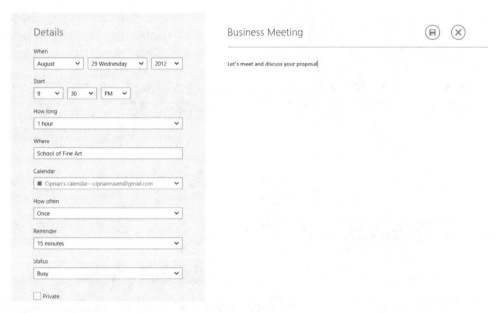

4   Select the calendar on which the event is added and invite the people who need to attend (if any).

5   On the right side of the window, type a name for the event and any other important details.

6   Click or tap the **Save** or **Send invite** button, depending on whether you invited people to the event.

✖ CLEAN UP Close the Calendar app.

The event you have created is added to your calendar and you will be reminded about it, depending on how you set the reminder.

Using the Messaging App

The Messaging app acts as a complement to the People app. In the People app, you can manage your list of contacts and add your friends from social networks such as Facebook. From the Mail app, you can send them email messages, and from the Messaging app, you can chat with them. Use the Messaging app to chat with your Facebook friends and those who are using the Messenger service.

When you open the app, you see the discussion threads that were previously started. If you added your Facebook account to the People app, you can also view the latest messages you received.

At the top right of the window is the Connected To notice, followed by some icons that represent the messaging services to which you are connected.

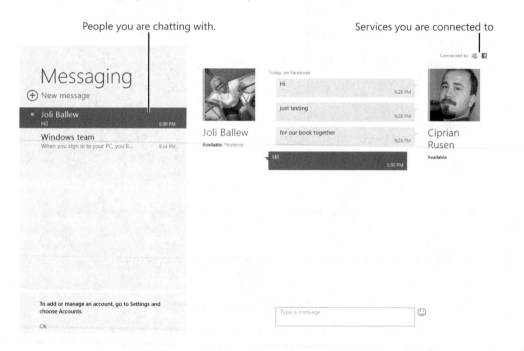

If you want to change your status or delete a messaging thread, right-click or swipe from the bottom edge. A menu appears with these options:

- **STATUS** Change your status on the messaging services to which you're connected. It can be set to Online or Invisible.

- **INVITE** Invite your friends to use the Messaging app or view invitations you received to chat through the Microsoft service.

- **DELETE** Delete the active messaging thread.

By using the Settings charm, you can change the accounts you're using and the options and permissions for the Messaging app. If you want to use a webcam and a microphone during chat sessions, you must change the Webcam and Microphone permissions from Off to On.

As you can see, the Messaging app is very similar to the other apps covered in this chapter.

Starting a Conversation with the Messaging App

It's easy to start conversations with the Messaging app. After you select the people with whom you want to talk, you can view the conversation thread on the left-side column. On the right, you see the picture of the person with whom you're talking, his or her status, your picture, your status, and the messages exchanged so far. To send a message, type it in the text box at the bottom of the window and press Enter. Type your replies in the same text box and press Enter to send them to the other person.

The status of the
person with whom
you are talking

Your status,
as visible
to others

Joli Ballew

Ciprian Rusen

Here you type your
message and replies

You can start conversations on Facebook only with your online friends; you can't leave them offline messages from the Messaging app. However, you can leave offline messages to people by using the Microsoft Messaging service (Windows Live Messenger).

In this exercise, you'll learn how to start a conversation by using the Messaging app.

 SET UP Make sure your Windows 8 device is connected to the Internet and then open the Messaging app.

1   Click or tap the **New message** option, found in the column on the left.

2 Wait for the People app to load and display all your contacts.

3 Click or tap **Online only** to view the people with whom you can start a conversation at this moment.

4   Browse through the list of people and select the person with whom you want to start the conversation.

5   Click or tap **Choose** to display the Messaging window.

6   Type your message and press Enter in the chat window to start the conversation.

❌ CLEAN UP After your chat, close the Messaging app.

The Messaging app saves the conversation you just started. You can delete it later if you don't want to save it.

Use the same procedure to leave an offline message.

Using the Camera App

You can use the Camera app if you have a webcam installed on your Windows 8–based computer or device. Record videos, take quick pictures, or use it in your messaging sessions.

When you launch it for the first time, you are asked whether you want to allow this app to use your webcam and microphone. If you click or tap Allow, you can use the Camera app.

The app offers very few customization options. To display them, right-click or swipe from the bottom edge.

The three buttons that appear offer the following options:

- **CAMERA OPTIONS** Use this button to set the webcam resolution, whether you want to use its built-in microphone, and so forth.

- **TIMER** Use this button to set a time when you want to take a picture or make a recording.

- **VIDEO MODE** Use this button if you want to set the camera to take pictures or make video recordings.

As you can see, this app is straightforward.

Key Points

- The Mail, Calendar, People, and Messaging apps are well integrated and easy to use, even with a mouse and keyboard.
- When you add an account in the Mail app, you can access it from the other apps.
- You can lower your inbox space usage by using SkyDrive to share email attachments.
- You can access the latest updates from your Facebook friends by using the People app.
- By using the Messaging app, you can chat with your Facebook friends or with people using the Windows Live Messenger service from Microsoft.

Chapter at a Glance

Access

Access the Top Free apps, page 235

Search

Search for an app by name, page 236

Install

Install apps, page 238

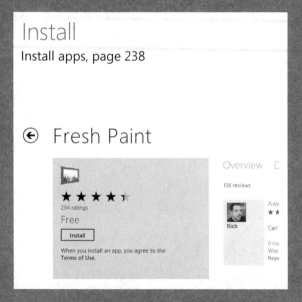

Use

Use apps, page 241

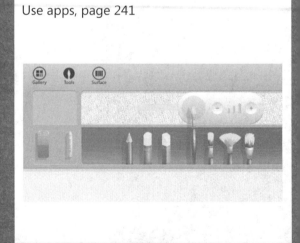

Shopping in the Windows Store

8

IN THIS CHAPTER, YOU WILL LEARN HOW TO

- Search and browse the Windows Store.
- Explore an app's listing page.
- Obtain, install, and use an app.
- Update and reacquire apps.
- Write a review for an app you own.
- Understand subscriptions and in-app purchases.

You know about apps. You've explored the apps on the Start screen, including Music, People, Internet Explorer, and others. You can easily obtain more apps from the Windows Store.

In this chapter, you'll learn how to access the Store, browse and install apps, update the apps you obtain, and more. Note that as the Store evolves, more categories, apps, and other items will likely be added. What you see here is what was available very early, when the Store was in its infancy.

TIP Microsoft has complete control over the apps that are available in the Store and approves and tests all apps before they appear there. This helps ensure that they are safe and functional and do not contain adware or spyware, among other things.

PRACTICE FILES You do not need any practice files to complete this chapter. For more information about practice file requirements, see "Using the Practice Files" at the beginning of this book.

Exploring the Landing Page

To enter the Store, you just click or touch the Store icon on the Start screen. If you're connected to the Internet and have logged on with a Microsoft account, you'll be taken to the landing page of the Store.

TIP Any time you see a number on a tile on the Start screen, it means new data that affects you is available. A number on the Store tile means updates for apps you own are available.

After you enter the Store, you can explore the landing page, which includes categories such as Spotlight, Games, Social, and more. If you have compatible hardware, you can use touch techniques to navigate the Store. Otherwise, you'll need to use your mouse and the scroll bar that appears across the bottom of the screen to navigate.

As you explore the Store's landing page, use the scroll wheel on your mouse or flick with your finger to explore the categories. Some of the categories are listed here.

- **SPOTLIGHT** This category holds apps deemed "great" by the Windows Store team. You'll find subcategories here, too, including Top free and New releases.

- **GAMES** This category offers games for kids (and adults) of all ages.

TROUBLESHOOTING Although you will see tiles for some apps on the landing page, you won't see all the apps in a category until you click the category name.

- **SOCIAL** This category holds apps for social networking websites.

- **ENTERTAINMENT** This category holds apps that are meant to entertain (such as Xbox SmartGlass) or that pertain to entertainment.

- **PHOTO** This category offers apps for photo-sharing sites, apps that work with a built-in webcam, and apps that enable you to fix your photos by removing red-eye, cropping, and so on.

- **MUSIC & VIDEO** This category offers apps for listening to Internet radio, learning song lyrics, listening to podcasts, and more.

- **SPORTS** This category offers apps for keeping up with your favorite sports teams and learning more about the sports you play or watch.

8

- **BOOKS & REFERENCE** This category offers apps such as third-party e-readers and dictionaries, bibles, and similar reference books.

- **NEWS & WEATHER** This category offers apps that involve news and weather, often from well-known national entities.

- **HEALTH & FITNESS** This category offers apps that can help you stay or get fit, lose weight, keep track of diet and exercise, and so on.

- **FOOD & DINING** This category offers apps for cookbooks and finding restaurants, reading restaurant reviews, and more.

- **LIFESTYLE** This category offers apps that help you sell a car, keep a journal, participate in an auction, and so on.

- **SHOPPING** This category offers apps that make it easy to shop by using an app. Look for apps from popular auction sites, phone directories, and shopping sites.

- **TRAVEL** This category offers apps about travel, including hotel locations, maps, and more.

- **FINANCE** This category offers apps to help you manage your finances, review stock prices, and so on.

- **PRODUCTIVITY** This category offers apps to help you be more productive. Here you'll find online storage solutions, note-taking apps, and so on.

- **TOOLS** This category holds apps that are tools with which you can compress files, connect your cell phone, manage computer resources, and more.

- **SECURITY** This category holds apps that will help you protect your computer or device and keep your data secure.

- **BUSINESS** This category holds business apps, including apps that help you look for a job, create presentations, and so on.

- **EDUCATION** This category holds apps that are related to education, including those to help you learn about planets, learn to spell words, and so on.

- **GOVERNMENT** This category holds apps related to governing and government entities.

At the landing page, if you see an available app that you like, you can click it to learn more. If you do this, the app's listing page appears. You'll learn more about listing pages later, but know that a Back button appears on the screen to take you back to the landing page if you want to explore now.

Browsing the Store by Category and Top Free

As you know, the landing page of the Store is the starting point. It offers some apps directly from the page, but usually you'll need to click a category name or Top free or perform some kind of search to find the apps you want. For example, if you click Games from the landing page, a new screen appears on which you can view all the available games or set search criteria for culling the list.

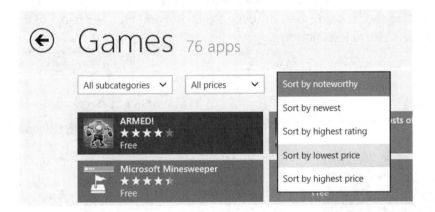

If, instead of clicking Games, you click Top free in any category, the top free apps appear in a similar listing. If you're unsure where to start, click Top free in any category that appeals to you. If you see an app you like, click it to learn more.

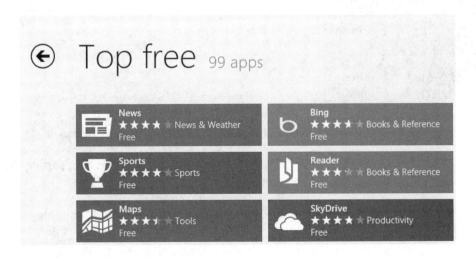

Searching the Store

Browsing the Store might work fine for you, at least for now, but as more apps become available, browsing by Top free or by category will become cumbersome. A time might come when there are hundreds of thousands of apps! With this in mind, note that there are two ways to search the store for a specific app or to sort the available apps. You can use the built-in Search charm in Windows 8, or you can use the sorting options in the Windows Store.

To use the Search charm, from any Store screen, position your cursor in the bottom-right corner to access the Search charm. Click or touch the charm and type the name of the app or app manufacturer you're looking for.

TIP See the section titled "Using Charms," in Chapter 1, "Introducing Windows 8."

If you see an app you want, click it. If you aren't sure of the name of the app, sorting the apps from inside the Store is another option.

In this exercise, you'll use the search features that are built into the Windows Store.

SET UP If you are not on the Start screen, position your mouse in the bottom-left corner of the screen and click the Start screen thumbnail that appears. You do not need any practice files to complete this exercise.

1 From the **Start** screen, click or touch **Store**.

2 If necessary, click any **Back** buttons to return to the landing page.

3 Click any title name that appeals to you (except Spotlight). Click **Entertainment** or **Games**, for example.

Search options appear.

Store

Entertainment

TROUBLESHOOTING If you don't see the built-in search options, make sure you clicked the category name and not a specific app or Top free. Click Back to try again if necessary.

4 From the available drop-down lists, set your options.

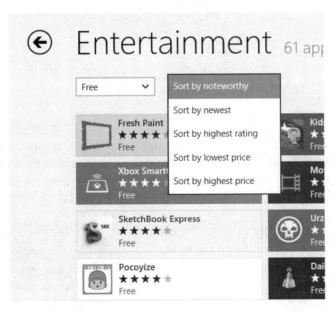

5   Click or tap the desired app to access its listing page.

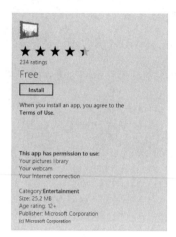

CLEAN UP Leave this screen open until you've read the next section.

TROUBLESHOOTING Many of the apps you'll acquire get their information from the Internet (such as those that give you up-to-date weather and news); thus, a working Internet connection must be available to retrieve accurate information.

Exploring an App's Listing Page

Because Microsoft requires all new apps to pass its certification process successfully before they can be listed in the store, you probably won't run across apps that don't work or that cause your Windows 8–based computer or tablet to freeze or fail. However, it never hurts to read the reviews of apps, just in case. You might find that the app is only mediocre, or that to access all features of an app you have to purchase the full version of it.

There are many other types of information on an app's listing page beyond reviews. You can also get an overview and details about the app and learn what permissions the app needs to work properly. For example, an app that offers the weather will certainly need permission to access your location. Of course, you'll be able to access an app's Terms of Use information, too. You can use all this information to decide whether the app is right for you.

You can access this information and more on every listing page. Here's some of what you will find from each of the available tabs on an app's listing page.

- **OVERVIEW** From the Overview tab, you can access a full description of the app, a list of features, and the developer's website.

- **DETAILS** From the Details tab, you can view the release notes, supported processors (x86, x64, ARM), supported languages, and more.

- **REVIEWS** From the Reviews tab, you can access user reviews and ratings and sort those reviews by Newest, Oldest, Highest rated, Lowest rated, and Most helpful.

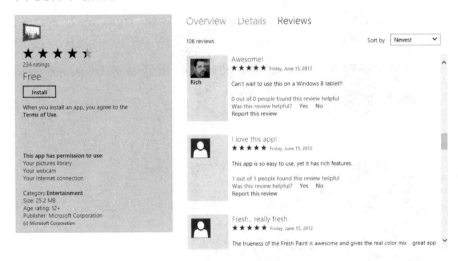

TIP The developers who read the reviews will take note of your suggestions. If you get an app and have a suggestion, write a review and then add your suggestion to the end of it.

Obtaining and Installing an App

Many of the apps from the Windows Store are free. However, paid apps start at $1.49 and run to $999.99. Apps can also have a trial window of anywhere from 24 hours to 30 days.

In this exercise, you'll obtain a free app.

→ SET UP If you are not on the Start screen, position your mouse in the bottom-left corner of the screen and click the Start screen thumbnail that appears. You do not need any practice files to complete this exercise.

1   From the **Start** screen, click or touch **Store**.

   TROUBLESHOOTING If you leave the Store app and return to it, you'll be in the Store at the position you left. Therefore, if you left the app while in the Music & Video section, you'll return there. To get back to the main screen, click the appropriate Back button.

2   Locate an app to install by using any method introduced so far. Click the **app name** to access its listing page.

3   From the listing page, click **Install**. You can follow the progress in the top-right corner of the screen.

4   When the installation completes, access the **Start** screen to view it.

   TIP Newly installed apps appear on the far right of the Start screen, after other installed apps. You'll probably have to scroll to locate your new apps, but you can reposition them on the Start screen if desired.

5   Click or tap the app to open it.

   TROUBLESHOOTING An app must complete the installation process before you can use it.

 **CLEAN UP** Leave the app open and available while you read through the next section.

Using Apps

The first time you open an app from the Start screen, you might be prompted to do something. You might need to log on with an existing user name and password or be instructed to click Play or view the various options. You might only see the various charms that offer access to the features.

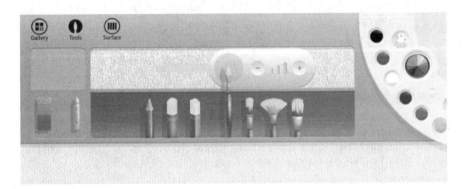

You might be prompted to allow permissions, too. If you want the weather for your current location, you'll need to let the app know your location. Your location is also necessary if you want a news app to offer local information. At times, though, you might encounter an app that asks for permissions you feel are unnecessary, and you might want to block permissions for such an app.

After you've worked past any logon screens, granted permissions, or otherwise reviewed information about an app, you're ready to use it. It's up to you to learn how to use a specific app, and many come with instructions. If you don't see what you need, try right-clicking the app's landing page and any subsequent pages, or use your finger to flick upward from the bottom of the app's interface.

In other instances, if you click Options, Settings, or something similar, a familiar Windows sidebar might appear. These options enable you to view settings, learn about the app, and rate and review it. Again, try right-clicking various screens, tapping and holding, and performing similar techniques.

TIP To remove an app from the Start screen, right-click it and choose Unpin From Start. To uninstall it from your computer, choose Uninstall.

Updating Apps

App developers are constantly creating apps and updating the apps they've already released. App updates might fix bugs, add new features, and offer additional data or options. You can tell that updates are available from the right corner of the Store. If you see that updates are available, you should install them for the apps you use. (You should uninstall apps you don't use.)

In this exercise, you'll check for updates and install them if necessary.

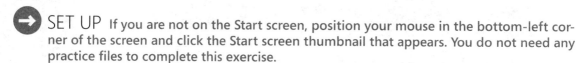 SET UP **If you are not on the Start screen, position your mouse in the bottom-left corner of the screen and click the Start screen thumbnail that appears. You do not need any practice files to complete this exercise.**

1   From the **Start** screen, click or touch **Store**.

2   Click any **Back** buttons to return to the Store's landing page.

3   Click **Update** or **Updates** if it is available in the top-right corner of the page.

The App updates page appears.

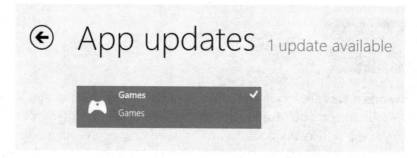

4   If there's an app you do not use, click it to clear the check mark.

5   Click **Install**.

 CLEAN UP No cleanup is required for this exercise.

Reacquiring Apps

You can uninstall apps that come with Windows 8 and apps you acquire from the Windows Store directly from the Start screen. You just right-click the app and choose Uninstall. You can also unpin the app, which is a better choice if you think you'll use the app again at a later date. By using this option, you can pin it again if desired. However, if you've actually uninstalled apps and now decide you want them back, you can reacquire them from the Store.

To reacquire an app, use any search method to locate it in the Store. From the app's listing page, choose Install. If you think you uninstalled an app but really didn't, you'll see that you already own the app when you access the app's listing page.

 Camera

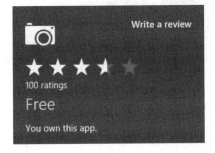

Write a Review

You can write reviews for apps you own. You'll see the option from the app's listing page. Some apps offer an option to write a review from inside the app through Options or Settings. However, one sure way to locate the Write A Review option is to locate the app in the Store.

In this exercise, you'll write a review for an app you own.

SET UP From the Start screen, look at your installed apps. Choose an app for which to write a review.

1   From the **Start** screen, click or touch **Store**.

2   Click any **Back** button to return to the landing page of the Store.

3   Use any method to locate the app's listing page; click **Write a review**.

    TROUBLESHOOTING You won't see Write A Review if you don't own the app.

⊖ Travel

4   Click the applicable number of **stars** to apply a rating, write a **title**, and then write your **review**. Click **Submit**.

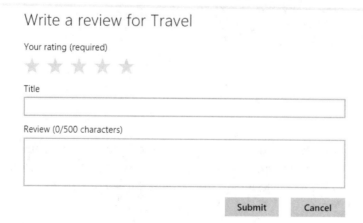

TIP After you click Submit, you'll have to wait for your review to become available.

❌ **CLEAN UP** No cleanup is required.

Understanding Subscriptions and In-App Purchases

Some apps will include apps that offer in-app purchasing and subscriptions. In-app purchases are those you make while using an app. For instance, in the case of a game, you might need to purchase "bombs" or farm animals to reach the next level or to beat an opponent. You can also subscribe to a particular app; for example, a newspaper or magazine. We'll have to wait to see what the future holds!

Key Points

- The Windows Store offers apps that are sorted by category, such as Games and Music & Videos.
- You can browse for apps in the Store through their categories or by the top free apps, or you can search for an app by name.
- You can sort apps in a category in many ways, including by ratings and release date.
- The listing page for an app offers information, reviews, and the option to install the app, among other things.
- You can reinstall apps you've previously uninstalled.
- You can update apps you own and write reviews as applicable.

8

Chapter at a Glance

View

View videos in Windows Media Player, page 252

Use

Use Windows Media Player to rip your CD collection, page 254

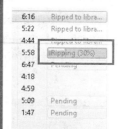

Create

Create playlists and burn the to CDs, page 251

Add

Add features such as the Windows Media Center add-on, page 260

Having Fun with Multimedia

9

IN THIS CHAPTER, YOU WILL LEARN HOW TO

- Explore Windows Media Player.

- Use Windows Media Player to rip your CD collection.

- Create playlists and burn them to CDs.

- Configure streaming options.

- Obtain Windows Media Center.

- Learn about Windows Media Center features.

Windows 8 offers many options for viewing and managing your media. Media include photos, videos, music, television, and more. You already learned quite a bit about accessing media from the various media apps on the Start screen, including Photos, Music, and Video; these were covered in Chapter 3, "Using Apps on the Start Screen." In this chapter, we'll look at two desktop apps with which you can view and manage media: Windows Media Player and Windows Media Center. Both open on the desktop in their own windows.

TIP Windows Media Center currently does not ship with Windows 8. It's an add-on. You'll learn how to obtain Windows Media Center later in this chapter.

By using both Windows Media Player and Windows Media Center, you can access the media stored on your computer and in shared network libraries and browse, play, and view music, photos, and videos. You can create playlists of music and view photos in various ways. However, these apps are different in many ways.

Windows Media Player was created to enable users to easily sync portable music devices, burn and rip music CDs, listen to music, and create music playlists. Windows Media Center offers many more options, including the ability to create slide shows of pictures, watch and record live TV, and browse and play media with a compatible remote control. Windows Media Player is just that, a player, whereas Windows Media Center is in essence an entertainment center. Usually, Windows Media Player requires less setup and is easier to use because you generally use it only to listen to and manage music. Windows Media Center requires more setup but offers more features and configuration options, including the ability to watch and record live TV.

In this chapter, you'll learn how to use Windows Media Player and how to obtain Windows Media Center and a little about the features it offers. Remember, however, that the Music, Photos, and Video apps are available from the Start screen, and those are much easier to use and more streamlined than Windows Media Player and Windows Media Center. You should try out all the apps and Windows Media Player and then decide what you prefer to use (or need to use) for managing and playing specific types of media.

PRACTICE FILES You don't need any practice files to complete the exercises in this chapter. For more information about practice file requirements, see "Using the Practice Files" section at the beginning of this book.

Exploring the Windows Media Player Interface

You open Windows Media Player like you open any app or desktop application; you just start typing its name at the Start screen. You'll see Windows Media Player in the results and can open it there. After it opens, if you're prompted to choose a setup option, choose the recommended settings; you can always go back and customize them if desired. Depending on the options you choose, the types of media already on your Windows 8–based computer, and other factors (such as other media programs you've installed and the type of media you've collected with them), you might see that some media (but perhaps not all of it) is already available from your computer. By default, Media Player populates itself automatically with compatible music from the My Music and Public Music folders (the Music library) and will do the same with media from the Pictures library and Videos library. You'll also see an entry in the Navigation pane if there's a CD in the CD/DVD drive.

TIP To pin Windows Media Player to the Start screen, type Media at the Start screen, right-click Windows Media Player in the results, and click Pin To Start.

You might also notice entries under Other Libraries while using Windows Media Player. If you do, media sharing is already set up on your network, and media stored in those libraries is available to you on your Windows 8–based computer. You must specifically state that you want to share media with other networked computers before you can access those media from your Windows 8–based computer. To do that, open Windows Media Player at the desired networked computers and click Stream to configure sharing.

TIP If you store all your music, pictures, or videos somewhere other than in the default libraries, you'll have to tell Windows Media Player where to look for the media. You can do that from the Organize, Manage Libraries tab.

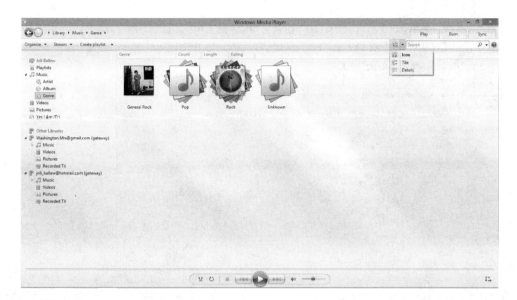

When you look closely at Windows Media Player, you'll see that several items run across the top of the interface. There are Back and Forward buttons, a Search window, and an icon to change the view. These probably look familiar to you if you've read other chapters in this book.

The titles you see (such as the name of your media library, the library that is currently selected, and how the data in that library is currently sorted) will differ from what you see here. You can click the arrow beside any title name to change the library you are in or the media you are browsing. What you see when you click a right-facing arrow depends on which arrow you click. To change from the current library (for example, Music) to another (for example, Recorded TV), you click the arrow in front of Music. (Depending on the type of media you own, you might see an option for Other Media.)

TROUBLESHOOTING If you do not see multiple titles, you have something other than a default library selected in the Navigation pane. You might have a CD selected, for instance. Select Music in the Navigation pane to rectify this.

To cull what's shown in any selected library, such as Music, click the arrow that appears after the name of the selected library. For example, you could show only music from a specific genre rather than all your music.

Beyond the drop-down lists for Organize, Stream, and Create Playlist detailed later in this chapter, there are tabs for Play, Burn, and Sync.

- **PLAY** Click this tab and use the resulting area to drag songs, create a playlist of songs, and save it. You can play any song by clicking it once, and songs in a playlist will continue to play in order unless Shuffle is enabled.

- **BURN** Click this tab and use this area to drag songs and create a list of songs to burn to an audio CD you can play in most CD players (such as the one in your car).

- **SYNC** Click this tab and use this area to drag songs and sync them to a compatible portable music device.

The commands that that run across the interface under the previously discussed titles enable you to perform tasks on the media in your library, configure preferences, share your media, change the Windows Media Player layout, and even customize the Navigation pane, among other actions.

- **ORGANIZE** Click the arrow by Organize to add folders to existing libraries (to expand your library), apply media information changes, sort the data currently visible, customize the Navigation pane by adding or removing elements, change the layout, and configure options.

9

- **STREAM** Click the arrow by Stream to allow devices on your network to access the media stored on your Windows 8–based computer and play it. You can also let those devices control Windows Media Player, and you can enable access to your media over the Internet. You'll learn more about this later in this chapter.

- **CREATE PLAYLIST** Click the arrow by Create Playlist to create a playlist or an auto playlist. You'll learn about this later in this chapter.

- **RIP CD** You'll only see the Rip CD option if you have inserted a CD in the CD/DVD drive and if that CD has not already been copied (ripped) to your computer.

- **VIEW OPTIONS** Click the arrow by the Views icon to change how media is displayed on the screen. The choices include Icon, Tile, and Details.

Finally, Windows Media Player has several items in the Navigation pane.

- **PLAYLISTS** Offers access to the playlists you've created, copied, or synced. A playlist is a group of songs that you place together. You might have a workout playlist, a sleep playlist, and a dinner playlist, for example. Click any playlist to begin playing it.

- **MUSIC** Offers access to music that is stored on your local computer. Click any song or album to access and play it.

- **VIDEOS** Offers access to videos that are stored on your local computer. Click any video to play it.

- **PICTURES** Offers access to pictures that are stored on your local computer. Click any picture to view it.

- **CD OR DVD (THE NAME APPEARS)** Only offers access if you have a CD or DVD in the CD/DVD drive.

- **OTHER LIBRARIES** Offers access to media that's been shared on your local network through other computers and compatible devices.

Ripping Your CD Collection

There are many ways to populate your Windows 8–based computer with music. You can buy music and other media from the Windows Store. You can copy the media from another computer, you can access the media from a shared drive on your home network, and you can copy music from a portable music player. You can also copy the music from CDs you currently own in a process known as ripping.

When you rip a CD, you have several settings you can configure prior to copying the songs; you'll use these options to change the default settings. For instance, when you rip a CD, the songs are formatted by using the default Windows Media Audio format. This is fine unless you later want to copy the songs to a generic MP3 player. In this case, you'd want to rip the songs as MP3s, not as Windows Media Audio files. You might also want to increase or decrease the Audio Quality settings. Lower quality takes up less storage space, but higher quality sounds better. You might also opt to eject the CD automatically after the rip has completed, which is a good option if you plan to sit down and rip your entire music collection. As you would guess, there are even more options from which to choose.

TIP See Chapter 8, "Shopping in the Windows Store," and Chapter 4, "Saving, Browsing, and Organizing My Files and Folders."

9

In this exercise, you'll rip a CD, format the songs as MP3s, and opt to eject the CD after the rip is complete.

 **SET UP** Open Windows Media Player. Locate a music CD that you own. You do not need any practice files for this exercise.

1   Place the music CD in the CD/DVD drive and shut the bay door.

2   If the CD is not selected in the Navigation pane, select it.

3   **Cancel the selection** of any songs you do not wish to copy.

4   Click **Rip settings**. You might have to click a right-facing arrow to access this.

5   Click **Format** and choose **MP3**.

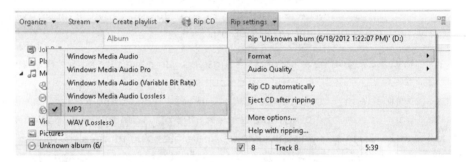

6   Repeat steps 1 through 4 and click **Eject CD after ripping**.

7   Click **Rip CD**.

The ripping process starts.

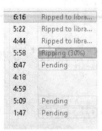

❌ CLEAN UP Repeat the process as desired.

Creating and Burning Playlists

You are likely to be familiar with playlists. A list of songs on a CD or album is a playlist. The older mixed tapes with which you might be familiar were playlists too, and you can create playlists that consist of your own music in Windows Media Player. You can create playlists for almost any occasion, including parties, workout routines, or even meditation sessions. After a playlist is created, you can sync it to other devices, burn it to a CD, and share it across your home network.

Creating a playlist is simple if you don't have any playlists yet. Click Playlists in the left pane, and you are prompted to Click Here to create your first one. After you've done that, you name the playlist, locate the songs to add to it, and drag them there. You'll use a similar dragging process to create a playlist to burn to a CD, detailed later in this section; read that section if you aren't sure how to drag the files to the new playlist.

Click here to create
your first playlist

If you already have playlists, the option to Click Here to create one will no longer be available. In that case, you can either add songs to an existing playlist or create a new one.

To add songs to an existing playlist, locate the song to add, drag it on top of the playlist's name, and drop it there. Note that songs you drag to playlists aren't moved there; only the titles are added to the list. The music remains in its current position in folders on the hard disk.

TIP If you aren't sure how to drag songs to create a playlist, work through the upcoming exercise to burn songs to a CD. The process is similar.

9

TIP To select multiple songs at one time, hold down the CTRL key while selecting.

If you want to create a new playlist, click Playlists in the left pane and notice the option to drag songs to create the list in the right pane. Drag the songs and then click Save List. You'll be prompted to name it, and it's done!

TROUBLESHOOTING If there are already songs in the Playlist area in the right pane, click Clear List.

You can also create another kind of playlist—an auto playlist. When you create an auto playlist, you name it and then set criteria. Criteria can be almost anything, and Windows Media Player will use the criteria you set to create a playlist automatically. For instance, you can create an auto playlist that contains only songs added to your library before or after a specific date or songs that you've played the most in the past year. After criteria are set, your playlist will be created and automatically managed. You start an auto playlist from Create Playlist | Auto Playlist.

You can burn any playlist you create to a CD, provided it will fit and you have the required rights to copy the music. Common CDs hold about 80 minutes of music. If your playlist won't fit on one CD, you'll be prompted to span it over several (which is often the case with audio books and auto playlists). If you don't already have a playlist created that you want to copy to a CD, you can create one on the go during the CD creation process.

In this exercise, you'll burn a CD that contains music you like in the form of a playlist.

➜ SET UP **You will need a computer that includes a CD-recordable drive, a blank CD, and music that you own available in Windows Media Player.**

1　Open **Media Player**.

2　Insert a blank, recordable CD into the recordable CD/DVD drive.

3　Click the **Burn** tab.

4　Browse to the songs to add and drag them to the **Burn list**.

> **TROUBLESHOOTING** If you drag a song to the Burn list and see a red circle with a line through it, you can't add that song to the burn list. There are many reasons this can happen, but it is usually because you don't have the proper permissions or haven't purchased the song.

5　When the list is complete, click **Start burn**.

✖ CLEAN UP **Remove the CD from the CD/DVD drive and test it in a CD player.**

Now that you understand the interface, how to navigate to various music tracks, and how to create playlists, spend some time playing the music you have on your computer. Playing music here is the same as playing music in the Music app you've already explored; you just select the song to play and use the controls to manage playback.

Sharing Media with a Network

You can share the media you've acquired on your Windows 8–based computer with compatible computers and devices on your network. Devices can include tablets, media centers, smart phones, and Xbox sets. For these other devices to gain access, however, you must enable streaming options in Windows Media Player. You do this from the Stream button.

There are four options from the Stream button, and you must click them to access their features and settings.

- **ALLOW INTERNET ACCESS TO HOME MEDIA** Select this option to stream music, pictures, and videos from your home computer to a computer outside your home (such as one at a vacation home). You can configure this computer to send your media over the Internet. After you configure this option on your home computer, you must configure the same option on the outside computer so that it can receive the media.

- **ALLOW REMOTE CONTROL OF MY PLAYER** Select this option to allow other computers and devices on your home network to push music, pictures, and videos to Windows Media Player and to remotely control Windows Media Player.

- **AUTOMATICALLY ALLOW DEVICES TO PLAY MY MEDIA** Select this option to enable other computers and devices on your home network to access the media you store on this computer. This is most likely the first option you'll want to choose.

- **MORE STREAMING OPTIONS** Select this option to choose media-streaming options for specific computers and devices on your network. You might allow access to your Xbox 360 while preventing access from your child's computer.

Choose media streaming options for computers and devices

Name your media library: Joli
Choose default settings...

Show devices on: Local network ▼   [Allow All]   [Block All]

🔘 Media programs on this PC and remote connections... Allowed access using default settings.	Customize...	☑ Allowed
🖥 compaq Device access is blocked.		☐ Allowed
🖥 Joli (WINDOWS7 : Windows Media Player) Allowed access using default settings.		☑ Allowed
🖥 Xbox 360 Allowed access using default settings.		☑ Allowed

Home group computers are automatically allowed access.

Choose homegroup and sharing options
Choose power options
Tell me more about media streaming
Read the privacy statement online

After it is configured, your media library will appear on allowed network devices.

Obtaining Windows Media Center

So far, you've learned about Windows Media Player. As you learned in the introduction, Windows Media Center is another media option that offers access to, management of, and ability to play and watch any media that are available to you. It offers more features than Media Player, including the ability to record live TV and watch Internet TV, provided your computer is equipped with the proper hardware. You can use Windows Media Center instead of your current DVR if you decide you like it.

9

You have to get Windows Media Center yourself; it's an available add-on feature. It's not included with Windows 8 by default.

1   At the **Start** screen, type add features and then, from the results in **Settings**, tap or click **Add features to Windows 8**.

2   Tap or click **I want to buy a product key online** or **I already have a product key** as applicable.

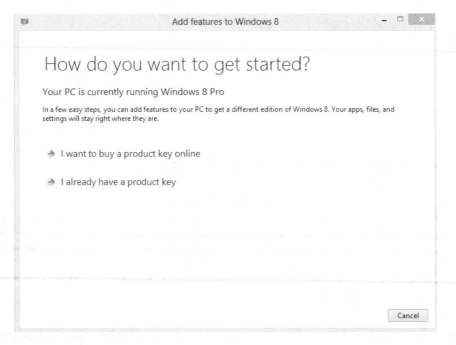

3   Work through the resulting process, which might involve purchasing the add-on and/ or inputting a product key.

4   Wait while the add-on installs.

When you start Windows Media Center, the setup process begins. You can choose Express or Custom. Because there are so many choices, it's generally best to choose Custom. When you choose Custom, you'll set up Windows Media Center by walking through each step of the configuration process.

During setup, you might be prompted to:

- Connect to the Internet.

- Allow Media Center to download album cover art, music and movie information, and TV Program Guide listings automatically and periodically.

- Optimize how Windows Media Center looks on your specific display.

- Set up or configure speakers.

- Set up or configure media libraries.

- Configure advanced settings for your specific setup.

- Configure your live TV signal.

Learn About Windows Media Center Features

You can navigate the Windows Media Center interface by using touch (if you have a compatible monitor), by using the arrow keys, by using a mouse, and even by using a compatible remote. At the main landing page, move up and down and left and right to see everything that's offered. You'll see various categories that enable you to view and manage all of your media libraries.

- With Windows Media Center you can:
  - Access all the pictures available to you, including shared pictures; add libraries; and create slideshows, tag and rate pictures, and sort pictures in various ways.
  - Access and watch videos available to you, including shared videos. You can add video libraries and sort videos in various ways, too.
  - Access your music library, sort music, create playlists, add libraries, and view album art, among other things.
  - Automatically play music that you've configured as your favorite music. You can right-click here to go to a specific artist or genre or to configure your favorite music. You can also access various settings and options, including the ability to buy music.

9

- Listen to FM radio and configure presets. You must have the proper hardware configured for this to work.

- Search for specific music.

- Access movies in your library. You can sort movies by genre, year, parental ratings, and more.

- Access the movie guide. If a TV tuner is configured and Live TV has been set up, you'll see the movies that are currently playing.

- Play a DVD you place in the CD/DVD drive.

- Access the TV guide and schedule recordings. One way to record TV is to right-click the show you want to record. You'll have myriad settings to explore.

- View TV programs you've recorded. You can sort by date recorded, title, and original air date, and you can access shared recordings.

- Watch Live TV and access playback controls, record what's on, and browse the guide. You can also pause Live TV. If you haven't set up Live TV, the option will be named Live TV Setup.

TROUBLESHOOTING If, after setting up your TV tuner, Live TV doesn't appear, restart your computer. Often this resolves the problem.

- View sports events, see scores, follow players, and more.

- Perform tasks such as shut down Windows Media Center, shut down the computer, restart the computer, and so on.

  - Access all Windows Media Center settings. If you want to change something about Windows Media Center, you do it here.

  - Sync Windows Media Center content to a compatible portable device.

  - Add a media extender so you can view your media on other devices on your home network.

Key Points

- Windows Media Player is most often used for playing music but can also be used to view pictures, videos, and other compatible media.

- You can rip and burn CDs by using Windows Media Player.

- With Windows Media Player, you can share media across your home network and access media shared by other computers on the network.

- Windows Media Center is most often used for watching and recording television, although it's also used to view and listen to other media, including pictures, videos, and music.

- Windows Media Center takes longer to set up, start, and find media than Windows Media Player does, but it offers more features than Windows Media Player.

- With Windows Media Center, you can watch, pause, and record Live TV; and play back those recordings.

9

Chapter at a Glance

Find

Find games in the Windows Store, page 267

Explore

Explore Xbox games from Windows 8, page 267

Calculate

Calculate your Windows Experience Index, page 269

Rate and improve your computer's performance

The Windows Experience Index assesses key system components on

Component	What is rated
Processor:	Calculations per second
Memory (RAM):	Memory operations per second
Graphics:	Desktop graphics performance
Gaming graphics:	3D business and gaming graphics performance

Connect

Connect Windows 8 to your Xbox, page 273

Playing Games 10

IN THIS CHAPTER, YOU WILL LEARN HOW TO

- Determine whether you can play a specific game on your Windows 8 PC or device.

- Find and purchase, download, and install games with Windows 8.

- Calculate your Windows Experience Index.

- Connect Windows 8 to your Xbox console.

We use computers, gadgets, and devices to be productive and do our work but also to have fun. Playing games can be an entertaining activity, and with Windows 8 you can play more games than ever. You can play not only desktop games but also touch-enabled games that use the new interface of Windows 8.

Windows 8 also enables you to connect to your Xbox console so that you can find, purchase, and download games to your console more quickly than when using your Xbox controller.

In this chapter, you'll first learn how to evaluate whether you can play a specific game on your computer or device. Then, you'll learn how to find games with Windows 8, how to calculate your Windows Experience Index, and how to connect to your Xbox console.

PRACTICE FILES You don't need any practice files to complete the exercises in this chapter. For more information about practice file requirements, see "Using the Practice Files" at the beginning of this book.

What's Required for Playing Games

Gaming just got richer with Windows 8: you can play the Desktop games you know and love but also new types of games designed for the new interface or for touch devices (for instance, tablets) with Windows 8.

Just like operating systems that have a very clear set of system requirements that must be met for them to work, games have individual system requirements depending on their size, complexity, and other criteria. If your computer or device can run Windows 8, it doesn't mean it can run all games that work on Windows 8. That's why before purchasing and installing a game you need to be aware of its system requirements. If your system doesn't meet at least the minimum requirements, you won't be able to play the game without problems.

Those requirements are always shared by the developers of each game. If you bought a game from a shop, the requirements will be on the back or side of its cover. If you purchase a game online, the requirements are listed with the description of the game on its dedicated page.

Unlike other types of software, gaming performance is closely related to having the latest drivers installed for your system's most important hardware components. If you want to play three-dimensional games with advanced graphics, it is important to update your video card's drivers regularly. In such scenarios, using the latest video card driver offered through Windows Update is not enough to ensure smooth game performance in all games. Therefore, you must download the latest drivers from the website of your video card's manufacturer for your specific video card model.

Where to Find Games

With the introduction of the Windows Store and the Games app for Windows 8 you now have even more platforms and ways to find and purchase games, both for your computer and for your Xbox console.

The Windows Store has a section dedicated to games where you can find diverse titles for computers and devices running Windows 8. For each game, you are shown important information about its size, rating, and publisher. A brief description and some screenshots are provided that give you an idea of what the game is about. In the Details section you can view the system requirements of the game, and in the Reviews section you can view what others had to say about the game.

With the help of the Games app, you can find, purchase, and install Xbox games from your Windows 8 PC or device. This app works with the Xbox SmartGlass app so you can connect your Windows 8 PC or device to your Xbox. After Xbox SmartGlass is set up and working, you can start browsing the list of available Xbox games.

TIP To learn how to set up the Xbox SmartGlass app, read the "Connecting Windows 8 to Your Xbox" section later in this chapter.

When you open the page of a game, you are shown information about the game and given options to buy the game for your Xbox (if the game is not free), view more details about the game, play it on your Xbox, play its trailer, or get the demo for your Xbox. (Some titles offer a demo or trailer, but others do not.)

Calculating Your Windows Experience Index

The Windows Experience Index is the Microsoft measurement of how well a computer can run Windows. To calculate a computer's Windows Experience Index score, Windows rates certain components and gives them a subscore. Those components are defined by the following areas.

- Processor Calculations per second

- Memory Memory operations per second

- Graphics Desktop performance in Windows

- Gaming graphics 3D business and gaming graphics performance

- Primary hard disk Disk data transfer rate for your primary hard disk

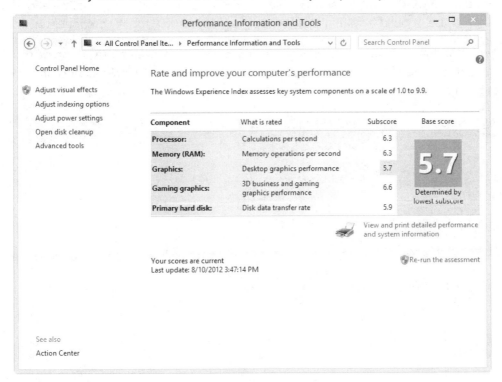

These components are examined and given a score that ranges between 1.0 and 9.9. The key part of the Windows Experience Index definition, which can be confusing, is the base score. The Windows Experience Index isn't an average of the subscores; it's only the lowest subscore your computer earns.

Microsoft defines a computer with a base score of 2.0 as one that can run general computing tasks, but it would not be powerful enough to run advanced multimedia features in Windows. A computer with a base score of 3.0 can run many Windows features at a basic level, but it might have issues running higher-level functions such as playing high-definition content or displaying themes at higher resolutions.

Computers sold with Windows 8 should have a score of 4.5 and higher. At this level, they are guaranteed to run all features of Windows. Scores of 6.0 and higher are generally given to higher-end computers.

10

For the best performance in games, the most important indicator is the Gaming Graphics subscore. The higher it is, the better your computer will perform. If you want to build a computer on which to play games with advanced graphics, it is highly recommended that you purchase or build a system that has scores of at least 6.0 for all components.

If your Windows 8 PC or device has not been evaluated, each subscore will be marked as (unrated). A message will be displayed saying that, "Your Windows Experience Index has not yet been established."

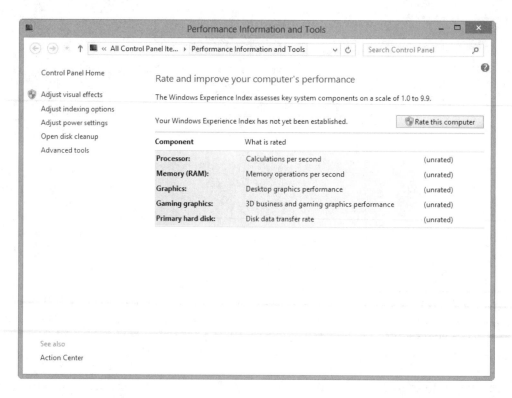

It is best to run the assessment when no other applications and processes are running so that they don't affect the evaluation and lower your scores. After you have assessed your system, you don't need to reassess it unless you change some of its hardware components, install new drivers, or improve some of its performance-related settings.

In this exercise, you'll learn how to assess (or reassess) your Windows Experience Index.

 SET UP Open Control Panel.

1   Click or tap **System and Security** and then click or tap **System** to view the System window, where your overall system rating is displayed.

2   Click or tap the link in the **Rating** row of the **System** area.

The link will be named **Windows Experience Index** if your system has been rated previously or **System rating is not available** if it hasn't. The Performance Information And Tools window opens.

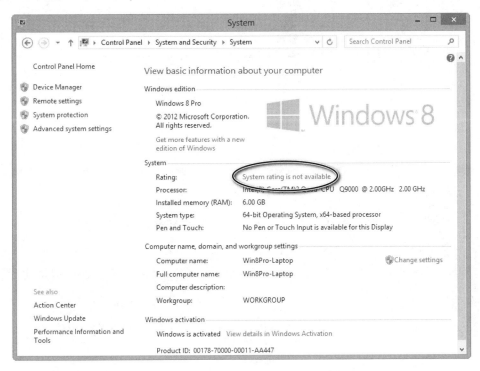

3   Click or tap **Re-run the assessment** if the system was previously assessed or **Rate this computer** if it hasn't.

10

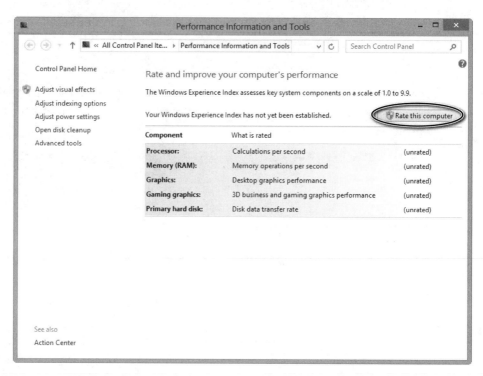

4.   Wait for the assessment to finish.

The overall base score and each individual subscore are displayed in the appropriate fields.

❌ CLEAN UP **Close the Performance Information And Tools window.**

Connecting Windows 8 to Your Xbox

It was mentioned in a previous section that you can connect to your Xbox console from any Windows 8 PC or device connected to the same network and using the same Microsoft account. You do this with the help of the Xbox SmartGlass app, which needs to be down-loaded and installed from the Windows Store.

TIP To learn more about the Windows Store and how to download and install apps, read Chapter 8, "Shopping in the Windows Store."

In this exercise, you'll learn how to connect your Xbox to your Windows 8 PC or device through the Xbox SmartGlass app.

SET UP First, install the Xbox SmartGlass app from the Windows Store if you don't have it installed yet. Start your Xbox console and log on with your Microsoft account. The Xbox LIVE gamer tag must use the same Microsoft account as the Windows 8 PC or device to which you want to connect it.

1   On your Xbox, click **Settings** and then choose **System**.

2   Click **Console Settings** and then choose **Xbox Companion**.

3   Select **Available**.

4   On your Windows 8 PC or device, launch the Xbox SmartGlass app while your Xbox console is still turned on.

5   Click or tap **Get started**.

Ready for Xbox SmartGlass?

To get started, make sure your Xbox 360 console is turned on.
Don't have an Xbox 360? Get one on Xbox.com.

Get started

10

6   Read the instructions displayed and click or tap **Next**.

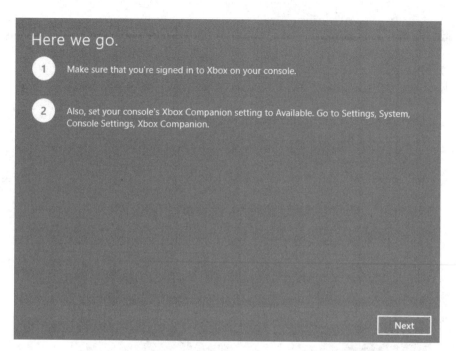

Xbox SmartGlass automatically connects to your console. A confirmation of the connection will be displayed both in the Xbox SmartGlass app and on your Xbox console.

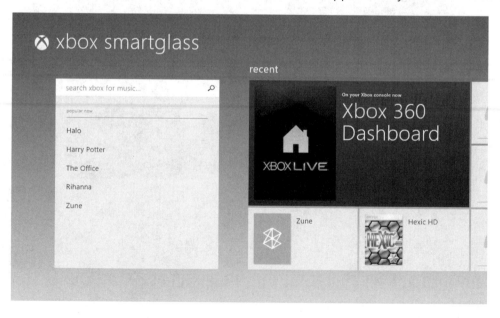

Now you can start using the Games app and purchase games, download demos, customize your Xbox profile, and so on. You won't need to reconnect the app each time you use it. After you have set it up, each time you run Xbox SmartGlass it searches for your Xbox console. If it finds it online, you can start using the Xbox SmartGlass and Games apps. If it doesn't find the console, you are informed and given advice on how to fix the problem.

Key Points

- Prior to purchasing and installing a game, check its system requirements to learn whether you can play it on your Windows 8 PC or device.

- You can find games in the Windows Store or with the Games app.

- The Windows Experience Index is the Microsoft measurement of how well a computer can run Windows. It gives a good perspective on the overall performance of your Windows 8 PC or device.

- You can connect your Windows 8 PC or device to your Xbox console through the Xbox SmartGlass app.

10

Chapter at a Glance

Use

Use the Network and Sharing Center, page 282

Connect

Connect to a wireless network, page 289

Work

Work with a hidden wireless network, page 292

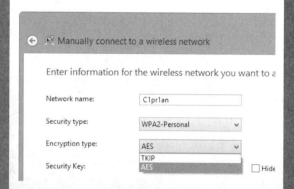

Change

Change the profile of a network, page 290

Connecting to a Network and the Internet

11

IN THIS CHAPTER, YOU WILL LEARN HOW TO

- Open the Network and Sharing Center.

- Connect to a wireless network.

- Connect to a hidden wireless network.

- Update the profile of your active network connection.

In this chapter, you'll first learn the jargon used when working with network connections. As you will see, it isn't as scary as it sounds, and the basic concepts can be understood by anyone with a little computing experience. Then, you'll learn about the Network and Sharing Center and its importance in managing network connections and settings. Finally, you'll learn how to access different configuration panels that you'll find in the Network and Sharing Center and how to change the active network profile depending on the type of the network to which you are connected.

You'll also learn how to connect to wireless networks, including those that are hidden and cannot be detected automatically by Windows 8.

PRACTICE FILES You don't need any practice files to complete the exercises in this chapter. For more information about practice file requirements, see "Using the Practice Files" at the beginning of this book.

Understanding the Jargon: Router, ISP, Network Adapter, and Other Terminology

Before connecting to the Internet and your home network, you need to learn a little bit of computer networking jargon. Don't worry! It isn't as difficult as it might seem when you hear it the first time.

First and foremost, you need a working Internet connection provided by an Internet Service Provider (ISP). The ISP will connect its Internet service either to a single computer in a home or to a home networking device, such as a router, that shares the Internet connection with computers and devices in your home.

The router is a device that handles the data being sent between the computers in your network and between those computers and the Internet. You will need a router if you want to create your own home wireless network even if you have only one computer. If you have a router, you need to be sure it's correctly configured so your computers can connect with each other and with the Internet. Instructions for doing this are provided in the router's manual and by your ISP.

For a computer to connect to the network and the Internet it needs a network adapter or network card. In tech-talk, this is also called a Network Interface Card (NIC). Desktop computers generally have a network card that is connected to the router through a standard network cable, which can be bought at any computer shop. You plug one end into your computer and the other end into the router. The router does all the settings, and you are connected.

However, mobile computers such as laptops, netbooks, or tablets need a wireless network adapter (wireless network card) that detects and works with wireless network signals.

The trouble with network adapters (both wired and wireless) is that they need appropriate Windows 8 drivers installed. A driver is a computer program that enables other programs to interact with the device for which it was created. For example, the driver for your computer's video card allows games to interact with it and generate the advanced graphics shown on your screen. Drivers for your network card enable Windows 8 to interact with the card and use it to connect to a network and the Internet.

If you have bought your computer with Windows 8 preinstalled, you won't need to worry about drivers. They are already installed and working. However, if that is not the case, you need to use another computer that is connected to the Internet and search for the latest network drivers developed for the specific computer model and network card you own. When you find them, download and install them on your Windows 8–based computer. Only then can you connect to your home network and the Internet.

One last item you should learn about is the security of wireless networks. Wireless networks can be either secured or unsecured. A secured network transmits data by using advanced encryption algorithms and, to connect to it, you need to know its security key or password. There are many types of wireless network security, each with a gibberish name such as WPA2-PSK, WPA-PSK, or WEP. If you know the appropriate password, you should be able to connect to it no matter the type of security it uses. Unsecured networks don't have any encryption and do not require passwords to connect to them. However, you should be wary about connecting to such networks, especially those found in public places. They might be used to access data on your computer.

Now that you know the basics, it is time to get practical and learn how to get connected to the Internet in Windows 8.

TIP If you want to know more about creating and securing home networks, read *Network Your Computers & Devices Step by Step.*

Using the Networking and Sharing Center

All the important network and sharing configuration settings are done from a panel called the Network and Sharing Center. It was first introduced in Windows Vista, and it has been fine-tuned in both Windows 7 and Windows 8.

The Network and Sharing Center panel is split in two areas: a central area and an area on the left.

11

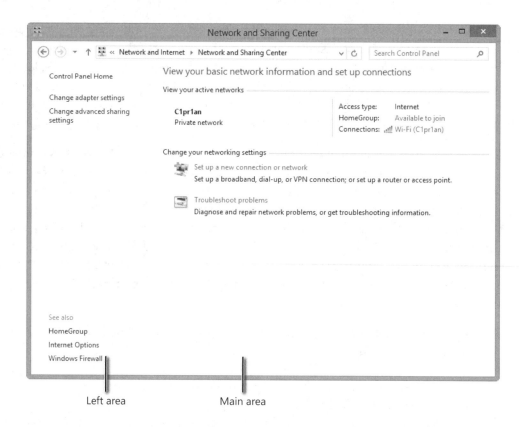

Left area   Main area

In the main area, you can see information about your active network connection (if any): the name of the network to which you are connected, the network profile (Private or Public) assigned to it, and the access type (Internet access, limited access, and so on). You can also learn whether a HomeGroup is available in your network and whether your computer has joined it. Below that, there are shortcuts for setting up a new connection or another network and for starting troubleshooting wizards, which help fix all kinds of networking problems.

In the area on the left side, you have shortcuts for changing the settings of your network adapter or network card, changing your network sharing settings, and accessing the configuration of HomeGroup, Internet Options, and Windows Firewall.

In this exercise, you'll learn the fastest way to open the Network and Sharing Center.

SET UP Open the Start screen.

1 Type **network sharing** so that Windows displays the appropriate search results.

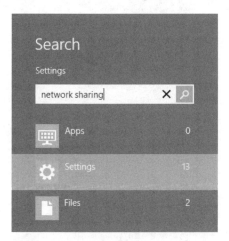

2 Click or tap **Settings**.

Windows displays only shortcuts to Windows panels and settings.

3 Click or tap the **Network and Sharing Center** search result.

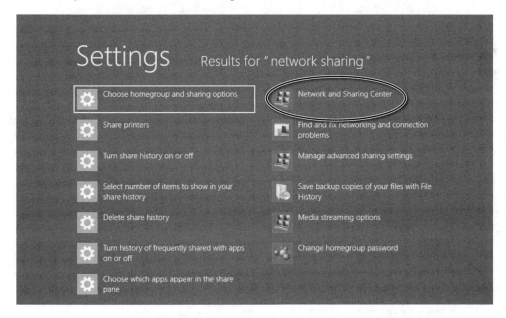

The Network and Sharing Center is now open and can be used to configure different networking aspects.

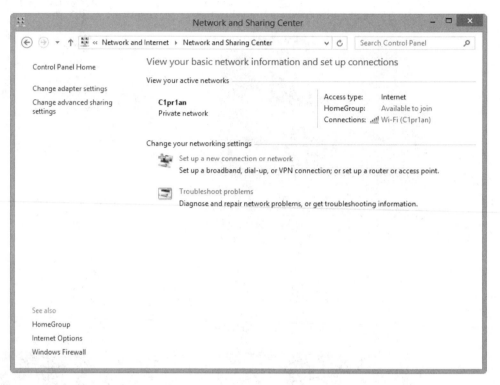

CLEAN UP Close the Network and Sharing Center by clicking the little red X button on the top right after you finish working with it.

TIP You can open the Network and Sharing Center in many other ways. If you prefer to use the mouse instead of the keyboard, first open the Control Panel, select Network and Internet, and then choose Network and Sharing Center.

Connecting to a Wireless Network

In today's world, a growing number of people use laptops, netbooks, or tablets instead of desktop computers. As a result of this trend—plus the growing number of devices such as smart phones—more people use wireless networks on a regular basis. Windows 8 offers all you need to connect to wireless networks as easily as possible.

Viewing and accessing available wireless networks is done from the Networks panel. For each network, the panel shows its name, the strength of its signal, and whether it is secured. All unsecured wireless networks have an exclamation mark on top of the icon that indicates their signal strength.

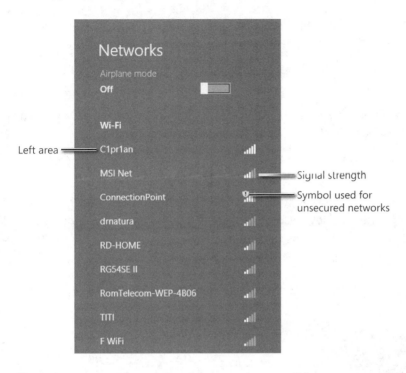

If you hover over the name of a network, a small box appears with details about the type of security that wireless network uses.

Before you try to connect, be aware that you can connect only to networks for which you have the appropriate connection details: the name of the network and the security key if the network is secured against unauthorized access. This means that you can connect only to the following types of wireless networks.

- Your home's wireless network, if you have one set up correctly, for which you should know the connection details

- The wireless networks of friends and neighbors who have shared their network connection details with you

- The wireless network of your workplace, for which the connection details are available from the network administrator or the IT support department

- Public wireless networks (that are generally unprotected) found in places such as airports, libraries, bars, cafes, and so on

After you are connected to a network for the first time, you are asked whether you want to enable sharing and connect to devices on that network. If you are connecting to a public, unsecured network, you should always be cautious and choose No, Don't Turn On Sharing Or Connect To Devices when the Network Connection Wizard asks.

Furthermore, you must have a security solution active and running on your system to make sure your computer is protected from attacks and unauthorized access. Windows Defender and Windows Firewall, included with Windows 8, should provide a good level of protection. Make sure to keep them turned on if you have not installed security solutions provided by companies other than Microsoft.

TROUBLESHOOTING If Windows 8 has not detected any connections, and you know that there is at least one wireless network available in your area, you should check whether your wireless network card has the appropriate drivers installed and whether the network card is enabled.

When connecting to a wireless network, a check box appears that says Connect Automatically. If you select it, the next time you log on to Windows and the same network is detected, Windows automatically connects to it by using the same details you provided the first time you connected.

If the connection is successful, Connected appears near the icon of the network in the Networks panel. Available networks to which you have not connected don't display status. Networks to which you connected but for which Windows 8 identifies issues will display Limited near their icons.

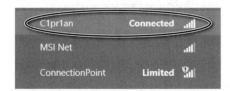

On the Desktop, similar icons appear in the taskbar. If network connectivity issues are found, they are signified by a yellow exclamation mark.

11

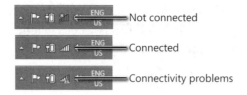

Not connected

Connected

Connectivity problems

If you cannot connect to a wireless network from your Windows 8–based computer, but all your computers with earlier operating systems can connect, you might need to upgrade the firmware on your wireless router. Consult the webpage of your router's model to see whether any upgrades are available. If they are, download and install the latest version of firmware. Unfortunately, some older router models do not work very well with computers that use newer versions of Windows unless you perform a firmware upgrade.

Another useful resource is the Windows 8 Compatibility Center, found at *http://bit.ly /xoI5fr*. There you can check the compatibility with Windows 8 for many applications and hardware devices.

The Networks panel can be launched by using several methods. If you are using a desktop computer, the simplest way is to click the network icon from the taskbar on the Desktop. If you're using a tablet or a computer with touch, use the Settings charm accessible from the Start screen.

In this exercise, you'll learn how to open the Networks panel, view all the available wireless networks in your area, and connect to one of them.

 SET UP First, make sure a wireless network is available for which you know the connection details (network name and security password) and then go to the Start screen.

1 Swipe from the right side of the screen or press **Windows+C** to open the charms.

2 Click or tap **Settings** to open the contextual settings for the Start screen.

3   Click or tap the **wireless network icon** (the first of the six icons at the bottom of the Settings charm).

The Networks panel opens.

4   Click or tap the network to which you want to connect.

5   Select **Connect automatically**.

6   Click or tap **Connect**.

You are prompted to type the security key.

TIP If the network to which you are connecting is not secured, you are not asked for a password. If this is the case, skip the next step.

7   Type the **security key** and then click or tap **Next**.

You are asked whether you want to turn on sharing.

TIP If you typed an incorrect password, Windows 8 informs you that it cannot connect to the network. If this happens, repeat the procedure, starting with step 1, retyping the password.

11

8   Click or tap **Yes, turn on sharing and connect to devices**.

Windows takes a few seconds to connect to the network you selected.

⊗ CLEAN UP If the Networks panel doesn't disappear, click or tap anywhere in the empty space on the Start screen.

Connecting to a Hidden Wireless Network

Hidden wireless networks are networks that do not broadcast their names, called Network ID or Service Set Identifier (SSID) in tech-talk. Although few people use such networks, some people feel a bit more secure if they have their home wireless network hidden from unwanted guests.

If you've set your wireless network this way, be aware that, according to the Microsoft TechNet community and other reputable websites, hidden wireless networks are not actually undetectable or more secure. On the contrary, computers and devices configured to connect to such networks are constantly disclosing the Network ID of those networks, even when they are not in range. As a result, using such a network actually compromises the privacy of the computers connected to it. If you still want to use and connect to such networks, this section shows how it is done, but you should know where to get the important technical details.

First and foremost, you need to know all the identification and connection details of the hidden wireless network to which you want to connect. To do this, open your router's configuration page and open the Wireless Configuration menu. Write down the values for the Network ID (SSID) and Security fields. Routers love to use intimidating tech talk, so prepare to encounter some weird-sounding acronyms. Routers have very different interfaces, depending on their model and manufacturer. There is no standard way to access this information. If you don't know how to find it, check the manual of your router for help and instructions.

Depending on what type of security your wireless network has, you need to write down the value of the following important fields.

- For WEP security, note the value of the WEP Key field.
- For WPA-PSK, WPA2-PSK(AES) security, note the value of the Preshare Key field.

These key fields store the password for connecting to the wireless network.

If your wireless network has no security enabled, you need to know only the network name (the value of the Network ID (SSID) field).

When completing all the required details to connect to the hidden wireless network, consider the following aspects.

- When asked about the security type of the network, you must make the correct selection; otherwise the connection won't work. You must select WEP for WEP security, WPA-Personal for WPA-PSK security, or WPA2-Personal for WPA2-PSK(AES) security. If the hidden network has no security enabled, select No authentication (Open).

11

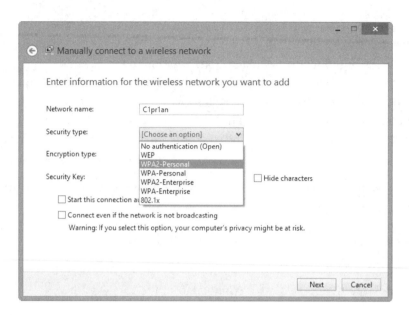

- For networks that have security enabled, select the encryption type. If this information is not shared by your router, leave the default value given by Windows for the
selected security type. In most cases, this works well.

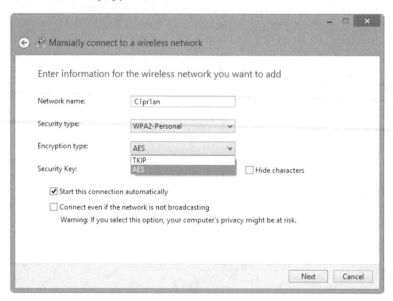

- Because Windows 8 cannot detect hidden networks, select Start This Connection
Automatically and Connect Even If The Network Is Not Broadcasting. Windows cannot detect a hidden network to connect to it.

☑ Start this connection automatically

☑ Connect even if the network is not broadcasting

    Warning: If you select this option, your computer's privacy might be at risk.

> **TIP** WPA2-Enterprise, WPA-Enterprise, and 802.1x are not covered in this book because they are specific to business networks. If you need to connect to a hidden business network, contact the network administrator or the IT help desk team for guidance.

In this exercise, you'll learn how to connect to hidden wireless networks.

SET UP Make sure you have a hidden wireless network available for which you know the connection details (network name, security password, and so on). Open the Network and Sharing Center.

1   Click or tap **Set up a new connection or network**.

    The Set Up A Connection Or Network window opens.

2   Select **Manually connect to a wireless network** and then click or tap **Next**.

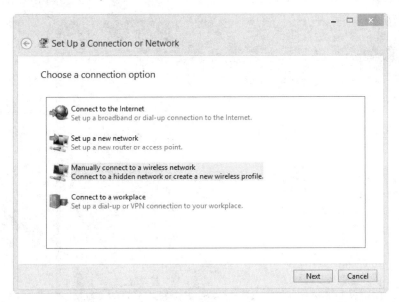

3   In the **Network name** field, type the name of the wireless network to which you want to connect.

4   In the **Security type** field, choose the type of security your wireless network uses.

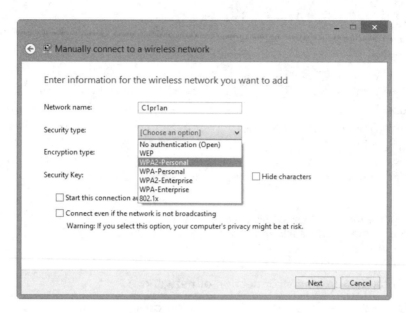

5   In the **Encryption type** field, choose the type of encryption used by the network to which you are connecting.

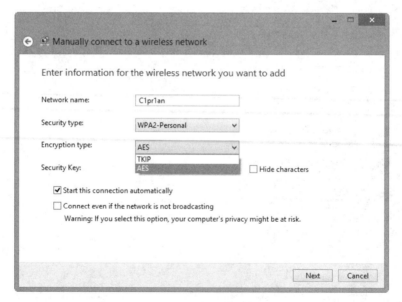

6   In the **Security Key** field, type the password used to connect to the wireless network.

7   Select **Start this connection automatically**.

8 Select **Connect even if the network is not broadcasting**.

9 Click or tap **Next**.

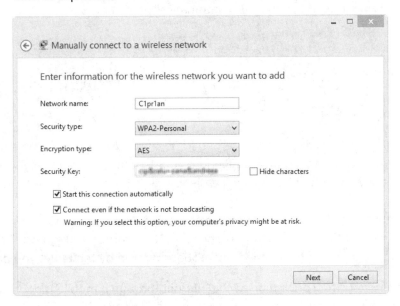

A message appears, indicating that you have successfully added the wireless network to your computer.

10 Click **Close**.

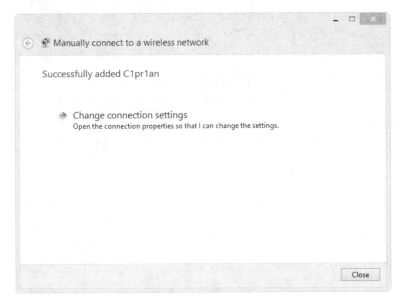

CLEAN UP Close the Network and Sharing Center.

If the network is in range, Windows 8 will automatically connect to it.

Connecting to the Internet through a Mobile Modem

Another option for connecting to the Internet, for example, when you are on a trip, is to use a mobile Internet modem that you plug into your laptop or netbook. If you are using a tablet with Windows 8, connecting is even easier because the operating system offers support for inserting a SIM card from your mobile operator, so you can use it to stay connected through its network. Although most tablets can use SIM cards, some models don't offer hardware support for them and can only connect to the Internet through wireless networks. Make sure you are aware of the connectivity options offered by the tablet you purchase.

Even though the steps for connecting to the Internet through a mobile modem are different, depending on the modem model and your mobile operator, the principles are always the same.

- You need a mobile Internet modem that you can plug into your computer.

- After it's plugged in, you need to install the drivers for the modem and the software that will connect to the Internet. They are always provided by your mobile operator in the package with the modem itself or on the manufacturer's website.

- Major mobile operators, such as AT&T, Verizon, and Vodafone, are likely to offer a Windows 8 app through the Windows Store, so check for such an app.

AT&T Communication Manager

- To connect to the Internet, you need to use the application provided by your mobile operator, which is specifically designed for this task. The application will ask for the PIN of the SIM card used with your modem and then connect to the Internet.

- The quality and speed of the connection will vary depending on where you are and the quality of the infrastructure your mobile operator has in that area.

If a Windows 8 app is not available, don't worry. Your mobile operator probably offers a desktop application that you can use to connect to the Internet.

Changing the Network Profile of a Network

A network profile in Windows 8 is just a collection of network and sharing settings that are applied to your active network. Setting this correctly is important to protect you when connecting to public networks and using network-sharing features when connected to trusted home or work networks.

When you connect for the first time to a network, you are asked whether you want to enable sharing and connect to other devices.

11

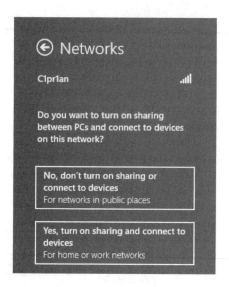

Depending on your answer, one of the two available network profiles is assigned to that network connection.

- **PRIVATE NETWORK** This profile is assigned if you select Yes, Turn On Sharing And Connect To Devices. You should set a network as private if it is your home or work network used by people and devices you trust. By default, network discovery will be turned on, and you will be able to see other computers and devices that are part of the network. This allows other computers from the network to access your computer, and you will be able to create or join a HomeGroup.

- **PUBLIC NETWORK** This profile is perfect when you are in public places such as airports, bars, libraries, and so on. Network discovery and sharing are turned off. Other computers from the network will not be able to see your computer. This setting is also useful when your computer is directly connected to the Internet (direct cable/modem connection, mobile Internet, and so on). To assign this profile, select No, Don't Turn On Sharing Or Connect To Devices when connecting for the first time to the network.

TIP There is a third network location profile, called Domain Network, which cannot be set by a normal user. It is available for enterprise workplaces and can be set only by the network administrator. Under this profile, the network and sharing settings applied are the setttings set by your workplace, and you cannot change them.

The default settings can be changed for both profiles. To learn how to do this, check the instructions detailed in Chapter 13, "Sharing Files and Folders with My Network."

These network profiles are useful to people who are very mobile and connect their computers to many networks. For example, you could use your work laptop to connect to your company network, take it home at the end of the day and connect to your home network, or connect to a few public networks at the airport and in a hotel while on a business trip. Each time you connect to a new network, Windows 8 asks about assigning the correct profile. With one choice, you get the entire set of network settings correctly updated; you won't compromise your security, and you have enabled only the network features that you need for each network connection.

If you made a mistake when setting the network profile for the network to which you are connected, you can change it later. In this exercise, you'll learn how.

SET UP Open the Networks panel. It doesn't matter whether you open it from the Start screen or the Desktop.

1   Right-click or press and hold (if you have a device with touch) the name of the network to which you are connected to access the contextual menu.

2   Click or tap **Turn sharing on or off.**

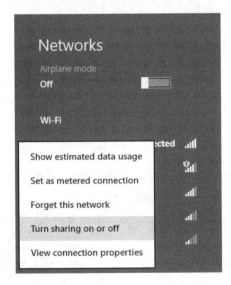

3   Choose the option you prefer.

11

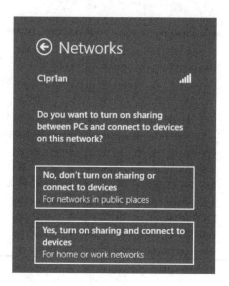

CLEAN UP If the Networks panel doesn't disappear, just click or tap somewhere in the empty space on the Start screen or the Desktop.

The network profile is updated along with the relevant network and sharing settings based on the choice you made.

Key Points

- Before working with network connections, it's best to understand the basic jargon so that you know what each term means when you encounter it.
- The Network and Sharing Center is the panel from which most network configuration settings can be accessed.
- Most wireless networks require a password (also called a security key) to connect to them successfully.
- Before connecting to a hidden wireless network, make sure you know all the important connection details.
- The network profile contains a collection of network and sharing settings that are applied to the network to which you are connected, depending on how you set it.

Chapter at a Glance

Find

Find the settings related to your user account in the new Users panel, page 308

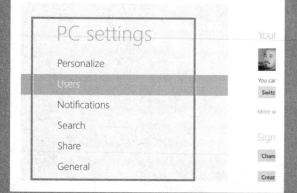

Use

Use your Microsoft account to access your Windows 8–based computer and all Microsoft services, page 314

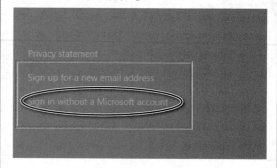

Create

Create a picture password to use instead of your normal password, page 328

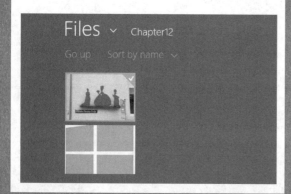

Delete

Delete a user account, page 344

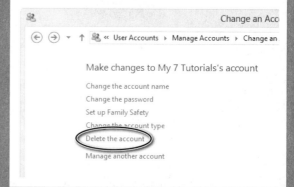

Allowing Others to Use the Computer

12

IN THIS CHAPTER, YOU WILL LEARN HOW TO

- Access the panels for managing user accounts.

- Create a new user account.

- Switch between user accounts.

- Create picture passwords and PINs.

- Change a user account password, picture, name, and type.

- Delete a user account.

In a typical family, there might be only one person who uses one or more computers. For these computers, you need only the user account you created when you first started using them. However, you might have a computer that more than one person uses; it can be a computer your children, your parents, or the whole family uses. If that's the case in your house, it is best to create a user account for each person so that settings, files, and folders don't get mixed up, which can be frustrating for everyone.

In this chapter, you'll learn what user accounts are, understand how many you need to have on a computer, and learn how to manage user accounts and configure them.

PRACTICE FILES Before you can complete the exercises in this chapter, you need to copy the book's practice files to your computer. The practice files you'll use to complete the exercises in this chapter are in the Chapter12 practice file folder. A complete list of practice files is provided in "Using the Practice Files" at the beginning of this book.

What Is a User Account and How Many Do I Need?

User accounts enable multiple people to share a computer, with each person having his or her own private Documents folder, email inbox, Windows settings, and so on. When you have your own account, you can do all the customization you want to your Windows 8 environment without affecting other user accounts. Other users will have their own visual customization, their own application settings, and so forth.

Multiple types of user accounts can be used in Windows 8. The Microsoft account (also known as a Windows Live ID) can be used across multiple computers with Windows 8 and a local account, defined only on your computer. These accounts can then have administrator permissions, and Administrator is specified near their name. A user account that is not an Administrator account is considered a standard user account and has limited permissions. A third type of user account is the Guest account.

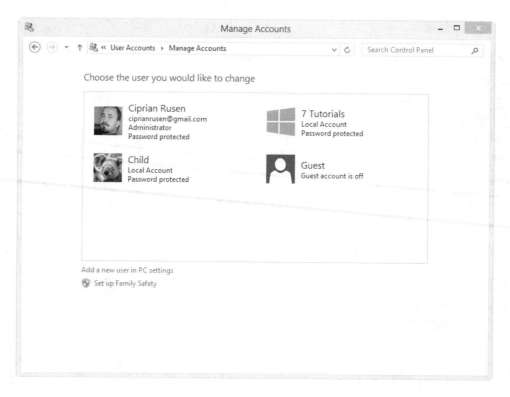

The administrator has full access to all user accounts. He or she can create and delete user accounts and change the name, password, and account types for other accounts. The administrator can also install software and hardware and configure every aspect of the operating system. As a rule, every computer must have at least one administrator.

A user with standard rights has access to programs that have already been installed on the computer and cannot install other software without the administrator password. A standard user can change his or her password but cannot change the account name or type without the administrator password.

The Guest account is a special type of limited user account that has the following restrictions:

- It does not require a password.

- The user can't install software or hardware.

- The user can't change the account type.

- The user can't create a password for the account.

When you install Windows 8 or when you use it for the first time (as is the case with devices that have Windows 8 installed already), you are prompted to create a default user account. That user account always has administrator permissions. A new account should be created when another person needs to work on the same computer.

For example, if you are a parent sharing the computer with your child, it is best to have two user accounts: one for you with administrator permissions and one for your child with standard user permissions. By doing this, you make sure that your child can use the computer but cannot change important configuration aspects.

TIP If children use a computer, consider using Family Safety. If you want to know more about Family Safety, read Chapter 16, "Supervising a Child's Computer Use."

If you have temporary guests who need to use one of your computers to browse the Internet, check their email, and perform other light computing activities, it is best to enable the Guest account for them to use.

12

Introducing the Microsoft Account (Windows Live ID)

A major change in Windows 8 from earlier versions of Windows is the introduction of the Microsoft account and its mandatory use for working with features such as synchronizing of your settings across the many computers you use or accessing the Windows Store to purchase applications. In addition, each time you create a user account, Windows 8 first asks for a Microsoft account.

The Microsoft account, formerly known as Windows Live ID, is an ID composed of an email address and password, which you can use to log on to most Microsoft websites, services, and properties such as Hotmail, Outlook.com, Xbox Live, and all Microsoft services (including SkyDrive and Messenger). It is also used in Windows 8 for synchronizing your PC settings, using the Windows Store to purchase applications, and other activities.

How do you know whether you have a Microsoft account? If you are already using any of these services—Hotmail, Windows Live Messenger, or Xbox Live—you already have a Microsoft account. Use the same email address and password in Windows 8.

If you don't have a Microsoft account, you can easily create one in Windows 8 or on the Microsoft websites.

Using such an account in Windows 8 is highly recommended if you want to access without problems or limitations all the features it has to offer. In addition, a Microsoft account gives you access to almost all Microsoft products, services, properties, and websites. The Microsoft account will be useful also when:

- You want to use any of the tools included in the Windows Live Essentials suite.
- You want to use devices such as Xbox consoles, Zune media players, or Windows Phones.
- You need a free email account from Microsoft on Hotmail, Outlook.com, or Live.com.

Accessing the User Accounts Settings

Windows 8 offers two places from which you can manage user accounts on your computer. In PC Settings, in the Users section, you can manage settings related only to your user account (password, picture password, and PIN) and add new user accounts.

12

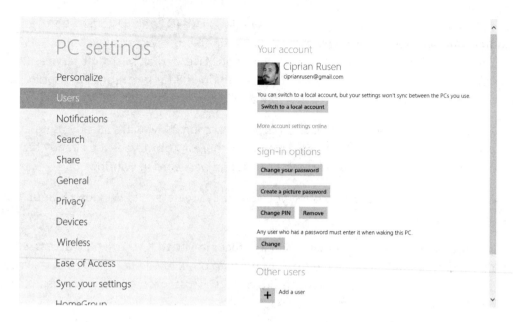

In Control Panel, you can manage other existing user accounts, change your account type, or configure the settings for User Account Control (UAC).

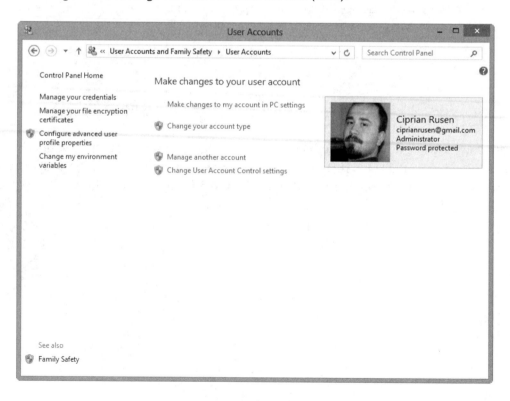

TIP If you want to know more about the User Account Control (UAC) and how it works, read the dedicated section in Chapter 14, "Keeping Windows 8 Safe and Secure."

In this exercise, you'll learn how to access both panels for managing user accounts, starting with the one found in Control Panel and ending with the one found in PC Settings.

SET UP Open Control Panel.

1 Click or tap **User Accounts and Family Safety.**

2 Click or tap **User Accounts**.

The User Accounts panel, with settings related to your user account, opens.

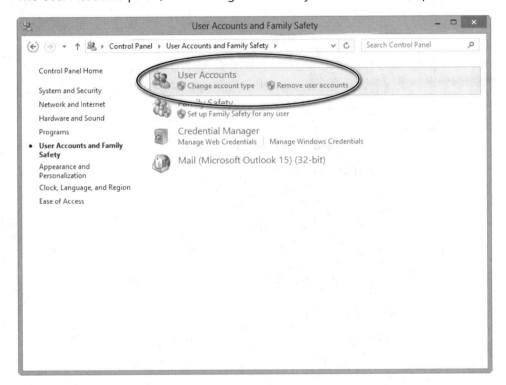

3 Click or tap **Make changes to my account in PC settings**.

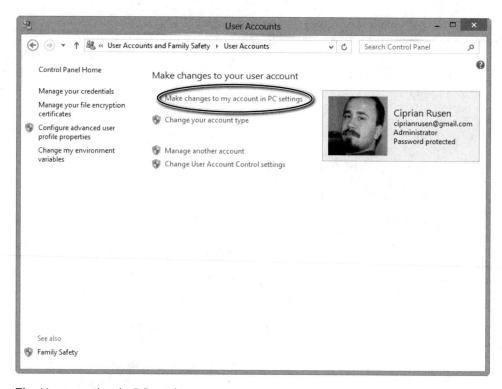

The Users section in PC settings opens.

The Users section in PC Settings can be opened directly, without going first to Control Panel and following the steps in the preceding procedure. This exercise was meant to familiarize you with each panel and its location before you learn how to manage the user accounts defined on your computer.

Adding a New User Account

Anyone with administrator permissions can add a user account from PC Settings. When a user is added, Windows 8 first asks for a Microsoft account. If one is provided, the user is immediately given access to the computer and can log on by using the password associated with that Microsoft account.

When adding a user, however, your computer must have an active Internet connection when the user is added and when he or she logs on for the first time.

If you are not interested in using a Microsoft account, you can create a local account, which will be created on your computer and can log on and use Windows 8. However, it won't be able to use any synchronization features provided by Microsoft for Windows 8 and won't be able to make purchases in the Windows Store unless a Microsoft account is associated with it later. Another important difference is that a local account can have a blank (empty) password, whereas a Microsoft account does not allow blank passwords. Further, a local account does not need an active Internet connection to log on for the first time or for subsequent logons.

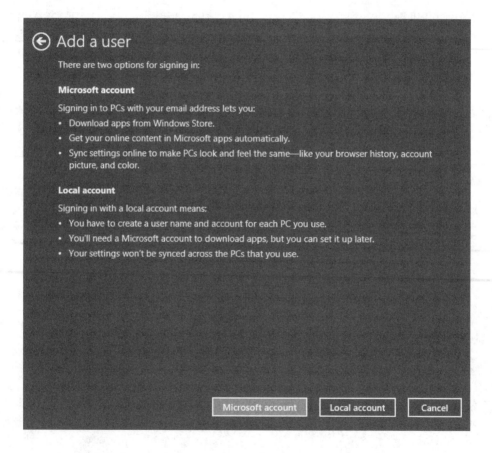

After the user account is created, a new folder with the new account name is created in the C:\Users folder, where all the personal files of the new user are kept. No users except administrator(s) and the newly added user have access to this folder.

In this exercise, you'll learn how to create a new local user account on your computer.

➡ SET UP Log on as a user who has administrator permissions and then open PC Settings.

1 Click or tap **Users**.

2 Click or tap the **Add a user** button from the **Other users** section.

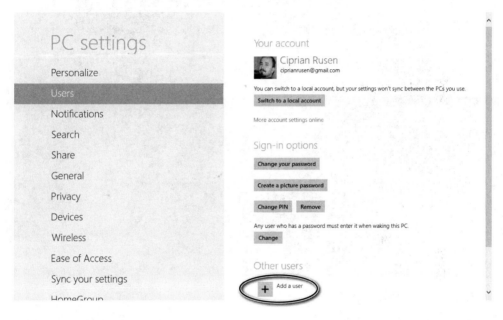

The Add A User Wizard opens.

12

3   Click or tap the **Sign in without a Microsoft account** link.

You are shown more information about the options for adding a user.

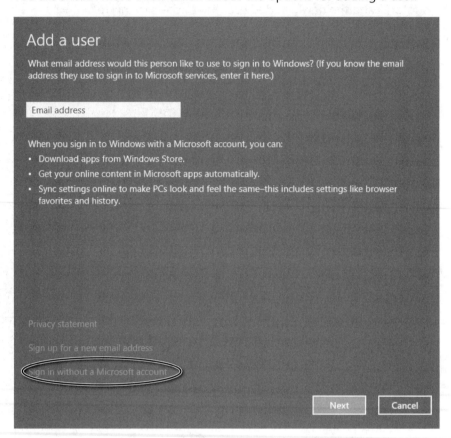

Add a user

What email address would this person like to use to sign in to Windows? (If you know the email address they use to sign in to Microsoft services, enter it here.)

Email address

When you sign in to Windows with a Microsoft account, you can:
• Download apps from Windows Store.
• Get your online content in Microsoft apps automatically.
• Sync settings online to make PCs look and feel the same—this includes settings like browser favorites and history.

Privacy statement

Sign up for a new email address

Sign in without a Microsoft account

Next   Cancel

4   Click or tap **Local account**.

You are asked to type the user name, password, and password hint.

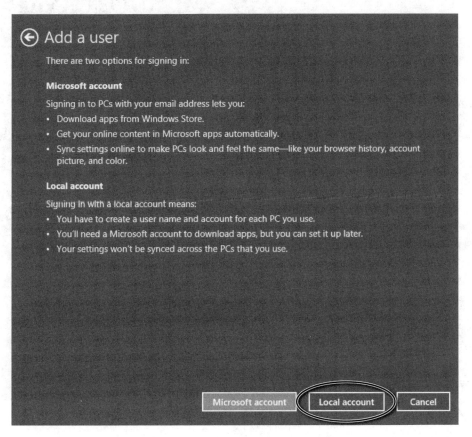

12

5 Complete all the fields and click or tap **Next**.

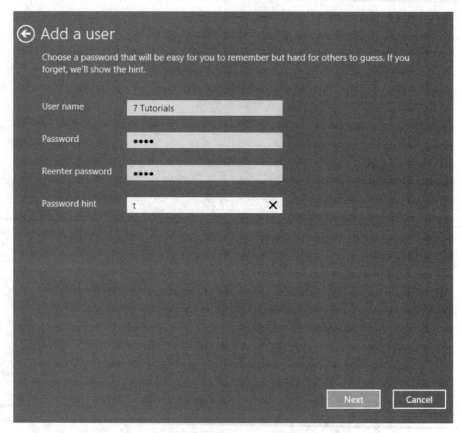

6 Click or tap **Finish**.

Windows 8 returns you to the Users panel.

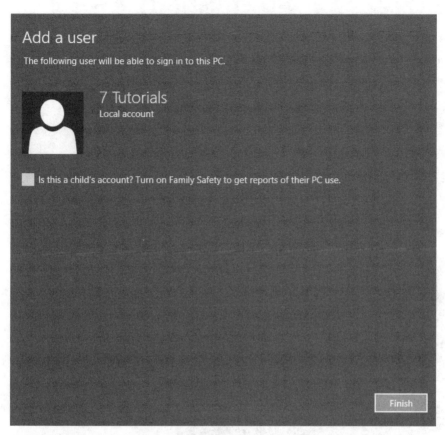

Add a user

The following user will be able to sign in to this PC.

7 Tutorials
Local account

☐ Is this a child's account? Turn on Family Safety to get reports of their PC use.

[Finish]

❌ CLEAN UP Close PC Settings.

The user account has been created using the password you have set.

Creating a Microsoft Account

You can create a Microsoft account in several ways. One way is to do it from Windows 8 during the Add A User procedure.

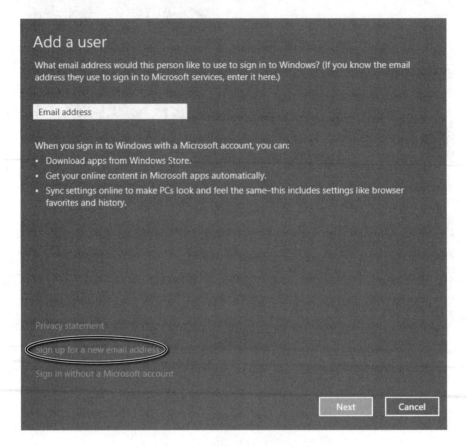

If Windows 8 has a connection to the Internet, it will ask for all the required details for creating such an account, send them to Microsoft to confirm your details, and allow the newly created account to log on to your computer.

Sign up for a new email address

You can use your Microsoft account to sign in to Xbox LIVE, Windows Phone, and other Microsoft services.

Email address	ciprian	@ hotmail.com ▾
New password	••••••••••••	
Re-enter password	••••••••••••	
First name	Ciprian	
Last name	rusen	
Country/region	United States ▾	
ZIP code	132323 ✕	

[Next]   [Cancel]

As an alternative, by using any web browser, visit *https://signup.live.com*, and enter all the details requested. If you use this method, you can create a Microsoft account without creating a Live.com or Hotmail.com email address. You can use your current email service and associate it with your Microsoft account. However, you can't do this if you create a Microsoft account by using the Add A User Wizard in Windows 8.

Switching between User Accounts

12

When you switch between user accounts, you leave the current user account logged on (with all running applications) and log on to a separate user account. You can switch back and forth between user accounts whenever you want. The user account from which you switched remains active with all applications running, and you can switch back to it any time without having to log off and log on again. This can be useful if you need to work on multiple accounts at once.

In this exercise, you'll learn how to switch between two user accounts. This is possible only if you have two or more user accounts defined on your computer.

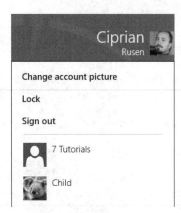 SET UP **Log on using one of the user accounts defined on your computer and open the Start screen.**

1   Click or tap the icon on the top right of the screen representing your user account.

A contextual menu with several options opens.

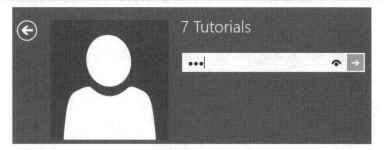

2   Click or tap the user account to which you want to switch.

You are asked to complete login details for the selected user.

3   Type the password for the selected user account and click or tap the **Submit** arrow.

You are now logged on to the selected user account.

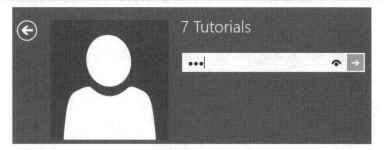

TIP Depending on how the user account you selected is set up, you'll need to type one of the login details, such as password, PIN, or picture password, at step 3. For example, if you have set up a PIN, you will be requested to type the PIN instead of the password.

 CLEAN UP **When you finish working with this user account, sign out.**

Changing the Password for Your User Account

Every user account except Guest can change its password. Making the change doesn't require any administrator permissions as long as you do not want to change the password of a user account other than your own.

If you are using a user account associated with a Microsoft account, the password change is applied to both your Windows 8–based computer and all Microsoft services that account uses. If you are using a local user account, the password change applies only to the user account defined on your computer.

TIP To keep your account safe, it is recommended that you use strong passwords: passwords that contain a combination of letters, numbers, and special characters (such as @, #, or &). Ideally, the password should be something that is easy for you to remember but difficult for anyone else to figure out.

In this exercise, you'll learn how to change the password of a local user account.

➜ SET UP **Open PC Settings.**

1 Click or tap **Users**.

2 Click or tap **Change your password**.

The Change Your Password Wizard opens.

12

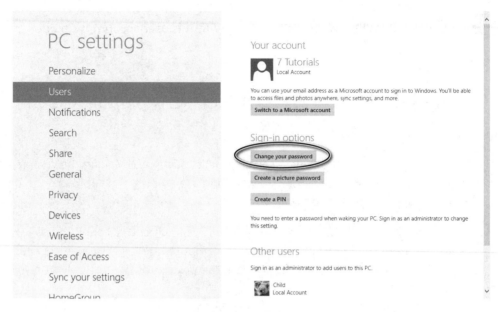

3   Type your current password and click or tap **Next**.

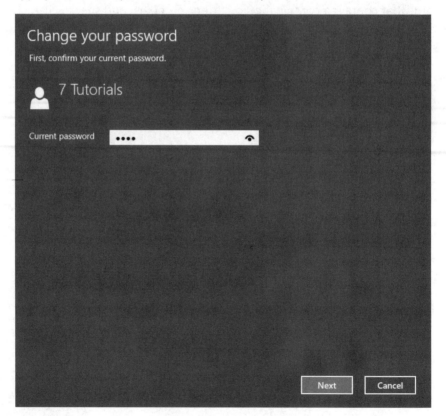

4   Type the new password in the **New Password** and **Reenter Password** fields.

5   Type a password hint, if you want to use one, in the **Password Hint** field.

6   Click or tap **Next**.

You are informed that the password has been changed successfully.

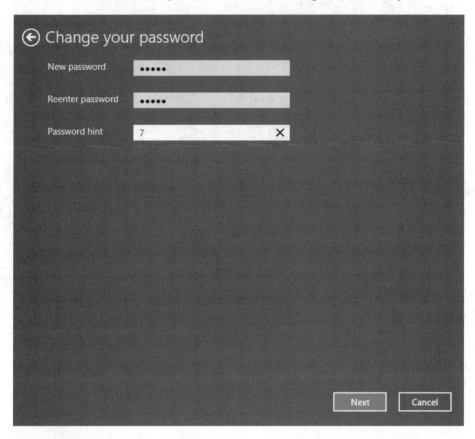

7   Click or tap **Finish**.

CLEAN UP **Close PC Settings.**

TIP If you are changing the password for a Microsoft account, the data requested at steps 3, 4, and 5 is requested in one window instead of in separate windows.

Removing the Password for a User Account

Unlike in earlier versions of Windows, in Windows 8 you cannot remove the password of a user account if a Microsoft account is associated with it. Having a password is critical to a Microsoft account and secures it from unauthorized access to your computer and all Microsoft services you are using. However, you can create local user accounts, which have no password, or change their existing password to a blank (empty) one.

Creating a Picture Password for Your User Account

One of the great features introduced in Windows 8 is the use of picture passwords. This concept entails using a specific picture on which you draw gestures. These gestures can be simple taps or clicks, circles, or lines. If your user account is using a Microsoft account with a complicated password, creating a picture password to be used as a complement can be a great way to make it easy to log on to your Windows 8–based devices.

Even though this feature is recommended for use on touch-enabled devices such as tablets, it can be used on a desktop computer by using a mouse.

In this exercise, you'll learn how to create a picture password for your user account. To make things fast and easy, the exercise will use only taps or clicks.

 SET UP To complete this exercise, you need the PictureA.jpg file, found in the Chapter12 folder in your practice files. When you have this file available, open PC Settings.

1   Click or tap **Users**.

2   Click or tap **Create a picture password**.

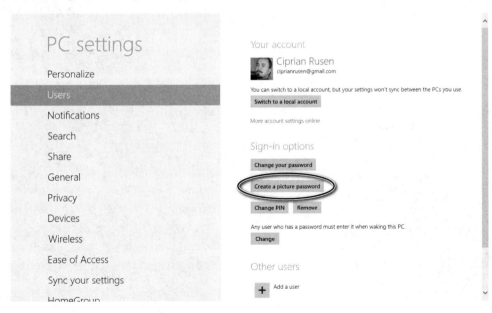

The Create A Picture Password Wizard opens.

3   Type your user account password and click or tap **OK**.

You are informed about picture passwords.

4   Click or tap **Choose picture**.

The Files browsing window opens.

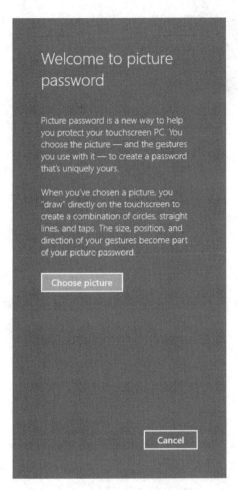

5   Click or tap **Files** and navigate to where you stored the PictureA.jpg practice file.

12

6   Select PictureA.jpg and click or tap **Open**.

You are asked whether to use the picture as is.

7   Click or tap **Use this picture**.

You are asked to set up the three gestures that will serve as your picture password.

8   Click or tap the picture as highlighted in the preceding screenshot, on the head of each figure, one by one.

You are immediately asked to confirm your gestures.

9   Click or tap the picture again as you did before on the head of each figure, one by one.

You are informed that the picture password has been created successfully.

10   Click or tap **Finish**.

Congratulations!

You've successfully created your picture password. Use it the next time you sign in to Windows.

Finish

Wilhelm-Glässing-Straße

CLEAN UP Close PC Settings.

The picture password is now set and can be used instead of your normal user account password each time you log on to your computer.

Creating a PIN for Your User Account

To further simplify the way you log on to your computer, especially if you are using a Microsoft account with a long password, Windows 8 allows the creation of a four-digit PIN associated with your user account. After you create a PIN, you can use it to log on quickly to your user account.

In this exercise, you'll learn how to create a PIN for your user account.

12

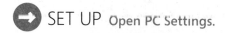 SET UP Open PC Settings.

1   Click or tap **Users**.

2   Click or tap **Create a PIN**.

     The Create A PIN Wizard opens.

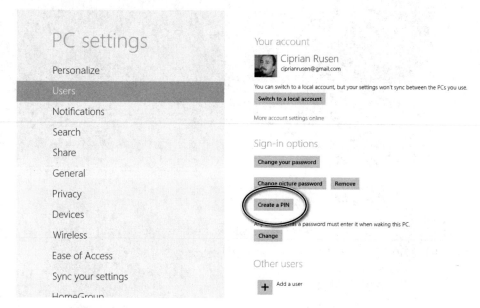

3   Type the password for your user account and click or tap **OK**.

     You are asked to type the four-digit PIN you want to use.

4   Type the same PIN in the **Enter PIN** and **Confirm PIN** fields.

5   Click or tap **Finish**.

❌ CLEAN UP   Close PC Settings.

The PIN you just set can now be used instead of your password to log on to your user account.

Changing the Picture Password or the PIN

You can change both your picture password and PIN if you decide to use these features. The change process is always started from the Users panel.

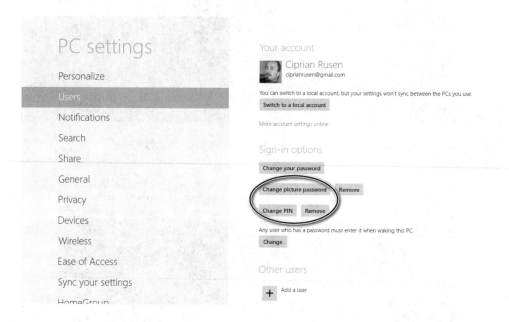

Windows 8 first asks you to type the current password associated with the user account and then allows you to change the picture password and the PIN. From here on, the procedures for changing them are the same as for creating them.

Changing a User Account Picture

As with any earlier version of Windows, you can change the picture for your user account at any time. The procedure involved is not complicated.

In this exercise, you'll learn how to change a user account picture.

➜ SET UP To complete this exercise, you need the PictureB.jpg file in the Chapter12 folder in your practice files. When this file is available, open the Start screen.

1   Click or tap the icon representing your user account on the top right of the screen.
    A contextual menu with several options opens.

2   Click or tap **Change account picture**.
    The Personalize section in PC Settings opens.

3   Click or tap **Browse**.
    The Files browsing window opens.

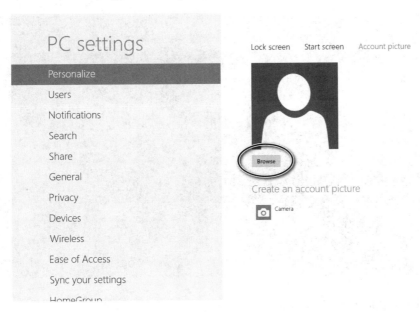

4   Click or tap **Files** and navigate to where you stored the PictureB.jpg practice file.

5   Select **PictureB.jpg** and click or tap **Choose image**.

You return to PC Settings.

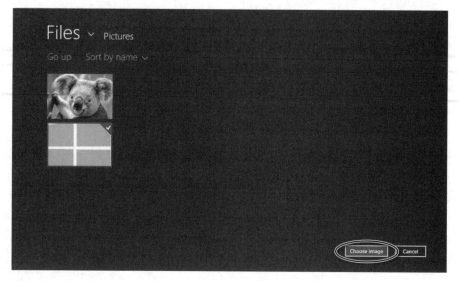

 CLEAN UP Close PC Settings.

Your user account picture has been changed.

Changing a User Account Name

In Windows 8, changing the name of a user account is possible only for local accounts. User account names associated with a Microsoft account cannot change without administrator permissions. It is best to make the change from another user account with administrator permissions.

In this exercise, you'll learn how to change the name of a local user account.

SET UP Log on with a user account that has administrator permissions. In Control Panel, open the User Accounts window by clicking User Accounts, Family Safety, and then User Accounts.

1   Click or tap **Manage another account**.

A list of all the existing user accounts opens.

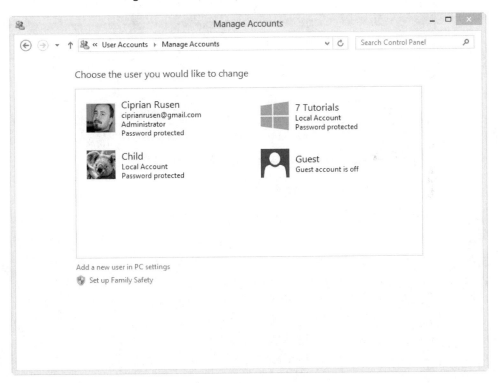

2   Click or tap the user account whose name you want changed.

The Change An Account window opens.

3   Click or tap **Change the account name**.

The Rename Account window opens.

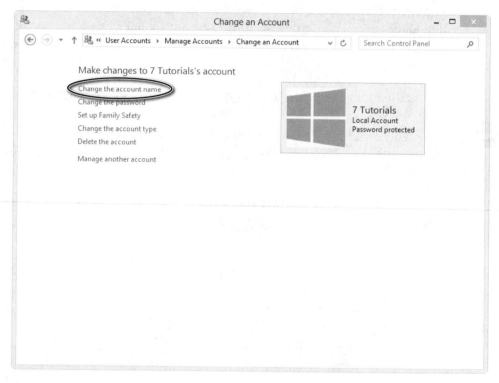

4   Type the new name you want to use for that user account.

5   Click or tap **Change Name**.

You return to the Change An Account window.

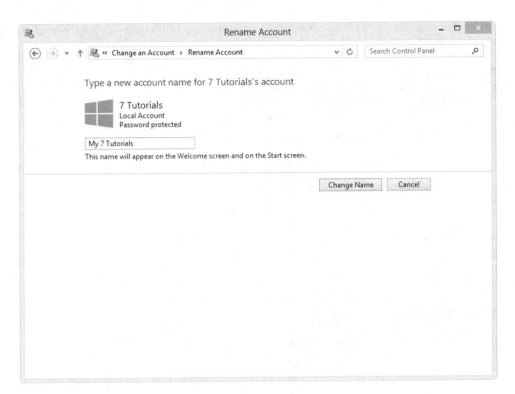

CLEAN UP Close the Change An Account window.

The name of the selected user account is now changed.

Changing a User Account Type

Every user except Guest can change his or her user account type. However, making the change requires administrator permissions. If you are trying to change the type for a user account with standard permissions, you need to know the password of the Administrator account or have someone log on with the Administrator account and change the account type.

You must have at least one user account with administrator permissions on your Windows 8–based computer. If you have only one such user account, you can't change its type to standard user. However, you can change any number of standard user accounts to Administrator.

12

In this exercise, you'll learn how to change the type of a user account from standard to Administrator.

SET UP Log on with a user account that has administrator permissions. In Control Panel, open User Accounts.

1   Click or tap **Manage another account**.

A list of all the existing user accounts opens.

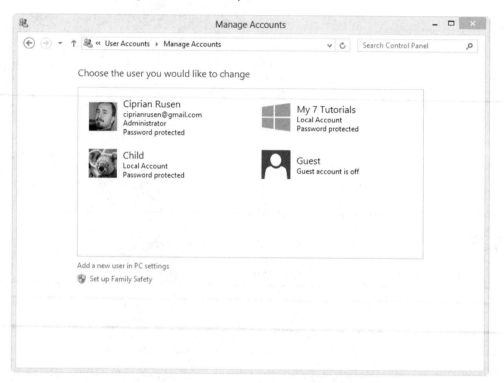

2   Click or tap the user account whose type you want to change.

The Change An Account window opens.

3   Click or tap **Change the account type**.

The Change Account Type window opens.

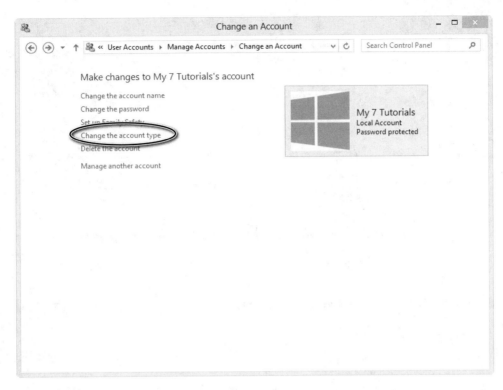

4　Select the new account type you want to use, in this case, **Administrator**.

5　Click or tap **Change Account Type**.

　　You return to the Change An Account window.

12

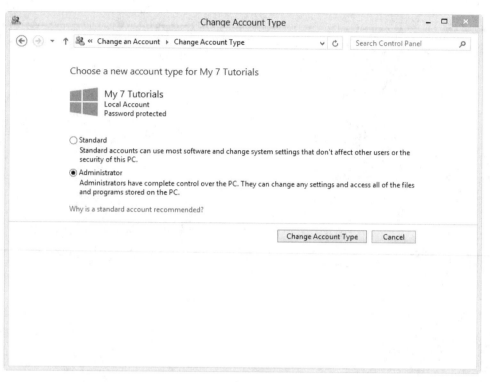

CLEAN UP Close the Change An Account window.

The type of the selected user account is now changed.

Deleting a User Account

Deleting user accounts is a task that administrators only can do. When an account is deleted, all the settings and files belonging to that user account are also deleted. This activity is best done by logging on to another user account and making the deletion from there. Make sure that the user account you are about to delete is not logged on when executing the deletion.

Before you delete a user account, make sure you back up all the important files created in its user files and folders so they can be used later.

In this exercise, you'll learn how to delete a user account.

SET UP Log on with a user account that has administrator permissions. In Control Panel, open the User Accounts window.

1 Click or tap **Manage another account**.

A list of all the existing user accounts opens.

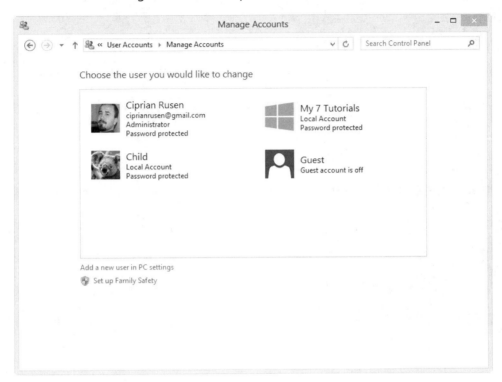

2 Click or tap the user account you want to delete.

The Change An Account window opens.

3 Click or tap the **Delete the account** link.

The Delete Account window opens.

12

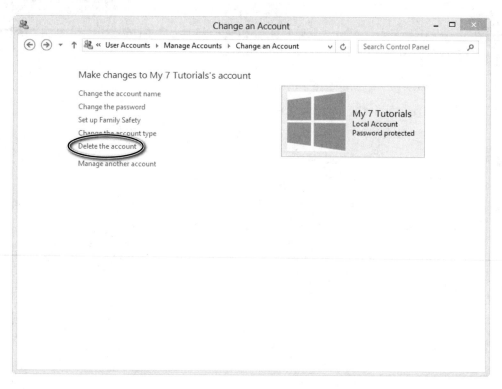

4   Click or tap **Delete Files**.

You are asked to confirm the deletion.

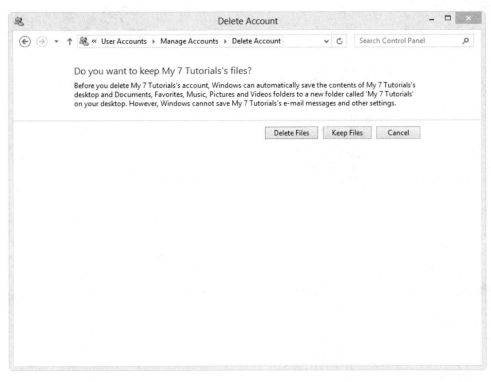

5   Click or tap **Delete Account**.

You return to the Manage Accounts window.

12

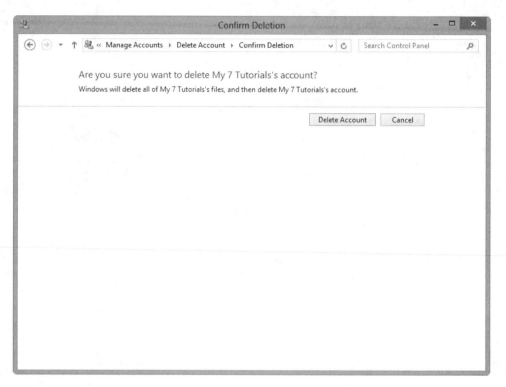

![Confirm Deletion dialog] Confirm Deletion

Manage Accounts ▸ Delete Account ▸ Confirm Deletion

Search Control Panel

Are you sure you want to delete My 7 Tutorials's account?

Windows will delete all of My 7 Tutorials's files, and then delete My 7 Tutorials's account.

Delete Account   Cancel

❌ CLEAN UP Close the Manage Accounts window.

The selected user account is now deleted.

TIP If you decide to keep the user's files, they will be saved in a folder on the Desktop of the user account from which you are making the deletion. The folder name will be the name of the deleted user account.

Key Points

- If more than one person is using a computer, it is best to create a separate user account for each person.

- Windows 8 allows you to use Microsoft accounts as user accounts on your device.

- With a Microsoft account, you can use all the features included in Windows 8, including the Windows Store.

- Any user can create picture passwords or PINs for quicker logon procedures.

- To create a user account, change user account names or types, and delete user accounts, you need administrator permissions.

- The deletion of a user account is best done from another user account and only after you have backed up all the important files created by that user.

12

Chapter at a Glance

Find

Find the Advanced Sharing Settings window that contains all your network-sharing settings, page 353

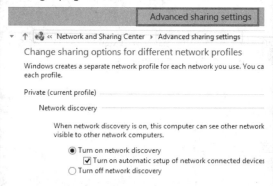

Create

Create a homegroup to easily share libraries, folders, and devices, page 359

Use

Use the Sharing Wizard for quick file sharing, page 374

Share

Share all printers and devices with one setting, page 383

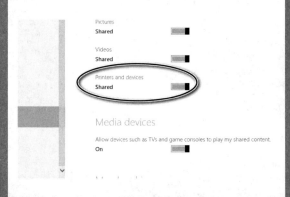

Sharing Files and Folders with My Network

13

IN THIS CHAPTER, YOU WILL LEARN HOW TO:

- Find the network sharing settings.

- Set up a homegroup.

- Join other computers and devices to the homegroup.

- Share files and folders.

- Share printers.

- Stop sharing files, folders, or printers.

- Enable the Sharing Wizard.

In Windows 8, Microsoft continued its efforts to simplify the network sharing experience. Features such as HomeGroup have been further improved, and network sharing settings and wizards have been simplified so that they require a smaller number of steps.

In this chapter, you'll learn about the default network sharing settings and how they affect your network sharing experience. You'll learn everything about the HomeGroup feature: how to create one, join other computers to it, find and change the current password, and leave an existing homegroup. Finally, you'll learn about sharing your libraries, folders, and devices such as printers, including how to stop sharing them when necessary.

PRACTICE FILES You do not need any practice files to complete the exercises in this chapter. For more information about practice file requirements, see "Using the Practice Files" at the beginning of this book.

Understanding the Default Network Sharing Settings

Windows 8 organizes your network sharing settings in the Advanced Sharing Settings window in the the Network And Sharing Center, covered in detail in Chapter 11, "Connecting to a Network and the Internet."

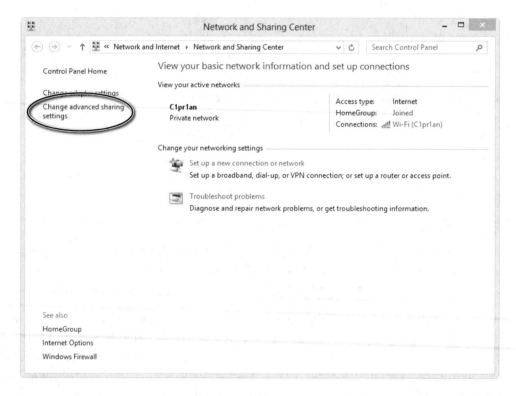

To access it, just click or tap the Change Advanced Sharing Settings link in the left sidebar of the Network And Sharing Center.

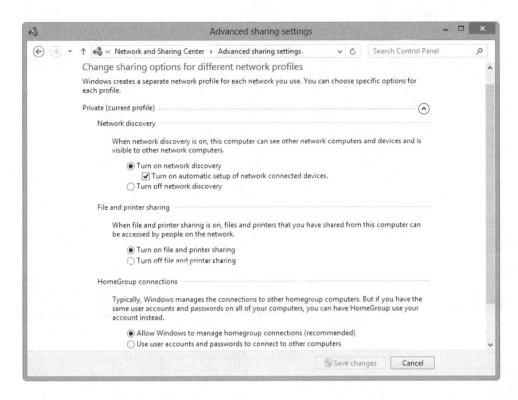

In Windows 8, the network sharing settings are split by network profile. Each network profile has different settings, and a combination of settings is applied to all networks to which you connect. The profile assigned to your current network connection is indicated by the **Current Profile** statement beside the name of one of the two profiles. If you want to access the settings for only one of the network locations, use the arrows to the right of each profile. Clicking or tapping the arrow once minimizes the list of settings for that network location. Clicking or tapping it again maximizes the list.

13

The profile assigned to the
active network connection

Minimize/Maximize
list of settings

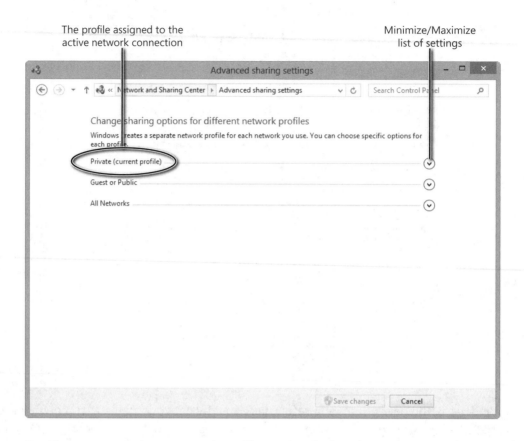

TIP To learn more about network profiles and assigning them to a network connection, see the "Setting the Network Profile" section in Chapter 11.

The Private profile has, by default, the following settings.

- **NETWORK DISCOVERY IS TURNED ON** When this setting is applied, Windows 8 can search for other devices on the network to which it is connected, and it allows other computers and devices on the same network to find your Windows 8–based computer or device.

- **FILE AND PRINTER SHARING IS TURNED ON** When this setting is applied, you can share content and printers with other computers and devices on your network.

- **WINDOWS IS ALLOWED TO MANAGE HOMEGROUP CONNECTIONS** After you join or create a homegroup, Windows 8 automatically manages homegroup connections. If you choose the other available option, you must manually type a user name and password when you connect to other computers.

The default settings for the Private profile are very effective and do not need changing unless you don't want to or don't need to use the available network sharing features on the network to which you are connected. If this is the case, it is best to switch the network profile to Guest or Public instead of changing the default settings of the Private profile.

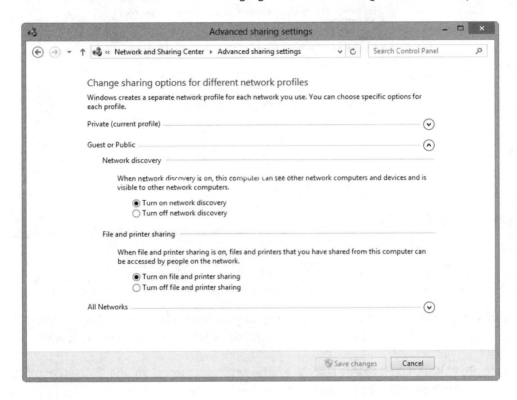

The Guest or Public profile has, by default, the following settings.

- **NETWORK DISCOVERY IS TURNED OFF** When this setting is applied, other computers and devices on the network can't discover your Windows 8–based computer or device unless they know its direct network address.

- **FILE AND PRINTER SHARING IS TURNED OFF** When this setting is applied, all network sharing features are disabled and can't be used on this network. If your computer is accessed by others, they cannot view any files, folders, or devices being shared.

These default settings are great when connecting to networks you don't trust and with which you do not want to share any folders, libraries, or devices.

13

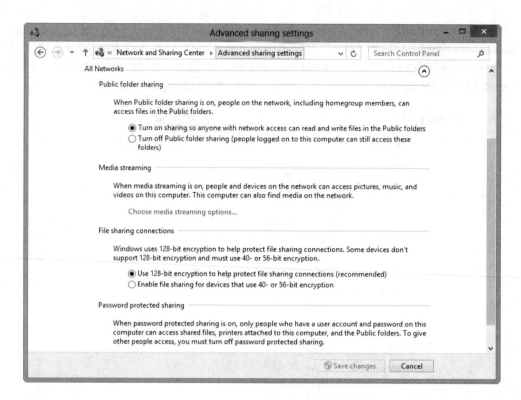

Last, a combination of settings is applied to all network connections. They are found in the All Networks section and can be customized. The available settings are the following.

- **PUBLIC FOLDER SHARING** When this setting is turned on, the C:\Users\Public\ folder is shared with all the computers and devices on the network. This folder contains the following subfolders: Public Documents, Public Downloads, Public Music, Public Pictures, and Public Videos. Other folders are also contained here, but they are not displayed to users. Users on the same computer or from other computers and devices can read the contents of the Public folder and write files inside it and its subfolders. When this setting is turned off, this folder is not shared with your network. Turning off Public folder sharing is recommended unless using this folder for sharing is useful to you. Depending on your personal preference, you might choose to share files and folders directly with others instead of copying them to the Public folder.

- **MEDIA STREAMING** With this setting, you can stream multimedia files (pictures, video, and music) by using Windows Media Player. When this setting is turned on, you can stream your media with the network and the Internet. When it's turned off, no media streaming is possible by using Windows Media Player. You should only turn on this feature if you plan to use it.

- **FILE SHARING CONNECTIONS** This setting determines the type of encryption used for file sharing connections. By default, it's set to 128-bit encryption. You can also set it to the less secure 40-bit or 56-bit encryption. However, it is best to leave this set at 128-bit encryption unless you have issues with older devices or computers that cannot properly access your shared files and folders.

- **PASSWORD PROTECTED SHARING** With this setting, people can only access your shared files and folders if they have a user account and password set on your computer. If they don't have these details, they cannot connect to your shared folders and devices unless the shared folders and devices are shared with everyone. Turning off this feature is useful only when connecting to trusted home or work networks with diverse operating systems that have trouble connecting to your Windows 8 shared folders and devices. However, this setting should be used only as a last resort.

If you make any changes to the default network sharing settings, don't forget to press the Save Changes button so that they are applied. Also, keep in mind that making changes to these settings requires administrator permissions. User accounts with no administrator permissions cannot modify them in any way.

Setting Up a Homegroup

HomeGroup is a network feature introduced first in Windows 7 and further improved in Windows 8. It aims to simplify the process of sharing content and devices on trusted small networks. In earlier versions of Windows, sharing content was a tedious and sometimes painful process.

By using the HomeGroup feature, you can access all shared files and devices in your network with very few clicks and without typing user names and passwords. The homegroup manages all security and authentication for you and makes sure that computers and devices outside the homegroup cannot access what you are sharing. This feature is designed primarily for computers and devices connected to a small home or work network.

Each time you connect the computer to a new network, Windows 8 asks you to set network sharing. If you turn on sharing and connect to devices, you are in a trusted and private network of computers and devices. In this scenario, Windows 8 enables you to use the HomeGroup feature. If you do not turn on sharing, this feature will not be available.

13

TIP To learn more about network profiles and assigning them to a network connection, see the "Changing the Network Profile of a Network" section in Chapter 11.

Even though this feature is useful and easy to use, it has an important limitation: It is available only for computers and devices running Windows 7 and Windows 8. Only these operating systems can join a homegroup and take advantage of it without any special configuration.

After you have connected to your network and customized the network sharing settings, you can create the homegroup for your network computers to join and exchange libraries, files, folders, and devices.

You can create the homegroup from either Control Panel or PC Settings. However, the creation process is slightly faster when done from PC Settings.

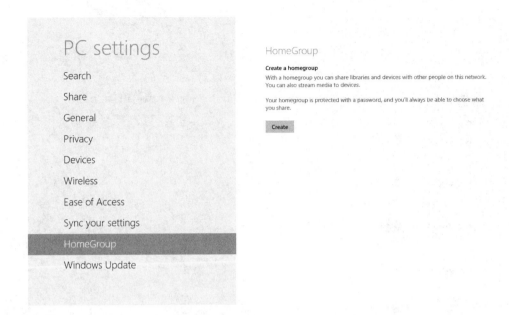

When you create a homegroup, Windows automatically generates a random and secure password that will be used by all computers and devices to join the homegroup and share items among them. You can't set this password when creating the homegroup, but you can change it after you create the homegroup.

Membership

If someone else wants to join your homegroup, give them this password:

e3w5Pe1bl8

If you leave the homegroup, you won't be able to get to shared libraries or devices.

Leave

After the homegroup is created, you can select from a standard list of items to share with others. A limited list of libraries is available for sharing: Documents, Music, Pictures, and Videos. You can also share installed printers and devices (scanners, multifunctional printers, and so on) and allow devices such as TVs and game consoles to play the content you have shared with the homegroup.

13

Libraries and devices

When you share content, other homegroup members can see it, but only you can change it.

Documents
Not shared   ◼▨▨

Music
Not shared   ◼▨▨

Pictures
Not shared   ◼▨▨

Videos
Not shared   ◼▨▨

Printers and devices
Not shared   ◼▨▨

Media devices

Allow all devices on the network such as TVs and game consoles to play my shared content

Off   ◼▨▨

TIP To learn more about libraries in Windows 8, read the "Understanding Files, Folders, and Libraries" section in Chapter 4, "Saving, Browsing, and Organizing Files and Folders."

Sharing other libraries, folders, or devices can be set up after you create the homegroup.

In this exercise, you'll learn how to create a homegroup.

 SET UP Open PC Settings.

1 Click or tap **HomeGroup** at the bottom of the **PC Settings** window.

TROUBLESHOOTING If, when you click the HomeGroup link, you do not see a window similar to the one shown here, but something with the settings of an existing homegroup, the computer is already part of a homegroup. In this scenario, you either keep the computer as part of that homegroup or leave that homegroup and create a new one. To learn how to leave a homegroup, read the "Leaving a Homegroup" section later in this chapter.

2 Click or tap **Create**.

Windows 8 takes a few seconds to create the homegroup.

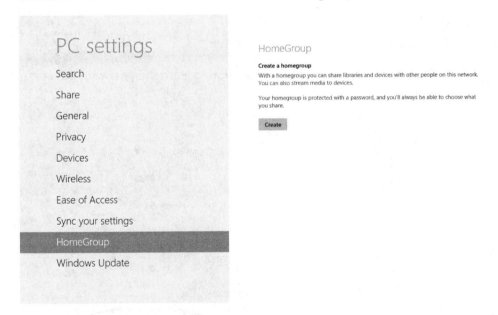

3 Set the permissions to **Shared** by changing the positions of the switches for the items you want shared with the homegroup.

13

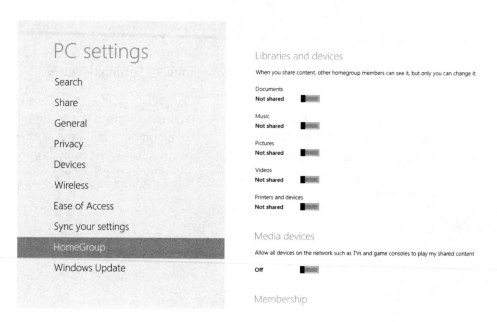

4   Scroll down to the Membership section to learn the password generated for your homegroup.

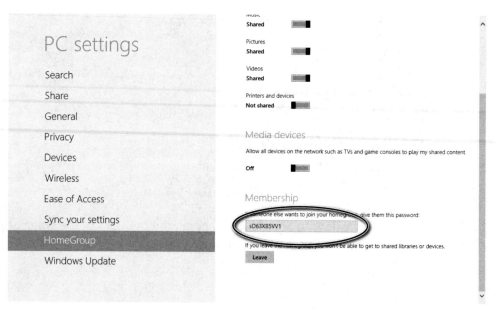

5   Write down the password.

❌ CLEAN UP Close PC Settings.

The homegroup is now created, and other computers and devices with Windows 7 or Windows 8 can join it by using the same password.

Joining a Homegroup

After the homegroup is created, you can join others so that you can exchange files, folders, and devices. Any computer on the network can be part of a homegroup, but it can be in only one homegroup at a time.

When you open the HomeGroup section in PC Settings, Windows 8 tells you whether it detects a homegroup created by another computer. If it does, it mentions the name of the user account and the computer that created the homegroup.

HomeGroup

A homegroup is available

Ciprian on CIPRIAN-PC has created a homegroup. Join the homegroup to share files and devices with other people on this network.

When joining a homegroup, you are asked to type the password that was generated during its creation. If you remember the password from the previous section, use that one. If not, ask the person who created the homegroup for the password.

In this exercise, you'll learn how to join a computer running Windows 8 to a previously created homegroup.

➡ SET UP Open PC Settings.

1   Click or tap **HomeGroup** at the bottom of the **PC Settings** window.

2   Type the homegroup password and click or tap **Join**.

     Windows 8 takes a few seconds to join you to the homegroup.

13

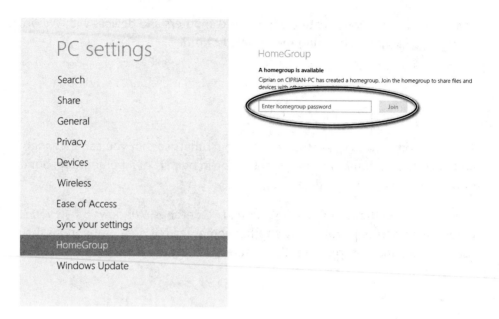

3   Set the permissions to **Shared** for the items you want shared with the homegroup.

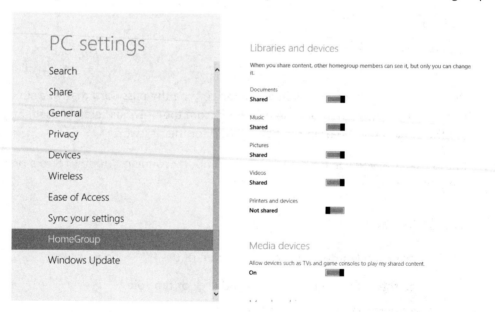

⊗ CLEAN UP Close PC Settings. Repeat this procedure for all the computers and devices on your network that you want in the homegroup.

The computer is now part of the homegroup and has shared the items you selected.

Finding Your Homegroup Password

If you want to add another computer or device to the homegroup and you forgot the password, you can access it easily on the computers that are part of the homegroup.

In this exercise, you'll learn how to find the password for your homegroup so that you can share it with the people who need to know it.

➡️ SET UP Open PC Settings.

1   Click or tap the **HomeGroup** section at the bottom of the **PC Settings** window.

2   Scroll down to the **Membership** section where the homegroup password is displayed.

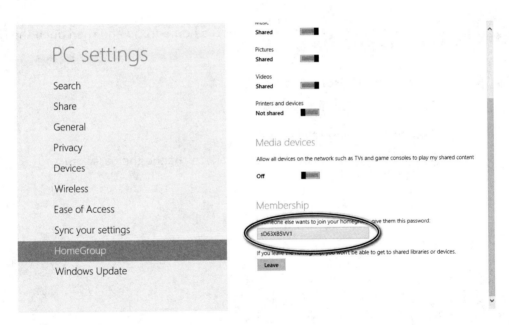

3   Write down the password.

✖️ CLEAN UP Close PC Settings.

13

Changing the Password of a Homegroup

You can change the password of a homegroup from any computer that joined it, but only from Control Panel, not from PC Settings. If you change the password after other computers and devices have joined the homegroup, the password change will disconnect the other computers and devices. After the password is changed, all the other computers and devices must rejoin the homegroup by using the new password.

When changing the password, Windows generates a new random and secure password for you, but you can type a password of your own. The only condition is that the password is at least eight characters long; otherwise, Windows won't accept it as a valid password.

In this exercise, you'll learn how to change the password of an existing homegroup to one you choose.

 SET UP **Start a computer that is part of the homegroup and then open the Network And Sharing Center.**

1   Click or tap the **HomeGroup** link.

    The HomeGroup window opens.

2   Click or tap **Change the password**.

    You are asked to confirm that you want to change the password.

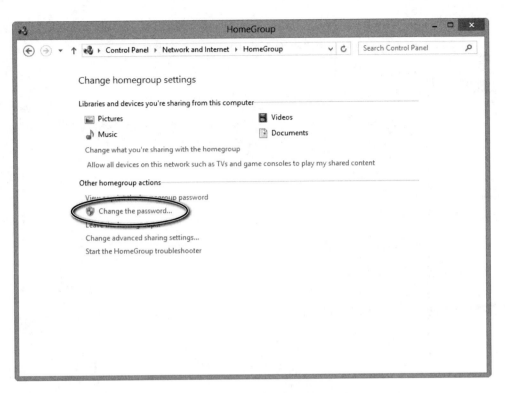

3   Click or tap **Change the password**.

Windows generates a new random password.

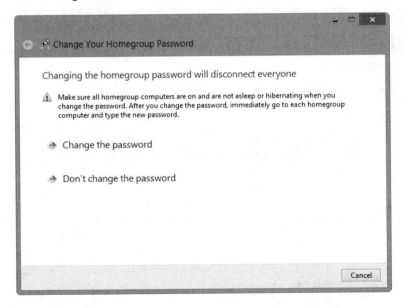

13

4   Type a new password that is at least eight characters long in the field where the random password is displayed.

5   Click or tap **Next**.

Windows 8 makes the necessary changes.

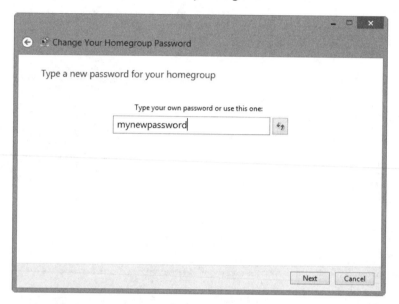

6   Click or tap **Finish**.

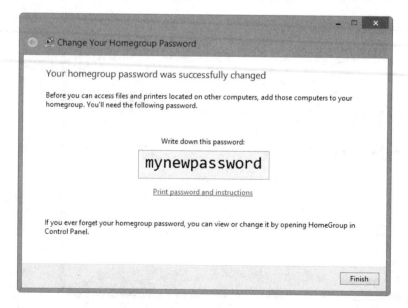

CLEAN UP Close the HomeGroup window. Rejoin all computers and devices that were disconnected due to the password change.

The password for the homegroup is now changed.

Accessing Homegroup Computers and Devices

After the homegroup is created and all computers and devices are joined, accessing their shared content is simple. All it takes is a few clicks or taps. You no longer need to type any user names and passwords to access what is being shared.

Just open File Explorer and click or tap the homegroup. You'll see a list of computers and user accounts that are part of the homegroup and running at that moment. Double-click or tap any of the shared folders and libraries to access their content.

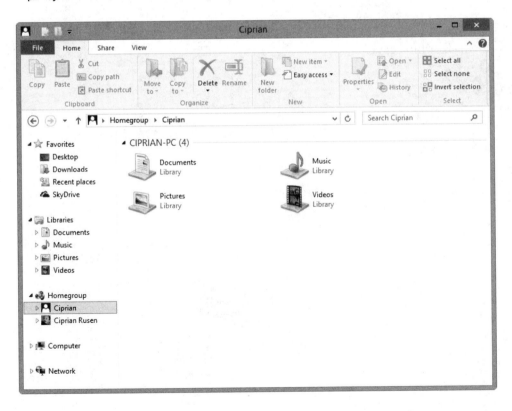

TIP By default, libraries and folders are shared with the other homegroup computers as Read Only. Therefore, you can access them or copy their content to your computer, but you can't delete them or change them unless the permissions are changed to Read/Write.

Leaving a Homegroup

Leaving a homegroup is as easy as joining one. If you leave a homegroup, you stop sharing files, folders, and devices with other members of the group, and you won't be able to access what is shared as part of that homegroup. You can create another homegroup or join the existing one again at any time.

In this exercise, you'll learn how to leave a homegroup to which your computer is joined.

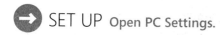 **SET UP** Open **PC Settings**.

1   Click or tap the **HomeGroup** section at the bottom of the **PC Settings** window.

2   Scroll down to the **Membership** section.

3   Click or tap **Leave**.

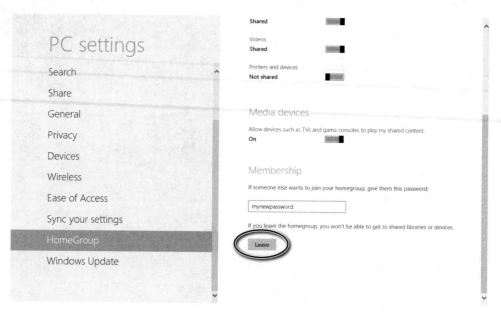

 CLEAN UP Close PC Settings.

Your computer is no longer part of the homegroup.

Using the Sharing Wizard to Share with the Homegroup

If you have set up a homegroup and you want to share something with other computers that have joined it, the Sharing Wizard makes the procedure simple. The sharing options are in the Share tab of File Explorer.

For any library or folder you select for sharing, you have the following options.

- **HOMEGROUP (VIEW)** This option shares the selected item with the homegroup and gives Read-Only permissions to all computers and devices in the homegroup. The item will be shared only when you are connected to the homegroup, and others will be able to view and read the shared item but not to modify it or delete it.

- **HOMEGROUP (VIEW AND EDIT)** This shares the item with others in your homegroup and gives full permissions to modify it or delete it. The item will not be shared when you disconnect from the homegroup or connect to another network.

- **USER ACCOUNTS NAMES** You will see other user accounts you defined in Windows 8 in the list. If you select a user account name, you will share the item (with Read-Only permissions) with that user account.

- **SPECIFIC PEOPLE** With this option, you can share the selected item with whomever you want, including with computers that are not part of the homegroup or specific user accounts. This option is described in more detail in the next section of this chapter.

13

In this exercise, you'll learn how to use the Sharing Wizard to share a folder with the homegroup.

SET UP Open File Explorer and browse to the folder you want to share. Maximize the ribbon, if it is minimized, with a double-click or double-tap.

1   Select the folder without opening it.

2   Click or tap the **Share** tab.

The list of sharing options opens.

3   Click or tap **Homegroup (view)** in the **Share with** section.

The File Sharing window opens.

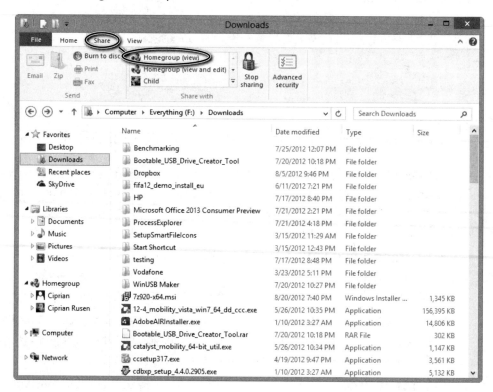

4   Click or tap **Yes, share the items**.

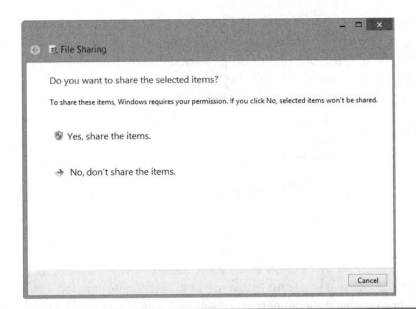

IMPORTANT Depending on what you have shared, you might not see the File Sharing window. In that case, you won't have to go through step 4, and the selected folder will be shared with the homegroup without additional confirmation.

CLEAN UP Repeat the procedure for all the items you want to share. When you have finished, close File Explorer.

The selected folder is now shared with the homegroup.

Using the Sharing Wizard to Share with Specific People

If you have computers that are not running Windows 8 or Windows 7, you can use the Sharing Wizard to share libraries and folders with them without using the homegroup. However, the procedure takes slightly longer than sharing items with the homegroup.

During the sharing procedure, a drop-down menu appears that shows all the user accounts defined on your computer, the homegroup you have joined, and a user account called

13

Everyone. The homegroup user account represents all the computers from your home-group, whereas Everyone is a generic user account; this can be any user on the list. If you want to share something with computers that have different operating systems installed, it is best to share items by using the Everyone user account. The other operating systems will have an easier time accessing what you have shared.

Choose people to share with

Type a name and then click Add, or click the arrow to find someone.

Child
Ciprian Rusen (ciprianrusen@gmail.com)
seventutorials@live.com (seventutorials@live.com)
Everyone
Homegroup

By default, all the user accounts with which you choose to share are granted **Read** permis-sions to the shared item. If you want to change that, click the **Permission Level** assigned. A list appears showing the available permission levels.

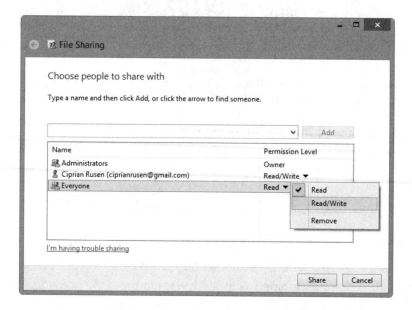

In this exercise, you'll learn how to use the Sharing Wizard to share a folder with everyone and assign Read/Write permissions.

SET UP Open File Explorer and browse to the folder you want to share. Maximize the ribbon, if it is minimized, with a double-click or double-tap.

1 Select the folder without opening it.

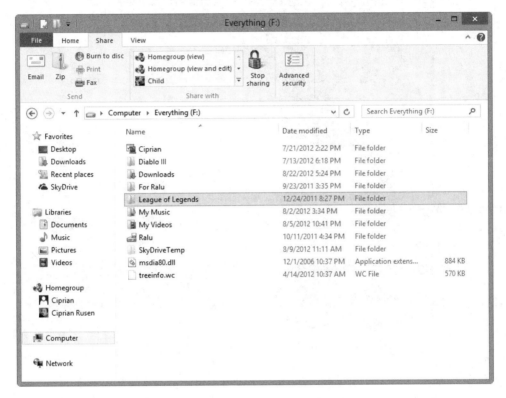

2 Click or tap the **Share** tab.

The list of sharing options opens.

3 Click or tap the arrow pointing down, found at the bottom of the **Share with** list of options.

4 Click or tap **Specific people**.

The File Sharing Wizard opens.

13

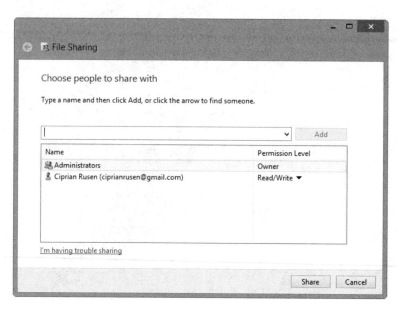

5 Click or tap the drop-down menu to open the list of user accounts with whom you can share.

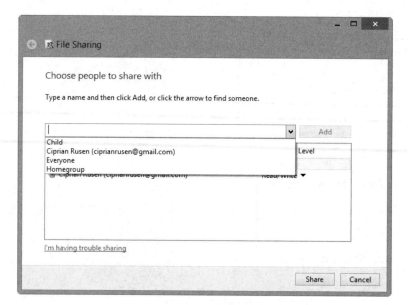

6 Select the user account named **Everyone**.

7 Click or tap **Add**.

The user account is added to the list below the drop-down menu.

8 Click or tap **Permission Level** for **Everyone** and select **Read/Write**.

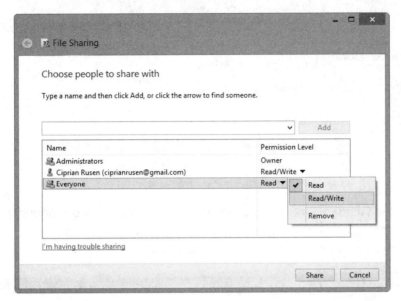

9 Click or tap **Share**.

You are informed that the selected folder has been shared.

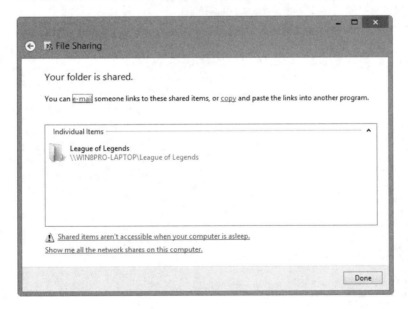

13

10   Click or tap **Done**.

✖ CLEAN UP Close File Explorer.

The selected folder is now shared with everyone on your network.

Stop Sharing a Library or Folder

At some point in your networking experience, you might want to stop sharing a folder or library. The procedure for this is the same as for sharing it. The only difference is that you need to click or tap the Stop Sharing button on the Share tab.

Without any other prompts or windows, the item you selected is no longer shared with the network to which you are connected.

Sharing a Printer with Computers on Your Network

Installed devices such as printers and scanners are accessible in the Devices And Printers panel; from here, you can configure everything, including sharing devices with the other computers on your network.

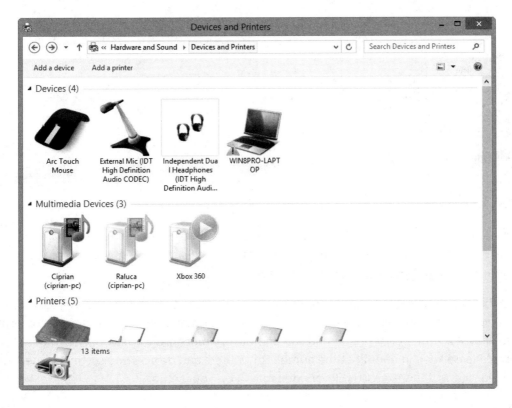

When sharing a printer, its default **Share name** is its model name. If you want to change it, you can type a new name during the sharing procedure.

13

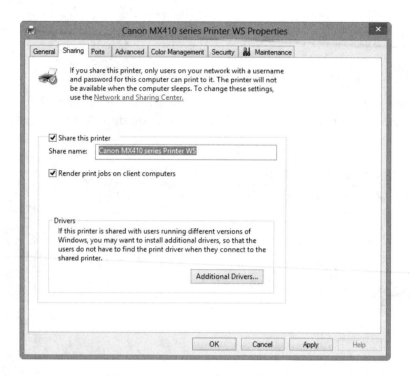

A shared printer on the network is shared with the entire network, including computers and devices that are outside the homegroup. If you want to share a printer with only the homegroup, check the instructions in the next section.

In this exercise, you'll learn how to share a printer with your network. The exercise and illustrations were created using a Canon Pixma MX410 printer; however, the same steps apply to almost any model of printer and should not vary much from what you see in this exercise. Please keep in mind that the number of printers and devices you see mentioned in the screenshots of this exercise will vary depending on your setup.

SET UP Connect the printer to your computer, start it, and install the latest drivers for it.

1 Open **Control Panel**.

2 Click or tap **View devices and printers** beneath the **Hardware and Sound** section title.

The Devices And Printers panel opens.

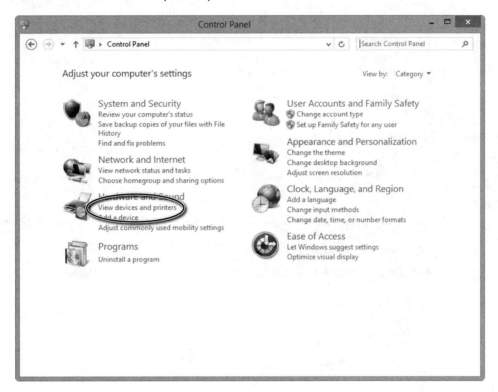

3 Scroll down to the **Printers** section to view the printers installed on your computer.

13

4   Right-click or press and hold the printer you want to share.

A menu with contextual options relevant to your printer opens.

5   Click or tap **Printer properties**.

The Printer Properties window opens.

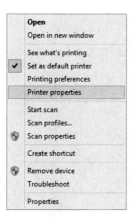

6　　Click or tap the **Sharing** tab.

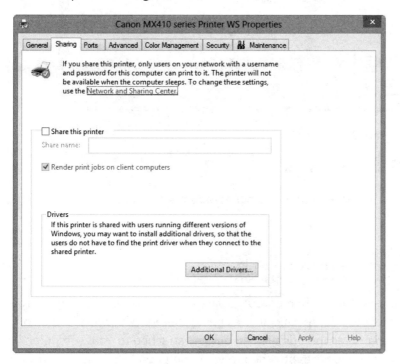

7　　Select the **Share this printer** check box.

13

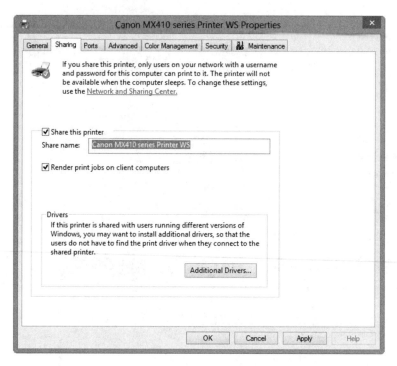

8   Click or tap **OK**.

CLEAN UP **Close Devices And Printers.**

The printer is now shared with the other computers on your network.

Sharing a Printer with Your Homegroup

Sharing a printer with your homegroup is very easy. However, the sharing procedure does not offer control over the specific devices being shared. With one setting, you can share with the homegroup all the printers and devices attached to your computer. If you want to share only one of the devices attached to your computer, it is best to follow the procedure detailed in the previous section.

In this exercise, you'll learn how to share all your connected printers and devices with others on the homegroup.

SET UP **Open PC Settings.**

1   Click or tap **HomeGroup** at the bottom of the **PC Settings** window.

2   In Libraries And Devices, click or tap the **Printers And Devices** switch.

3   Change the position of the switch from Not Shared to **Shared**.

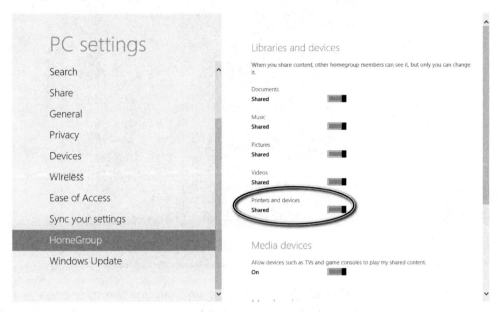

⊗ CLEAN UP Close PC Settings.

All your printers and devices are now shared with the homegroup.

Stop Sharing the Printer

If you want to discontinue sharing a printer, use the same steps you took to share. For example, if you shared a printer with the network, to stop sharing it go through the steps detailed in the "Sharing a Printer with Computers on Your Network" section and clear the Share This Printer box at step 8. All the other steps are the same.

13

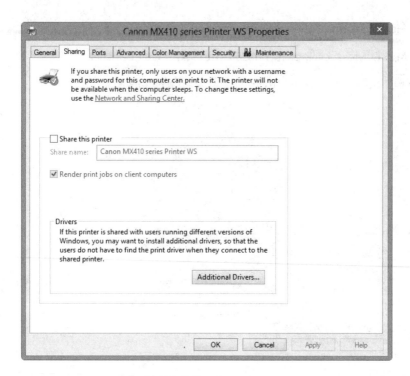

To stop sharing a printer with the homegroup, go through the same steps you took to share it and turn the switch to Not Shared instead of to Shared. All the other steps are identical.

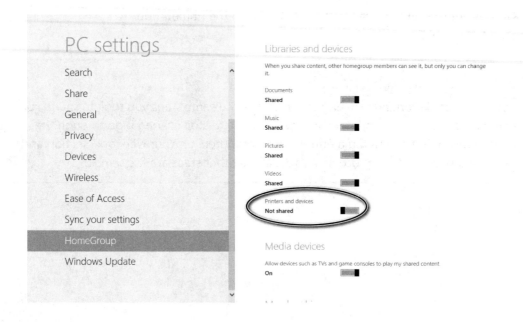

Enabling the Sharing Wizard

The Sharing Wizard in Windows 8 is designed so that you can easily share anything you want with the other computers and devices on the network. By default, the wizard is enabled in Windows 8. However, if it is disabled on your computer, the exercises included in prior sections about sharing over the network won't work, and you will see a completely different set of sharing options and buttons. Therefore, this section shows how to enable the Sharing Wizard so that you can complete the previous exercises without problems and have the easiest network sharing experience possible with Windows 8.

In this exercise, you'll learn how to enable the Sharing Wizard.

➡ SET UP Open File Explorer and maximize the ribbon by double-clicking it.

1   Click or tap the **View** tab.

2   Click or tap the **Options** button on the right side of the ribbon.
    The Folder Options window opens.

3   Click or tap the **View** tab.

4   Scroll down the **Advanced settings** list and select the **Use Sharing Wizard (Recommended)** check box.

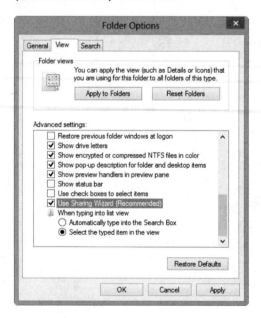

5   Click or tap **OK**.

You return to the File Explorer window.

❌ CLEAN UP Close File Explorer.

The Sharing Wizard is now enabled and can be used to complete the exercises detailed in this chapter.

Key Points

- The appropriate network sharing settings are applied automatically to the network to which you are connected, depending on whether you turned on sharing when first connecting to it.

- The homegroup works only on computers running Windows 7 and Windows 8. It allows easy sharing of files, folders, libraries, and devices without having to type user names and passwords each time you want to access something that is shared over the network.

- To join a homegroup, you need to type the homegroup password defined on the computer on which it was created.

- A computer can join only one homegroup at a time. To join another homegroup, the computer must first leave the current one.

- You can share your printer with both your homegroup and the computers that are not in your homegroup but are part of the network to which you are connected.

- The Sharing Wizard makes it easy for you to share libraries and folders with your home network.

13

Chapter at a Glance

Change

Change the UAC level, page 395

Choose when to be notified about changes to your computer

User Account Control helps prevent potentially harmful programs from making
Tell me more about User Account Control settings

Always notify

Notify me only when apps try to make changes to computer (default)

- Don't notify me when I make changes to Wind settings

Work

Work with Windows Firewall, page 404

Allowed apps

↑ 📷 « System and Security ▸ Windows Firewall ▸ Allowed apps

Allow apps to communicate through Windows Firewall
To add, change, or remove allowed apps and ports, click Change settings.
What are the risks of allowing an app to communicate?

Allowed apps and features:

Name
☑ Bing
☐ BranchCache - Content Retrieval (Uses HTTP)
☐ BranchCache - Hosted Cache Client (Uses HTTPS)
☐ BranchCache - Hosted Cache Server (Uses HTTPS)
☐ BranchCache - Peer Discovery (Uses WSD)

Restore

Restore Windows Firewall settings to their
defaults, page 410

Restore Defaults Confirmation

 Restoring the default settings will delete all settings of Windows Firewall
that you have made since Windows was installed. This may cause some
apps to stop working

Do you want to continue?

 Yes   No

Use

Use Windows Defender to secure your
system, page 411

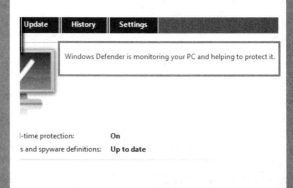

Update	History	Settings

Windows Defender is monitoring your PC and helping to protect it.

l-time protection: **On**
s and spyware definitions: **Up to date**

Keeping Windows 8 Safe and Secure

14

IN THIS CHAPTER, YOU WILL LEARN HOW TO

- Work with the User Account Control (UAC).

- Use Windows Firewall.

- Use Windows Defender.

- Enhance the security of your passwords.

Security is very important in the modern era of computers and devices. Microsoft has spent quite a bit of effort to enhance the security provided by Windows 8. This operating system offers improved versions of all its main security tools: User Account Control, Windows Firewall, and Windows Defender.

In this chapter, you'll learn how the User Account Control (UAC) works, how to tweak it, and why you should never disable it. In addition, you'll learn the basics of working with Windows Firewall to secure your network and Internet traffic and about the new and much improved Windows Defender and how to use it to keep your system safe from viruses and spyware. Finally, you'll learn how to improve your passwords to make it more difficult for unwanted people to access your Microsoft account, your email, and other important accounts you use and the Internet.

PRACTICE FILES You don't need any practice files to complete the exercises in this chapter. For more information about practice file requirements, see "Using the Practice Files" at the beginning of this book.

Understanding the User Account Control (UAC)

User Account Control (UAC) is a security feature that was introduced in Windows Vista and improved in all subsequent versions of Windows. It is present in Windows 8 as well, and it helps prevent unauthorized changes to your computer. These changes can be initiated by users, applications, viruses, or other types of malware. UAC makes sure these changes are made only with approval from the administrator of the computer. If these changes are not approved by the administrator, they will never be executed, and the system will remain unchanged.

Unlike in Windows XP, applications in Windows 8 do not run with administrator permissions and cannot make any changes to the operating system. When an application wants to make system changes such as modifications that affect other user accounts, modifications of system files and folders, or installation of new software, UAC prompts the user to ask for permission.

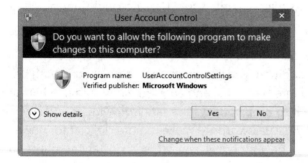

If the user clicks No, the changes won't be performed. If the user clicks Yes, the application receives administrator permissions and makes the system changes it is programmed to make. These permissions will be granted until the application stops running or is closed by the user. The next time it runs, it starts without receiving any administrator permissions.

To illustrate this process, the UAC algorithm is explained in the following diagram.

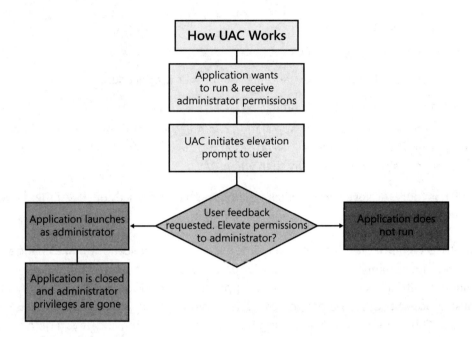

How UAC Works

Application wants to run & receive administrator permissions

UAC initiates elevation prompt to user

User feedback requested. Elevate permissions to administrator?

Application launches as administrator

Application does not run

Application is closed and administrator privileges are gone

Many changes require administrator privileges and, depending on how UAC is configured on your computer, they can cause a UAC prompt to ask for permissions. These changes are the following.

- Running an application as an administrator
- Changes to system-wide settings or to files in the Windows and Program Files folders
- Installing and uninstalling drivers and applications
- Installing ActiveX controls
- Changing settings to Windows Firewall
- Changing UAC (User Account Control) settings
- Configuring Windows Update
- Adding or removing user accounts
- Changing a user's account type
- Configuring parental controls

14

- Running the Task Scheduler

- Restoring backed-up system files

- Viewing or changing the folders and files of another user account

- Changing the system date and time

If UAC is turned off, any user and any application can make any of these changes without a prompt for permissions. This would allow viruses and other forms of malware to infect and take control of your system more easily than when UAC is turned on.

Windows 8 has four UAC levels from which to choose. The differences between them are the following.

- **ALWAYS NOTIFY** At this level, you are notified before applications make changes that require administrator permissions or before you or another user changes Windows settings. When a UAC prompt appears, your desktop is dimmed, and you must choose *Yes* or *No* before you can do anything else on your computer. Security Impact: This is the most secure setting but also the most annoying. If you do not like the UAC implementation from Windows Vista, you won't like this level either.

- **NOTIFY ME ONLY WHEN APPS TRY TO MAKE CHANGES TO MY COMPUTER (DEFAULT)** This is the default level; it only notifies you before programs make changes to your computer that require administrator permissions. If you manually make changes to Windows, UAC doesn't notify you. This level is less annoying because it doesn't stop the user when making changes to the system; it only shows prompts if an application wants to make changes. When a UAC prompt appears, the desktop is dimmed, and you must choose *Yes* or *No* before you can do anything else on your computer. Security Impact: This is less secure because malicious programs can be created that simulate the keystrokes or mouse moves of a user and change Windows settings. However, if you are using a good security solution, these scenarios should never occur.

- **NOTIFY ME ONLY WHEN APPS TRY TO MAKE CHANGES TO MY COMPUTER (DO NOT DIM MY DESKTOP)** This level is identical to the preceding one except that, when a UAC prompt appears, the desktop is not dimmed, and other programs might be able to interfere with the UAC dialog box. Security Impact: This level is even less secure because it is easier for malicious programs to simulate keystrokes or mouse moves that interfere with the UAC prompt. Again, a good security solution can compensate for the slight decrease in security.

- **NEVER NOTIFY** At this level, UAC is turned off and offers no protection against unauthorized system changes. Any user or application can make system changes without any prompts for permission. Security Impact: If you don't have a good security solution, you are very likely to have security problems. With UAC turned off, it is easier for malicious programs to infect your computer and take control of it and its settings.

> **IMPORTANT** Use either of the first two levels. The third level can be used when you have a very good security solution in place. The fourth level should always be avoided because it has a negative impact on the security of your system.

Changing the UAC Level

Now that you know what this feature does and how it works, you'll learn how to configure it to offer the level of security you desire. In this exercise, you'll learn how to change the UAC level.

> **IMPORTANT** Before changing the UAC level, review the previous section in this chapter, "Understanding the User Account Control (UAC)." It is very important to understand the differences among the levels before making any changes.

➜ SET UP Open Control Panel.

1   Click or tap **System and Security**.

    The System And Security window opens.

2   In the Action Center section, click or tap **Change User Account Control settings**.

    The User Account Control Settings window opens.

14

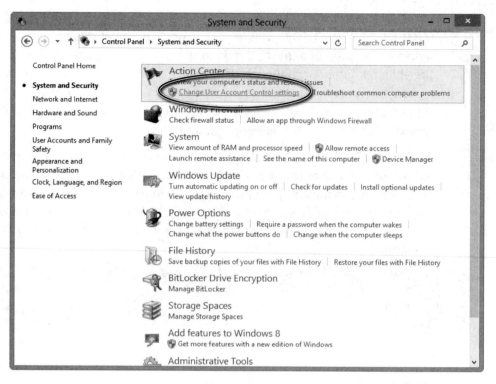

3   Move the slide to the UAC level you want to use.

4   Click or tap **OK**.

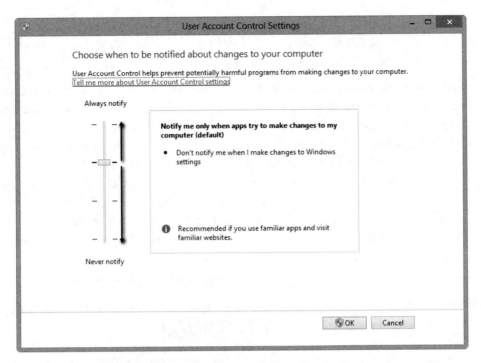

5   Depending on the UAC level set before making the change, you might receive a UAC prompt. Click or tap **Yes** if you do.

✖ CLEAN UP Close the System And Security window.

The UAC is set to the level you selected and will provide you with the appropriate security level according to the choice you made.

14

Should I Disable UAC When I Install My Applications and Turn It On Afterward?

The biggest annoyance UAC causes is when you install all your daily applications. At this time, you can receive many UAC prompts (one for each application you install). You might be tempted to disable UAC temporarily while you install your applications and enable it again when you're finished. In some scenarios, this can be a bad idea. Certain applications, which make many system changes, can fail to work if you turn on UAC after their installation even though they work if you install them with UAC turned on. These failures happen because, when UAC is turned off, the virtualization techniques UAC uses for all applications are inactive. This causes certain user settings and files to be installed to a different place and no longer work when UAC is turned back on. To avoid these problems, it is better to have UAC turned on at all times.

Using the Windows Firewall

Windows Firewall is a security application built into Windows 8 that helps block unauthorized access to your computer while permitting authorized communications to and from your computer. This application has been improved in each new version of Windows.

Windows 8 allows this tool to filter both inbound and outbound traffic or set rules and exceptions, depending on the type of network to which you're connected. If you aren't using a third-party security suite that includes a firewall, it is highly recommended that you use Windows Firewall because it provides a good level of security.

Windows Firewall has a predefined set of rules that is applied as soon as it is turned on. By default, it allows you to do many things: browse the Internet; use instant messaging applications; connect to a homegroup; share files, folders, and devices with other computers; and so on. The rules are applied differently depending on the network profile set for your active network connection.

TIP For more information about network profiles, see the "Changing the Network Profile of a Network" section in Chapter 11, "Connecting to a Network and the Internet."

Most applications you install on your computer automatically add an exception to Windows Firewall so that they receive network and Internet access as soon as you launch them. However, if they don't add such an exception, Windows Firewall asks you to allow them access to the network. At this point, you receive a security alert similar to the following one, in which you are asked to select the network profiles to which you allow access for the application: private networks (such as home and work networks) or public networks (such as those in airports, coffee shops, and so on).

By default, Windows Firewall selects the box relevant to the network you are currently using. However, you can select either of the options or both, depending on what you want to do. When you've decided, click Allow Access, and the application is allowed to communicate on the selected type(s) of network. To block access, just click Cancel.

> **IMPORTANT** If you do not have administrator access, you can't set any exceptions, and the programs that do not comply with the standard set of rules are automatically blocked.

Windows Firewall is turned on by default in Windows 8, and it runs silently in the background as a service. It prompts you whenever you need to make a decision, and you don't need to open this application unless you want to see its status or configure it to better meet your needs.

To open Windows Firewall, type firewall at the Start screen and click or tap the Windows Firewall search result. As an alternative, you can open Control Panel and click System And Security to open the System and Security window, which has all tools and configuration options available for this category.

14

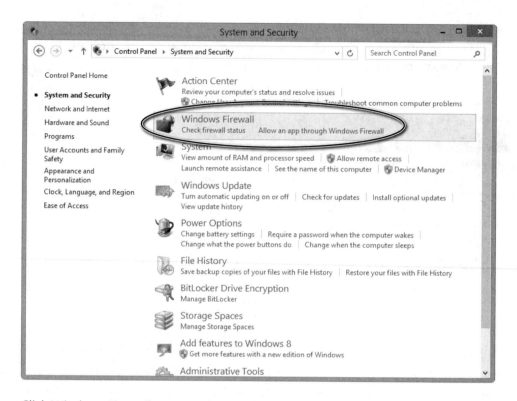

Click Windows Firewall to open the Windows Firewall application and its main window. In the center of the window, you can see information about the status of your network connections and how Windows Firewall is set for each type of connection.

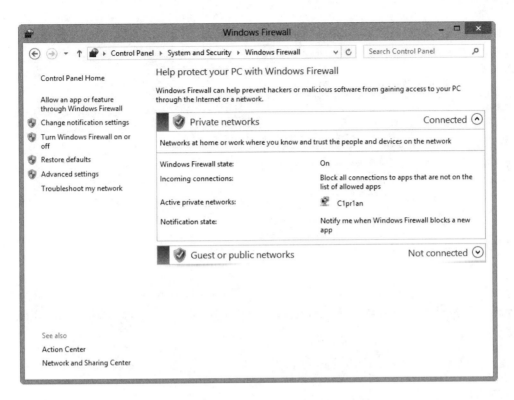

In the left column are links to different configuration options for Windows Firewall and other tools such as the Action Center.

Turning Windows Firewall Off or On

By default, Windows Firewall is turned on for both types of network profiles, private and public. You can turn it on or off for one or both the network locations from the Customize Settings window.

If you choose to install a third-party security application, such as a complete Internet security suite or another firewall, it is best to disable Windows Firewall so that it doesn't create conflicts and problems.

14

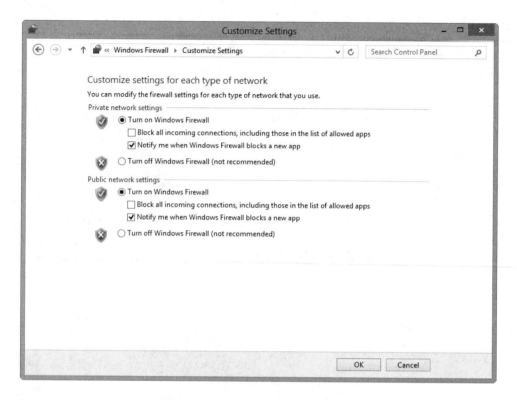

Beneath the Turn On Windows Firewall option, there are two other settings you can choose. The first is to block all incoming connections to your computer. Don't choose this unless you want your computer to be unavailable to anyone or any application. The second is to receive notifications when Windows Firewall blocks a new program. You should enable this; otherwise, you won't know why an application doesn't access the network or the Internet correctly.

In this exercise, you'll learn how to disable Windows Firewall.

 SET UP Log on with a user account that has administrator rights and open Windows Firewall.

1   Click or tap **Turn Windows Firewall on or off** in the left-side column.

    The Customize Settings window, which shows whether the application is turned on, opens.

2   Select **Turn off Windows Firewall (not recommended)** for both **Private network settings** and **Public network settings**.

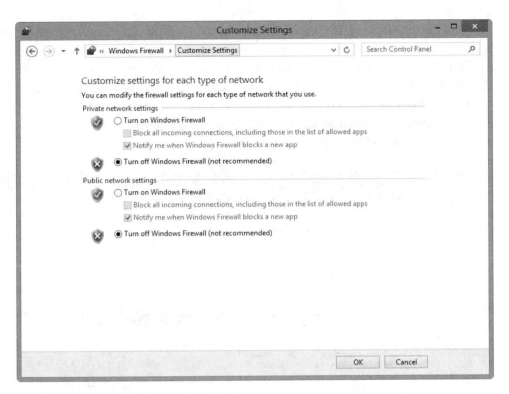

3   Click or tap **OK**.

You return to the Windows Firewall window.

CLEAN UP Close the Windows Firewall window.

> **IMPORTANT** You can only turn Windows Firewall on or off if you are logged on as an administrator. This setting will apply to all users defined on your computer. Also, if you disable Windows Firewall, make sure your user account and others have proper security alternatives installed.

To turn Windows Firewall on, perform the same steps. The only difference is that at step 2, you select Turn On Windows Firewall for both Private Network Settings and Public Network Settings.

14

Customizing the List of Allowed Programs

The Allowed Apps window contains all the programs that are allowed to go through Windows Firewall. By default, the list is editable; however, it can be dimmed and not editable. If that's the case, click or tap the Change Settings button to edit the list of allowed apps. The button will then be dimmed, and the list of allowed apps, programs, and features will become editable.

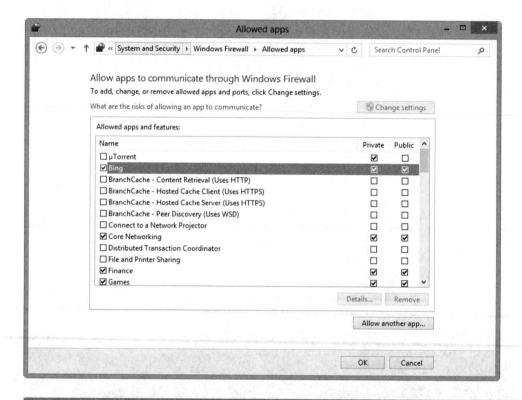

IMPORTANT Some apps have check marks before their names, indicating that the rules defined for those apps are active and used by Windows Firewall. The apps with no check marks before their names don't have any active rules used by Windows Firewall. There are also check marks in the Private and Public columns. If a check mark exists in any of these columns, it means that the rule defined for that app is applied to the network profile that is selected. Some apps have rules for one network profile, whereas others have rules for both. The rules are active only for the network profiles that are selected.

Windows Firewall allows you to edit its communication rules so that you can permit or deny network access for certain applications or services. In this exercise, you'll learn how to customize the list of allowed apps.

SET UP Log on with a user account that has administrator rights and open Windows Firewall.

1   Click or tap the **Allow an app or feature through Windows Firewall**.

    The Allowed Apps window opens.

2   Find the program with permissions you want changed and select it.

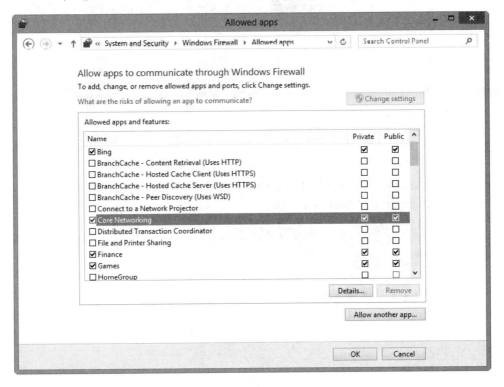

3   Click or tap **Details**.

    A window with its properties opens.

14

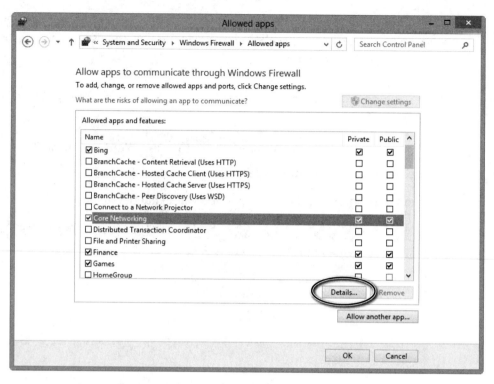

4   Read the information to confirm that this is the program with permissions you want changed and click or tap **OK**.

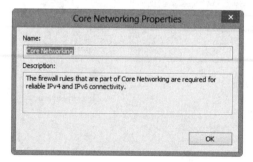

5   Clear the Private and Public check boxes for the program to block its access to both network profiles.

6   Click or tap **OK**.

⊗ CLEAN UP Close the Windows Firewall window.

The changes you made for the selected program are now applied.

Adding New Apps to the Allowed List

You can easily add new apps to the list of apps allowed through Windows Firewall. In this exercise, you'll learn how to add new apps to the allowed list.

➡ SET UP Log on as administrator and open Windows Firewall. In the Allowed Apps window, make the list of allowed apps, programs, and features editable by clicking or tapping the Change Settings button if necessary.

1   Click or tap **Allow another app**.

The Add An App window opens.

2   Select the app you want to add and click or tap Network types.

The Choose Network Types window opens.

> **IMPORTANT** If you don't find the app you want to add in the Add An App list, click Browse and browse to its location. Select it and then continue with the instructions in this exercise.

3   Select the network locations through which you want to allow the app to communicate and click or tap **OK**.

14

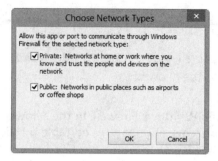

4   Click or tap **Add**.

You return to the Allowed Apps window, in which you can see the newly added app on the list.

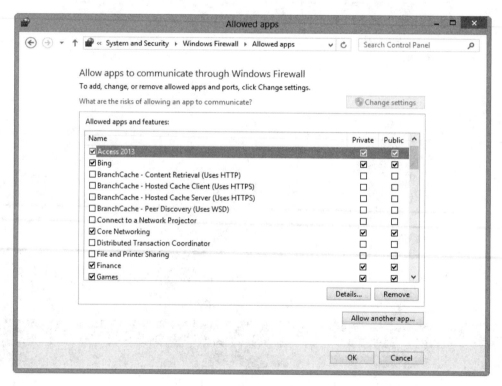

5   Click or tap **OK**.

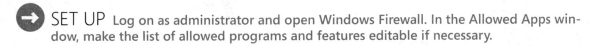

CLEAN UP Repeat this procedure for all the apps you want to add and then close the Windows Firewall window.

The change is now applied to the list of active rules Windows Firewall uses.

Removing Apps from the Allowed List

Removing apps from the list of allowed apps through Windows Firewall or disabling access to certain types of networks is easy. Both tasks are done from the Allowed Apps window. If you want to disable a rule allowing access to a certain app or feature, simply clear the box on the left side of its name. Windows Firewall will no longer use it.

If you only want to disable network and Internet access for an app when connected to a certain type of network profile, clear the box in the column of that network profile. For example, if you want to prevent an app from receiving network and Internet access when you are connected to a public network, clear the box in the Public column. If the Private column is selected for that app, it will only have access to private networks.

When removing entries from the allowed list, keep in mind that you can remove only apps and entries that were not included with Windows 8. For example, you cannot remove an entry about Windows Media Player because it is part of Windows 8, although you can remove an entry about a third-party app you installed, such as Steam or uTorrent. The entries that are included in the default configuration of Windows Firewall can only be disabled, not removed.

In this exercise, you'll learn how to remove an app from the allowed list.

SET UP Log on as administrator and open Windows Firewall. In the Allowed Apps window, make the list of allowed programs and features editable if necessary.

1   Select the app or feature you want to remove.

14

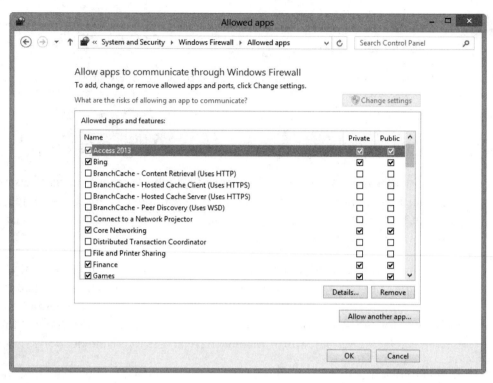

2   To remove it from the list, click or tap **Remove**.

You are asked to confirm the removal.

3   Click or tap **Yes**.

You return to the Allowed Apps window.

4   Click or tap **OK**.

⊗ CLEAN UP Close the Windows Firewall window.

The change is now applied to the list of active rules Windows Firewall uses.

Restoring the Windows Firewall Default Settings

If you have used this tool for a long time and you have made many changes to its settings, chances are some things might stop working. In such cases, it is best to reset all rules to the default settings and values created by Microsoft. Then you can start from the beginning, defining the rules that apply to your apps so that everything works as it should.

In this exercise, you'll learn how to restore the default settings of Windows Firewall.

 **SET UP** Log on with a user account that has administrator rights and open Windows Firewall.

1   Click or tap **Restore defaults**.

The Restore Defaults window opens.

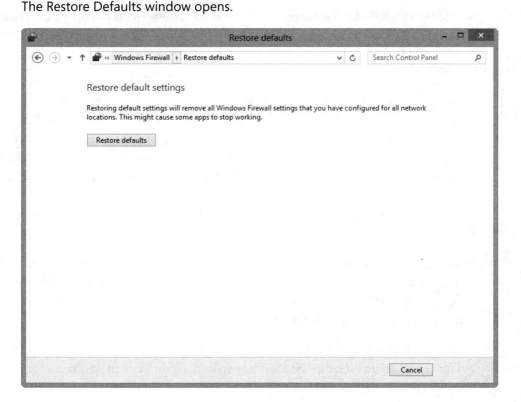

14

2   Read the information shown and click or tap **Restore defaults**.

You are asked to confirm your choice.

3   Click or tap **Yes**.

You are returned to the Windows Firewall window.

✖ CLEAN UP Close the Windows Firewall window.

All the Windows Firewall settings you created are deleted. Everything is now reset to the initial settings and values existing when Windows 8 was installed on your computer.

Using Windows Defender

Windows Defender was originally a tool that provided protection only against spyware threats. Then Microsoft launched Microsoft Security Essentials, a product that added anti-virus protection to the Windows Defender protection. It quickly became one of the most popular free anti-malware products among Windows users. With Windows 8, Microsoft has decided to include the features initially released in Microsoft Security Essentials in the earlier Windows Defender product.

In Windows 8, Windows Defender provides basic anti-malware protection that will keep you safe from viruses, spyware, and other types of malware. It doesn't compare in number of features and efficiency with most commercial security solutions, but it is one of the best free security solutions you can find for Windows 8.

Windows Defender is enabled by default in Windows 8, and it can be launched by searching for the word *defender* in the Start screen and clicking or tapping the appropriate search result.

Its interface is simple and easy to use. At the top of the Windows Defender window, four tabs are available.

■ **HOME** This tab shows an overview of Windows Defender: whether any threats and problems were detected, whether the real-time protection is turned on, and whether the virus and spyware definitions are up to date. On the right side, you can start a manual scan for malware; on the bottom, you can view when the last scan was made.

Green means no problems were detected.
Red means problems were found, while orange means there are warnings to consider.

Options for starting a manual scan.

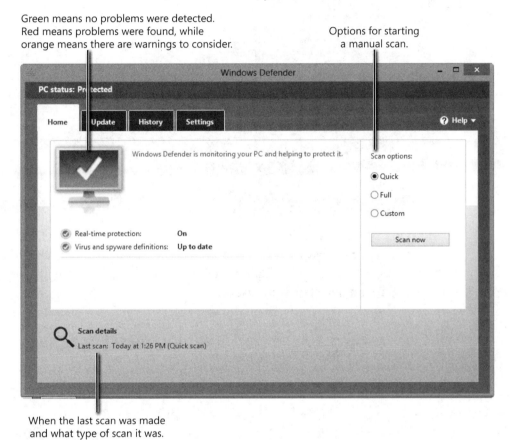

When the last scan was made and what type of scan it was.

■ **UPDATE** This tab displays details about the latest update of definitions Windows Defender made. You can also manually start an update if the definitions are more than a day or two old.

14

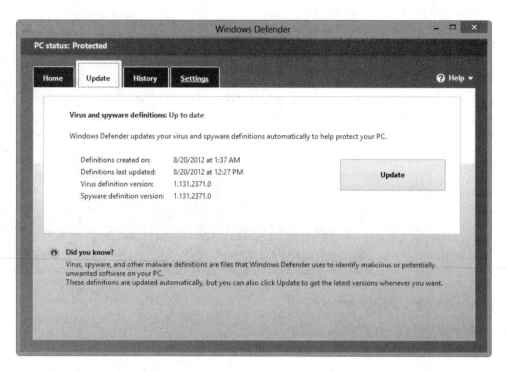

■ **HISTORY** This tab is for viewing details about the threats Windows Defender has detected. You can view the items that were quarantined, the items that you allowed to run despite the recommendations received from Windows Defender, and all the items that were detected as malicious.

- **SETTINGS** On this tab, you can customize how Windows Defender runs. You can enable or disable its real-time protection engine; exclude files, locations, or processes from being scanned; tweak more advanced settings; choose whether you want to join the Microsoft Active Protection Service; or completely disable Windows Defender.

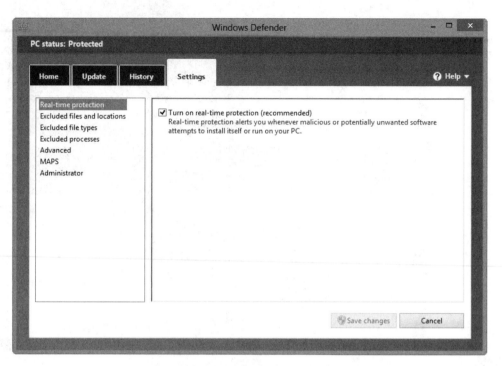

Windows Defender automatically scans all the files and folders through which you browse. If a threat is identified, it is immediately quarantined and you are informed that action was taken.

Removing Quarantined Files

Each time you see a warning similar to the following one, Windows Defender cleaned some threats it detected.

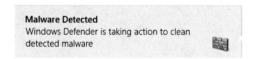

Detected threats are automatically isolated and placed into quarantine. You can only access the items that were quarantined from Windows Defender and decide whether you want to remove them completely from your system or keep them and set Windows Defender to allow them. However, to remove them or keep them you need to have administrator permissions.

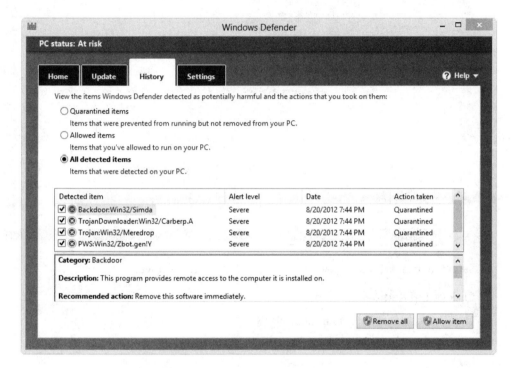

In this exercise, you'll learn how to access the items that were detected as malicious by Windows Defender and remove them from your computer.

 SET UP Log on with a user account that has administrator rights and open Windows Defender.

1   Open the **History** tab.

2   Choose the **All detected items** button.

3   Click **View details** to view all the items that were detected as malware.

14

4   Select all the detected malware items you want to remove.

5   Click or tap **Remove all**.

The list of selected items is cleaned.

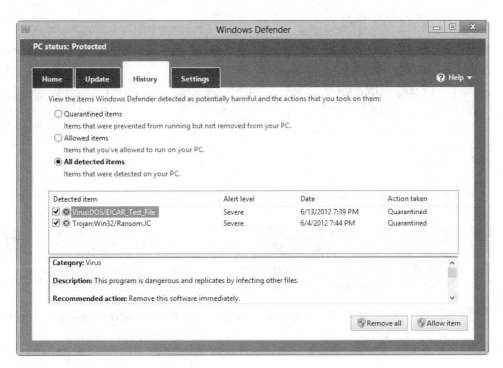

CLEAN UP Close Windows Defender.

The items that were detected as threats have now been completely removed from your computer.

14

Don't Ignore the Warnings and Recommendations from SmartScreen Filter

In Chapter 5, "Using Internet Explorer 10," the section "Understanding SmartScreen Filter in Internet Explorer" covers in detail how the SmartScreen feature included in Internet Explorer and Windows 8 can help prevent security problems with your computer or device.

This chapter reinforces that recommendation to consider the warning messages from SmartScreen Filter.

In Windows 8, File Explorer also uses this feature to scan the files you are running. If you see a warning similar to the following one when trying to launch a file, make sure to scan that file with Windows Defender or any other security product you have installed prior to launching it.

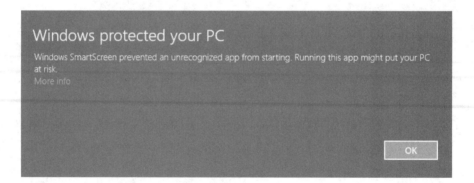

Following this recommendation will help keep your Windows 8 system safe and secure.

Improving Your Password Habits

No matter how good the security products you are using are, you are still vulnerable to many security problems if your habits related to password use are poor. Many people tend to use the same one-two-three passwords everywhere. This is a sure recipe for security problems, including security problems with your Microsoft account (Windows Live ID), your Facebook and Google accounts, and any other accounts. If you use the same password everywhere, a malicious user might break into a forum or social website you are using and steal your password from there. That user can then use the same password and the email address with which you registered to access more of your personal data and information from your Inbox, accounts on social networks, and so on.

To make sure it is much more difficult for unwanted parties to access your Windows 8–based computer, your Microsoft account, your email inbox, and any online services you are using, consider the following recommendations regarding password use.

- Do not use passwords with fewer than six characters. They are especially easy to break.

- Ideally, your passwords should be at least eight characters long and include letters, numbers, and special characters such as +, #, $, and so on.

- Do not use the same password twice or more.

- Having different passwords for different accounts can be difficult to manage, so using password management solutions such as LastPass, KeePass, or Roboform is also recommended. You can find them easily with a search on Bing. These solutions help you identify your duplicate passwords, change them to new random passwords, generate secure passwords automatically, and store them safely so that you can use them whenever needed and not lose them again.

Reasons to Consider Commercial Security Solutions

Windows Defender together with Windows Firewall and Internet Explorer can provide a good level of security. If you are not willing or able to invest in security software, they are the best free security tools available for Windows 8, and you won't need to install other free products.

14

However, if you want the maximum level of security possible and premium features such as anti-spam ad blockers for your Internet browser, remote location of your computers and devices if they are stolen, the possibility to command a remote wipe of your data (if your computers and devices are stolen), and more advanced malware detection algorithms and other features, it is best to consider purchasing and installing security products provided by specialized vendors. The best way to be fully protected is to use a complete security package, generally called an Internet Security Suite. These packages include antivirus, anti-spyware, and firewall protection plus other security modules such as the ones previously mentioned.

Before making a choice, it is best to understand which options are available. To make an informed decision, it is recommend that you check the following Internet sources.

- **ANTIMALWARE APPS FOR WINDOWS 8** (*http://www.microsoft.com/en-us/windows/compatibility/en-US/CompatCenter/Home*) This Microsoft page lists all the security software providers that offer solutions compatible with Windows 8.

- **SECURITY FOR EVERYONE AT 7 TUTORIALS** (*http://www.7tutorials.com/security-everyone*) The 7 Tutorials website provides a series of reviews for Internet security suites. The team from the website regularly tests the latest offerings from both a security and a usability perspective. The aim of the team is to highlight solutions that provide the best mix of effective security and user friendliness.

- **AV COMPARATIVES** (*http://av-comparatives.org*) This is the website of an independent security organization that regularly tests the quality of security provided by antivirus products. Its tests are very professional and evaluate all the important security aspects for an antivirus solution. If you want to know which security company has the best detection engine for viruses, this website is the place to visit.

- **AV TEST** (*http://www.av-test.org*) This website is run by the AV-Test GmbH company, which offers security testing and consulting services. It runs regular reviews of the latest security products on the market and publishes the results of its evaluations. Just like AV Comparatives, this website is a great destination for learning how effective the latest security offerings are.

Key Points

- Never turn off User Account Control (UAC); it's a key feature that contributes to a good level of security on your system.

- Windows Firewall filters both inbound and outbound traffic depending on the type of network to which you are connected. It is an important tool in securing your network and Internet traffic.

- Windows Defender now includes both antivirus and anti-spyware protection.

- Improving your password habits is a key component of a secure computing experience.

14

Chapter at a Glance

Check

Check for Windows updates, page 427

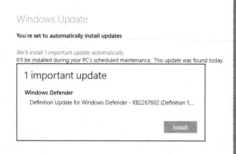

Learn

Learn File History and how to use it, page 432

Restore

Restore your system to a previous state with System Restore, page 446

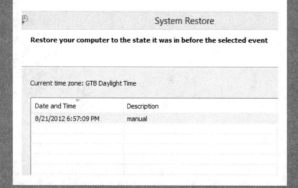

Use

Use the Action Center to prevent problems, page 450

Review recent messages and resolve problems
Action Center has detected one or more issues for you to review.

Security

Spyware and unwanted software protection (Important)
Windows Defender is turned off.
Turn off messages about spyware and unwanted software protection
Find an app onlin

Virus protection (Important)
Windows Defender is turned off.
Turn off messages about virus protection
Find an app onlir

Preventing Problems

15

IN THIS CHAPTER, YOU WILL LEARN HOW TO

- Keep your system up to date.

- Check for Windows updates and install them.

- Turn on File History.

- Restore files with File History.

- Use System Restore to revert Windows 8 to a previous state.

- Use the Action Center to prevent problems.

Prevention is an important part of having a safe and pleasant computing experience. Windows 8 offers a few tools to help you stay away from trouble for as long as possible and, if you do have trouble, restore your lost user files.

The first and most important tool for preventing problems is Windows Update. In this chapter, you'll learn about its role in keeping your computer running smoothly, how it works, and how to use it to keep your system up to date. You'll learn how to use the new File History feature in Windows 8 to make automated backups of your user folders, libraries, and files and to restore files from those backups. In addition, you'll learn about System Restore and how to use it to revert to an earlier and more stable state if you encounter problems and how to use the Action Center to stay informed about the maintenance and security of your system so you can spot problems before they have a major impact on your system.

PRACTICE FILES You don't need any practice files to complete the exercises in this chapter. For more information about practice file requirements, see "Using the Practice Files" at the beginning of this book.

Keeping Your System Up to Date with Windows Update

Keeping your system up to date is important for keeping it as secure and trouble-free as possible. Viruses and other forms of malware that exploit security problems in Windows and other operating systems appear on a daily basis. Being up to date means having fewer security issues and fewer chances for your computer to become infected and exploited by unauthorized parties.

Windows Update also includes stability and compatibility fixes that solve problems you might encounter with your system; other updates can add functionality. One good example is service packs, which help maintain your security, add new features to Windows, and keep your performance levels up to date. Another important type of update is drivers for your computer's components. Windows Update automatically installs the newest versions of signed drivers for your system's components, which keep your system's performance at good levels.

All these are good reasons for you to have Windows Update turned on at all times and configured to install the most important updates automatically. It is enabled by default in Windows 8, and it should be active and working on your system. The only exceptions are business computers and devices on which the updates and the update policy are handled by the IT support staff.

You can find Windows Update in both PC Settings and Control Panel. In PC Settings, you have a simplified version of the tool that shows information about available updates and enables you to check for new updates manually and install those that are available.

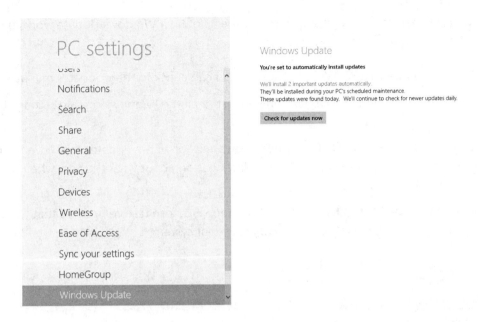

In Control Panel, open System And Security and then Windows Update.

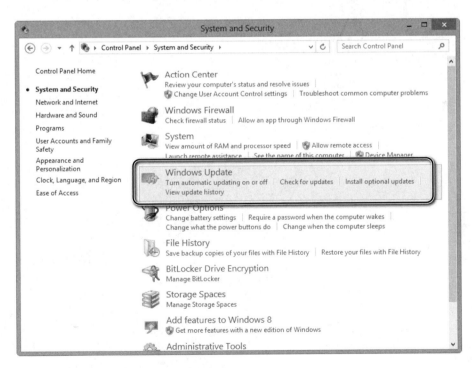

From Control Panel, you can customize many aspects of how Windows Update works by using the options found in the left-side column.

- **CHECK FOR UPDATES** With this option, you can check for new updates manually.

- **CHANGE SETTINGS** This option opens a list of all the Windows Update settings that can be customized.

- **VIEW UPDATE HISTORY** This option shows a list of all the updates that have been installed on your system with complete information about what they do, when they were installed, and so on.

- **RESTORE HIDDEN UPDATES** With this option, you can restore updates that have been hidden and marked as unavailable for your system.

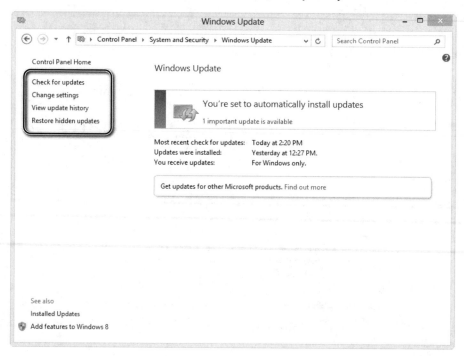

Checking for and Installing Available Updates

Windows handles the installation of updates automatically. However, you can check for updates manually and install them at any time. PC Settings only shows you the important updates that are available, and you can install them at one time.

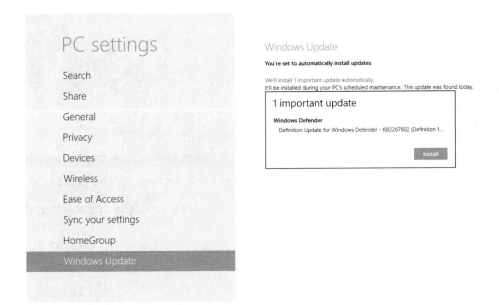

However, you cannot select individual updates to be installed. This can be done only from the Control Panel. There, you can clear the updates you don't want installed. From the Control Panel you can also install optional updates that are available for Windows 8. These updates are not shown in PC Settings.

In this exercise, you'll learn how to check for updates manually and install the available updates from PC Settings.

→ SET UP Make sure you have a working Internet connection. Open PC Settings.

1 Click or tap **Windows Update.**

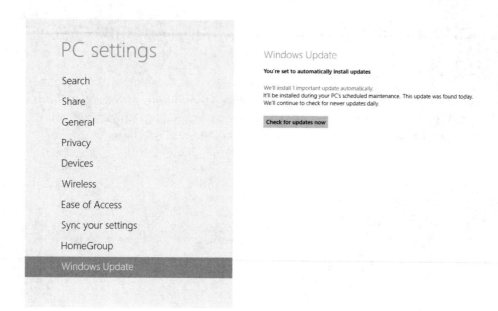

2   Click or tap **Check for updates now** and wait a few seconds for the process to finish.

3   Click or tap the line summarizing the results to view a list of the updates found.

4   Click or tap **Install.**

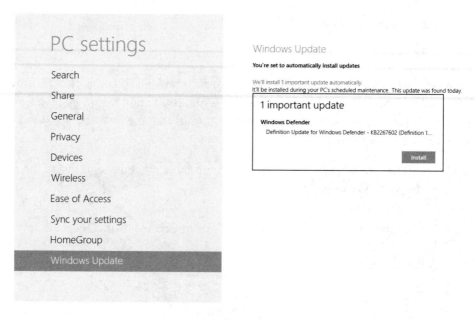

CLEAN UP Close PC Settings at any time, even if the updates are still being downloaded and installed.

The download and installation process for all the available updates is handled in the background by Windows Update. Its window does not need to remain open. You can continue your normal computing activities while the updates are installed.

Using File History in Windows 8

File History is a new feature introduced in Windows 8 that allows users to back up the files in their libraries, contacts, favorites, and desktop. The backup is handled automatically by Windows 8 after this feature is turned on and the backup location is available.

File History backs up only your users' libraries and the folders specified in the preceding paragraph. If you want to have file copies made for other folders, you must include them in one of your user libraries.

TIP To learn more about libraries and how to create a library and add folders to it, see Chapter 4, "Saving, Browsing, and Organizing Files and Folders."

File History also stores the versions you create for any file, depending on how you set it, so you can revert to a previous version of a file if you need to.

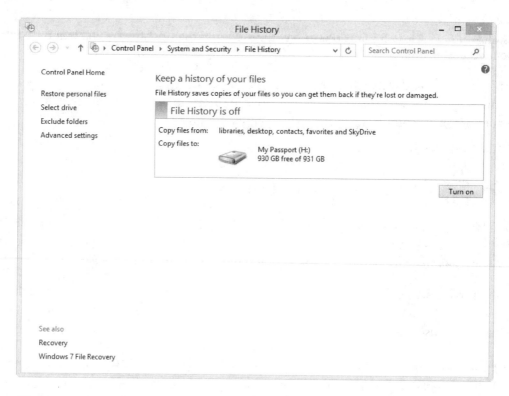

File History works best with external drives such as hard disk drives or large USB memory sticks that have sufficient space for the file copies. You can also make copies on network locations such as folders from another computer or a home server if you have one available.

File copies can be restored at any time on the same computer or on other Windows devices and computers. This can be useful if your system crashes or encounters problems with data corruption. By using File History, you can make sure that your important data is always backed up and available.

The file copies are made on the target drive (or network location) by using the following folder structure: File History>Your User Account Name>Your Computer Name. There you will find two folders.

- **CONFIGURATION** Files with File History settings
- **DATA** The file copies

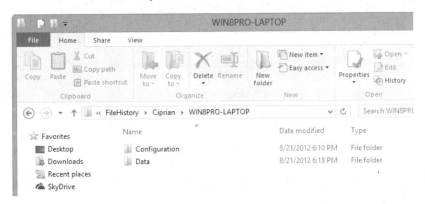

The File History window is organized simply.

- On the left is a column that gives you access to different configuration options.
- In the center you can view its status: on or off.
- In the center you can also see where file copies are stored.
- Beneath that you can view when the last file copies were made.
- On the right is a button for turning File History on and off.

Access to different
configuration options

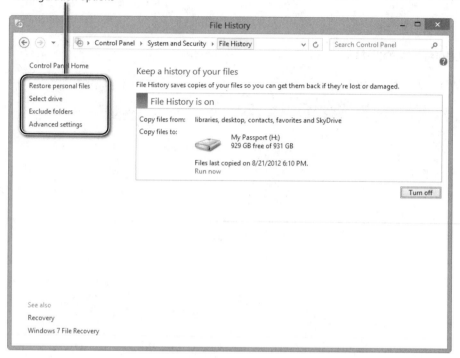

The column on the left side of the File History window has the following links.

- **RESTORE PERSONAL FILES** Starts the wizard for restoring files using the existing copies. This will be covered in a step-by-step exercise later in this chapter.

- **SELECT DRIVE** Enables you to change the drive on which file copies are made. You can also add a network location if that suits your needs better.

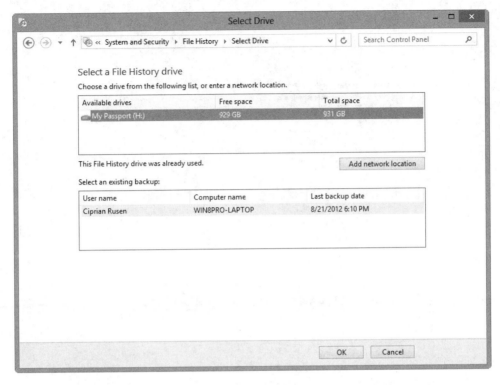

- **EXCLUDE FOLDERS** Enables you to exclude specific folders and libraries from backup by File History.

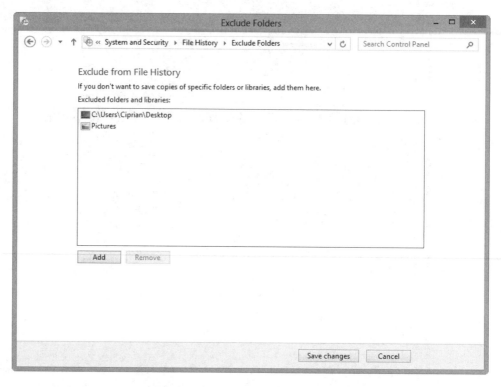

- Advanced Settings Enables you to change the following settings.

    - **SAVE COPIES OF FILES** Sets how often file copies are made. The default is to save copies of files every hour. The interval can be changed to almost anything from every 10 minutes to daily.

    - **SIZE OF OFFLINE CACHE** Sets the percentage of disk space file copies can occupy on the target drive. The default is 5 percent of disk space. It can be changed to values ranging from 2 percent to 20 percent of disk space.

    - **KEEP SAVED VERSIONS** Sets how long you want to keep the different versions of files. The default is to keep file versions forever. It can be set to keep versions until space is needed on the target drive or for a set time ranging from one month to two years.

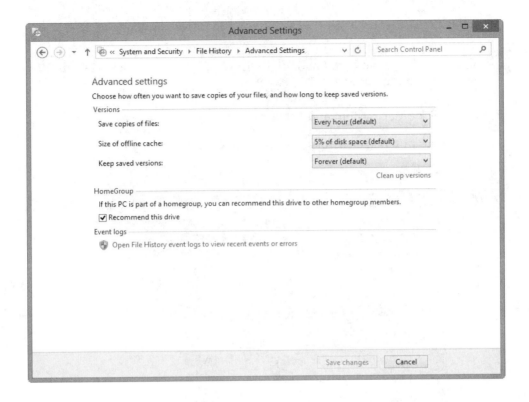

Turning On File History

After File History is turned on, it automatically starts creating copies of your files based on its default schedule settings. When files are copied for the first time, you are informed in a line of text just above the Turn Off button. If copies were created, you are shown the date and time when they were last copied.

One important aspect to keep in mind is that File History is turned on only for your own user account. If you want the files in other user accounts on the same Windows 8–based computer or device to be backed up, turn on File History for each account.

In this exercise, you'll learn how to turn on File History in Windows 8.

SET UP Plug in an external hard disk or a USB memory stick. Wait for Windows 8 to detect it and then open Control Panel.

1   Click or tap **System and Security.**

2   Click or tap **File History** to open the File History window.

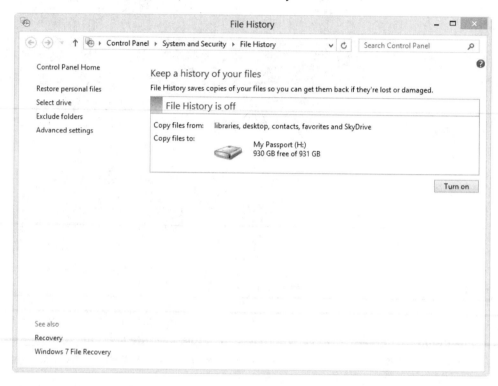

3   Click or tap **Turn on**.

File History asks whether you want to recommend this drive to other members of your homegroup.

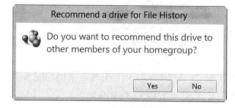

4   Click or tap **Yes.**

CLEAN UP Close the File History window and leave the external drive plugged into your computer or device until the file copies are created.

15

File History is now turned on and will automatically save copies of your files according to its default settings and when the external drive is available for making the copies. In addition, Windows 8 will make the drive visible to other computers and devices on the homegroup so that they can use it to back up their files, folders, and libraries with File History.

You can turn off File History by using the steps in the preceding exercise and clicking Turn Off instead of Turn On.

Restoring Files with File History

Restoring files with File History is an easy process and can be done at any time. You can restore complete folders and libraries as well as individual files. If you want to restore a library, you select it. If you want to restore only one file, browse to its location and select it.

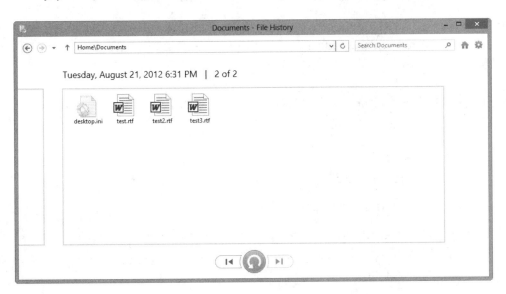

To select more than one item, press and hold the CTRL key on your keyboard while selecting each item with the mouse.

You can restore files to the location on your computer from which files were initially copied or to a different location. If you want to restore a file to a different location, select it, click the Options button, and then click or tap Restore To.

Options button

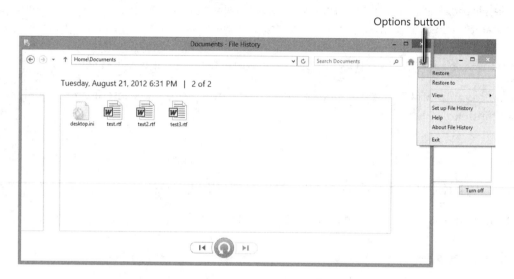

In this exercise, you'll learn how to restore folders and libraries previously backed up with File History. Restore individual files by using the same steps but selecting files instead of folders or libraries.

SET UP Plug in the drive on which your file history is stored. Wait for Windows 8 to detect it and then open File History.

1   Click or tap **Restore personal files.**

    The File History Wizard opens.

2   Select the libraries and folders you want restored.

3   Click or tap the **Restore** button to start the restoration procedure.

    You are asked to confirm that you want to replace the existing files with the ones from your backup.

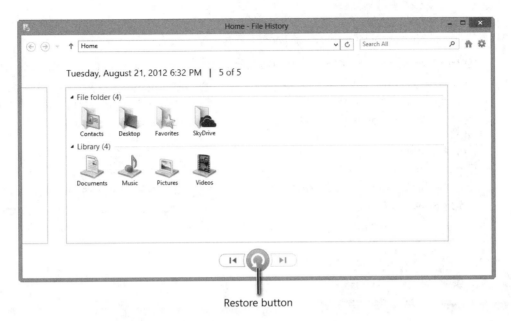

Restore button

4   Click or tap **Replace the files in the destination** and wait for the files to be copied.

After the copying process completes, a File Explorer window opens, showing the files, folders, and libraries you copied.

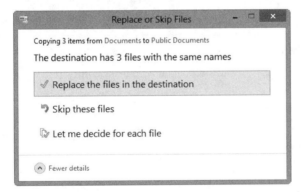

CLEAN UP Close File Explorer and the File History window.

The selected folders and libraries are now restored to their original location.

Using System Restore

System Restore is an old and useful Windows application that can restore your system and settings to a previous state. It can be used when you encounter problems and you need to revert quickly to a previously working state without removing all your installed applications, as is the case when using the Refresh feature introduced in Windows 8.

This feature is turned on by default in Windows 8 for the partition in which the operating system is installed. It automatically creates a new restore point each time you install a new application or make important changes to your system such as installing a long list of updates and drivers. These restore points can then be used to restore your system to an earlier but stable state if you hit some stability or performance issues later.

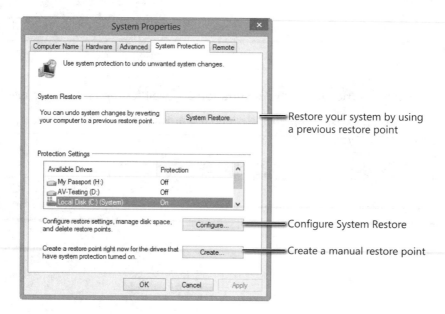

System Restore has one tab, System Protection, in the System Properties window. The tool is straightforward and easy to use.

- Use the System Restore button to start the wizard for restoring your system by using a previous restore point.

- The Protection Settings section contains a list of all the partitions available on your computer or device. You can see whether the System Restore protection is turned on or off in each partition.

- When you select a partition, you can change its protection settings by using the Configure button.

- Use the Create button when you want to create a manual system restore point.

Having System Restore turned on is a good prevention practice. If you encounter issues, the first and easiest step is to use this tool to restore your system to a previous and more stable state.

Launching System Restore

In Windows 8, the System Restore tool is hidden behind menus and options, so it is not easy to find. In this exercise, you'll learn how to launch System Restore.

SET UP Open the Control Panel.

1   Click or tap **System and Security**.

2   Click or tap **System**.

    The System window, which contains information about your system's hardware and software configuration, opens.

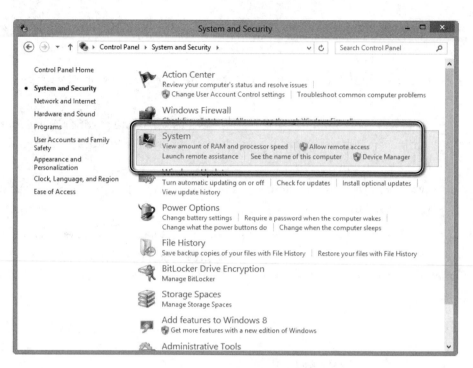

3   Click or tap **System protection** in the left column.

The System Properties window, which contains System Restore, opens.

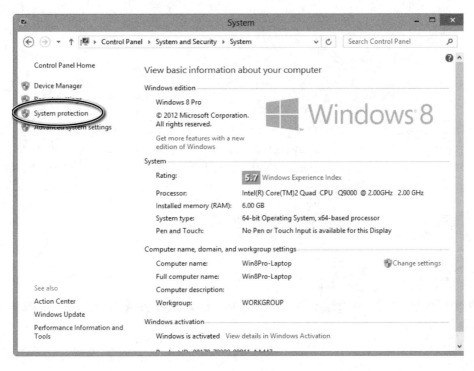

CLEAN UP When done working with System Restore, close the System Properties window.

The System Properties window is opened directly at the System Protection tab, where you can find System Restore.

Restoring to a Previous State with System Restore

If you have installed some new drivers that make your system unstable or you have some performance issues, you can use System Restore to revert to an earlier and hopefully more stable state.

Before starting the restoration process, you can click or tap Scan For Affected Programs.

This opens a new window in which you are shown a summary of the changes that will be made to your system when the restoration process is complete. If you don't like the number of changes that will be executed, you can select a more recent restore point (if available) that makes fewer changes.

After the restore process is started, it cannot be interrupted. It also involves a restart, so before you go ahead with the process it is best to close any applications and current work.

In this exercise, you'll learn how to use System Restore to restore Windows 8 to a previous state.

→ SET UP Open System Restore.

1   Click or tap **System Restore**.

The System Restore Wizard is opened.

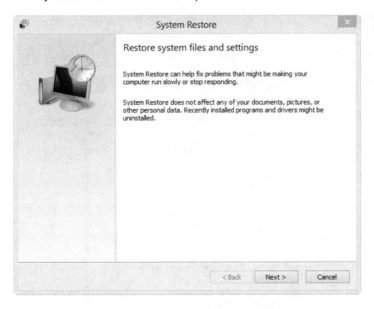

2   Click or tap **Next**.

You are asked to select the restore point to which you want to restore.

3   Select the restore point you want to use and click or tap **Next**.

You are informed of the changes that will be made.

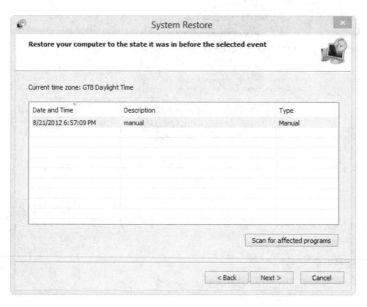

4   Click or tap **Finish**.

You are asked to confirm that you want to continue the process.

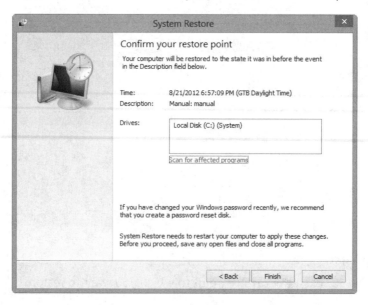

5   Click or tap **Yes** and wait for Windows 8 to restart and revert to the selected restore point.

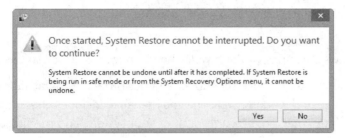

CLEAN UP Log on to Windows 8 and resume your computing activities.

Windows 8 is now restored to the selected restore point. Any changes made to your system since that point are not available. Also, any applications that were installed after the restore point was created are no longer available.

Using the Action Center

Windows 8 comes with a convenient way to help you review the state of your system and find solutions to security and maintenance issues. The feature that facilitates this is called Action Center, and it is built upon the foundation set by the Windows Security Center, which was first introduced in Windows XP Service Pack 2 and then improved in Windows Vista and Windows 7.

Action Center continuously monitors the state of your system. If it notices any kind of problem related to the security or good maintenance of your system, it immediately notifies you so that you can take corrective action. Action Center monitors the following aspects of Windows 8.

- Whether Windows Update is turned on and working well.

- Whether all Internet Security settings are set to their recommended levels.

- Whether the network firewall is actively protecting your computer or device.

- Whether your Microsoft account is working properly.

- Whether you have an active tool providing spyware and related protection.

- Whether User Account Control (UAC) is turned on.

- Whether virus protection exists and is working well.

- Whether the SmartScreen technology used in Internet Explorer and File Explorer is turned on.

- Whether Windows Backup is working well when Windows 8 users use this feature.

- Whether automatic maintenance scheduled and performed automatically by Windows 8 is active and working well. This maintenance includes checking for the latest software updates, making a security scan of your system, and running some quick system diagnostics to search for new problems.

- Whether all your drives are working well.

- Whether you need additional drivers and software installed for some of your computer's hardware devices.

- Whether there are any ongoing problems that can be fixed by using Windows troubleshooting tools.

- Whether a homegroup is available.

- Whether File History is turned on and working well.

- Whether Storage Space is working well when Windows 8 users use this more advanced feature.

When a problem is detected, the user is notified and guided in what he or she could do to fix it. As you can see, Action Center is an important tool for preventing problems with your system.

On the Desktop, in the notification area of the Windows 8 taskbar, there's always a little white flag icon. This is the icon of Action Center. When there are messages for the user, it is overlaid by other icons: a red x or a black clock. The red x overlay means there is at least one important message, so you need to pay attention. The black clock overlay means a scheduled task is running in the background (for example, a scheduled Windows Defender scan).

Hover over the flag icon to see a tooltip, giving you some brief information about what is happening with your system.

Solve PC issues: 3 important messages
4 total messages

US   8/21/2012

To see the list of messages you should read, click or tap the Action Center icon (the white flag).

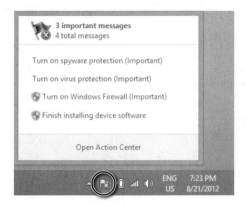

To open Action Center and view more details, click or tap Open Action Center.

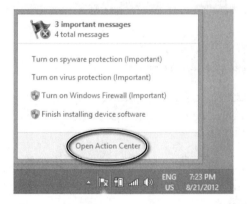

As an alternative, you can search for the words *action center* in the Start screen and click or tap the appropriate search result.

Reviewing the list of messages displayed by Action Center is simple. No complicated jargon is involved, and you just see what the tool recommends to keep your computer in top shape. Each message has a button that takes you directly to where you need to fix things. For example, in the following screenshot, Action Center says Turn On Windows Firewall. A click or tap of the Turn On Now button, visible for this warning, quickly turns on this security feature of Windows 8.

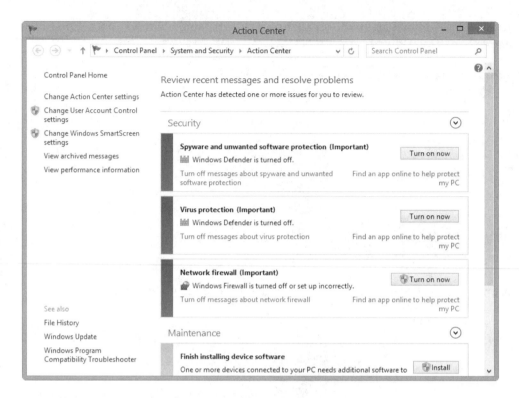

The same thing happens with the recommendation to install software for your devices. Clicking or tapping Install automatically starts the download and installation process for that missing software.

TIP All messages that Action Center displays have the following color coding: Red means a very important message that you should not ignore; yellow means a recommendation that can be ignored if you do not consider it important.

Configuring the Messages Action Center Shows

Another great thing about Action Center is that it is very configurable. You can easily customize which types of alerts and messages you want to receive, depending on how you have configured your Windows 8 installation and the additional software you have installed.

In this exercise, you'll learn how to configure the list of messages Action Center shows you.

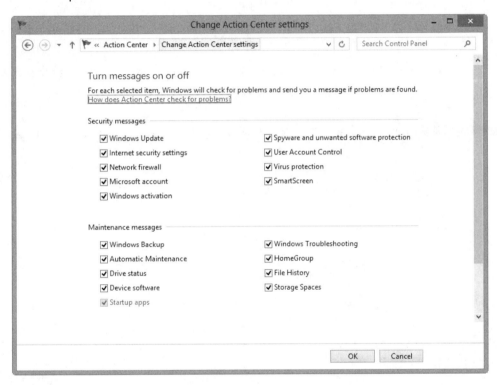

SET UP Open Action Center.

1　Click or tap **Change Action Center settings** on the upper-left side of the Action Center window.

2　Select the boxes for the messages you want to receive.

3　Clear the boxes for the messages you do not want to receive.

4　Click or tap **OK**.

CLEAN UP Close Action Center.

Action Center will now show only messages for the items you allow it to check on a continuous basis.

IMPORTANT It's strongly recommended not to disable the messages from the Security category. If there are security issues with your computer, you would miss important alerts that could help you fix them.

Key Points

- Windows Update is a key feature for preventing problems and for securing your system.

- File History can be set to back up your important user folders, libraries, and files automatically.

- You can restore files with File History to the location where they were originally stored or to a new, custom location.

- You can use System Restore when you have stability or performance problems to revert to an earlier and more stable system state.

- Action Center keeps you informed of the status of your system's security and regular maintenance tasks.

Chapter at a Glance

Enable

Enable Family Safety, page 461

e

or

Set up how Child will use the PC

Family Safety:
- ○ On, enforce current settings
- ○ Off

Activity reporting:
- ◉ On, collect information about PC usage
- ○ Off

Windows settings:

Web filtering
Control the websites Child can access online

Time limits
Control when Child uses the PC

Set

Set time limits and application restrictions, page 460

- ○ Child can use the PC all day
- ◉ Child can only use the PC during the time ranges I allow

Set times when Child can't use PC at all

	Midnight (AM) 12 1 2 3 4 5 6 7 8 9 10 11	Noon (PM) 12 1 2 3 4
Sunday		
Monday		
Tuesday		
Wednesday		
Thursday		
Friday		
Saturday		

☐ Allowed
☐ Blocked

Define

Define restrictions for games and apps, page 471

Rating Level

Allow or Block Games

Allow or block games and Windows Store a[

Set game and Windows Store ratings

Maximum allowed rating: EVERYONE 10

Allow or block any game on your PC by nan

Allow or block specific games

Always blocked: No

Always allowed: None

Create

Create restrictions for websites and downloads, page 475

Control Panel Home

Allow or block specific websites f

| User Settings |
| Web Filtering |
| Web Restrictions |
| **Allow or Block Websites** |

Enter a website to allow or block.

Allowed websites:

http://en.wikipedia.org/wiki/main_page

Supervising a Child's Computer Use

16

IN THIS CHAPTER, YOU WILL LEARN HOW TO

- Enable Family Safety.

- Set time limits and application restrictions.

- Define restrictions for games.

- Create restrictions for websites and downloads.

Children use computers and gadgets at a very young age for many purposes: to have fun, to learn, to communicate, to socialize, and so on. In today's world, such devices are an integral part of their life. That's why, as a parent, it is important to educate children about how to use these devices and how to stay safe, but also about the implications of using them for long periods of time.

Windows 8 has a great feature, Family Safety, that can help parents educate children and control their computing habits. This feature helps parents define when children can use the computer, what games they are allowed to play, which apps they are allowed to use, and what kinds of websites they can browse on the Internet.

In this chapter, you'll learn how to turn on Family Safety; how to define time limits; and how to apply restrictions for games, applications, websites, and downloads.

PRACTICE FILES You don't need any practice files to complete the exercises in this chapter. For more information about practice file requirements, see "Using the Practice Files" at the beginning of this book.

Turning on Family Safety

Before setting up Family Safety, you need to create a standard user account with no administrator permissions for your child. If your child's user account has administrator permissions, he or she will have all the required rights to override any controls you apply.

TIP To learn more about user accounts and how to set them up, see Chapter 12, "Allowing Others to Use the Computer."

After you have created a user account for your child, you can enable Family Safety and configure all the limitations that can be defined (allowed websites, time limits, game, and apps ratings). At the beginning, the setting for these limitations is Off, so even if Family Safety is enabled no limitations are defined for your child's user account. He or she is free to do anything on the computer, so configure the limitations you want applied one by one. You'll learn how to do this throughout the sections of this chapter.

In this exercise, you'll learn how to enable Family Safety.

 SET UP Open Control Panel.

1   Click or tap **User Accounts and Family Safety** to access all the settings related to administering user accounts.

2   Click or tap **Family Safety** to see a list of the user accounts for which Family Safety can be set up.

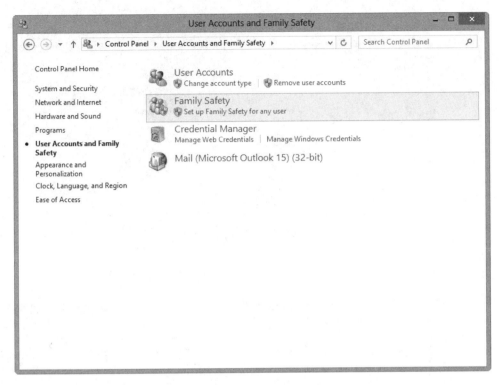

3   Select your child's user account (which, for the purposes of illustration in this exercise, is named **Child**) to open User Settings.

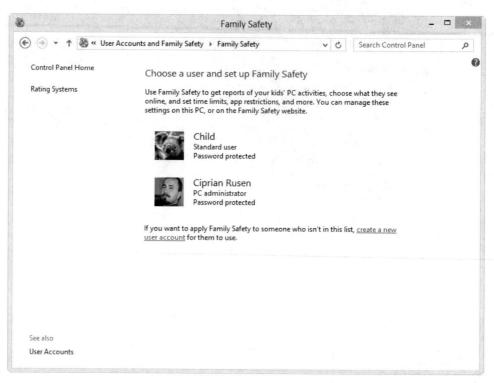

4   Select **On, enforce current settings**.

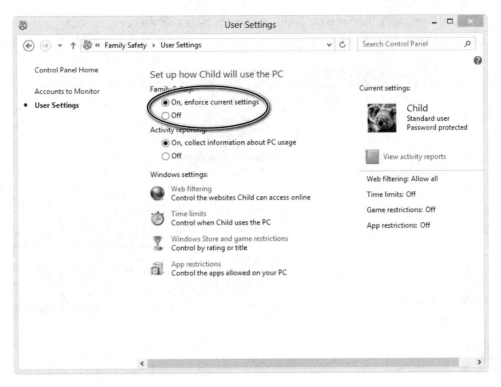

5   Select **On, collect information about PC usage**.

CLEAN UP Close the User Settings window.

Family Safety is now enabled using the default settings, which do not impose any restrictions.

Setting Time Limits and Application Restrictions

Now that Family Safety is enabled, define the restrictions you want. The easiest restrictions you can define are related to the times when your child can use the computer and which applications he or she is allowed to use.

Time restrictions can be defined for each day of the week and for the hours in a day. A simple table displays the hours you want to block. When selected, all the blocked hours appear blue. The hours that appear white represent hours when computer usage is allowed. You can change a time slot from allowed to blocked and vice versa by clicking or tapping it.

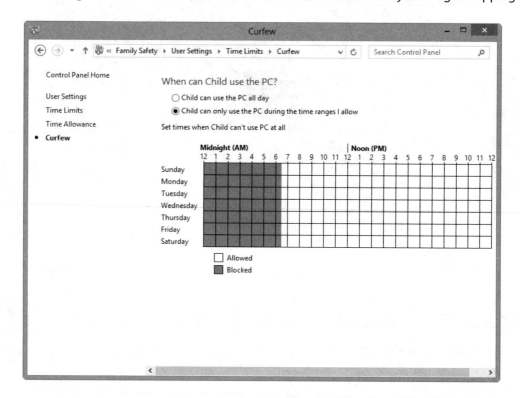

You can also set restrictions on how many hours and minutes your child is allowed to use the computer each day. The restrictions can be set independently for each day of the week or for weekdays and the weekend.

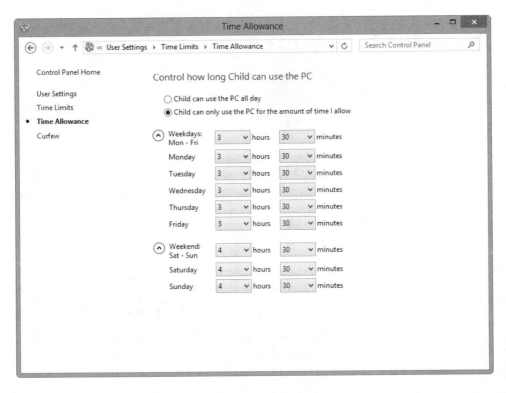

When you turn on Family Safety, no application restrictions are enforced; you need to create such restrictions and manually select which applications your child is allowed to use. The list of applications is split into two columns, File and Description, and into sections based on their locations on the disk. In a list of the most common folders, you can find applications and, for each folder, the executable files of each application. Based on all this information, you can figure out which applications to allow and block. The applications that are not selected are blocked by default.

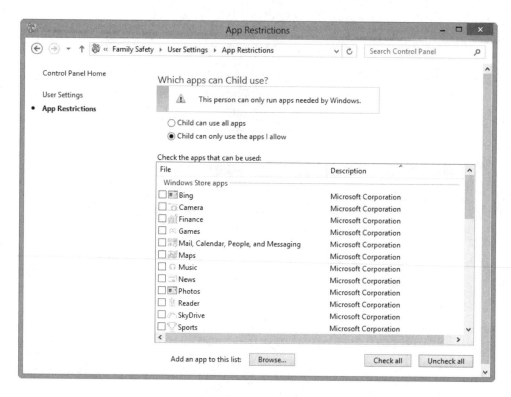

When defining restrictions for applications, keep in mind that all the new Windows 8 apps have their own section, called Windows Store apps. It's at the top of the list of apps.

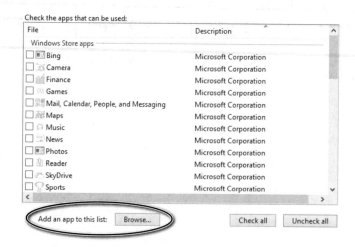

You might not find some apps included in this list. In that case, scroll to the bottom of the window, click or tap Browse, navigate to the app you want to allow, and then select it.

In this exercise, you'll learn how to set restrictions for time limits and set allowed applications. The exercise will start by setting time limits to block computer usage for your child's user account between 10 P.M. and 7 A.M. each day. Then you'll allow usage of specific subset of all the apps available in Windows 8.

➡ SET UP Open Family Safety and select your child's user account.

1   In **Windows Settings**, click or tap **Time Limits**.

The Time Limits window opens.

2   Click or tap **Set curfew.**

The Curfew window opens.

Control when Child can use the PC

Set the number of hours Child can use the PC per day

   Set time allowance

Set the time of day Child can use the PC

   Set curfew

3   Click or tap the option that starts with your child's user name followed by **can only use the PC during the time ranges I allow.**

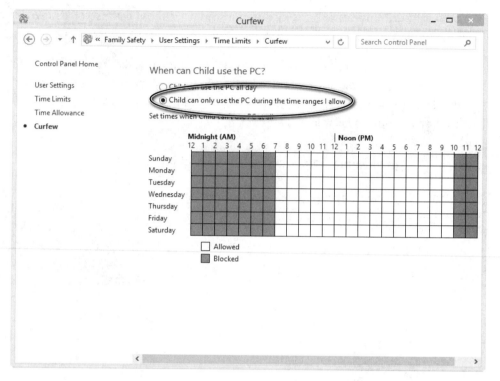

4   Highlight the squares in the table so that your child is not allowed to use the computer each day between 10 P.M. and 7 A.M. The table should look similar to the preceding screenshot.

5   When you have finished setting the time slots, click or tap **User Settings** on the left-side panel.

You return to the User Settings window.

6   To set app restrictions, click or tap **App restrictions**.

You are asked to choose whether your child can use all apps or only those you allow.

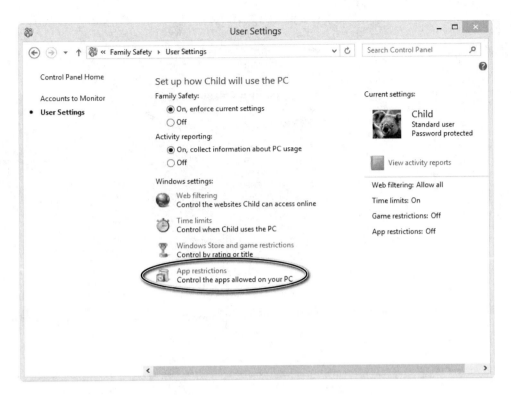

7   Select **can only use the apps I allow** appended to the name of the user account (in this exercise, **Child can only use the apps I allow**).

A list of all the applications installed on your computer appears.

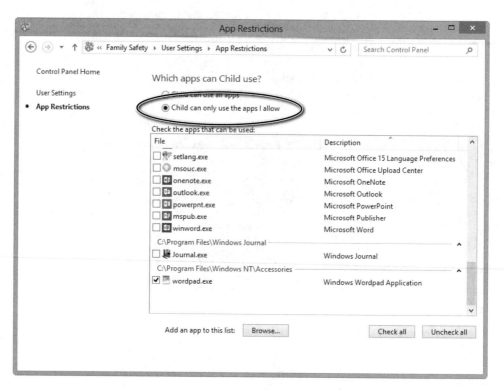

8   For this exercise, select **wordpad.exe** in C:\Program Files\Windows NT\Accessories.

9   Scroll to **Windows Store apps** and view all the new Windows 8 apps.

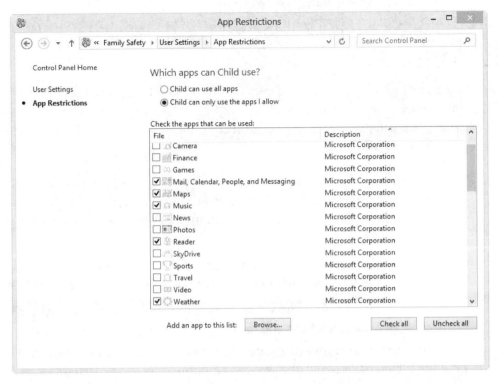

10   Select the following apps to allow your child to use them: **Mail**, **Calendar**, **People and Messaging**, **Maps**, **Music**, **Reader**, and **Weather**.

✕ CLEAN UP Close the App Restrictions window.

> **IMPORTANT** The tricky part about blocked apps is that Family Safety will allow some of the Windows-specific apps to run even if they are not marked as allowed (such as Calculator and Internet Explorer). However, any third-party apps that are installed on the computer won't be allowed to run on your child's user account unless marked as allowed. In addition, when you want to allow an application that uses more than one executable file while you run it, it is best to allow all its executable files, not just the main one. This helps ensure that an application won't fail because only some of its executable files are allowed to run.

Setting Restrictions for Games and Windows Store Apps

Another control feature that you might want to use sets up restrictions on the kinds of games your child can play. This can be very important, especially if he or she is very young. Family Safety makes it very easy to set such restrictions. All the options you need are in the Game Controls window.

- You can approve and block games based on their ESRB (Entertainment Software Rating Board) rating: Early Childhood, Everyone, Everyone 10+, Teen, Mature, and Adults Only. You have a detailed description of what each rating means so that you can make an informed choice.

- You can block games that are not rated by ESRB. This can be very useful if your child plays games from smaller independent studios whose games are not rated by ESRB.

- You can allow or block individual games. The individual overrides you choose overrule other general restrictions you have set for games.

The restrictions you set for ratings are also applied to the apps that your child can install from the Windows Store. Apps that don't conform to the rating you set won't be allowed.

In this exercise, you'll learn how to set restrictions for the games and apps your child is allowed to play. You'll allow games and apps that have a rating of up to Everyone 10+ and block games that have no rating. You'll also block your child from playing any of the games installed on the computer.

 SET UP Open Family Safety and select your child's user account.

1   In **Windows Settings**, click or tap **Windows Store and game restrictions**.

    You are asked to set the games and apps your child may use.

2   Select **can only use games and Windows Store apps I allow** appended to the name of the user account (in this exercise, **Child can only use games and Windows Store apps I allow**).

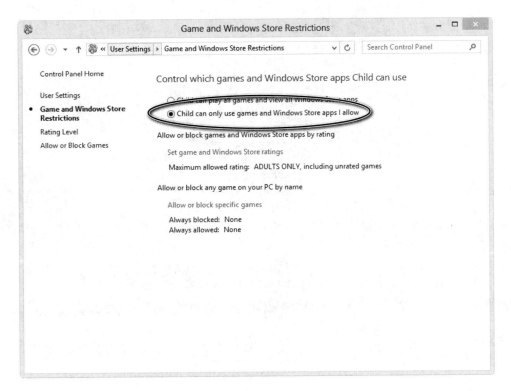

3   Click **Set game and Windows Store ratings**.

The Rating Level window opens, displaying a list of restrictions you can define.

4   Select **Block games with no rating**.

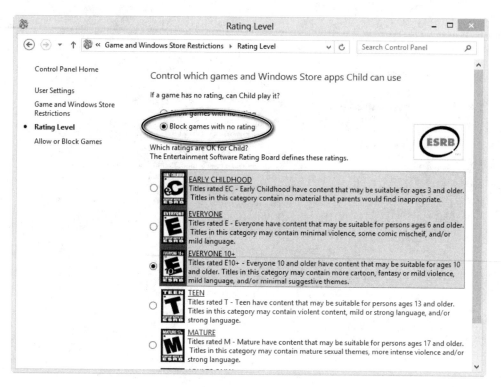

5   Scroll down a bit and select **EVERYONE 10+** to allow titles with this maximum rating.

6   Click or tap **Game and Windows Store Restriction** in the left-side column.

7   Click **Allow or block specific games**.

The Allow Or Block Games window opens.

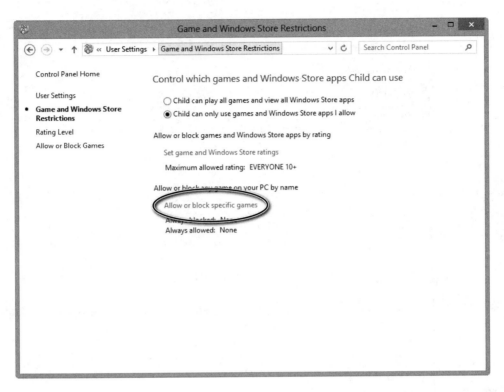

8   Select **Always block** for each game you want to block.

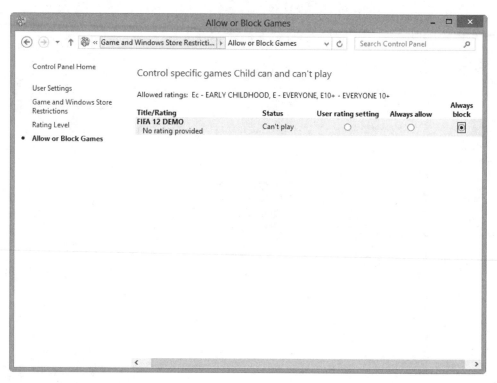

CLEAN UP Close the Allow Or Block Games window.

The game and apps restrictions you have defined are now applied to your child's user account. Before setting these restrictions, take the time to look through all the types of content that can be blocked and select all those you consider appropriate. The preceding exercise showed only the steps involved in this procedure and was not making recommendations for the types of content that should be blocked for a child depending on his or her age.

Setting Restrictions for Websites and Downloads

Another important feature in Family Safety is the ability to filter the websites to which your child has access. Microsoft has a large database that can categorize websites and the type of content found on them. By using just one setting, you can ensure that your child is blocked from accessing websites that are not appropriate for his or her age. Turning on web restrictions also turns on the SafeSearch settings found in all popular search engines such as Bing and Google. The web searches your child initiates will be filtered to prevent access to adult content of any kind.

16

You have five restriction levels from which to choose.

- **ALLOW LIST ONLY** Your child can view only the websites you have added to the Allow List. All other sites, including adult sites, are blocked.

- **CHILD-FRIENDLY** Your child can view only websites you specifically marked as allowed and those with child-friendly content. Adult sites are blocked.

- **GENERAL INTEREST** Your child can view only websites you specifically marked as allowed, those with child-friendly content, and those with content of general interest. Adult sites are blocked.

- **ONLINE COMMUNICATION** This setting applies the same restrictions as the previous level, but it also allows social networking sites, web chat, and webmail. Adult sites are blocked.

- **WARN ON ADULT** Your child is allowed to view all websites but receives a warning when a site has adult content.

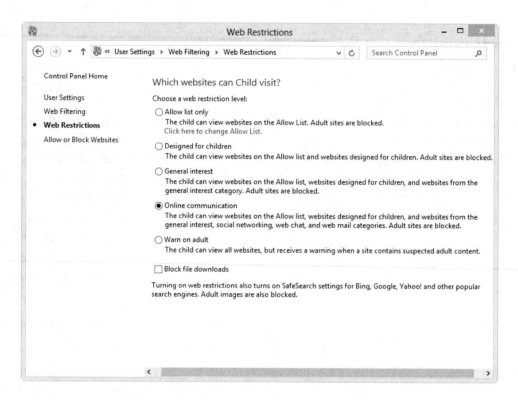

You can also block file downloads by selecting Block File Downloads to make sure your child can't view files you do not approve.

You can add specific websites to be allowed or blocked from the Allow Or Block Websites window. As with games, these individual overrides overrule other general restrictions you have set for websites.

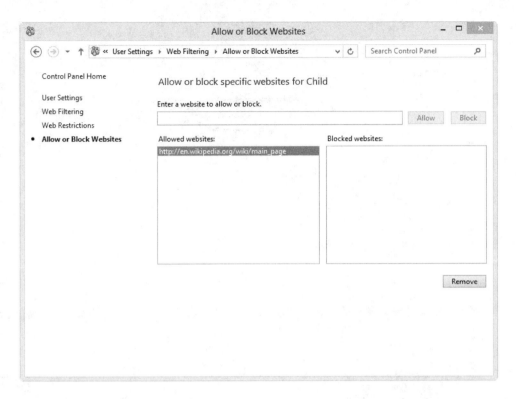

The restrictions you define are applied to all major browsers. For example, if your child is using Mozilla Firefox or Google Chrome instead of Internet Explorer, the restrictions will be working. Your child doesn't have to use Internet Explorer for the restrictions to work.

In this exercise, you'll learn how to block web content automatically and how to block file downloads.

SET UP Open Family Safety and select your child's user account.

1 In **Windows Settings**, click or tap **Web Filtering**.

You are asked to set the websites your child can view.

2 Click or tap **Child can only use the websites I allow**.

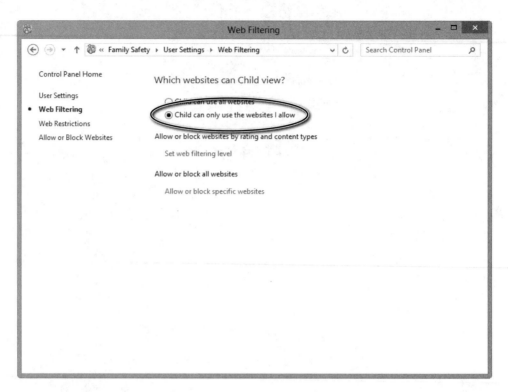

3　Click or tap **Set web filtering level** to open the Web Restrictions window.

4　Choose **General interest**.

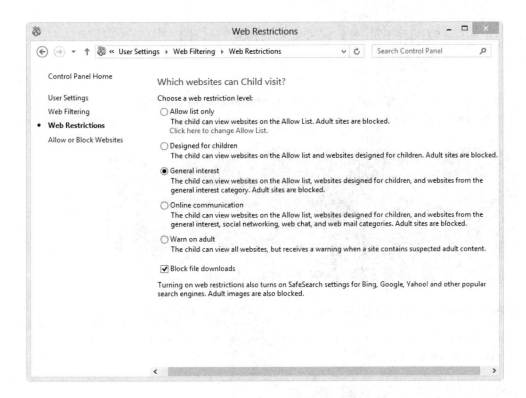

5   At the bottom of the Web Restrictions window, select **Block file downloads**.

❌ CLEAN UP Close the Web Restrictions window.

The web restrictions you have set are now applied to your child's user account.

Understanding Messages Family Safety Shows

When your child wants to log on to the computer during a time slot that is blocked, he or she receives the following message: "Time's up! It's past the curfew time your parent set."

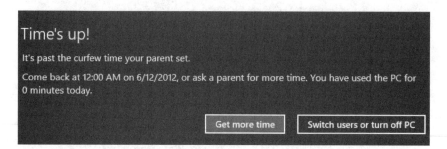

Your child cannot log on unless you set that specific time slot as allowed.

If your child tries to run a blocked app or game, a pop-up appears with the message, "Blocked by Family Safety."

If your child tries to access a blocked website, that website will not be loaded and he or she is notified that "This page is blocked."

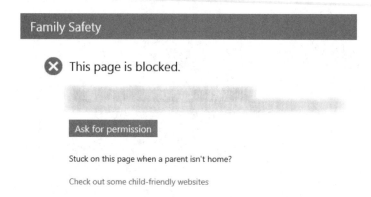

When he or she tries to download a file and downloads have been blocked, a notification says, "Family Safety has blocked this download." The download does not proceed.

Family Safety

Family Safety has blocked this download

To find out why this download is blocked, check your Family Safety settings. If you need access to this download, ask permission from the person who set up Family Safety.

Each time something is blocked, your child is given the chance to ask for permission and receive access. Parents can review his or her permission requests approve them when appropriate.

Managing Family Safety Settings and Viewing Activity Reports

You can view your child's activity from both the computer he or she is using and a remote computer through the Family Safety website.

In the User Settings window, after you select your child's user account, click View Activity Reports on the right side of the window.

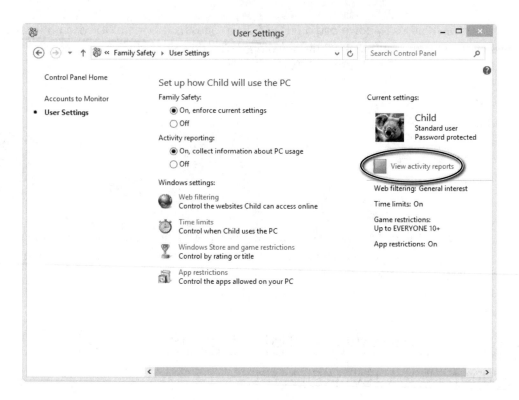

The reports include much useful information, including the most popular websites your child has visited, the latest pages that were blocked, how much time the PC was used during the past week, and the apps and games he or she used the most.

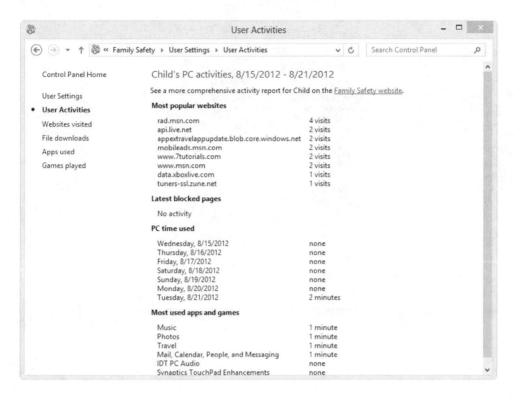

You can also manage the settings for Family Safety online. Click Manage Settings On The Family Safety Website at the bottom of the Family Safety window or browse to *https:// familysafety.microsoft.com* and log on with your Microsoft account.

On the Family Safety website, you can view activity reports for your child, approve or deny the requests he or she sends you, and change the settings for all the restrictions that can be set in Family Safety.

Key Points

- You can only turn on Family Safety if your child has a standard user account.

- You can easily set time limits and restrictions on applications and games.

- Restrictions for games and apps can be set by using their ESRB rating.

- Setting restrictions on the types of websites that can be visited helps ensure that your child doesn't visit websites with content that is inappropriate for his or her age.

- Your child is notified each time he or she tries to log on at a restricted time or run a blocked game or application.

- You can view reports about your child's activity and approve his or her requests by using the Family Safety website.

Chapter at a Glance

Apply

Apply high contrast if you have a visual disability, page 487

Use

Use the Magnifier, page 492

Write

Write a letter using the on-screen keyboard, page 502

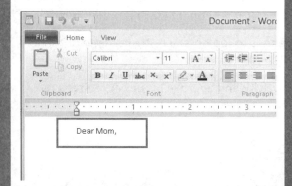

Give

Give commands with Windows Speech Recognition, page 505

Making My Computer Accessible

IN THIS CHAPTER, YOU WILL LEARN HOW TO

- Explore ease of access options.

- Let Windows suggest ease of access settings.

- Use the magnifier.

- Use Narrator.

- Use the on-screen keyboard.

- Set up and use Windows Speech Recognition.

Windows 8 offers several options to help you use your computer if you have any kind of impairment or disability. These are referred to cumulatively as ease of access features; there are many ease of access features and options from which to choose.

If you have to wear reading glasses to see what's on the screen, you can make the text larger; if you are blind, you can turn on Narrator to have what's on the screen read to you. If you are hard of hearing, you can turn up the volume on your speakers or turn on text captions for spoken dialogue; if you are deaf, you can enable visual notifications with Sound Sentry. If you have difficulty using the mouse or keyboard, options exist to help you, including Toggle Keys, Sticky Keys, Filter Keys, and so on. You can also enable and configure Windows Speech Recognition so that you can talk to your computer to give commands and perform tasks.

PRACTICE FILES You do not need any practice files to complete this chapter. For more information about practice file requirements, see "Using the Practice Files" at the beginning of this book.

Accessing the Ease of Access Center

There are several ways to access and configure ease of access options. You can enable a specific option by searching for it from the Start screen. For instance, you can type High Contrast and, from the results in Settings, select Turn High Contrast On Or Off. You can use the ease of access options from PC Settings; you've explored many of the options there already, including personalizing the Lock screen with your favorite picture and adding users. You can use the desktop app Ease Of Access Center, which offers access to all the ease of access options in one place. You will find quick access to common features from PC Settings.

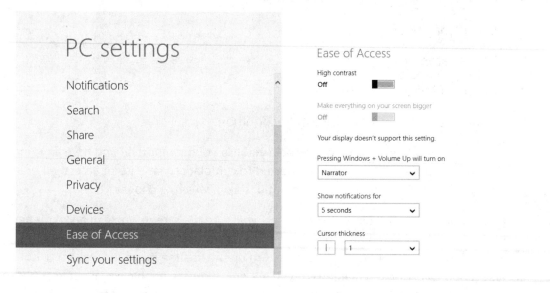

From here, you can turn on or configure the following.

- **HIGH CONTRAST** When this is applied, the background is changed to black, the text and dialog box outlines to white, and selected menus to purple. Other colors appear as applicable.

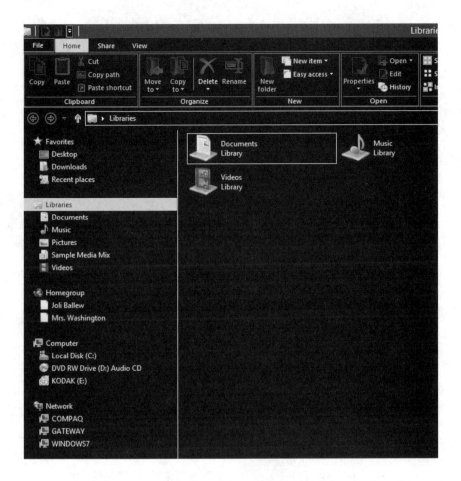

- **MAKE EVERYTHING ON YOUR SCREEN BIGGER** When this option is enabled, everything on the screen appears larger. This is not the Magnifier detailed later; this is an option to make what's on the screen easier to see (perhaps to keep you from needing to wear reading glasses while using your computer). Your display must be able to support this setting. If it does not, increase the screen resolution.

- **PRESSING WINDOWS + VOLUME UP WILL TURN ON** You can set what happens when you press the Windows key and the Volume Up key at the same time. Choices include Nothing, Magnifier, Narrator, or On-Screen Keyboard.

- **SHOW NOTIFICATIONS FOR** You can set how long notifications remain on the screen. You can choose from several options, the longest being five minutes. If notifications disappear before you've had a chance to read them, increase this setting.

- **CURSOR THICKNESS** Use this setting to set how thick the cursor is on the screen. Settings range from 1 to 20, and a preview is available.

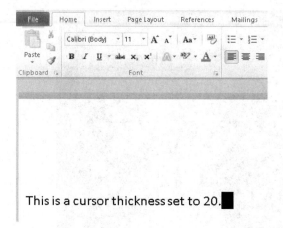

This is a cursor thickness set to 20.

TIP Many more accessibility settings are available than the five shown here. To see everything that's available, open Control Panel and then click Ease Of Access. You can then select Ease Of Access Center or Speech Recognition. You'll learn more about this later in the chapter.

In this exercise, you'll view all the ease of access options available from the Start screen and then open the PC Settings app and enable High Contrast.

 SET UP **Start your computer and unlock the Lock screen. You need access to the Start screen.**

TIP When an instruction requires you to click something with a mouse, note that you can generally tap the item on a compatible touch screen to achieve the same result.

1   From the **Start** screen, type **Ease**.

2   Click **Settings**.

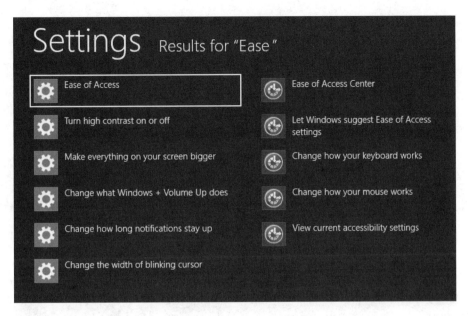

Settings Results for "Ease"

Ease of Access

Ease of Access Center

Turn high contrast on or off

Let Windows suggest Ease of Access settings

Make everything on your screen bigger

Change how your keyboard works

Change what Windows + Volume Up does

Change how your mouse works

Change how long notifications stay up

View current accessibility settings

Change the width of blinking cursor

3   Click **Ease of Access**.

4   Click the slider next to High Contrast to change the setting to **On**.

✖ CLEAN UP **Change the High Contrast setting to Off.**

Letting Windows Suggest Ease of Access Settings

Because you can't access all the Ease of Access options from the PC Settings hub, and because you might not even be sure what options to enable, it's often best to let Windows suggest the settings it deems best for you based on a series of questions you answer. The five questions are easy to understand, and after you answer them options to enable the suggested accessibility options are presented. For example, if you work through the wizard and state only that you are hard of hearing, Windows will suggest that you turn on Sound Sentry and choose a visual warning. (If you state that "it is often difficult for me to concentrate," more options are presented.)

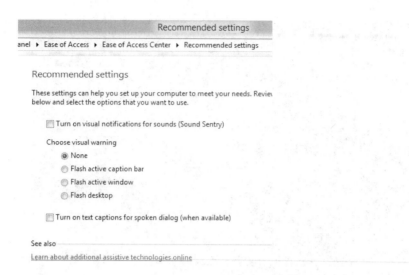

There are several ways to access the wizard that helps you decide which options are best for you, but the best way is to open Control Panel and then open Ease Of Access. You can access Control Panel from the Start screen by typing **Control** and selecting Control Panel from the results.

From Control Panel, under Ease Of Access Center, you can select Let Windows Suggest Settings. The rest is simple; you just answer the questions as they pertain to you and let Windows figure out what needs to be enabled.

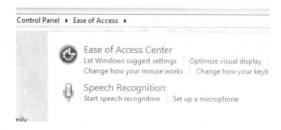

Here are a few of the items (and a few related items) that you might be prompted to enable based on the answers you give in the wizard.

- **NARRATOR** Narrator reads aloud any text on the screen. You'll need speakers. (You might also want to turn on audio descriptions to hear what's happening on the screen when that feature is available for the items being viewed.)

- **MAGNIFIER** Magnifier zooms in anywhere on the screen and makes everything in that area larger. You can move the magnifier around on the screen just as you would if you had a magnifying glass in your hand. (You might also want to turn on High Contrast, change the thickness of the cursor, adjust the color and transparency of the window borders, and so on.)

- **ON-SCREEN KEYBOARD** Use the on-screen keyboard to type using the mouse, your finger (on a touch screen), or another pointing device, such as a joystick, by selecting keys that appear on the screen.

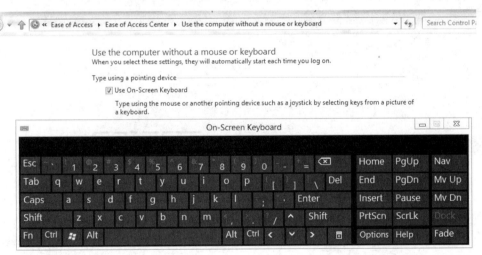

- **SPEECH RECOGNITION** Use speech recognition to speak into a microphone to control the computer, open programs, and dictate text.

- **MOUSE KEYS**, **STICKY KEYS**, and **FILTER KEYS** With Mouse Keys, you use the numeric keypad to move the mouse around the screen; with Sticky Keys, you press keyboard shortcuts such as Ctrl+Alt+Del one key at a time instead of at once; enabling Filter Keys causes Windows to ignore or slow down brief or repeated keystrokes and adjust keyboard repeat rates. (You might also try Toggle Keys, which sound a tone when you press specific keys such as Caps Lock, Num Lock, or others.)

- **VISUAL NOTIFICATIONS** and **TIME LIMITS** Sound Sentry enables visual notification for sounds, and you can enable visual warnings that flash on the screen when a notification is active. You can also turn off time limits and flashing visuals if you find it difficult to concentrate, or set how long Windows notification boxes should stay open. (You might also want to turn off unnecessary animations, prevent windows from being automatically arranged when you move them to the edges of the screen, or turn on caret browsing.)

Using the Magnifier

You can turn on Magnifier from the Ease of Access Center in Control Panel. Start Magnifier is an option from the landing page.

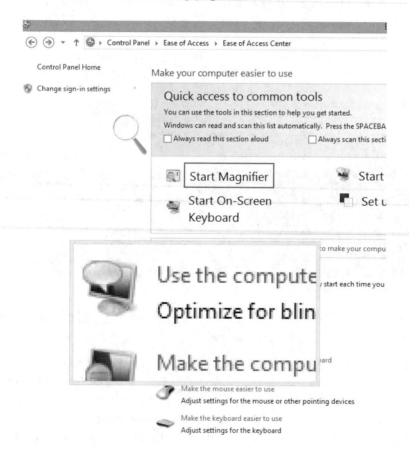

You can also type **Magnifier** on the Start screen to access options to enable it. Whatever you choose, when you turn on Magnifier a window appears for a second or two that contains options to change the magnification level and how Magnifier shows its magnified data.

If you don't immediately click any option from this window, it changes to a magnifying glass. (You click or tap the magnifying glass to access this window when you need it.) With the settings configured, you just move your cursor around the screen to use Magnifier. As you can see here, the image degrades and pixelates at higher settings.

Many keyboard shortcuts are available for Magnifier, including those you can use to start and exit it.

- **START MAGNIFIER** Windows+Plus Sign

- **ZOOM OUT OR IN WHILE MAGNIFIER IS RUNNING** Windows+Plus Sign or Minus Sign

- **EXIT MAGNIFIER** Windows+Esc

You'll want to explore each available view (under the Views tab) and the settings available from the Settings icon in the Magnifier window if you decide to use Magnifier regularly. One view is Full Screen. When you use it, the entire screen is magnified at the percentage you select, and you move around the screen with your mouse or finger.

Docked view is another viewing option. In this view and while on the desktop, you'll see an area at the top of the screen that shows what's being magnified (where you've placed your cursor). Docked is not an option from the Start menu or while using an app. Docked is available only on the desktop.

If you aren't on the desktop but instead on the Start screen or in an app, you can choose between Lens and Full Screen. You've seen Full Screen; Lens offers a rectangle on the screen that holds the magnified data.

In this exercise, you'll enable Magnifier and use it at 200% and 300% in Full Screen view. You'll then exit the Magnifier application.

➔ SET UP Start your computer and unlock the Lock screen. You need access to the Start screen.

1   While at the **Start** screen, press **Windows** and the **+ key**.

2   Move the cursor over the magnifying glass, click the right-facing double arrows, and
     click the arrow by **Views**.

     Verify that **Full Screen** is selected.

3   If it disappears, click the **magnifying glass icon**. Then click the **+** sign.

4   Using the keyboard, press **Windows + -** two times.

5   Press **Windows+Esc** to close Magnifier.

❌ CLEAN UP No cleanup is required.

Using Narrator

You can start Narrator from Ease of Access Center in Control Panel. You can also start
Narrator from the Start screen. Just start typing the word *Narrator* and then click Narrator
when it appears.

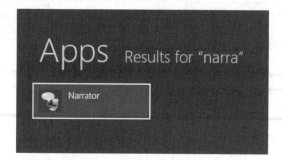

You can use Narrator Touch, a new feature, if you have a touch screen that supports four-
finger input. Otherwise, you can control and use Narrator with a keyboard and mouse.
You'll be prompted either way. To get started, click Close in the prompt box that appears.
An introductory screen appears. Read this information before continuing.

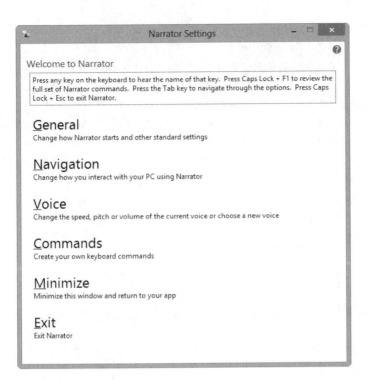

As you'll learn, you can press any key on the keyboard to hear the name of the key. You can press Caps Lock+F1 to review and have read to you a full set of Narrator commands. You can also change the various settings, including the speed, pitch, and volume of the narrator and how and when the program starts. Each time you click an option, you are prompted to save or discard the changes before you can return to the previous screen. To use Narrator, use the computer as you normally would, using the keyboard and mouse or the touch screen.

Understand that Narrator won't read all of the *content* you encounter; however, it will always let you know what's happening on the screen itself. It might read what's on a web-page, and it will read URLs, dialog boxes, text entry boxes, and so on. When you open a program, it will announce that you've opened a window, available tool tips, and the name of the program you've opened. It won't read the content of documents or tell you what's on a Microsoft PowerPoint slide. It will state which key you press on the keyboard, such as Print Screen (PrtSc), but it won't describe what you've copied. It won't read locations on maps (in fact, it'll announce that Maps is not supported by screen readers), describe what's shown in a photo, or tell you what's happening on a video. Instead, it tells you when those programs and apps are opened and closed, the commands available under your cursor, the com-mands you've selected, and other pertinent information.

Narrator does work with some apps. This is an ever-expanding technology, so you can expect more features and functionality as time goes by. As an example of what is available now, however, you can open the Weather app and click the current temperature; Narrator will read the temperature aloud to you if you place the cursor appropriately. In fact, when you open the Weather app, Narrator will announce that there is "explorable text". If you open Calendar and create an event, it will read some of the information, such as the month you select, the number of hours you configure for the event, and so on.

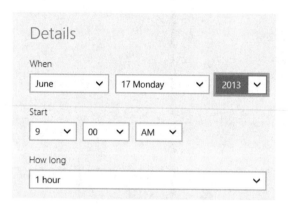

If you decide to use Narrator regularly, you'll need to spend some time exploring the features, configuring the settings, and learning about keyboard, mouse, and touch screen shortcuts.

TIP If you've started Narrator and want to stop it, return to the Narrator window and click Exit. Click Yes to confirm.

Using the On-Screen Keyboard

The on-screen keyboard is an accessibility option in the Ease of Access Center. The on-screen keyboard is available on all computers, even those that do not support touch, and you can use the keyboard with a mouse or input device designed for people with disabilities. Start On-Screen Keyboard is an option in Control Panel from the Ease Of Access Center. An easier way to open the on-screen keyboard is to type Keyboard while on the Start screen and click On-Screen Keyboard in the results. (You can also press Windows+Volume Up on many keyboards, provided you have changed the defaults in PC Settings under Ease Of Access.) The keyboard appears immediately when you do this and offers a Minimize button so you can easily hide it when you aren't using it.

TIP You can drag from the corners of the keyboard to make it larger and easier to use. It can be configured to be quite large.

The keyboard is similar to most: you tap or click keys to use them, and there are specialty keys such as Tab, Caps, and Shift; Alt, Ctrl, and Del; the Windows key; arrow keys; and PgUp, PgDn, PrtScn, and so on. This keyboard has a few extra entries such as Nav, Mv Up, Mv Dn, Dock, Fade, Help, ScrLk, and Options. To get the most from the on-screen keyboard, you need to know how most of these extra entries are used.

TIP If you plan to use the on-screen keyboard regularly, start it and then right-click it on the taskbar. Click Pin This Program To Taskbar.

The on-screen keyboard special keys include:

- **NAV** To hide the full keyboard and show only the navigation options. Click General to return to the full on-screen keyboard.

- **MV UP** To reposition the on-screen keyboard near the top of the screen.

- **MV DN** To reposition the on-screen keyboard near the bottom of the screen.

- **DOCK** To dock the on-screen keyboard to hide it, show it, or otherwise manage it. This option is dimmed on PCs but might be available on tablets.

- **FADE** To make the keyboard transparent. Click Fade again to show it.

- **HELP** To get help using the on-screen keyboard.

- **SCRLK** The Scroll Lock key you find on many keyboards. When the ScrLk key is enabled, it is white.

- **OPTIONS** To configure options for the on-screen keyboard. These include but are not limited to setting a click sound when keys are pressed, enabling a numeric keypad, using text prediction, and enabling the option to hover over a key for a specific amount of time to use it (versus actually clicking the key with a mouse or other device).

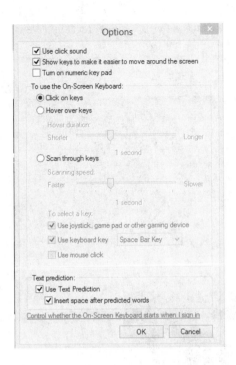

TIP To open the on-screen keyboard by using keyboard shortcuts, press Windows+R and, in the Run dialog box, type **osk** and press Enter.

In this exercise, you'll open the on-screen keyboard from the Start screen and use it to type a short note by using WordPad.

SET UP Open WordPad by using any method desired. Return to the Start screen.

1 From the **Start** screen, type **Keyboard**. From the results, click **On-Screen Keyboard**.

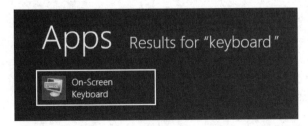

2 If desired, drag from **any corner** of the keyboard to enlarge it.

3 Position WordPad and the on-screen keyboard where you can access both easily.

4 Click inside **WordPad** to place your cursor there.

5   Use your mouse or another pointing device (such as your finger) to select keys on the keyboard. Note that they appear on the screen in WordPad.

6   Use the **Shift** and **Enter** keys as required.

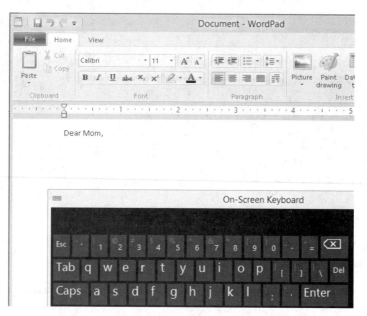

❌ CLEAN UP Close WordPad and save the document if desired.

Set Up and Use Windows Speech Recognition

Like Narrator, Windows Speech Recognition will take a little time to master. You have to set it up, train it to understand your voice, and then learn the commands for using it. Then you can use Windows Speech Recognition to start and close programs, open and select items from menus, click buttons and objects, and even dictate text. Just about everything you can do with a keyboard and mouse can be done with only your voice.

You must set up Speech Recognition. The wizard can take a while to get through, so it's best to start when you have at least 30 minutes for the process. You open Speech Recognition the same way you open any program, by typing related keywords at the Start screen.

Setup is the only option you have the first time you open Windows Speech Recognition. During the setup process, you'll be required to:

- **CONFIGURE A MICROPHONE** You choose and test a microphone. This can be one built into a headset, one that sits on the desk, or one built into your computer (or device).

- **ENABLE DOCUMENT REVIEW** Speech Recognition will work better if you let it review the documents and email that have already been indexed for search by Windows. The computer can learn words and phrases you use often and can understand better when you speak.

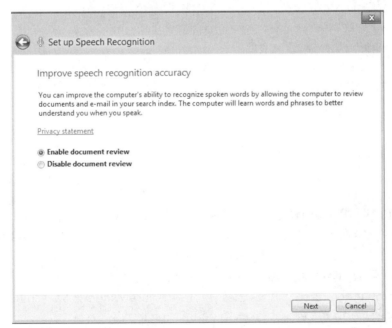

- **CHOOSE HOW TO ACTIVATE AND DEACTIVATE THE PROGRAM** Start Listening and Stop Listening are the two commands you'll learn to use first. You can choose what happens when you say these commands. You can configure it so that when you say "Stop listening," Windows Speech Recognition closes (Manual), or you can configure it so that when you say "Stop listening," it stays active and waits for you to use the Start Listening command to reactivate it.

- **PRINT THE SPEECH REFERENCE CARD** You can print the speech reference card if you have a printer so that you will always have a quick reference of the available commands. You can also view the reference sheet. If the sheet does not automatically appear, search for Controlling Your PC With Speech Recognition.

	Windows Help and Support

Any time you need to find out what commands to use, say "what can I say?"

To do this	Say this
Select any item by its name	Click *File*; *Start*; *View*
Select any item or icon	Click *Recycle Bin*; Click *Computer*; Click *file name*
Double-tap or double-click any item	Double-click *Recycle Bin*; Double-click *Computer*; Double-click *file name*
Switch to an open app	Switch to *Paint*; Switch to *WordPad*; Switch to *program name*; Switch application
Scroll in one direction	Scroll *up*; Scroll *down*; Scroll *left*; Scroll *right*
Insert a new paragraph or new line in a document	New *paragraph*; New *line*
Select a word in a document	Select *word*
Select a word and start to correct it	Correct *word*
Select and delete specific words	Delete *word*
Show a list of applicable commands	What can I say?
Update the list of speech commands that are currently available	Refresh speech commands
Turn on listening mode	Start listening
Turn off listening mode	Stop listening
Move the Speech Recognition microphone bar	Move speech recognition

- **RUN SPEECH RECOGNITION AT STARTUP** If you know you'll use Windows Speech Recognition every time you use your computer, enable this feature; otherwise, disable it.

- **WORK THROUGH THE TUTORIAL** After Windows Speech Recognition is set up, work through the tutorial. It teaches you how to use Windows Speech Recognition and is well worth the time it takes to go through it.

After you've worked through the tutorial, you're ready to use Windows Speech Recognition. You'll see the Speech Recognition window on the desktop and Start screen when it's running, and it will appear on top of any open windows (until you minimize it to the taskbar).

In this exercise, you'll start Windows Speech Recognition, use it to access the desktop, and use it to open and close the Recycle Bin on the desktop.

SET UP Start your computer and unlock the Lock screen. You need access to the Start screen.

TIP If you did not print out the list of commands offered in the Windows Speech Recognition tutorial, you can access commands from www.microsoft.com. Search for Speech Recognition commands. You can also say, "What can I say?" while Windows Speech Recognition is listening.

1   From the **Start** screen, type Speech.

2   Click **Windows Speech Recognition** to open it.

3   Say "**Click Desktop.**"

4   Say "**Double-click Recycle Bin.**"

5   Say "**Close Recycle Bin.**"

6   Say "**Stop listening.**"

CLEAN UP No cleanup is required.

Finally, understand that there are multiple ways to configure Windows Speech Recognition. You can access the options by right-clicking the Speech Recognition dialog box on the screen, from which you can access many configuration options, including but not limited to:

- Choosing how Windows Speech Recognition should start, stop, and listen.

- Starting or restarting the Speech tutorial.

- Getting help.

- Performing steps to improve voice recognition.

- Opening the Speech Dictionary and adding a word.

- Exiting Windows Speech Recognition.

TIP If you plan to use Windows Speech Recognition regularly, explore each option from the contextual menu.

Key Points

- You can configure basic accessibility options in the Ease of Access Center.

- If you're unsure of which accessibility options are right for you, you can work through the available wizard to let Windows make suggestions.

- To access all accessibility options, open the Ease of Access Center from Control Panel; this is the desktop version.

- Magnifier can be used in various modes and views; you can choose the one that's right for you.

- Narrator can read what's happening on the screen and can inform you when a program is opened or closed, name the URL of the website you're visiting, and read what's under your cursor. It can sometimes read content, although that feature is expected to become more robust in the future.

- The on-screen keyboard can be used with alternative input devices, with a mouse, and with touch (on compatible monitors).

- By using Windows Speech Recognition, you can say commands such as, "Click Desktop," "Double-click Recycle Bin," "Scroll up," "Scroll down," and so on.

17

Chapter at a Glance

Learn

Learn to use the Windows Mobility Center, page 510

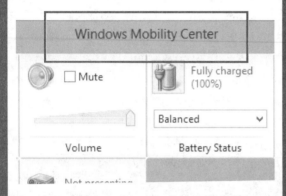

Turn on

Turn on presentation mode, page 514

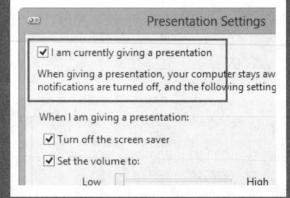

Encrypt

Encrypt the operating system drive with BitLocker, page 524

Secure

Secure removable data drives with BitLocker, page 527

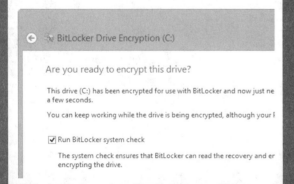

Using Windows 8 at Work

18

IN THIS CHAPTER, YOU WILL LEARN HOW TO

- Learn to use the Windows Mobility Center.

- Turn on presentation mode.

- Use BitLocker to encrypt the operating system drive.

- Use BitLocker to secure removable data drives.

Chances are you will also be using Windows 8 at your workplace. Although the tools covered in this book can be used both at home and at work, there are a few that you are likely to use mostly at work and not at home.

The first is Windows Mobility Center, which is targeted at laptop or netbook users who are mobile and need to connect to multiple devices and external displays. The second is BitLocker, a feature by which you can encrypt your computer and make sure your data is safe and accessed only by you and other authorized people.

In this chapter, you'll learn how to use the Windows Mobility Center, connect to external displays, and use presentation mode to deliver presentations without any unwanted interruptions. Then you'll learn how to encrypt drives with BitLocker and make sure your data is safe.

PRACTICE FILES You don't need any practice files to complete the exercises in this chapter. For more information about practice file requirements, see "Using the Practice Files" at the beginning of this book.

Using the Windows Mobility Center

The Windows Mobility Center is a tool that works only on mobile computers and devices such as laptops or netbooks. It is not available on desktop computers. Its role is to help users be mobile and quickly take the following actions.

- Changing the display brightness of the screen
- Changing the sound volume of the computer or device
- Changing the power plan
- Connecting or disconnecting external displays
- Setting sync partnerships with portable music players, USB memory sticks, or smart phones that provide support for this feature
- Turning presentation mode on or off

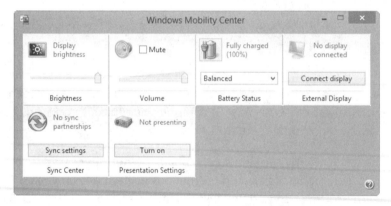

Although all the settings that you can manage through the Windows Mobility Center are important, two will be especially appreciated during office hours: the ability to connect external displays and to turn on presentation mode.

These settings are very useful when switching among different office rooms and connecting the laptop to different kinds of external displays, from monitors to TVs and projectors.

The Connect Display button is the equivalent of pressing the Windows+P keys on your keyboard. It opens a window asking how you want to set the second screen.

- **PC SCREEN ONLY** The second screen is ignored and no image is displayed on it.
- **DUPLICATE** The image on your laptop's screen is duplicated on the external display.

- **EXTEND** The second screen extends your laptop's screen and can be used as an additional desktop.

- **SECOND SCREEN ONLY** The second screen becomes your main screen, and the laptop's screen is turned off.

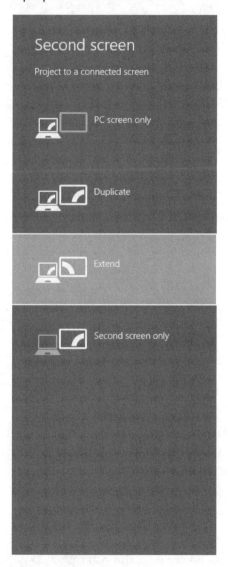

To launch the Windows Mobility Center, open Control Panel, choose Hardware and Sound, and then select Windows Mobility Center.

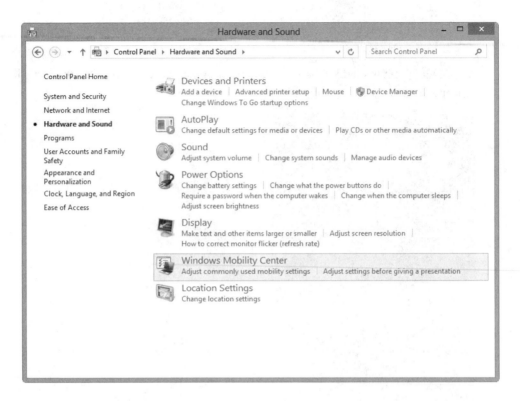

As an alternative, you can search for the word *mobility* on the Start screen and click or tap the appropriate search result.

Turning On Presentation Mode

Presentation mode is very useful when delivering any kind of presentation. Take some time to configure presentation mode exactly the way you want so your presentation runs smoothly without unwanted hiccups and interruptions (such as the screen saver showing up when you don't need it).

In this exercise, you'll learn how to turn on presentation mode and configure it.

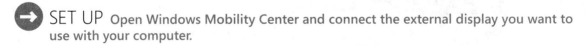

SET UP Open Windows Mobility Center and connect the external display you want to use with your computer.

1   Click or tap **Connect display** to set how you want to connect the second screen.

2   Click or tap **Extend**.

The second external display now acts as a second desktop.

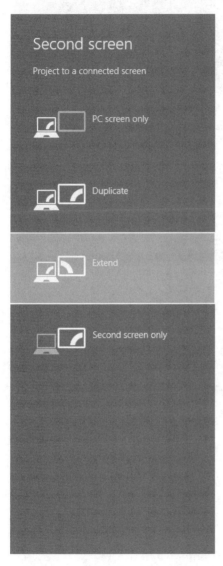

3   Click or tap the **projector icon** in **Presentation Settings** to open the Presentation Settings window.

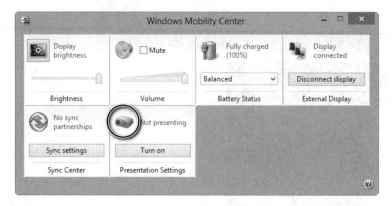

4   Select the boxes for **I am currently giving a presentation** and **Turn off the screen saver**.

5   Set the volume and the background as you want them to be.

6   Click or tap **OK**.

You return to the Windows Mobility Center window.

⊗ CLEAN UP After you have delivered your presentation, click or tap the Turn Off button under Presentation Settings and close Windows Mobility Center.

Now you can move the documents and presentations you want to show to the second display and start your presentation. You won't have to worry about unwanted screen savers turning on, distracting wallpapers being displayed, and so on.

Using BitLocker to Encrypt Drives

Many companies use different encryption solutions to ensure the security of the data stored on the companies' systems. If a business laptop is stolen or a USB memory stick with company data is lost, it's important for the stored data to be inaccessible to unwanted people. In such scenarios, encryption is the only solution that ensures that the data is accessed only by people who have the appropriate access keys and passwords. Some businesses also have policies that forbid the distribution of company data on removable media such as USB memory sticks. Be sure you comply with such policies. However, if you need to have important business data on a mobile device when you're away from the office and you won't break any company policies by doing so, use encryption. It is the only sensible solution to make sure the data is protected.

BitLocker is available only for business editions of Windows 8 such as Windows 8 Pro and Windows 8 Enterprise. That's why it is very likely that you will use it only on your work computers. In addition, it works only on computers with TPM (Trusted Platform Module) chips. These chips can store the cryptographic keys BitLocker and other encryption solutions use. TPM chips are included in most business computers but not in computers sold to consumers and home users.

BitLocker can be found by opening Control Panel, choosing System And Security, and then selecting BitLocker Drive Encryption.

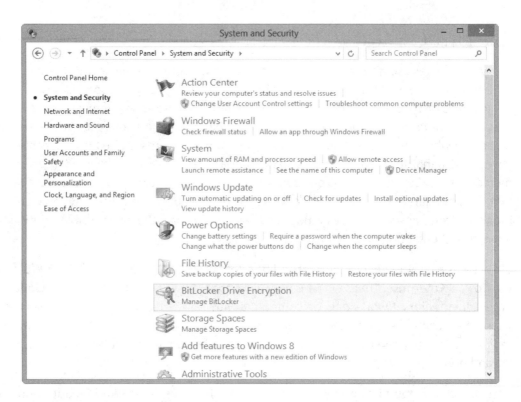

BitLocker's main window is well organized and easy to understand and use. First, you see the drive on which Windows 8 is installed, then other fixed data drives that might exist on your computer, and then the removable data drives that are plugged into your computer.

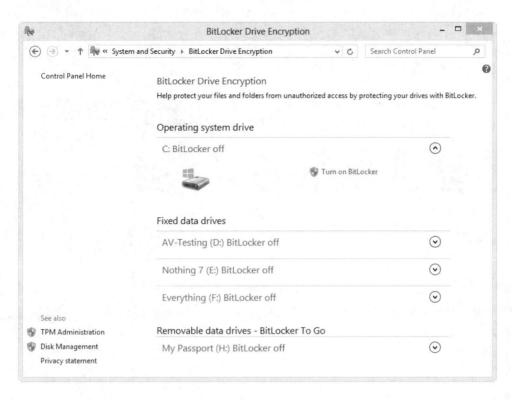

All these drives can be encrypted with BitLocker. After a drive is encrypted, its status changes from BitLocker Off to BitLocker On. In addition, you can perform tasks such as:

- Suspending the BitLocker protection for a time.

- Backing up the recovery key again in case you lose it.

- Changing the password used to access the encrypted drive.

- Removing the existing password.

- Turning off BitLocker and decrypting the drive.

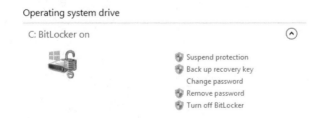

Encrypting the Operating System Drive with BitLocker

The encryption process is rather lengthy and first involves setting a password that will be used prior to launching Windows 8 and using any encrypted drive.

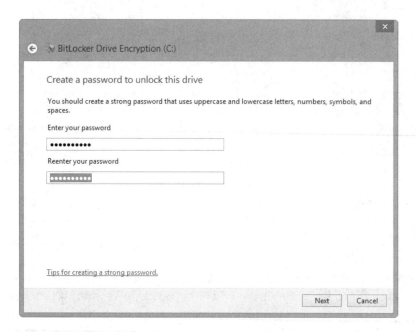

It is important to remember this password. Without it, you won't be able to access the encrypted drive. To prevent this from happening, the encryption process includes a step to save a backup recovery key you can use if you forget the password and need to recover the encrypted data. The recovery key can be saved automatically to your Microsoft account (if you log on to Windows 8 with a Microsoft account), to a file on a USB flash drive, or on a different drive, or it can be printed on a piece of paper.

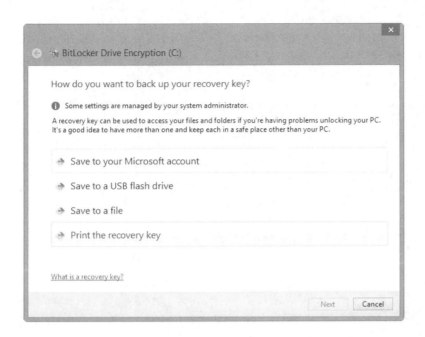

TIP When encrypting a drive other than the operating system drive, the text displayed will be slightly different. However, the options you can choose remain the same.

Before the encryption process starts, you are asked whether you want to encrypt only the used disk space or the entire drive. Both methods work well. If you have a newer computer with a fresh installation of Windows 8, it is best to choose the first option. If your computer has been used for quite some time, it is best to encrypt the entire drive. However, the second option will make the encryption process take longer than the first.

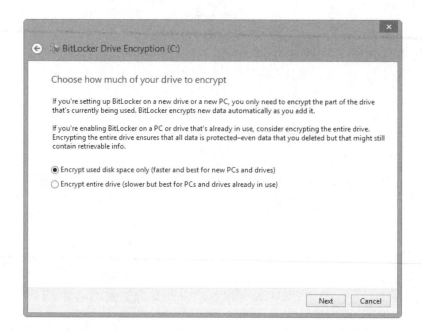

As soon as the encryption process starts, each time you start your computer you are asked to enter the password you set earlier. Without it, you can't start Windows 8 or access the encrypted drive.

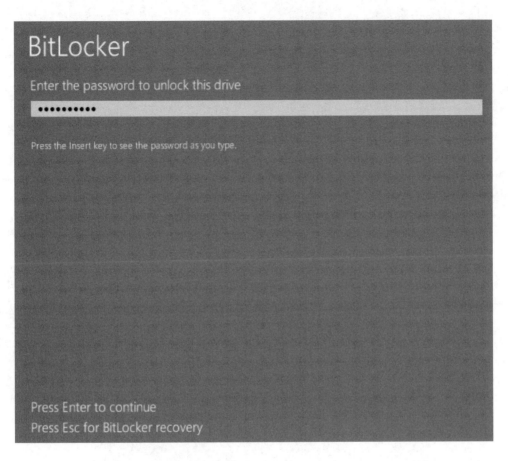

BitLocker

Enter the password to unlock this drive

••••••••••

Press the Insert key to see the password as you type.

Press Enter to continue
Press Esc for BitLocker recovery

Prior to encrypting the drive, you are asked to restart the computer. When you log on again, you see a small notification on the Desktop stating, "Encryption In Progress."

If you click or tap the notification, you see a progress indicator for the encryption process.

During the encryption process, you can use your computer normally. You can run applications, work on documents, and so on. You can restart your computer even if the encryption is not yet finished, and it will resume automatically the next time you start Windows 8.

In this exercise, you'll learn how to encrypt your operating system drive with BitLocker.

 SET UP Close any applications or work you have open and open the BitLocker Drive Encryption window.

1   Click or tap **Turn on BitLocker** next to the operating system drive to start the BitLocker Drive Encryption Wizard.

2   Enter the password you want to use twice.

3   Click or tap **Next**.

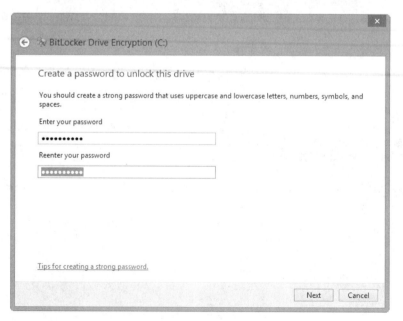

4   Save the recovery key by using the method you prefer and click or tap **Next**.

You are asked to choose how much of your drive you want to encrypt.

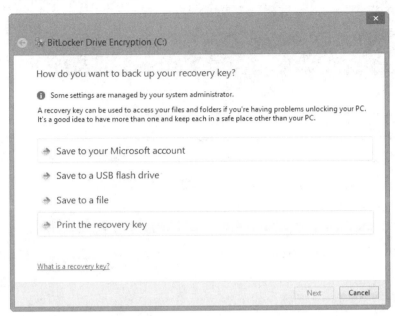

5   Select the option that fits your needs best and click or tap **Next**.

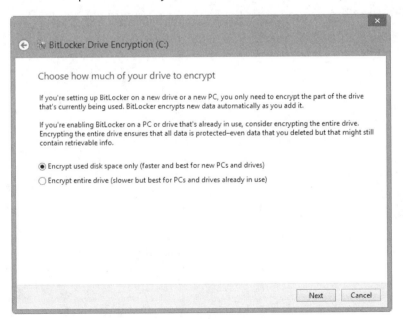

6   Leave the **Run BitLocker system** check box selected and click or tap **Continue**.

You are informed that the encryption will be completed after the computer is restarted.

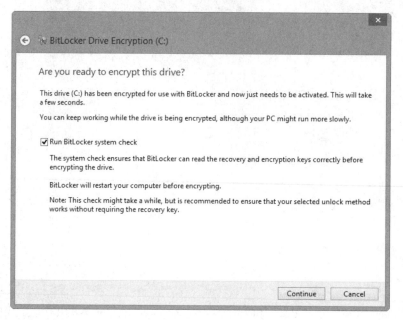

7   Restart the computer and enter the BitLocker password you set at step 2.

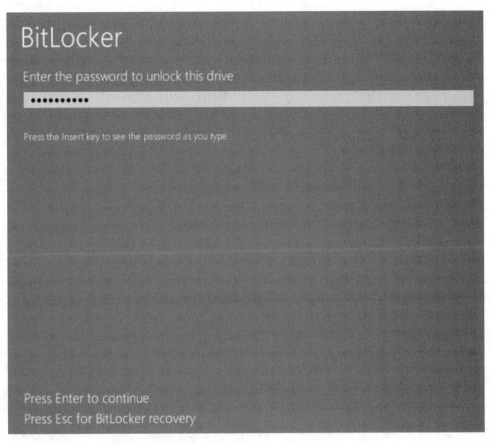

BitLocker

Enter the password to unlock this drive

●●●●●●●●●●

Press the Insert key to see the password as you type.

Press Enter to continue
Press Esc for BitLocker recovery

8   Log on to Windows 8.

You are notified that the encryption is in progress.

CLEAN UP Continue using your computer while the encryption process runs in the background.

The time it takes for the operating system drive to be encrypted depends on its size and how much data is stored. The performance of your computer's processor will also affect the speed of encryption. The faster the processor is, the faster the encryption process. It can take from 30 minutes to a few hours, so be patient.

Encrypting Removable Data Drives with BitLocker

Encrypting a removable data drive such as a USB memory stick doesn't take long, and it involves fewer steps than encrypting the operating system drive.

After the encryption process ends, each time you plug that drive into a Windows PC it will be displayed in File Explorer using a lock icon, signaling that it is encrypted. To access its content, you must enter the password that was set during the encryption process.

In this exercise, you'll learn how to encrypt a USB memory stick with BitLocker. The process is the same for other types of removable data drive, such as external hard disk drives.

 SET UP **Plug in the USB flash drive you want to encrypt and then open the BitLocker Drive Encryption window.**

1   Click or tap **Turn on BitLocker** next to the flash drive to start the BitLocker Drive Encryption Wizard.

TIP Depending on the USB memory stick you are encrypting, you might see an additional option on the screen, which says, "Automatically unlock this drive on this computer." If you are storing very sensitive data, it is best not to select this option.

2   Select **Use a password to unlock the drive**.

3   Enter the password you want to use twice.

4   Click or tap **Next**.

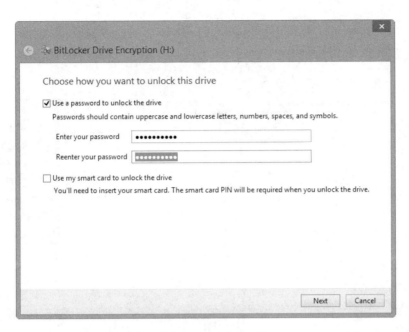

5   Save the recovery key by using the method you prefer and click or tap **Next**.

You are asked to choose how much of your drive you want to encrypt.

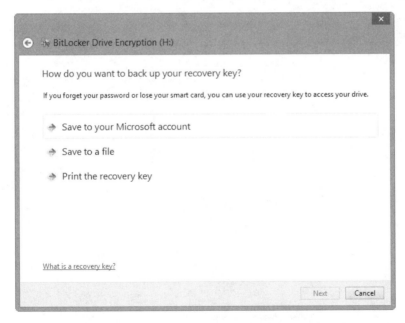

6   Select the option that fits your needs best and click or tap **Next**.

You are asked to confirm that you are ready to encrypt the drive.

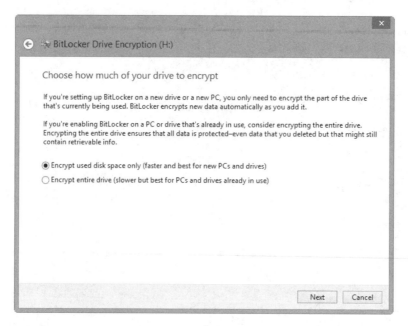

7   Click or tap **Start encrypting**.

A progress window appears.

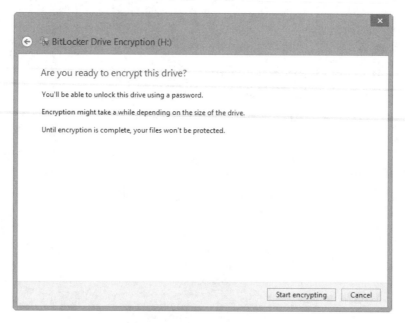

8   Wait for the process to finish and then click or tap **Close**.

CLEAN UP Close the BitLocker Drive Encryption window.

You can now use the USB memory stick as you normally would. All the data stored on it is now encrypted and can be accessed only with the password you have set. You can encrypt other removable drives, including external hard disk drives, by using the same procedure. The steps will be the same, but some of the options will appear slightly different depending on the device.

18

Accessing an Encrypted Removable Drive

Each time you plug the removable drive you have encrypted into any computer running Windows 8, including your own, a notification appears saying that the drive is BitLocker-protected.

Click or tap the notification, and you are asked to type the password you set during the encryption process. Type the password and click or tap Unlock. If you click or tap More Options, you can also set Windows to unlock this drive automatically each time you insert it.

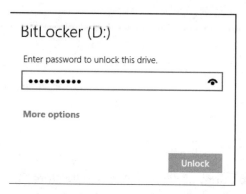

Only then can you view the data stored on it.

Decrypting a BitLocker-Protected Drive

The process for decrypting a BitLocker-protected drive is easy. Open the BitLocker Drive Encryption window and click Turn Off BitLocker for the drive you want to decrypt.

Confirm that you want to decrypt the drive and wait for the process to finish. BitLocker no longer protects the drive.

You can decrypt the drive only after you have unlocked it by providing the appropriate encryption password.

Key Points

- Windows Mobility Center is a helpful tool when you are mobile and you need to connect your laptop to multiple devices and displays.

- Turning on presentation mode is helpful when you need to deliver presentations at work or anywhere else.

- Encryption is a great solution for ensuring that your data is not accessed by unwanted people.

- With BitLocker, you can encrypt both your computer's drives and removable data drives such as USB flash memory sticks.

Chapter at a Glance

Calibrate

Calibrate your touchscreen, page 535

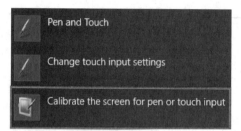

Flick

Flick to show charms, page 536

Swipe

Swipe slowly to show two apps at once, page 539

Write

Write an equation with the math input panel, page 547

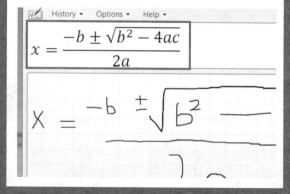

Using Windows 8 on Touch-Compatible Devices

19

IN THIS CHAPTER, YOU WILL LEARN HOW TO

- Set up your screen and calibrate it.

- Use general touch gestures.

- Explore and use multi-touch gestures.

- Change touch input settings.

- Use the math input panel.

If you have a Windows 8 PC, laptop, tablet, or other compatible device that accepts touch gestures, you can use the single-touch and multi-touch features available with Windows 8 in lieu of using a mouse or other pointing device. There are several features to explore beyond touch gestures, however; you can use a pen (stylus) to draw on the screen and use the on-screen keyboard to type (see Chapter 17, "Making My Computer Accessible"). You can use the Touch Keyboard on the Desktop. You can configure touch settings, too, including how you want to use a double-tap or long press. You should also configure and calibrate your display (even if it seems to work fine now). The touch and pen settings are configurable, so they can be personalized to suit your needs exactly.

PRACTICE FILES You do not need any practice files to complete this chapter. For more information about practice file requirements, see "Using the Practice Files" at the beginning of this book.

Setting Up Touch Hardware

If you've used touch before, you know you can touch app tiles to open their respective apps, double-tap desktop apps and desktop items such as Recycle Bin to open them, and use your finger to swipe and scroll while inside various apps and programs, including Microsoft Internet Explorer. You know you can tap and hold some items and swipe up from the bottom or down from the top to access an app's charms features. You might think that because touch works, your hardware does not need to be set up, but it does. At the very least, it should be calibrated.

During the calibration process, you'll be prompted to:

- **CHOOSE THE SCREEN TO USE** If more than one screen is available (or if Windows thinks there are multiple screens available), you choose which screen to use.

- **CALIBRATE THE SCREEN** You'll touch the screen in various places to make sure Windows 8 is calibrated properly.

- **CHOOSE A ROTATION OPTION** If your screen rotates, you can configure how the screen's orientation changes when you rotate it.

In this exercise, you'll access the touch options and work through the wizard to complete the setup process.

 SET UP **Start your computer and unlock the Lock screen. You need access to the Start screen.**

TIP In this book, if an instruction requires you to click something with a mouse, you can generally touch or tap the item to achieve the same result. If a right-click is required, you might need to touch and hold, swipe up from the bottom, or perform some other gesture.

1   At the **Start** screen, type **Touch**.

2   Click or touch **Settings**.

3   From the results, click or touch **Calibrate the screen for pen or touch input**.

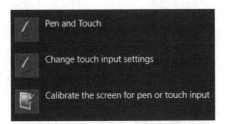

4   In the **Tablet PC Settings** dialog box, click or tap **Setup**.

5   Tap the screen to choose a monitor if prompted.

6   Tap **Calibrate**.

7   Work through the wizard as instructed. Tap **Yes** to save the calibration data.

8   If your screen rotates, tap **Go to Orientation**.

9   Configure orientation options as desired and then tap **OK** and **OK** again to close all dialog boxes.

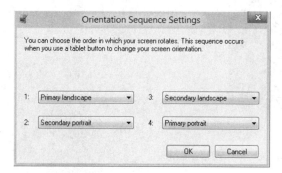

10   Tap the middle of the right side of the screen and flick left.

11   From the results, tap **Start** to return to the Start screen.

TIP It might take some practice to learn how to swipe from the right side of the screen to the left to access the charms. Keep trying; it will work!

✖ CLEAN UP No cleanup is required.

Learning General Touch Gestures

You might already be familiar with a few touch gestures; you can certainly tap a tile on the Start screen to open an app. You can apply many more touch techniques, too.

Here are the general single-touch gestures you'll want to learn right away.

- **ONE TAP** To open an app, to select a desktop icon, to apply a rating in the Store, to open a link in Internet Explorer, to use a Back or Forward button, to install an app, to select an email, or to perform any other task that can be applied with a single mouse click.

- **A DOUBLE-TAP** To open an item on the desktop, to zoom in on a webpage, or to perform any other task that can be applied with a traditional double-click with the mouse.

  TIP Use a pinching motion with your thumb and forefinger to zoom in and out of the screen. This works on the Start screen, too. Technically, this is a multi-touch gesture and is outlined in the next section.

- **A LONG TOUCH (TOUCH AND HOLD)** In some cases, to obtain results consistent with a traditional right-click with the mouse. Long-touch a folder on the desktop to access the contextual menu; long-touch a link in Internet Explorer to access options to copy and open the link. Use a long touch on the Start screen to drag an app to a new position.

- **A FAST SWIPE FROM THE LEFT EDGE INWARD** When multiple apps and desktop applications are open, this one-finger motion switches among them.

TROUBLESHOOTING If you have trouble getting the desired result when you swipe from the edges of the screen with a finger, try swiping with your thumb instead.

- **A FAST SWIPE FROM RIGHT TO LEFT OR FROM LEFT TO RIGHT (WHILE NOT AT THE EDGE OF THE SCREEN)** To scroll quickly through a map with the Maps app; to view additional information about the current weather from the Weather app; to change months quickly in the Calendar; to scroll through pages in the Store, Music, Video, and similar apps; to move among webpages you've visited in the Internet Explorer app; or to perform tasks such as scrolling from right to left with a traditional scroll bar and mouse.

- **A FAST SWIPE FROM THE RIGHT EDGE INWARD** To show the charms (Search, Share, Start, Devices, Settings).

  TIP To access settings for any app quickly, while in the app swipe from the middle right edge inward to show the charms and tap Settings.

- **A SLOW SWIPE FROM LEFT TO RIGHT (IN THE MIDDLE OF THE LEFT EDGE)** If you perform this gesture while using an app when multiple apps are open, you can snap one app so that it takes up a third of the screen and another app takes up the rest of it. This enables you to run two apps side by side (such as Calendar and Weather) and interact with both.

  TIP When you have two apps open at one time on the screen, use the bar that appears between them to make the smaller one larger and the larger one smaller. In this mode, you can still pinch to zoom and use other touch techniques.

IMPORTANT You won't be able to snap apps (and perform some other touch gestures) if your resolution is set too low or your monitor doesn't support the required resolution (which, at the current time, is 1366 × 768).

- **A FAST SWIPE OUT AND BACK FROM THE MIDDLE OF THE LEFT SIDE OF THE SCREEN** To show all running apps in a bar on the left side of the screen. (You can then tap any app to open it.)

- **PULL (FLICK) DOWN FROM TOP** Depending on your display and resolution and the app you have open, you might be able to pull down from the top of an app and drag it off the screen to close it or to view additional features.

  TIP Open the Internet Explorer app and pull down from the top to see additional options.

- **PULL (FLICK) UP FROM THE BOTTOM** While in an app, this gesture might display the available charms for that app.

- **TAP, HOLD, AND PULL SLIGHTLY DOWNWARD** To select an item in an app such as Photos or SkyDrive. This gesture selects the item and offers charms for managing the selected item. If you swipe down farther, the selected element can sometimes be moved to a new position.

TIP Try all these gestures before moving on.

Using Multi-Touch Gestures

In the previous section, you learned how to use the most common one-finger gestures. You learned about tapping, double-tapping, long-touching, swiping, and others. There are also a few multi-touch gestures you can use, and these require more than one finger to perform.

One of the most-used multi-touch gestures is the pinch. With two fingers, you can pinch inward and outward to zoom. You can do this even on the Start screen. When you pinch inward, all the icons on the Start screen become smaller; pinch outward, and they return to their original size. You can also perform this task with four or five fingers if desired.

If you have compatible hardware, a screen set to the proper resolution, and if you are using an app that supports it, you can use two fingers to rotate what's on the screen 90 degrees. In addition, as newer releases, updates, and hardware improvements become available, more multi-touch gestures will become available as well.

Changing Touch-Input Settings

Touch settings exist. If you use a tablet, you might have more settings than described in this section if they are provided by the manufacturer. Here, you'll be concerned only with what's available with Windows 8 and what is common to all Windows 8 computers, tablets, and devices.

TIP The manufacturer of your device might include additional features for it, such as a Windows button on the device itself (which returns you to the Start screen).

To see which touch features and configuration options are available, from the Start screen, type **Touch**. From Settings, view the results.

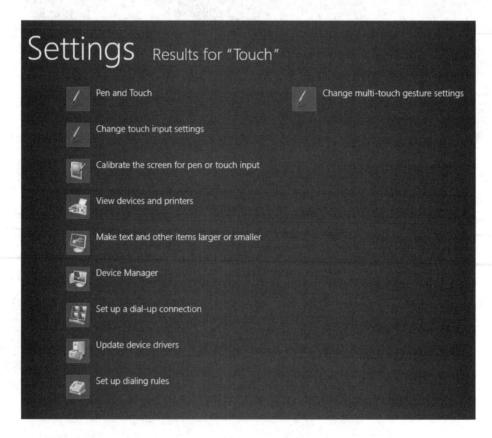

Settings — Results for "Touch"

- Pen and Touch
- Change touch input settings
- Calibrate the screen for pen or touch input
- View devices and printers
- Make text and other items larger or smaller
- Device Manager
- Set up a dial-up connection
- Update device drivers
- Set up dialing rules
- Change multi-touch gesture settings

The settings you'll want to explore include but might not be limited to:

- **PEN AND TOUCH (OR CHANGE TOUCH INPUT SETTINGS)** To configure options that require you to use your finger to interact with items on the screen. You can configure settings for Double-Tap and Press And Hold and settings to show visual feedback when touching the screen and when using a projector or external monitor.

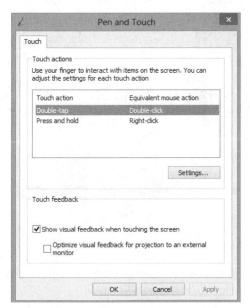

- **CALIBRATE THE SCREEN FOR PEN OR TOUCH INPUT** To access the Tablet PC Settings dialog box and its Display tab, introduced earlier in this chapter. You can calibrate your screen and configure the screen orientation options when your screen rotates (if it does). From the Other tab, you can access additional options to change multi-touch gestures.

- **CHANGE MULTI-TOUCH GESTURE SETTINGS** Access the Tablet PC Settings dialog box and its Other tab, to change handedness settings. Click Go to Input Panel Settings, to use gestures commonly used on handheld computers, the default, or use gestures from the Simplified Chinese standard.

You can access these settings and more from the traditional Control Panel, too. From Control Panel, Hardware And Sound, you have easy access to Mouse settings, Display settings, Pen And Touch input settings, and Tablet PC Settings.

In this exercise, you'll access Pen and Touch settings and configure how quickly you tap the screen when you double-tap and the tolerance for the distance you can move between taps.

→ SET UP Start your computer and unlock the Lock screen. You need access to the Start screen.

1   At the **Start** screen, type Pen. Tap **Settings**.

2   Touch **Pen and Touch**.

3   On the **Touch** tab, select **Double-tap** and touch **Settings**.

4   Move the slider for **Speed** to make the speed of the required double-tap faster or slower.

5   Double-tap in **Test Settings**. If the door opens and you are happy with the set speed, continue. Otherwise, repeat step 4 to change it.

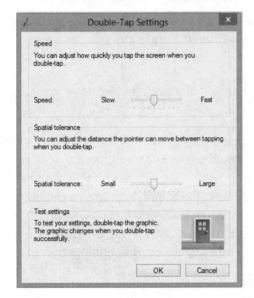

6   Repeat the process with **Spatial Tolerance**.

7   Tap **OK** and **OK** to close both dialog boxes.

TIP If you have a disability and find it difficult to use your hands effectively, increase the spatial tolerance to Large. This will give you the most leeway possible if your hands shake or you have other issues that keep you from tapping the screen the same place twice in a row.

Using the Math Input Panel

If you've ever tried to type a mathematical equation, you know how difficult it is. It's problematic to type something as simple as the Pythagorean theorem and almost impossible to type something as complicated as the Fourier series.

$$a^2 + b^2 = c^2; f(x) = a_0 = \sum_{n=1}^{\infty}\left(a_n \cos\frac{n\pi x}{L} + b_n \sin\frac{n\pi x}{L}\right)$$

Some programs such as Microsoft Word and Excel offer options that enable you to type common equations such as these, but other programs such as Mail don't. If you're creating your own formula, it wouldn't matter that these options were available.

You can use the math input panel to write math equations yourself, and you can write them with a stylus or your finger. After you've written the equation, you can insert it somewhere else easily.

TIP When exploring new apps, look for ones that accept text input by touch, specifically apps that enable you to "type" with your finger.

Learning to use the math input panel takes a little time, and it's important to know that as you type (or draw), what is shown in the preview area might not be what you meant. The math input panel is smart, and as you type, what appears might change automatically, based on what follows it. So, as you experiment, remember to write as legibly as possible and be patient. After you've typed the entire formula, you can use the eraser to remove what hasn't been interpreted correctly and retype it. After the formula is correct, tap Insert and then tap, hold, and paste your input into any other compatible program or app, such as a word processing program.

In this exercise, you'll type a common formula into the math input panel.

SET UP **Start your computer and unlock the Lock screen. You need access to the Start screen.**

1   At the **Start** screen, type Math. Touch **Math Input Panel**.

2   Note that **Write** is selected; use your finger to write the Pythagorean theorem.

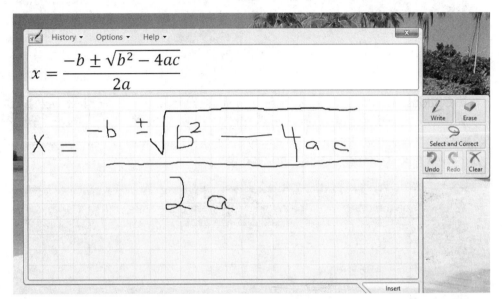

3   If necessary, tap **Erase** and drag your finger over the part of the equation that is not recognized. Tap **Write** and reenter the data.

   TIP If you only want to replace a single character in an equation, tap Select And Correct and circle the character. You can then reenter only that character.

4   If necessary, tap **Select and Correct**, select the entry to change, and choose from the list of options.

5   Tap **Insert**.

   The equation is now saved to the virtual clipboard.

6   If desired, open a program such as **Microsoft Word**, tap and hold, and select **Paste** to insert the formula.

   TIP Not all apps or applications currently support Paste in this scenario. Microsoft Office and other programs do, however.

CLEAN UP Leave the math Input panel open while you read the rest of this section.

After you've used the math input panel for a while, you can explore the tabs. On the History tab, you can access equations you've already created.

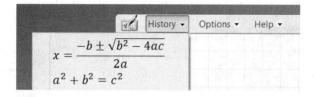

In Options, you can set preferences for using the math panel. For instance, by default, when you click Insert, the equation in the Write Math Here area disappears. In Options, you can disable this default feature. You can also change the side on which the buttons appear, show an on-screen keyboard, and hide the grid.

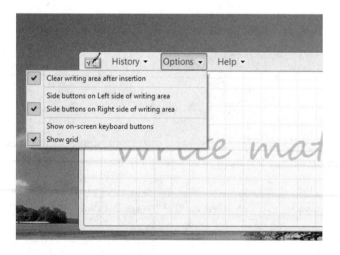

TIP You can get help from the math input panel on the Help tab.

Key Points

- You should calibrate your monitor even if it worked correctly right out of the box.

- You can use many single-touch and single-finger gestures to navigate Windows 8.

- A handful of multi-touch gestures, such as pinching, require more than one finger to perform.

- You can change many aspects of touch features, including how fast a double-tap should be and how close or far apart from each other those taps must occur.

- On the math input panel, you can write equations with your finger or a stylus and then copy and paste them into the desired program or app.

19

Chapter at a Glance

Add

Add the Shut Down, Restart, Sign Out, and other shortcuts to the Start screen, page 553

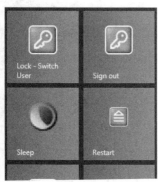

Place

Place a Show Start shortcut to the desktop, page 554

Name

Name groups of shortcuts on the Start screen, page 556

Optimize

Optimize startup items with Task Manager, page 594

20 Tips for Improving Your Windows 8 Computing Experience

20

IN THIS CHAPTER, YOU WILL LEARN HOW TO

- Add useful shortcuts for displaying the Windows 8 Start screen and Desktop.
- Customize the Windows taskbar.
- Use the hidden system menu.
- Use Task Manager to optimize the Windows 8 startup.

The learning doesn't stop with the tips mentioned in the preceding list. This chapter aims to teach you twenty useful tricks to optimize your Windows 8 experience.

Because the Start screen represents a major change from earlier versions of Windows, you'll find quite a few tricks to help you be more organized and productive when using it. You'll see some tips for the desktop and the Windows taskbar you've grown to love from earlier versions of Windows.

Next, you'll learn how to log on to Windows 8 automatically, without typing your password each time; run older apps as an administrator; add or remove features in Windows 8; turn off notifications; and optimize your disks. You'll learn a few tricks about using SkyDrive and the new Task Manager, too.

This chapter ends with tips on how to change the defaults for programs, file extensions, and AutoPlay dialog boxes.

PRACTICE FILES Before you can complete the exercises in this chapter, you need to copy the book's practice files to your computer. The practice files you'll use to complete the exercises in this chapter are in the Chapter20 folder. A complete list of practice files is provided in "Using the Practice Files" at the beginning of this book.

Adding Shut Down, Restart, Sign Out, and Other Shortcuts to the Start Screen

In the folder with practice files for this chapter are quite a few shortcuts for handy commands such as Shut Down, Restart, Sign Out, Sleep, Lock - Switch User, and Stop Shut Down.

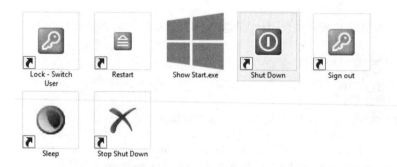

Each shortcut does what its name says, and all shortcuts work on all editions of Windows 8. There are a few things to keep in mind, though.

- The Shut Down shortcut won't shut down your system immediately. It initiates the shutdown procedure, which takes a few seconds to finish.

- The Stop Shut Down shortcut works only if you have used the Shut Down shortcut to shut down your system. If you have started the shutdown procedure by other means, running this shortcut probably won't have any effect on your system.

In this exercise, you'll learn how to add each of these shortcuts to the Start screen.

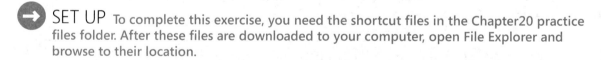

SET UP To complete this exercise, you need the shortcut files in the Chapter20 practice files folder. After these files are downloaded to your computer, open File Explorer and browse to their location.

1   Right-click or press and hold one of the shortcuts you want to pin to the Start screen.

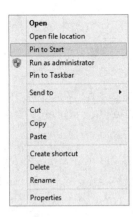

2   Click or tap **Pin to Start**.

3   Repeat steps 1 and 2 for all the shortcuts you want pinned to the Start screen and then open the Start screen.

4   Drag and drop the shortcuts on the Start screen so that they are in the same group and placed in the order you want.

⊗ CLEAN UP Close File Explorer.

Make sure you don't delete the shortcuts from the location to which you downloaded them. If you do, they will stop working because the Start screen will point to files that no longer exist.

Adding a Show Start Shortcut to the Desktop

The Windows 8 Start screen is so different from earlier versions of Windows that you cannot create normal shortcuts to take you from the Desktop to the Start screen. There is no Show Start shortcut on the Desktop that you can click or tap.

For this reason, the practice files contain a small executable file that opens the Start screen when you run it with a double-click. The file is named Show Start.exe; it's in the Chapter 20 practice files folder. Download it to your Desktop, and you can use it as a Show Start short-cut from the Desktop.

This shortcut will be useful especially while you are learning Windows 8 and all its new features and changes. It is also useful to people who prefer to use shortcuts they can click or tap instead of keyboard shortcuts. You can achieve the same effect as this shortcut by pressing the Windows key on your keyboard. If you are fine with using the keyboard, then you won't need this file.

If File Explorer is set so that it doesn't display file name extensions, you will see this file on your Desktop without the .exe extension.

Its name will be just Show Start.

When you no longer want to use this file as a shortcut, just delete it from your Desktop.

Adding a Control Panel Shortcut to the Start Screen

Another useful shortcut you might want to have on your Start screen is a shortcut for Control Panel. In this exercise, you'll learn how to add this shortcut to the Start screen.

SET UP Open the Start screen.

1 Type **control** and look for the Control Panel search result.

2 Right-click the **Control Panel** search result (or press and hold it while dragging slightly downward).

3 Click or tap **Pin to Start**.

CLEAN UP Switch from the list of search results back to the Start screen.

A Control Panel shortcut is now pinned and visible on the Start screen.

Naming Groups of Shortcuts on the Start Screen

On the Windows 8 Start screen you can drag and drop shortcuts into groups and name groups with custom names.

If you like your Start screen well organized, you'll want to name each group of shortcuts. In this exercise, you'll learn how to name these groups.

 SET UP Open the Start screen.

1   Note the minus sign on the bottom-right corner of the Start screen.

2   Click or tap the minus sign and notice a zoom-out effect.

3   Right-click the group of shortcuts you want to name (or press and hold it while drag-
     ging downward slightly).

4   Click or tap **Name group**.

5   Type the name of the group and then click or tap **Name**.

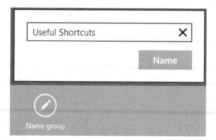

CLEAN UP Click or tap the empty space of the zoomed-out Start screen to return it to normal.

The selected group of shortcuts now has the name you set.

Adding Clocks and Time Zones to the Windows Taskbar

If you interact with people all over the world, it is useful to quickly access the time for more than just your time zone. You can set Windows 8 to display up to two additional clocks when you click or use the mouse to point to the clock shown in the taskbar.

In this exercise, you'll learn how to add two clocks to the Windows taskbar.

➡ SET UP **Open the Desktop.**

1   Click or tap the area of the taskbar where the clock is displayed to open a window with details about the current date and time.

2   Click or tap **Change date and time settings** to open the Date And Time window.

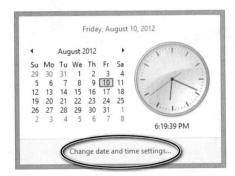

3   Click or tap the **Additional Clocks** tab.

4   Click or tap the **Show this clock** check box and select the time zone you want displayed for the first additional clock.

5   Type the name you want displayed for the first additional clock in the **Enter display name** field.

6   Repeat steps 4 and 5 for the second clock.

7   Click or tap **OK**.

❌ CLEAN UP No cleanup is required.

The additional clocks are now displayed each time you use the mouse to point to the clock in the taskbar or when you click or tap the taskbar.

Adding the Recycle Bin to the Windows Taskbar

If you are the type of user who likes to keep the desktop clean and without shortcuts, you might be interested in using the taskbar to keep shortcuts to apps and Windows features you use often.

In this exercise, you'll learn how to pin the Recycle Bin to the taskbar.

➡ SET UP To complete this exercise, you need the Recycle Bin shortcut found in the Chapter20 practice files folder. After you have downloaded this file, open File Explorer.

1   Browse to where you stored the Recycle Bin shortcut.

2   Right-click or press and hold the Recycle Bin shortcut to open the shortcut menu.

3   Click or tap **Pin to Taskbar**.

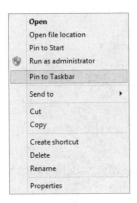

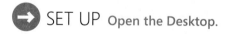 CLEAN UP Close File Explorer.

The Recycle Bin is now pinned to your taskbar. You can use the same procedure to pin other apps. You can use their shortcuts on the desktop or you can pin their main executable files directly to open the apps. The pinned entry will then act as a shortcut.

Using the Hidden System Menu

Microsoft removed the classic Start menu from Windows 8. In its place is a hidden system menu that provides quick and easy access to many useful tools such as Computer Management, the command prompt, Task Manager, Control Panel, the Run window, and many others. This is another feature Microsoft has added to make navigating Windows 8 easy for those who prefer using a keyboard and mouse.

The fastest way to open this menu is to press Windows+X on your keyboard.

In this exercise, you'll learn how to launch the hidden system menu by using the mouse or touch gestures.

SET UP Open the Desktop.

1   Using the mouse or your finger (if you have a screen with touch), point to the bottom-left corner of the screen until a Start tile appears.

2   Right-click the tile or press and hold it while dragging slightly downward to open the menu.

3   Click or tap the tool you want to launch.

❌ CLEAN UP No cleanup is required.

Don't hesitate to experiment with this procedure until you are comfortable launching and using this hidden menu.

Logging On to Windows 8 Automatically, Without Entering Your Password Each Time

If you are using only one user account on your Windows 8 PC or device, and you are using it where it is safe from strangers gaining unwanted access to it, you might want to set Windows 8 to log you on automatically, without entering your password each time. Even though this isn't a best practice recommended by Microsoft because it can lead to some complications detailed at the end of this section, it can make your life easier in certain scenarios.

In this exercise, you'll learn how to set Windows 8 to log on to your user account automatically.

➡ SET UP Open the Start screen.

1   Type netplwiz.

2   Click or tap the **netplwiz search result** to open the User Accounts window.

3   Select your user account.

4   Clear the **Users must enter a user name and password to use this computer** check box.

5   Click or tap **OK**.

You are asked to enter and confirm your password.

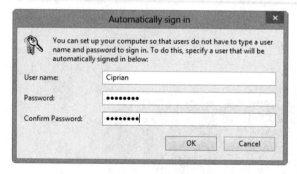

6   Type your user account password in the **Password** and **Confirm Password** fields.

7   Click or tap **OK**.

❌ CLEAN UP **No cleanup is required.**

The next time you start Windows 8, you will be logged on automatically to the user account you just selected. This user account will become the default logon user to Windows 8.

If you have multiple user accounts on your computer or device, setting this up might be an inconvenience. Windows 8 will always log on automatically to the user account you selected during this procedure. To log on with another user account, you need to wait for Windows 8 to start up and log on automatically. Then you must sign out and select the other user account to which you want to log on. If you want to reverse this setting, follow the same procedure and make sure you select Users Must Enter A User Name And Password To Use This Computer at step 4 in the exercise.

If your Windows 8 PC or device is part of a network domain, such as a corporate network, this procedure will not work. In network domains, the policies regarding the logon procedure are set by the network administrator and cannot be overwritten by users.

Running an Application as Administrator

In Windows 8, applications run by default without administrator permissions. This is a security feature that makes sure applications do not have the permission to make unwanted system changes. However, earlier applications that don't run so well on newer versions of Windows might need to be run with administrator permissions so that they function without problems.

If the application has a shortcut on the Start screen, right-click its shortcut or press and hold to select it. On the bottom menu, click or tap Run As Administrator.

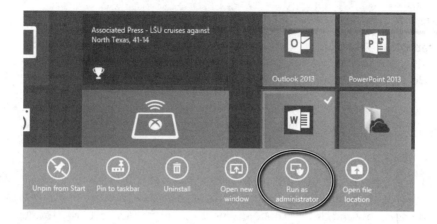

If you want to run the application from the desktop or File Explorer, right-click its shortcut or main executable (or press and hold) and select Run As Administrator from the shortcut menu.

In this exercise, you'll learn how to edit the properties of the application shortcut or main executable and have it always run as administrator.

➜ SET UP Open File Explorer.

1   Browse to where the main executable file of the application or its shortcut is stored.

2   Right-click or press and hold it and select **Properties** from the shortcut menu to open the Properties window.

3   Click or tap the **Compatibility** tab.

4   In **Privilege Level**, choose **Run this program as an administrator**.

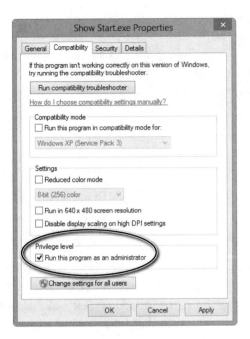

5   Click or tap **OK**.

⊗ CLEAN UP Close File Explorer.

From now on, each time you run the selected application a User Account Control (UAC) prompt appears asking for your permission to run the application as administrator. After you approve, the application is allowed to run with administrator permissions.

IMPORTANT Remember that the new Windows 8 apps don't run with administrator permissions and cannot be set to run with administrator permissions.

Adding or Removing Windows Features

Windows 8 comes with many features. Some of them are installed and enabled by default, whereas others are not and need to be added manually. You add or remove Windows features from the Windows Features window.

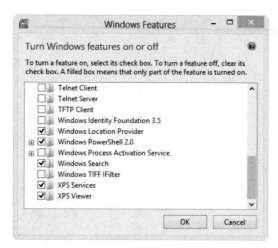

The features with a check mark near their name are turned on; those without a check mark are turned off. Similar features are grouped into folders that can be expanded. Clicking or tapping the plus sign near the folder name shows the individual features that are included. You can enable or disable the entire set of features in that folder or just individual features.

In this exercise, you'll learn how to remove a Windows feature. To demonstrate the procedure, you'll remove XPS Viewer, which you can add back after the exercise. However, for this exercise you can remove any Windows feature you don't plan to use.

 SET UP Open Control Panel.

1   Click or tap **Programs** and choose **Programs and Features**.

2   Click or tap **Turn Windows features on or off** to open the Windows Features window.

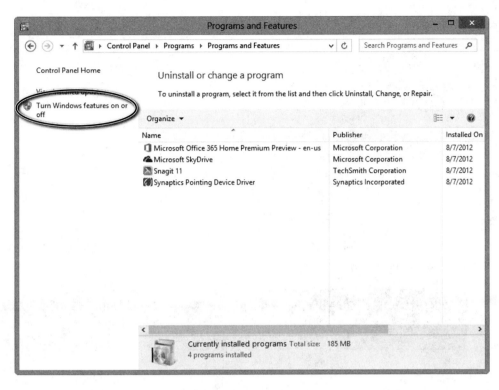

3   Clear the check mark for **XPS Viewer**.

You are warned that this might affect other Windows features and programs.

4   Click or tap **Yes** and then **OK**. Wait for Windows to complete the requested changes.

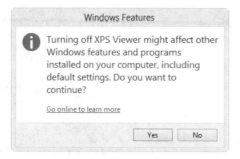

Windows Features

Turning off XPS Viewer might affect other Windows features and programs installed on your computer, including default settings. Do you want to continue?

Go online to learn more

| Yes | No |

5 Click or tap **Close**.

❌ CLEAN UP Close Programs And Features.

To add a Windows feature, go through the same steps. At step 3, you just choose the feature you want added.

> **IMPORTANT** Depending on the feature you are removing or adding, you might be asked to restart your system or to provide the Windows 8 installation disc for files to be copied from it. For most features, a disc won't be required.

Turning Off Notifications for Windows 8 Apps

Windows 8 has a new system for showing notifications that is more verbose than earlier versions of Windows, which you will notice after you download and install a number of apps.

You can customize in detail, at an app level, which notifications you receive. This customization is done from the Notifications area in PC Settings.

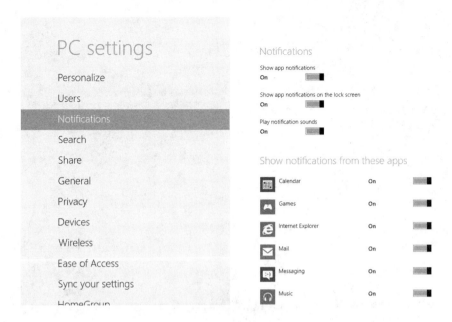

At the top are three settings with switches that affect all app notifications.

- **SHOW APP NOTIFICATIONS** When this is set to Off, you will stop receiving notifications from all apps.

- **SHOW APP NOTIFICATIONS ON THE LOCK SCREEN** When set to Off, no notifications appear on the lock screen.

- **PLAY NOTIFICATION SOUNDS** When set to Off, notifications will no longer be accompanied by sounds.

You have individual switches for all Windows 8 apps, too. Setting the switch for an application to Off stops notifications from that app. Keep in mind that the list of apps displayed depends on the apps you install on your computer or device. On your Windows 8 installation, you won't see the same number of apps listed as in the screen shots included in this section.

In this exercise, you'll learn how to disable notifications for a group of apps.

SET UP Open PC Settings.

1 Click or tap the **Notifications** area.

2 Browse through the list of notifications that can be turned on or off and identify those you want to turn off.

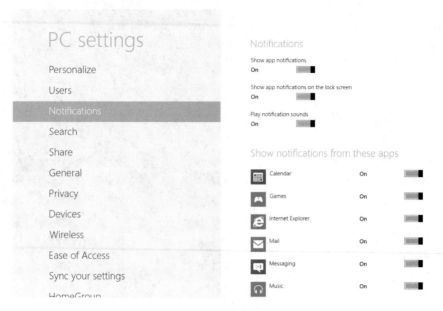

3   For the apps for which you no longer want to receive notifications, turn the switch from On to Off.

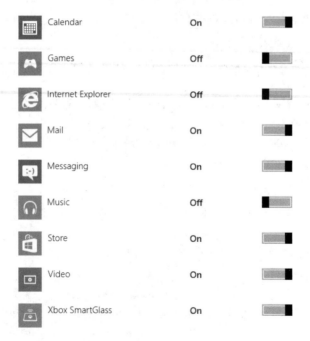

 CLEAN UP Close PC Settings.

Your notification settings are now applied.

Defragmenting a Disk Drive Manually

By default, Windows 8 automatically defragments all your disk drives once per week. The defragmentation process includes all your internal disk drives (except solid-state drives [SSD]) and all the external drives you have connected (such as USB memory sticks or external hard disks). SSDs are not included in the process because, due to the technology they use, defragmentation actually lowers their lifespan and doesn't provide any tangible speed benefit.

There might be times when you want to do this defragmentation ahead of schedule for the internal disk drives that make up your computer or for an external drive that you connected to the computer.

In this exercise, you'll learn how to perform a manual defragmentation of a disk drive.

 SET UP Open the Start screen.

1   Type **defrag** and click or tap **Settings** to view the search results.

2   Click or tap **Defragment and optimize your drives** to open the Optimize Drives window.

20

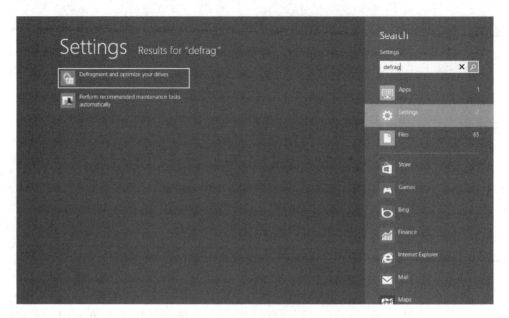

3   Select the drive you want to defragment and click or tap **Optimize**.

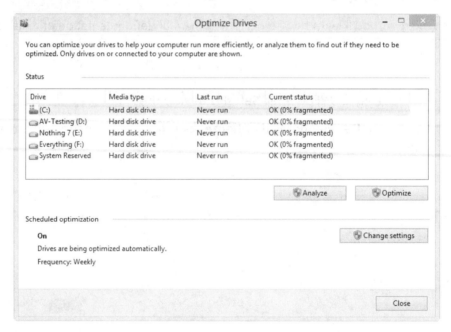

4   Wait for the process to finish.

❌ CLEAN UP Close Optimize Drives.

The selected drive has been defragmented.

You can use the steps detailed in this exercise to start the Optimize Drives tool and change its settings. Follow steps 1 and 2 and, at step 3, click or tap Change Settings.

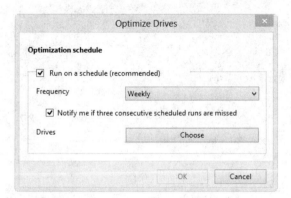

You will be able to change the schedule of when the defragmentation process runs and choose which drives are included in the process.

Freeing Up Disk Space with Disk Cleanup

When you are running out of space, a good solution to free up some space is to use the Disk Cleanup tool. This tool scans a selected drive and looks for temporary files and log files that are no longer needed, cache files used by different programs such as Internet Explorer, file history data, and so on.

It's recommended to use this tool once every few months to make sure your disk doesn't get overloaded with files that are not useful and to make more space available.

In this exercise, you'll learn how to use the Disk Cleanup tool to save space on your disk.

→ SET UP Open the Start screen.

1   Type **cleanup** and click or tap **Settings** to view the appropriate search results.

2   Click or tap **Free up disk space by deleting unnecessary files** to open the Disk Cleanup window.

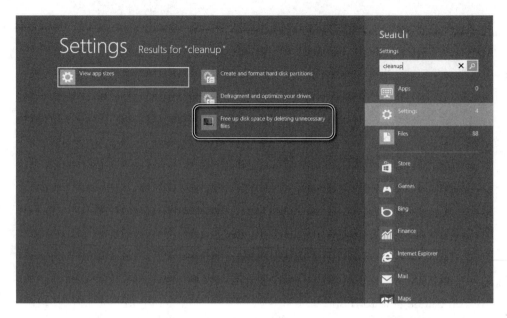

3   If you have more than one drive in your computer, select the drive on which Windows 8 is installed (by default, it's the C drive) and click or tap **OK**. Otherwise, skip to the next step.

4   Wait for the tool to scan the selected drive and present its suggestions for files to delete.

5   Select all the types of files that can be deleted.

6   Click or tap **OK**.

You are asked to confirm your choice.

7   Click or tap **Delete Files** and wait for the cleanup process to finish.

CLEAN UP No cleanup is required.

The selected files are deleted, and now more space is available on the selected disk. You can repeat the procedure on other disks in your Windows 8 PC or device.

Changing the Location of the Downloads Folder and Other User Folders

Windows 8 stores all your user files and folders in C:\Users, followed by your user name. There you will find folders such as Desktop, Downloads, My Documents, My Music, My Pictures, and so on.

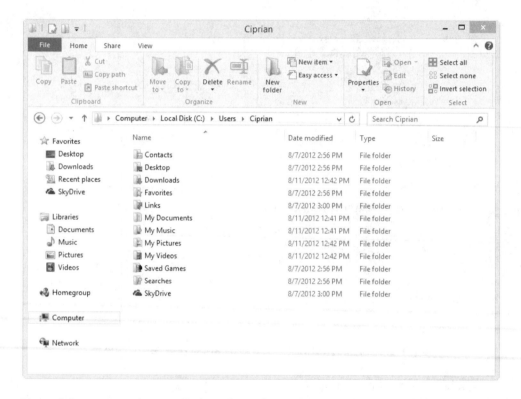

You might want to change the location of one or more of your user folders. For example, you might want to move the Downloads folder to the Desktop. Or, if you have more than one partition, you might want to move all your important user folders away from the partition on which Windows 8 is installed. This will help make sure your useful folders and their contents are safe if Windows 8 fails and you need to reinstall it.

In Windows 8, you can easily change the location of your user folders. In this exercise, you'll learn how to change the location of your Downloads folder.

➜ SET UP **Open File Explorer and navigate to where you user folders are stored (for instance, C:\Users, followed by your user name).**

1   Right-click or press and hold the Downloads folder to open the shortcut menu.

2   Click or tap **Properties** to open the Properties window for the Downloads folder.

3   Click or tap the **Location** tab.

4   Click or tap **Move** and select the new location for the Downloads folder.

5   Click or tap **OK**.

You are asked to confirm whether you want to move all the files from the old location to the new location.

6   Click or tap **Yes** and wait for the process to finish.

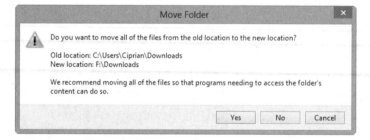

✖ CLEAN UP Close File Explorer.

The Downloads folder and all its content has been moved to the new location. You can repeat the same procedure for other user folders you would like to move to a different location. If you move them, make sure you don't select the same folder for more than one user folder. For example, don't have your Downloads and Desktop folders point to the same location. If you move two user folders to the same new folder, certain apps and Windows features will start to malfunction.

Burning a Disc with File Explorer

You can burn a disc directly from File Explorer without the need for a third-party solution. Even though third-party solutions are more complex and offer more features, File Explorer can do the job when you need to write a simple disc with files on it. When starting the burning process, you are prompted to choose between two types of discs.

- **LIKE A USB FLASH DRIVE (LIVE FILE SYSTEM)** Discs formatted with this method work like a USB flash drive or floppy disk, meaning you can copy files to disc immediately. They are a good choice if you want to keep a disc in the burning drive and copy files whenever you need to. These discs are compatible only with Windows XP and later versions of Windows.

- **WITH A CD/DVD PLAYER (MASTERED)** Discs formatted with this method don't copy files immediately, meaning you need to select the entire collection of files that you want to copy to the disc and then burn them all at once. They are convenient when you want to burn a large collection of files at one time. These discs are compatible with older computers and devices such as CD players and DVD players.

In this exercise, you'll learn how to burn a disc like a USB flash drive by using the Live File System.

SET UP Open File Explorer and insert an empty disc (CD or DVD) into the burning drive. Wait for the disc to be detected.

1   Click or tap **Computer**.

2   Double-click or tap the **DVR-RW Drive**.

You are asked how you want to use the disc you are about to burn.

3   Select **Like a USB flash drive**.

4   Type the title of the disc and press **Next**.

5   Wait for the disc to become ready for writing.

When the disc is ready, use File Explorer to access the disc.

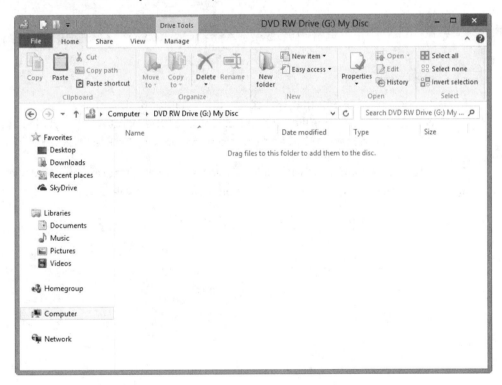

6   Drag the files and folders you want to burn to the disc.

7   Wait for the burn process to end.

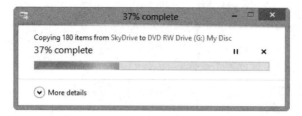

8   Eject the disc and wait for the burning session to be closed so that the disc can be used later.

⊗ CLEAN UP Close File Explorer.

You can continue to add content to the disc until it becomes full on the same computer on other Windows 8–based computers.

Accessing SkyDrive from the Desktop and File Explorer

By using the SkyDrive app that was covered in Chapter 6, "Using SkyDrive," you can access SkyDrive and manage your files with ease. However, the Windows 8 SkyDrive app is accessible only from the Start screen and not from the Desktop or File Explorer.

As an alternative, there is an official SkyDrive desktop application you can download, install, and use independently of the SkyDrive app included with Windows 8.

You can find it at *https://apps.live.com/skydrive*. Download it to your computer and install it.

SkyDrive apps

SkyDrive ▶ SkyDrive apps

SkyDrive for Windows

Keep important files on your PC in sync with SkyDrive.com.

Get the app

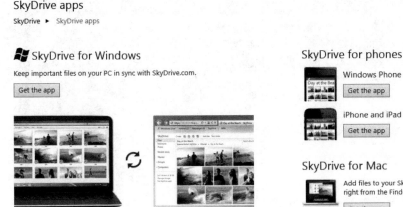

SkyDrive for phones

Windows Phone

Get the app

iPhone and iPad

Get the app

SkyDrive for Mac

Add files to your SkyDrive and organize them right from the Finder.

Get the app

If you are using a Microsoft account to log on to Windows 8, SkyDrive will use your account details automatically to sign in to the SkyDrive service. If you use a local account, you will have to enter the details of your Microsoft account manually.

After the application is set up, you can use its shortcut on the Desktop and access SkyDrive by using the SkyDrive shortcut in your File Explorer list of Favorites. The most important difference between the SkyDrive desktop application and the Windows 8 SkyDrive app is that by using the desktop application, you can access SkyDrive from File Explorer and the Desktop.

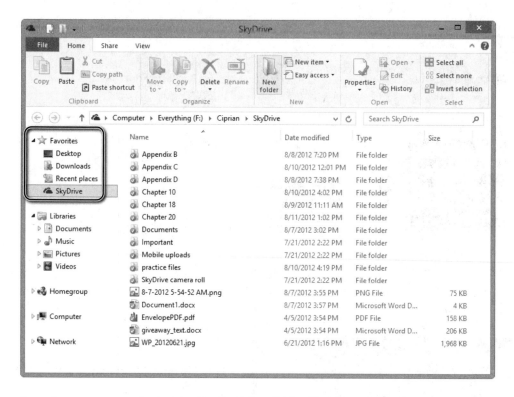

Any changes you make inside the SkyDrive folder listed in File Explorer will be automatically synced with the SkyDrive service and vice versa.

Unlike the Windows 8 app, the desktop SkyDrive application cannot be used to share files with others.

Using Shortened URLs When You Want to Share Files from SkyDrive

You can share files and folders from SkyDrive by using the SkyDrive app in Windows 8 and from the browser. When sharing a file from the browser, you have access to more options for sharing, including using a shortened URL instead of a complete one.

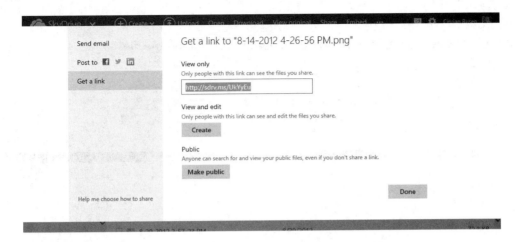

When generating the link for the file, you can also set permissions for accessing the file. The default is View Only permissions, but you can set them to View And Edit or to Public. Setting these kinds of sharing permissions is not available in the Windows 8 SkyDrive app. Therefore, if you want to share files and folders and set very specific permissions, it is best to use the browser and visit the SkyDrive webpage.

In this exercise, you'll learn how to share a file from SkyDrive by using a shortened URL.

SET UP Open Internet Explorer, browse to *https://skydrive.live.com*, and log on with your Microsoft account.

1   Select the file you want to share.

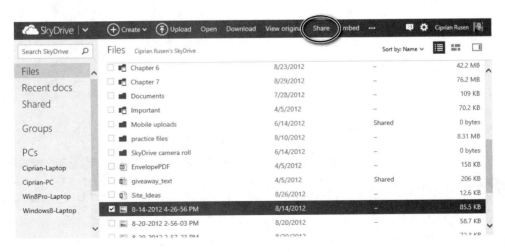

2   In the top toolbar, click or tap the **Share** button.

This opens a pop-up window with options for sharing the file.

3   Click or tap **Get a link**.

4   In the View Only section, click or tap **Create**.

5   Click or tap **Shorten**.

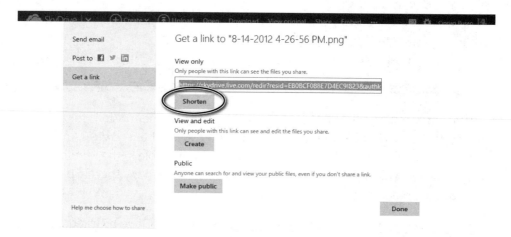

6   Copy the short URL and use it to share the file with others.

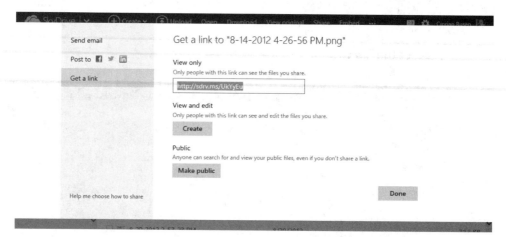

❌ CLEAN UP When you have shared the file by using the short URL, close the SkyDrive tab in Internet Explorer.

Five Ways to Launch Task Manager in Windows 8

The "Exploring Advanced Troubleshooting Tools" section in Chapter 21, "Troubleshooting Problems," covers the basics of using the new Task Manager to manage running applications and services. However, it does not cover in detail the many ways you can access this tool.

The first and best-known method to access Task Manager is not necessarily the fastest. It involves pressing Ctrl+Alt+Del followed by clicking or tapping Task Manager.

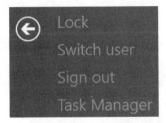

If you prefer to use your keyboard, the fastest way to launch Task Manager is to press Ctrl+Shift+Esc. That will open the tool without an additional click or tap.

Another rapid method is to use the hidden menu for power users, detailed in a previous tip in this chapter. Press Windows+X and then click or tap Task Manager.

You can also perform a search on the Start screen for the word *task* and click the search result.

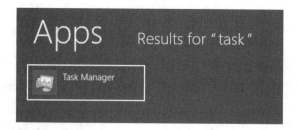

Last, you can use the All Apps list that can be launched from the Start screen. The Task Manager shortcut is in the Windows System area of shortcuts.

20

Optimizing Startup Items with Task Manager

When you open the new Task Manager for the first time, you might have the impression that it can be used to manage only the apps that are currently running due to the simplicity of the interface and the apparent lack of options.

Clicking or tapping More Details will make its window larger and display several tabs and options. In the Startup tab, you can view the apps that run at the Windows 8 startup. For each app, Task Manager shows its name, its publisher, its status (whether it is enabled or disabled to run at startup), and its impact on the startup procedure.

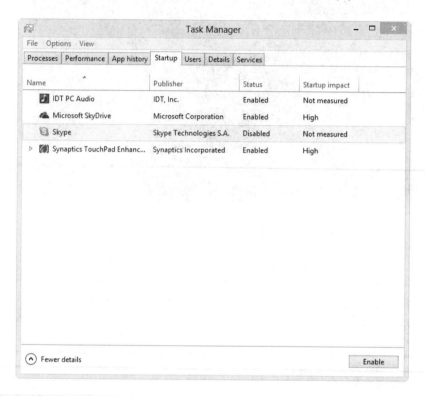

Based on this information, you can choose to disable some apps from running at startup so that Windows 8 starts up more quickly.

In this exercise, you'll learn how to disable apps from running at startup by using Task Manager.

SET UP Open Task Manager.

1   Click or tap **More details**.

2   Click or tap the **Startup** tab to view a list of all the applications running at startup.

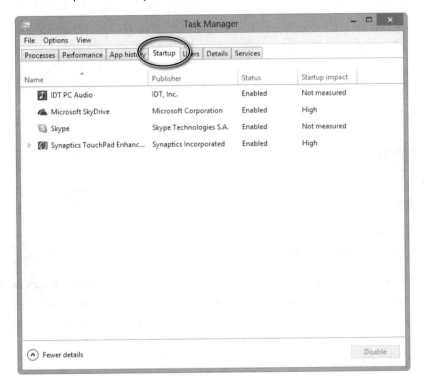

3   Select the app you want to disable from running at startup.

4   Click or tap **Disable**.

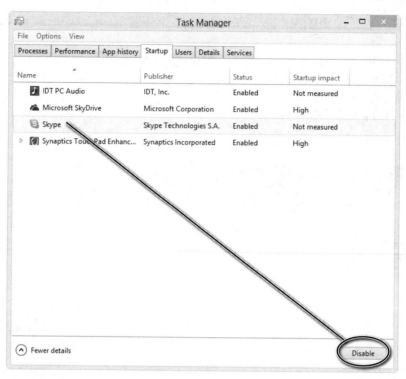

CLEAN UP Close Task Manager.

By using this method, you can disable all the items running at startup. However, when disabling items, it's recommended that you disable only apps you don't need to run at startup. Apps that are installed by the drivers of your hardware components (video card drivers, keyboard and mouse drivers, sound card drivers, and so on) should not be disabled. If you disable them, you might encounter issues with the functioning of your hardware components.

Changing the Defaults for Programs, File Extensions, and AutoPlay Dialog Boxes

Windows 8 users can change the defaults for programs, file types, and AutoPlay settings. The values can be changed from Control Panel by clicking or tapping Programs and choosing Default Programs.

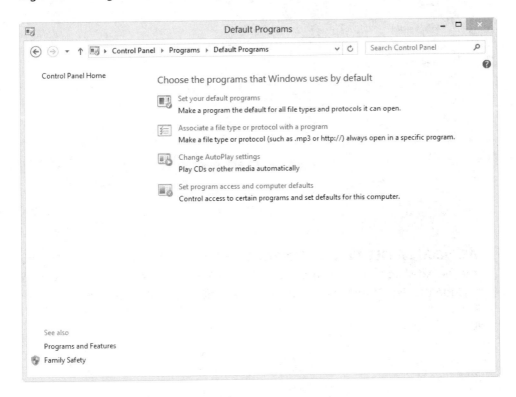

There you will find the following entries.

- **SET YOUR DEFAULT PROGRAMS** This setting lists all the programs and apps you have installed so you can choose the default files types and protocols that each program will open.

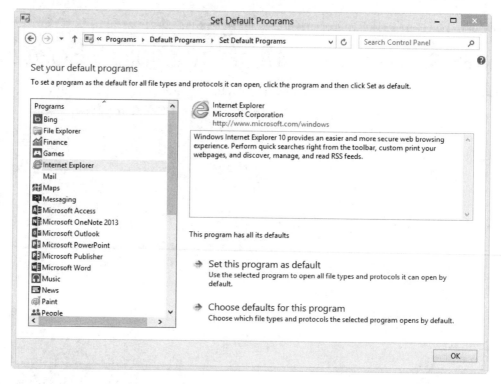

- **ASSOCIATE A FILE TYPE OR PROTOCOL WITH A PROGRAM** This setting lists all the file extensions registered on your Windows 8 computer or device so you can change the default program or app used to open each file extension.

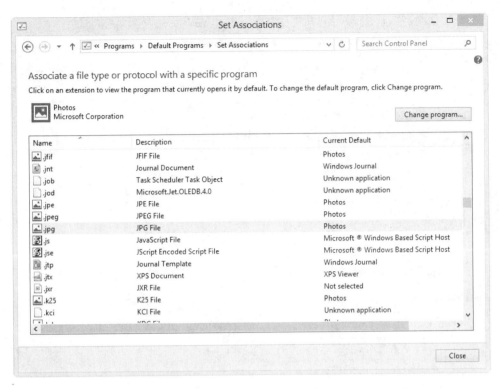

- **CHANGE AUTOPLAY SETTINGS** These settings determine the behavior of the AutoPlay dialog boxes displayed for the following types of media and devices: removable drives, video and photo storage, DVDs, Blu-ray discs, CDs, software, and games.

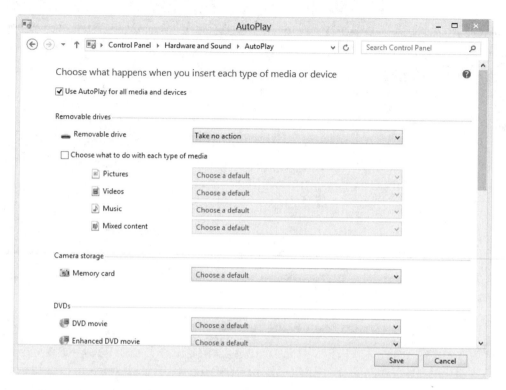

■ **SET PROGRAM ACCESS AND COMPUTER DEFAULTS** This setting changes the
default programs and apps you use for the most common computing activities: web
browsing, email, playing multimedia, instant messaging, and the virtual machine
used for Java. You can change the default programs so that they are the Microsoft
Windows defaults, third-party programs and apps you installed, or you can choose a
different program for each type of activity.

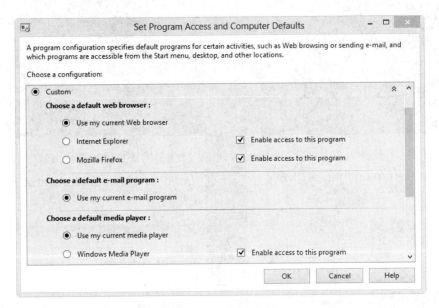

These tools come in handy after you have installed many programs and apps on your Windows 8 computer or device, which can cause your defaults to change in ways you don't want. You can use these tools to customize default programs and have the computing experience you want.

Key Points

- To ease your adjustment to the new Start screen, don't hesitate to use the shortcuts the first few tips suggest.

- If you would like to have a shortcut for the Start screen on your desktop, download and use the file provided near the beginning of this chapter.

- Notifications for Windows 8 apps can be set on a per-app level.

- You can use Task Manager not only to end programs that don't respond to your commands but also to optimize the list of apps running at startup.

Chapter at a Glance

Apply

Apply Advanced Startup options, page 604

Advanced startup

Start up from a device or disc (such as a USB drive or DVD), change firmware settings, change Windows startup settings, or restore system image. This will restart your PC.

Restart now

Troubleshoot

Troubleshoot hardware and sound problems, page 608

Explore

Explore advanced tools, page 616

Use these tools to get additional performance information

Performance issues

⚠ Performance can be improved by changing visual settings. View details.

View advanced information about your computer's performance

🖼 ⚙Clear all Windows Experience Index scores and re-rate the system
Force a complete re-run of all Windows Experience Index tests.

💾 ⚙View performance details in Event log
View details of problems affecting Windows performance.

◎ ⚙Open Performance Monitor
View graphs of system performance and collect data logs.

Use

Use Task Manager, page 618

	Task Manager			
Startup	**Users**	**Details**	**Services**	

Status	0% CPU	17% Memory	0% Disk	0% Network
	0%	20.7 MB	0 MB/s	0 Mbps
	0.1%	7.8 MB	0 MB/s	0 Mbps
▶	0%	40.8 MB	0 MB/s	0 Mbps

Troubleshooting Problems

21

IN THIS CHAPTER, YOU WILL LEARN HOW TO

- Resolve most problems with common solutions.

- Let Windows fix problems for you.

- Use Help and Support.

- Ask for Remote Assistance.

- Explore advanced troubleshooting tools.

- Refresh your computer or device.

- Reset your computer or device.

Your Windows 8 computer or device will likely run smoothly for quite some time. However, as your computer or device ages and you install new apps, acquire Windows and software updates, and save data and media to your computer's hard drive, problems might begin to appear. Most problems can be fixed by applying common solutions such as restarting the computer or uninstalling problematic apps, but others can take a little more effort.

In this chapter, you'll learn how to troubleshoot problems. In general, you should apply the techniques in this chapter in the order in which they are presented. Try to apply the most common solutions first and then see whether Windows can fix the problem for you. You might be able to resolve the problem by using Advanced Startup. If that doesn't work, you can look at Windows and Microsoft Help files, webpages, and forums. If you can't find a solution on your own, you can ask for Remote Assistance, experiment with advanced troubleshooting tools, and, finally, refresh or reset your computer or device.

PRACTICE FILES You do not need any practice files to complete this chapter. For more information about practice file requirements, see "Using the Practice Files" at the beginning of this book.

Resolve Most Problems with Common Solutions

Most problems can be resolved (at least in the short term) with one of a few common solutions. Restarting your computer is the first thing you should try. Restarting often resolves a problem temporarily and might allow you to get back to work quickly. You'll need to resolve the problem later and locate the root cause when you have more time.

Although there are several ways to restart your computer, the best way is to press the Windows+i key combination, click Power, and choose Restart.

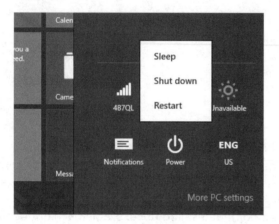

After you restart your computer, one of a few things will happen. Most likely, your computer will restart without incident, and the problem will be resolved. However, Windows 8 should run without incident, so whatever problem exists will still need to be resolved. If you've restarted the computer and you can access the Start screen, and you find that the problem persists, try these common fixes as they apply to your particular problem. (You'll try other options if these don't work.)

NOTE If your computer won't start, your only option is to start with the Windows 8 DVD or an available restore partition provided by the manufacturer and then run a repair option or perform an upgrade.

- **RESET DEVICES** Turn off, turn on, disconnect, and reconnect cables for problematic sound devices, monitors, printers, scanners, routers, and USB or FireWire devices. Turn off Bluetooth devices and resync or relink them.

- **RESTART YOUR NETWORK** Restart a problematic network by turning everything off and then turning hardware back on in the following order, letting each piece of hardware finish initializing before moving to the next one: modems first, then routers, and then computers, one at a time.

- **CHECK FOR SOLUTIONS FROM THE ACTION CENTER** Make sure Windows is up to date from the Action Center and let the Action Center check for solutions to problems it knows about already. See Chapter 15, "Preventing Problems," for more information.

- **UNINSTALL AND REINSTALL A PROBLEMATIC DESKTOP APP** If you are sure an installed desktop app is causing the issue, uninstall and reinstall it (or run its repair program). You can often click Help>Check For Updates in third-party programs to see whether known problems have been resolved by updates.

- **UNINSTALL AND REINSTALL A PROBLEMATIC APP** If you are sure an installed app is causing the issue, uninstall it. If the problem resolves, you can try reinstalling the app. If the problem reappears, uninstall the app permanently.

- **OPEN DEVICE MANAGER** Open Device Manager (type **Device** at the Start screen) and see whether specific hardware is the issue. If possible, install, reinstall, or roll back the driver. If prompted, let Windows search for the appropriate driver.

If your problem is not resolved, access the Advanced Settings. To start with advanced startup settings, type **Advanced** at the Start screen and choose Advanced Startup Options from the results available from Settings.

In PC Settings, scroll down to the bottom of the options on the General tab (which is selected), locate the Advanced Startup area, and then click Restart Now.

TIP You no longer press F8 during startup to access advanced startup options because many computers start too quickly to press F8 in time!

Advanced startup

Start up from a device or disc (such as a USB drive or DVD), change your PC's firmware settings, change Windows startup settings, or restore Windows from a system image. This will restart your PC.

Restart now

When you click Restart Now, you'll have access to the following options after the computer starts.

- **CONTINUE** Select this option to continue the start process. The only thing that happens is that the computer restarts.

- **USE A DEVICE** Select this option to start the computer with an alternate drive or device such as a Windows recovery DVD or startable USB drive.

- **USE ANOTHER OPERATING SYSTEM** If this option is available, you can select it to start with another operating system that is installed on your computer.

- **TROUBLESHOOT** Select this option to reset or refresh your PC or to use advanced tools.

- **TURN OFF YOUR PC** Turn off the PC and do nothing.

> **IMPORTANT** You will encounter problems if your computer's BIOS settings don't allow you to (or aren't configured to) start to a DVD or startable USB drive and you choose Use A Device in the advanced startup options. You might have to restart the computer again, enter BIOS settings (often by pressing F2 or some other key during startup), and change the start options so that you can start with the desired device.

In this exercise, you'll restart the computer, access the advanced options, and choose Automatic Repair. This will not harm your computer.

SET UP Start your computer and unlock the Lock screen. You need access to the Start screen.

1   From the **Start** screen, type Advanced.

2   Click **Settings** in the right pane and then click **Advanced startup options**.

3   Under **Advanced startup**, click **Restart now**.

4   From the Start options, click **Troubleshoot**, **Advanced options** and then **Automatic Repair**.

5   Wait while the computer restarts.

6   Follow the prompts to log on as required.

7   If problems are found, let Windows repair them. If not, click **Advanced options** when prompted. Click **Continue**.

CLEAN UP No cleanup is required.

TIP Read Chapter 14, "Keeping Windows 8 Safe and Secure," to learn how to use features such as System Restore, the Action Center, and Windows Defender.

Letting Windows Fix Problems for You

In the previous section, you worked through the most common solutions to problems, including restarting your computer or device, connected devices, and your network. In the exercise, you let Windows fix problems for you during the start process. You also learned that you can refer to Chapter 14 in this book to learn how to use System Restore, the Action Center, and Windows Defender if you have not tried those solutions yet and think they might work in your situation. However, if your computer starts properly, you've explored other options, and a problem persists, you'll need to try other solutions. (Sometimes a problem involves an inability to access the Internet, a printer not being recognized, or a program that is incompatible with Windows 8, which are situations System Restore, the Action Center, Windows Defender, and other options probably can't fix.)

Your next step in resolving problems is to explore the available troubleshooting wizards. To access the wizards, type **Fix** at the Start screen and, from the Settings results, choose Find And Fix Problems.

The resulting screen shows four categories; when you click one of these categories, new options appear.

- **PROGRAMS** Choose this option to run programs (now called desktop apps) that were made for previous versions of Windows on your Windows 8 computer or device. This opens Program Compatibility Troubleshooter. Work through the wizard to select the problematic program and choose the operating system for which it was designed. This resolves almost all problems with earlier programs because it lets those programs run in their native operating system space.

- **HARDWARE AND SOUND** Click this option to access troubleshooting wizards that relate to hardware and sound. You can choose from Sound, Device, Network, Printing, and Media Player options. Continue to work your way through these wizards by selecting the associated entry in this window.

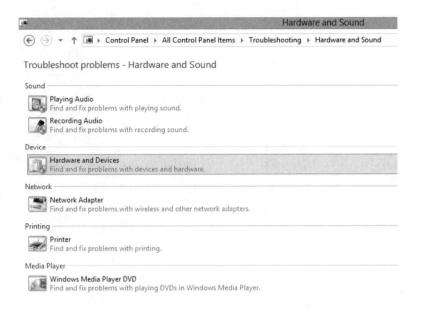

Troubleshoot problems - Hardware and Sound

Sound
Playing Audio
Find and fix problems with playing sound.

Recording Audio
Find and fix problems with recording sound.

Device
Hardware and Devices
Find and fix problems with devices and hardware.

Network
Network Adapter
Find and fix problems with wireless and other network adapters.

Printing
Printer
Find and fix problems with printing.

Media Player
Windows Media Player DVD
Find and fix problems with playing DVDs in Windows Media Player.

- **NETWORK AND INTERNET** Choose this option if you've restarted your network as detailed earlier but are still having problems. You can let Windows troubleshoot and fix advanced network problems, including those that deal with Internet connections, shared folders, homegroups, network adapters, incoming connections, and DirectAccess connections. You can also troubleshoot network printer problems.

   TIP If you receive an error announcing an IP address conflict or something similar, the Network And Internet Wizard can fix it.

- **SYSTEM AND SECURITY** Choose this option if you have problems with Internet Explorer, system maintenance, power, search and indexing, or Windows Update. As with the other options, when you open the desired wizard, it asks for input from you. Often, Windows will suggest a fix for your problem, and the fix will resolve it.

Troubleshoot problems - System and Security

Web Browser

Internet Explorer Safety
Find and fix problems with security and privacy features in Internet Explorer.

System

System Maintenance
Find and clean up unused files and shortcuts, and perform maintenance tasks.

Power

Power
Find and fix problems with your computer's power settings to conserve power and extend battery life.

Windows

Search and Indexing
Find and fix problems with Windows Search.

Windows Update
Resolve problems that prevent you from updating Windows.

Using Help and Support

Your Windows 8 operating system comes with built-in Help files for common problems and issues. You can access these files by typing Help at the Start screen.

When you click Help And Support, the Windows Help and Support Center appears. By default, the Help and Support feature accesses online Help files so that the results you get are the latest available. To get the most from Help and Support, you should be connected to the Internet.

You search for information and solutions in the Help and Support Center the same way you'd search for them on the Internet: type your keywords in the Search window and click the Search icon. You can use the Back and Forward buttons and access web links to more information. The Windows Help and Support Center offers access to both the Windows website and the Microsoft Answers website.

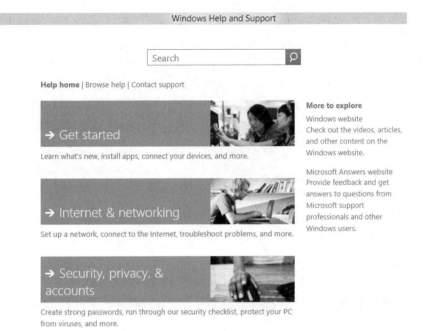

Search   🔍

Help home | Browse help | Contact support

→ Get started

Learn what's new, install apps, connect your devices, and more.

→ Internet & networking

Set up a network, connect to the Internet, troubleshoot problems, and more.

→ Security, privacy, & accounts

Create strong passwords, run through our security checklist, protect your PC from viruses, and more.

More to explore

Windows website
Check out the videos, articles, and other content on the Windows website.

Microsoft Answers website
Provide feedback and get answers to questions from Microsoft support professionals and other Windows users.

You can use Help and Support to troubleshoot hardware, network, and security issues, just as you can with the wizards, although most people find the wizards easier to use. However, the Help and Support pages also offer information related to more general problems. Suppose your child keeps accessing your user account and you can't figure out how to restrict such access. You can search Help and Support for information on how to create user accounts and create stronger passwords that your kids can't easily guess. That's a form of troubleshooting; it's resolving a problem!

In this exercise, you'll browse the Help and Support files to learn how to secure your computer with a user account for every user and to create strong passwords.

 SET UP **Start your computer and unlock the Lock screen. You need access to the Start screen.**

1   From the **Start** screen, type Help. Click **Help and Support**. Maximize the window if desired.

2   Click **Security, privacy, & accounts**.

3   Click **Create a user account**. Read the data and click the **Back** button.

4   In the **Search** window, type **Strong passwords**. Click the **Search** icon.

5   Review the results as desired.

❌ CLEAN UP Close the Help and Support window.

Asking for Remote Assistance

Remote Assistance is a feature available in Windows 8 (and previous operating systems) by which you can ask a friend, relative, colleague, or support professional for assistance in resolving a problem. After you ask for assistance and the other person agrees to give it, the helper can view your computer screen to see the problem in action. (He or she does this over the Internet.) By viewing your computer screen and the problem, he or she can often help you figure out how to fix it. After you're connected with a helper by Remote Assistance, you can also give him or her permission to take control of the screen and resolve the problem directly. It's a technology that enables someone who is not physically close to you to access your computer as if he or she were sitting in front of it.

Before you can use Remote Assistance, you must verify that Remote Assistance invitations can be sent from your computer. You can check this from the System Properties window. By default, this feature is enabled. If you click the Advanced button, you'll also see that the ability to let the helper control the computer remotely is also enabled by default.

TIP To access the System Properties dialog box, type **System** at the Start screen, click Settings, choose System from the results, and then click Advanced System Settings. Choose the Remote tab.

When you're ready to send a Remote Assistance invitation, you must access the option to send an invitation. You can do this by typing **Invite** at the Start screen. Click Settings, and the option to Invite Someone To Connect To Your PC And Help You, Or Offer To Help Someone Else appears.

When the Windows Remote Assistance window opens, select Invite Someone You Trust To Help You and then follow the rest of the prompts as required.

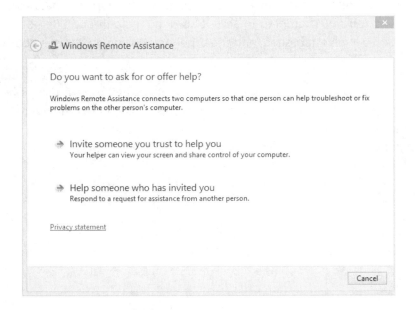

There are three ways to send the required invitation to ask for help by using Remote Assistance.

- **SAVE THIS INVITATION AS A FILE** Choose this option to send your invitation as an attachment when you use a web-based email account such as Google mail or Yahoo!.

- **USE EMAIL TO SEND AN INVITATION** Choose this option if you use a compatible email program on your computer, such as Microsoft Outlook or the Mail app, to send the invitation as an attachment.

- **USE EASY CONNECT** Choose this option if your helper also has access to Easy Connect. When you choose this option, you'll receive an Easy Connect password, which you'll relay to your helper by phone, email, fax, or text. (Try this option first and then work through the exercise offered later if this option doesn't work.)

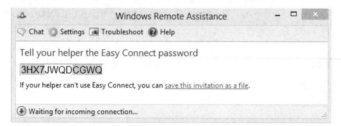

After your helper receives an invitation by email or as a message from you by another means, he or she will open Remote Assistance on that computer and type the password you've given him or her. You'll be prompted to accept his or her help through Remote Assistance, a connection will be established, and the other user will be able to see your screen.

During the session, the helper can see and take control of your screen by using his or her own monitor and mouse. You can hold chats to relay the problem, stop sharing your screen (if you are), pause the session, and so on. You're always in control and can stop the session at any time by clicking the red X in the Remote Assistance window.

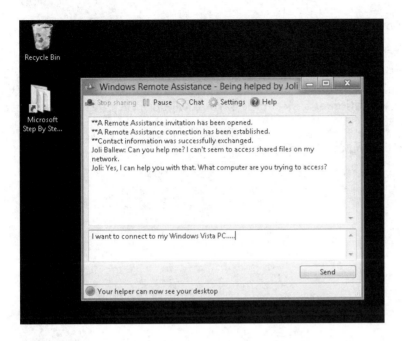

In this exercise, you'll create a Remote Assistance invitation code and relay that code to your helper by using your preferred method of communication.

 SET UP Start your computer and unlock the Lock screen. You need access to the Start screen.

1   At the **Start** screen, type Invite. Click **Settings**.

2   Click **Invite someone to connect to your PC and help you, or offer to help some-one else**.

3   Click **Invite someone you trust to help you**.

> **TIP** If you've received help from someone before by using Remote Assistance, that person will appear as an option after you invite someone to help you.

4   Click **Save this invitation as a file**. In the **Save As** window, click **Desktop** and then choose **Save**.

The invitation file and password opens.

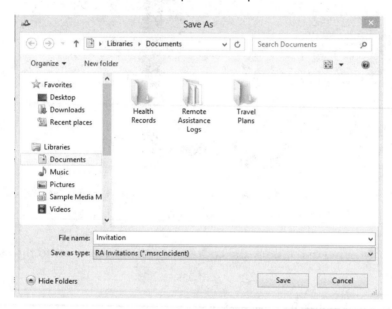

5   Relay the information to your helper as desired.

The helper inputs the 12-character password he or she receives, and a session begins.

6   Follow the helper's instructions to resolve your problem.

CLEAN UP If the helper responds with an offer to help, accept the offer. When desired, close the Remote Assistance window to end the session.

Exploring Advanced Troubleshooting Tools

Windows 8 comes with many more troubleshooting tools than can be detailed here. You can access the tools from the Start screen by typing **Troubleshooting**, **Diagnose**, **Performance**, **Repair**, or similar keywords. These options can be more complex than you are ready for, such as using Task Manager to close processes or services or viewing and drawing conclusions from what you see in event logs, Performance Monitor, Resource Monitor, and similar programs. However, it's important to know at least some of the advanced tools that are available in case your troubleshooting efforts continue to go unresolved or if a technician asks you to supply information you can get only by using these tools.

TIP Although advanced tools are detailed here, it is probably best to try to refresh your PC before you spend too much time working with these tools if you don't have professional help.

Here are a few of the tools you can use to troubleshoot difficult-to-diagnose problems.

- **PERFORMANCE INFORMATION AND TOOLS** To adjust visual effects, indexing options, and power settings and to access advanced tools. You can also view and print detailed performance and system information.

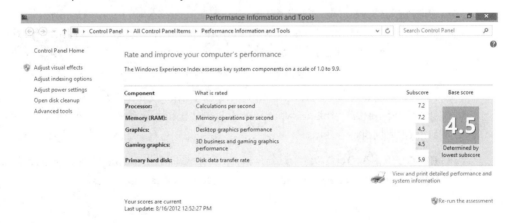

- **ADVANCED TOOLS** To view current known performance issues and to view information in event logs, Performance Monitor, Resource Monitor, Task Manager, System Information, and so on.

Use these tools to get additional performance information

Performance issues

⚠ Performance can be improved by changing visual settings. View details.

View advanced information about your computer's performance

🔧 Clear all Windows Experience Index scores and re-rate the system
Force a complete re-run of all Windows Experience Index tests.

🔧 View performance details in Event log
View details of problems affecting Windows performance.

🔧 Open Performance Monitor
View graphs of system performance and collect data logs.

🔧 Open Resource Monitor
View real-time system resource usage and manage active services and applications.

Open Task Manager
Get information about the programs and processes that are currently running on your computer.

View advanced system details in System Information
View details about the hardware and software components on your computer.

🔧 Adjust the appearance and performance of Windows
Select settings to change visual effects, processor and memory usage, and virtual memory.

🔧 Open Disk Defragmenter
Modify the schedule used to automatically defragment your hard disk.

🔧 Generate a system health report
View details about system health and performance.

- **EVENT VIEWER** To view information about errors that have occurred on your computer, warnings that have been generated, and critical events. Although the information here is rather cryptic, a technical support professional (or a good web search) might help you understand the information.

- **PERFORMANCE MONITOR** To view performance information in logs by configuring specific criteria detailing what you'd like to monitor. You can monitor memory, CPU, and other components.

- **RESOURCE MONITOR** To view live information about how resources are currently being used along with other data regarding those resources.

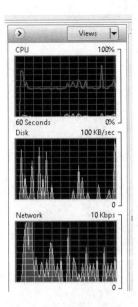

One other tool with which you'll want to become familiar is Task Manager. If you've used a computer running Windows before, you're probably already familiar with it. After you open Task Manager, click More Details. Task Manager offers seven tabs, and each performs specific functions.

21

TIP You can open Task Manager by using the Ctrl+Alt+Del key combination. When it opens, click More Details.

- **PROCESSES** To see which apps, background processes, and Windows processes are currently running. If an app is frozen, you can right-click it from this tab and end the task (close the app). You can also view how much of your computer's resources the app is using. Likewise, if you know that a particular process is unresponsive, you can exit that process.

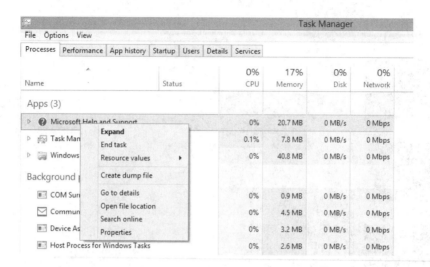

- **PERFORMANCE** To see how your computer's resources are currently being allocated. You have options for CPU, Memory, Disk, and likely Wi-Fi and Ethernet, although you might see others. You can use this information to find out which resource is being overworked or overwhelmed.

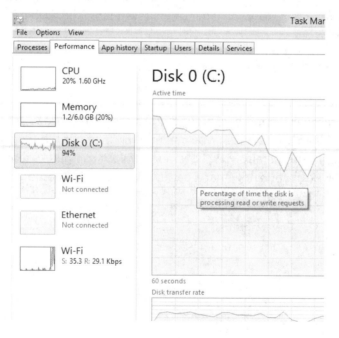

TIP There are some general rules for deciding whether a resource is overwhelmed. For instance, average CPU usage when the computer is idle or only running a word processing program should be around 10 percent, and when *average* usage hits 90 percent or higher, the CPU is working hard to keep up with the demands placed on it. You can expect spikes for components at any time, however; spikes are normal.

- **APP HISTORY** To view the total resources that your installed apps have used for the past month. You can use this tab to discover resource-intensive apps and uninstall them if you feel one app might be causing performance problems.

- **STARTUP** To see which applications start when your computer starts (and thus run in the background all the time). The more enabled apps you see here, the longer it will take the computer to start. You can right-click to disable any app so that it does not start when your computer starts to improve start time and computer performance.

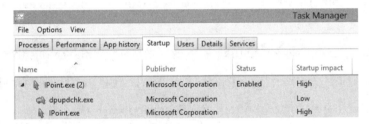

- **USERS** To view the users who are currently logged on and how many resources they are using.

- **DETAILS** To view details about running apps and programs, including how much CPU and memory they use, their status, and their descriptions. You probably won't make too many changes here; you'll use other tabs to troubleshoot.

- **SERVICES** To view the services that are currently running. Services run so that Windows features can work, including Plug and Play, Themes, Task Scheduler, and more. Programs and apps need services to run, so stopping a service could cause problems for the computer. Sometimes you can use this option to troubleshoot a nonworking service and start (or restart) the service if it's inadvertently been stopped or is not working properly.

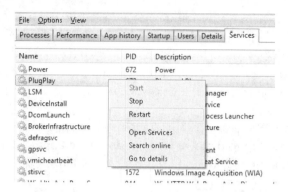

In this exercise, you'll explore Task Manager and view CPU usage as you perform calculations.

SET UP Start your computer and unlock the Lock screen. You need access to the Start screen.

1. From the **Start** screen, type Calculator. Click **Calculator** in the results to open it.

2. Press **Ctrl+Alt+Del** and then click **Task Manager**; click the **Performance** tab.

3. Position Calculator on top of the Task Manager window.

4. Perform several complex computations and note the change (if any) in the CPU's performance graph.

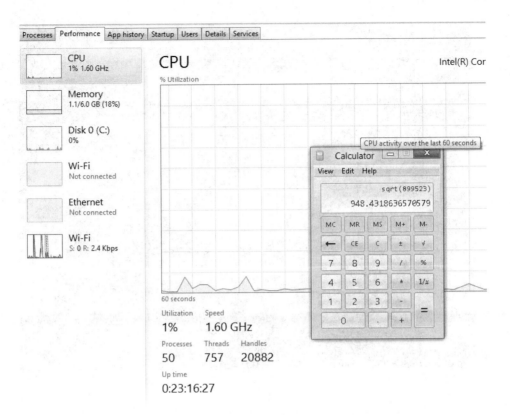

To view additional resources, type keywords on the Start screen. *Troubleshooting* is a great keyword to try. Try *Performance* and *Identify*, too, as time allows.

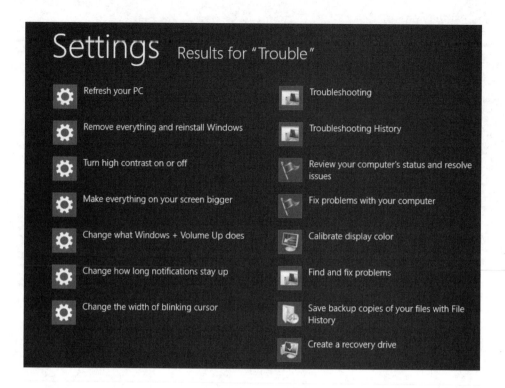

Settings   Results for "Trouble"

Refresh your PC

Remove everything and reinstall Windows

Turn high contrast on or off

Make everything on your screen bigger

Change what Windows + Volume Up does

Change how long notifications stay up

Change the width of blinking cursor

Troubleshooting

Troubleshooting History

Review your computer's status and resolve issues

Fix problems with your computer

Calibrate display color

Find and fix problems

Save backup copies of your files with File History

Create a recovery drive

Refreshing Your PC

If your PC just isn't running well, or if you have problems that you think are related to missing operating system files, third-party programs, malware, or some hard-to-fix Windows-related issue, you can refresh your PC.

Refresh will revert Windows 8 to its system defaults. This option also preserves user settings, user data, and applications bought through the Windows Store. It keeps all your photos, music, documents, and videos. It keeps your personal settings, too. However, everything else is removed, and the computer is restored to its defaults. Programs you've installed will be removed. Toolbars for Internet Explorer will be uninstalled. Third-party software, such as software you might acquire with a new printer or scanner, will be removed.

This is a good option if you've tried everything else and nothing seems to work. It isn't a new install; it's just a refresh of the operating system and a removal of potentially problematic third-party applications and add-ons.

In this exercise, you'll refresh your PC. Do not perform this exercise unless you have tried other troubleshooting techniques and you are sure this is the only option remaining.

SET UP Start your computer and unlock the Lock screen. You need access to the Start screen.

1   From the **Start** screen, type Refresh.

2   Click **Settings** and choose **Refresh your PC**.

3   Read the information and click **Next**.

4   Wait while the computer is prepared for the refresh and then follow any additional prompts.

5   When the process completes, enter your password on the **Lock** screen.

CLEAN UP Reinstall third-party programs as applicable.

Resetting Your PC

You reset your PC by using the same method you used to refresh it. Resetting is a good option if you've already tried all the other troubleshooting tips in this chapter and others, if you've refreshed your PC, and if you've been told by a professional that resetting is the only option (or if you plan to sell or give away your PC).

When you reset your PC, all your personal files, apps, and third-party programs are removed. All your personalization settings will be reset. Your network settings, Internet settings, installed hardware, and any other personalization you've made are erased, and all your PC settings are changed to their defaults. This option restores your computer to a like-new state.

Key Points

- Restarting your computer will resolve many problems in the short term without further troubleshooting. However, you'll need to get to the root of the problem to resolve it permanently.

- Resetting devices or your network can easily resolve many related problems.

- Advanced startup options are no longer available by pressing F8 during startup; instead, you restart the PC with Advanced settings enabled from Windows 8.

- Troubleshooting wizards are available that can help you fix all kinds of problems, including those that are related to program, hardware, network, Internet, security, and so on.

- The Windows Help and Support Center offers resources you can use to diagnose and resolve many types of issues.

- With Remote Assistance, you can easily ask a friend, colleague, relative, or other person for help.

- When all else fails, there are myriad advanced troubleshooting tools to try.

- Refresh and Reset are options to return your PC to a previous state.

Using Keyboard Shortcuts and Touch Gestures in Windows 8

IN THIS APPENDIX, YOU WILL LEARN HOW TO

- Use the keyboard shortcuts for Windows 8.

- Explore touch keyboard shortcuts.

- Use touch gestures in Windows 8.

As long as there have been Windows operating systems, there have been keyboard shortcuts. You might know some already. You might even know that you can press the Windows key to return to the Start screen from anywhere in Windows 8, for instance, or that Windows+C displays the default charms. There are many more shortcuts; you will likely be surprised at just how many there are and the extent to which they can be used.

In this appendix, you'll first learn all the keyboard shortcuts that work in Windows 8 and how to experiment with touch keyboard shortcuts. Then, you'll see the touch gestures you can use in Windows 8 when running it on a computer or device with touch capabilities.

PRACTICE FILES You do not need any practice files for this Appendix. A complete list of practice files is provided in the "Using the Practice Files" section at the beginning of this book.

Learning Keyboard Shortcuts for Windows 8

Some keyboard shortcuts are unique to Windows 8, such as pressing the Windows key to return to the Windows 8 Start screen, mentioned earlier. Some keyboard shortcuts are traditional, such as using Ctrl+x to delete selected text, Ctrl+z to undo what you've just done (perhaps restoring text you've just deleted), and so on, and have been around for decades and almost always produce the same results.

TIP See Chapter 17, "Making My Computer Accessible," for more information about personalizing the keyboard to use Sticky Keys, Toggle Keys, Filter Keys, Mouse Keys, and so on.

The following list contains a few keyboard shortcuts that are extremely useful in Windows 8, and you can use them no matter where you are (in an app, on the desktop, using Internet Explorer, and so on) on the computer.

TIP If you prefer the on-screen keyboard to a traditional keyboard, you can use these shortcuts there. However, because you can't hold down two keys at once, click the first required key (such as Windows) and then the second (such as D or C) when using the on-screen keyboard.

- **ACCESS THE START SCREEN** Press the Windows key
- **ACCESS THE DESKTOP** Windows+D
- **SHOW THE CHARMS** Windows+C. Shortcuts for charms are:
  - **SEARCH** Windows+Q or just start typing when you are on the Start menu
  - **SHARE** Windows+H
  - **START** Windows
  - **DEVICES** Windows+K
  - **SETTINGS** Windows+I

  TIP When you're ready to shut down your computer, use Windows+I and then click or tap the Power button, found on the bottom right.

- **SHOW THE APP BAR WHILE IN ANY APP** Windows+Z
- **CYCLE THROUGH OPEN APPS** Windows+Tab or Alt+Tab
- **ZOOM IN AND OUT** Ctrl+- to zoom out and Ctrl++ to zoom in
- **SNAP AN APP TO ONE SIDE OF THE SCREEN** Windows+period.

TIP You'll find that many of the traditional shortcuts you've always used still exist, such as Windows+L to lock and Windows+P to project to another display.

The complete list of keyboard shortcuts that you can use in Windows 8 follows.

- **WINDOWS** Opens the Start screen.
- **RIGHT SHIFT KEY** If you press it for eight seconds, it turns on Filter Keys. If you press it five times in a row, it turns on Sticky Keys.
- **CTRL+MOUSE WHEEL** When used on the desktop, it changes the size of your desktop icons. When used on the Start screen, it zooms in and out.
- **CTRL+A** Select all.
- **WIN+C** Open the charms.
- **CTRL+C** Copy.
- **WIN+D** Show the desktop.
- **ALT+D** Select the address bar in Internet Explorer.
- **CTRL+ALT+D** Enable the Docked mode in the Magnifier tool.
- **WIN+E** Open File Explorer.
- **CTRL+E** Select the search box in File Explorer.
- **WIN+F** Show Files in the Search charm.
- **WIN+CTRL+F** Open the Find Computers window, which can find computers on a network (used mostly in business networks).
- **WIN+G** Cycle through desktop gadgets.
- **WIN+H** Open the Share charm.
- **WIN+I** Open the Settings charm.
- **CTRL+ALT+I** Invert colors in the Magnifier tool.
- **WIN+J** Switch the focus between snapped apps and larger apps.
- **WIN+K** Open the Devices charm.
- **WIN+L** Lock the computer and display the Lock screen.
- **CTRL+ALT+L** Enable Lens mode in the Magnifier tool.
- **WIN+M** Minimize all the windows on the desktop.

A

- **CTRL+N** Open a new File Explorer window.
- **CTRL+SHIFT+N** Create a new folder in File Explorer.
- **WIN+O** Change the Lock screen orientation.
- **WIN+P** Open the project options for a second screen.
- **WIN+Q** Open the Search charm.
- **WIN+R** Open the Run window.
- **CTRL+R** Refresh.
- **WIN+T** Set the focus on the taskbar and cycle through the running desktop apps.
- **WIN+U** Launch the Ease of Access Center.
- **WIN+V** Cycle through notifications.
- **WIN+SHIFT+V** Cycle through notifications in backward order.
- **CTRL+V** Paste.
- **WIN+W** Open Settings in the search charm.
- **CTRL+W** Close the current window. It works only in desktop apps.
- **WIN+X** Open the hidden system menu.
- **CTRL+X** Cut.
- **CTRL+Y** Redo.
- **WIN+Z** Opens the app bar. It works only in Windows 8 apps.
- **CTRL+Z** Undo.
- **WIN+KEYS FROM 1 TO 9** Display the app at the given position on the taskbar.
- **WIN++ (PLUS SIGN)** Zoom in while using the Magnifier tool.
- **WIN+- (MINUS SIGN)** Zoom out while using the Magnifier tool.
- **WIN +, (COMMA)** Peek at the desktop.
- **WIN+. (PERIOD)** Snap a Windows 8 app to the right.
- **WIN+SHIFT+. (PERIOD)** Snap a Windows 8 app to the left.
- **WIN+ENTER** Launch Narrator.
- **WIN+ALT+ENTER** Launch Windows Media Center if installed.

- **ALT + ENTER** Open the Properties window for the item selected in File Explorer.

- **SPACE** Select or clear an active check box.

- **WIN+SPACE** Switch the input language and keyboard layout.

- **ALT+SPACE** Open a shortcut menu in desktop applications.

- **TAB** Move forward through options.

- **WIN+TAB** Cycle through Windows 8 app history.

- **WIN+CTRL+TAB+ARROW KEYS** Cycle through Windows 8 app history in the direction you specify by using the arrow keys.

- **CTRL+TAB** Cycle through Windows 8 app history (identical to **Win+Tab**).

- **ALT+TAB** Switch between opened apps (including desktop apps).

- **SHIFT+TAB** Move backward through options.

- **CTRL+ALT+TAB+ARROW KEYS** Switch between opened apps (including desktop apps) in the direction you specify by using the arrow keys.

- **ESC** Cancel.

- **WIN+ESC** Exit the Magnifier tool.

- **CTRL+ESC** Show the Start screen.

- **CTRL+SHIFT+ESC** Launch Task Manager.

- **PRTSCN** Copy an image of your screen to the Clipboard.

- **LEFT ALT+LEFT SHIFT+PRTSCN** Turn on High Contrast.

- **NUMLOCK** Press for five seconds to turn on Toggle Keys.

- **CTRL+INSERT** Copy (alternative to **Ctrl+C**).

- **SHIFT+INSERT** Paste (alternative to **Ctrl+V**).

- **WIN+HOME** Minimize inactive desktop windows.

- **WIN+PAGEUP** Move the Start screen to the left monitor.

- **WIN+PAGEDOWN** Move the Start screen to the right monitor.

- **WIN+BREAK** Open the System Properties window.

- **LEFT ARROW** Open the previous menu or close the current submenu.

- **WIN+LEFT ARROW** Snap the active desktop window to the left.

A

- **WIN+SHIFT+LEFT ARROW** Snap the active desktop window to the left monitor.

- **CTRL+LEFT ARROW** Show the previous word or element.

- **ALT+LEFT ARROW** Show the previous folder in File Explorer.

- **CTRL+SHIFT+LEFT ARROW** Select a block of text from the current cursor position to the left.

- **RIGHT ARROW** Open the next menu or submenu.

- **WIN+RIGHT ARROW** Snap the active desktop window to the right.

- **WIN+SHIFT+RIGHT ARROW** Snap the active desktop window to the right monitor.

- **CTRL+RIGHT ARROW** Show the next word or element.

- **CTRL+SHIFT+RIGHT ARROW** Select a block of text from the current cursor position to the right.

- **WIN+UP ARROW** Maximize the active desktop window.

- **WIN+SHIFT+UP ARROW** Maximize the active desktop window and keep the current width.

- **CTRL+UP ARROW** Show the previous paragraph.

- **ALT+UP ARROW** Advance up one level in File Explorer.

- **CTRL+SHIFT+UP ARROW** Select a block of text.

- **WIN+DOWN ARROW** Minimize the active desktop window.

- **WIN+SHIFT+DOWN ARROW** Minimize the active desktop window and keep the current width.

- **CTRL+DOWN ARROW** Advance to the next paragraph.

- **CTRL+SHIFT+DOWN ARROW** Select a block of text.

- **F1** Display Help if available.

- **WIN+F1** Launch Windows Help and Support.

- **F2** Rename the selected item.

- **F3** Search for a file or folder.

- **F4** Display items in the active list (works only for desktop apps).

- **CTRL+F4** Close the active document.
- **ALT+F4** Close the active item or app.
- **F5** Refresh.

Exploring Touch Keyboard Shortcuts

If you have a touch-based device, you can use the touch keyboard. It's available on the desktop taskbar. Tap or click the keyboard icon located there to show the touch keyboard on the screen. You can then use it to type in any compatible program.

You can configure the keyboard to display in different ways. The keyboard icon located on the touch keyboard offers access to the options. Below, a traditional keyboard is selected, but it's easy to see the others. If you don't like the traditional keyboard, you can select the split keyboard. You can also write with a pen in the designated writing area and hide the keyboard when you no longer need it.

You can also configure how you want the touch keyboard to work. From the Start screen, type **keyboard**. From the results, select Settings and then choose General.

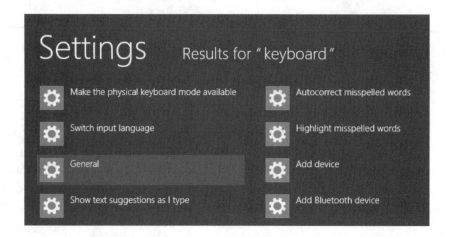

In the General options, located in the PC Settings window, you can configure the touch keyboard settings.

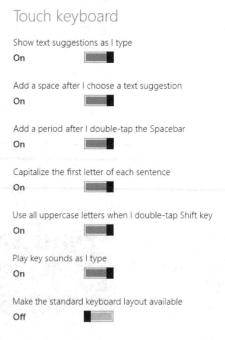

Touch keyboard

Show text suggestions as I type
On

Add a space after I choose a text suggestion
On

Add a period after I double-tap the Spacebar
On

Capitalize the first letter of each sentence
On

Use all uppercase letters when I double-tap Shift key
On

Play key sounds as I type
On

Make the standard keyboard layout available
Off

You might want to make note of the following particular options.

- Add A Period After I Double-Tap The Spacebar
- Capitalize The First Letter Of Each Sentence
- Make The Standard Keyboard Layout Available

Using Touch Gestures in Windows 8

You can use Windows 8 on a multitude of touch-based input devices such as tablets, compatible monitors, laptops with trackpad gesture support, and so on. Before using Windows 8 on such devices on a daily basis, becoming thoroughly familiar with the touch gestures and their mouse equivalents will quickly make you more productive.

The touch gestures you can use in Windows 8 are the following.

- Swipe from the right edge for system commands. Swiping from the right edge of the screen reveals the charms with system commands. Swiping from the left displays previously used apps.

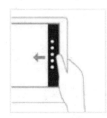

  Mouse equivalent Place the mouse pointer in the lower-right or upper-right corner of the screen and move your mouse on the right edge.

- Swipe in from the left to switch apps. Swiping in from the left reveals thumbnails of your open apps so you can switch to them quickly.

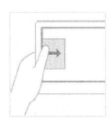

Mouse equivalent Place the mouse pointer in the upper-left corner of the screen and click to cycle through apps or in the lower-left corner of the screen to see the Start screen.

■ Swipe in and out on the left. Swiping in and back out on the left displays the most recently used apps, and you can select an app from that list.

Mouse equivalent Place the mouse in the upper-left corner and slide down the left side of the screen to see the most recently used apps.

■ Swipe from the bottom or top edge. App commands are revealed by swiping from the bottom or top edge.

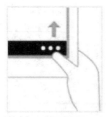

Mouse equivalent Right-click the app to see the app commands.

■ Drag an app down from the top to close it. You don't have to close apps. They won't slow down your computer or device, and they'll close on their own if you don't use them for a while. If you want to close an app, drag the app to the bottom of the screen.

Mouse equivalent Click the top of the app and drag it to the bottom of the screen.

- Press and hold to learn. You can see details when you press and hold an item. In some cases, pressing and holding opens a menu with more options.

  Mouse equivalent Point to an item to see more options. In some applications (for instance, File Explorer), it is the equivalent of right-clicking an item.

- Tap to perform an action. Tapping an item causes an action such as launching an app or following a link.

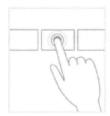

  Mouse equivalent Click an item to perform an action.

- Slide to drag. This is used mostly to pan or scroll through lists and pages, but you can use it for other interactions, such as moving an object or drawing and writing.

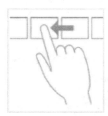

  Mouse equivalent Click, hold, and drag to pan or scroll. In addition, when you use a mouse and keyboard, a scroll bar appears at the bottom of the screen so you can scroll horizontally.

- Pinch or stretch to zoom. Zooming provides a way to jump to the beginning, the end, or a specific location within a list. You can start zooming by pinching or stretching two fingers on the screen.

A

Mouse and keyboard equivalent Hold down the Control key on the keyboard while using the mouse wheel to expand or shrink an item or tile on the screen.

■ Rotate to turn. Rotating two or more fingers turns an object. You can turn the whole screen 90 degrees when you rotate your device, too.

Mouse equivalent Support for rotating an object depends on whether the specific app supports it.

Key Points

■ You can use keyboard shortcuts to navigate in Windows 8 just as you could in previous versions of Windows.

■ If you have a touch screen, you can use the touch keyboard to type text, including keyboard shortcuts you would use on a physical keyboard.

■ Learn the touch gestures Windows 8 supports if you plan to use it and be productive on a device with touch input.

Enhancements for Using Multiple Displays in Windows 8

B

IN THIS APPENDIX, YOU WILL LEARN HOW TO

- Use Windows 8 with multiple monitors.
- Customize the way the image is displayed on multiple monitors.

One of the subtle but important changes to Windows 8 is that it can work with more display types than any other version of Windows. For example, it can be used on all the traditional displays that work with Windows 7 and earlier versions of Windows. In addition, it can work on touch displays with small sizes (such as the 10.6-inch display of the Microsoft Surface) on huge displays as large as 82 inches.

Windows 8 provides better support for dual or multiple-monitor setups than any previous version of Windows. For example, on a dual-monitor setup, you can display the Start screen on the main monitor and the Desktop on the second. You can also display the Desktop on both monitors, and unlike Windows 7, the taskbar can be visible on both.

In this appendix, you'll learn in detail how to use Windows 8 with a dual-monitor setup and how to customize how each display is used.

PRACTICE FILES You do not need any practice files for this Appendix. A complete list of practice files is provided in the "Using the Practice Files" section at the beginning of this book.

Using Windows 8 with a Dual-Monitor Setup

When using Windows 8 with a dual-monitor setup, the Start screen is displayed on the main monitor, and the Desktop is displayed on the second monitor.

With the Windows+P keyboard shortcut, you can open the projection options for the second display. You can choose to use only the main monitor, duplicate the image from the main monitor on the second monitor, extend the image from the main monitor to the second monitor, or use only the secondary monitor.

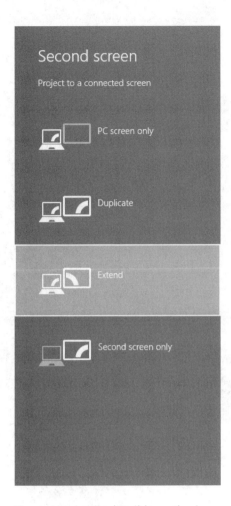

Second screen

Project to a connected screen

PC screen only

Duplicate

Extend

Second screen only

To customize in detail how the image is displayed on each monitor, right-click or press and hold the Desktop. Click or tap Screen Resolution.

This displays the Screen Resolution window, in which both monitors and their relative positions are displayed as identified by Windows 8.

You can drag and drop each monitor to a different position or switch between them.

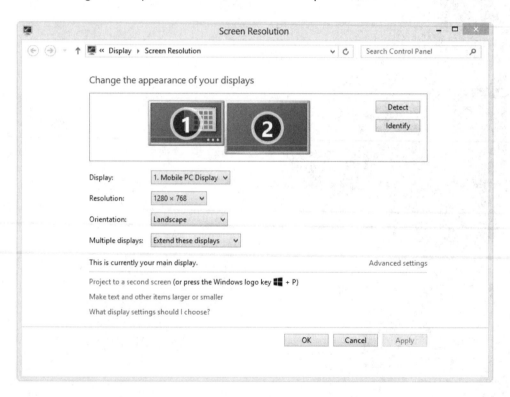

When selecting each monitor, you can also customize the following parameters.

- Display The display you want to customize
- Resolution The resolution of the selected display
- Orientation The orientation of the selected display
- Multiple displays How to use the available displays

After you make your changes, press or tap OK to apply them. Don't hesitate to experiment until you find the setup that works best for you.

Key Points

- Windows 8 provides support for more display types than any earlier version of Windows.
- Windows 8 can also work with touch screens with different sizes and aspect ratios.
- You can customize the available display options when using a dual-monitor setup so that everything is displayed the way you want it to be.

B

Installing and Upgrading to Windows 8

C

IN THIS APPENDIX, YOU WILL LEARN HOW TO

- Make a clean installation of Windows 8.

- Dual-boot Windows 8 with earlier versions of Windows.

- Upgrade to Windows 8 from earlier versions of Windows.

If you are the type of person who likes to configure your own computers and devices, you'll want to learn how to install Windows 8. In this appendix, you'll learn how to perform a clean installation of Windows 8 when you have a new computer or device on which you would like to install it. If you want to use Windows 8 alongside other operating systems that's entirely possible, and this appendix will show the basics you need to know about how to create a dual-boot setup.

In addition, you'll learn how to perform an upgrade to Windows 8 from an earlier version of Windows.

PRACTICE FILES You do not need any practice files for this Appendix. A complete list of practice files is provided in the "Using the Practice Files" section at the beginning of this book.

Installing Windows 8

Installing Windows 8 is not a complicated procedure. As long as your system meets at least the minimum Windows 8 hardware requirements to run, you can install it yourself.

TIP If you want to learn more about the hardware requirements of Windows 8, read Chapter 1, "Introducing Windows 8."

Before you start the installation procedure, look for the activation code (also called the product key) that is required for the whole process to start. Without it, you cannot install Windows 8. The code is distributed with your retail copy of Windows 8.

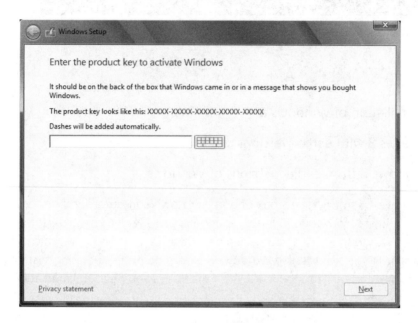

Insert the installation disc into your computer or device and boot your computer or device from it. Depending on how it is configured, you might need to edit the basic input-output system (BIOS) and change the boot order so that your system starts first from your DVD or Blu-ray drive.

Early in the installation process, you are asked to select the partition on which you want to install Windows 8. If you are installing it on a new computer or device, you'll see your hard disk drive as one chunk of unallocated space. You must create a new partition for it. When creating the partition, keep in mind that it is best to allocate at least 25 GB for Windows 8 to make sure you have space for it and the apps that you will install while using it. If you plan to install many apps and games, allocate even more space.

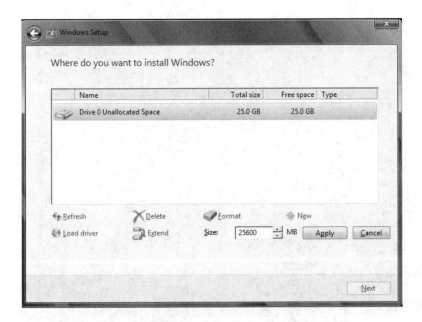

When creating this partition, Windows Setup automatically creates another partition named System Reserved, about 350 MB in size. Leave this partition untouched and don't delete it. It stores recovery tools that are necessary when encountering failures and problems.

If you have partitions, all you need to do is select the one on which you want to install Windows 8. It is best to format that partition so that there is no data on it, and Windows 8 can use all the space on it.

After the installation process is complete, start customizing your Windows 8 installation. You will be asked to select whether you want to use the express settings (the default settings) or customize things in detail.

C

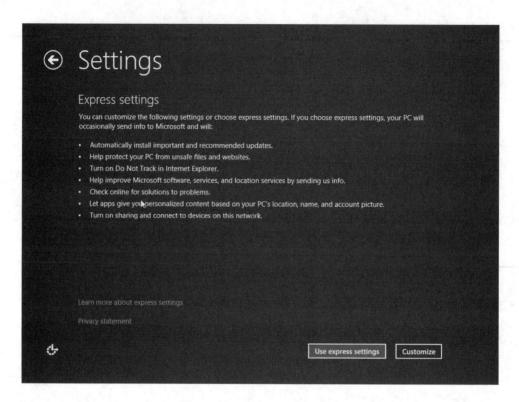

To make sure Windows 8 will work the way you want it to, select Customize and go through a few additional steps.

Prior to the first logon, you will be asked to enter the details of your Microsoft account (email address and password). If you do not have a Microsoft account, it is best to create one on a computer or device with an Internet connection prior to the installation process.

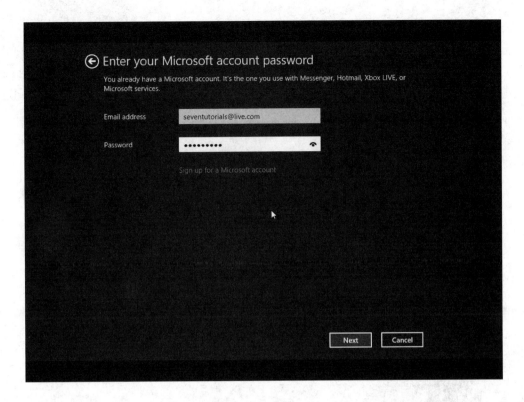

Enter your Microsoft account password

You already have a Microsoft account. It's the one you use with Messenger, Hotmail, Xbox LIVE, or Microsoft services.

Email address   seventutorials@live.com

Password   ••••••••••

Sign up for a Microsoft account

Next   Cancel

TIP If you want to learn more about the Microsoft account, see the "Introducing the Microsoft Account (Windows Live ID)" section in Chapter 12, "Allowing Others to Use the Computer."

In this exercise, you'll learn how to install Windows 8 from the beginning on a new computer or device.

SET UP Insert the Windows 8 installation disc into your DVD or Blu-ray reader. Start from the disc. Depending on how your system is set up, you might need to enter your computer's BIOS and set it to boot from the DVD or Blu-ray reader.

1   Press a key on your keyboard when asked to do so, to start the Windows 8 setup process.

2   Select the language you want to install, the time and currency format you want to use, and the keyboard or input method.

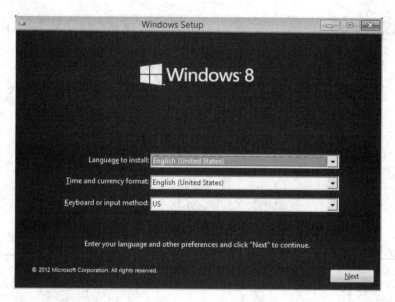

3   Click or tap **Next**.

4   Click or tap **Install now**.

You are asked to enter the product key.

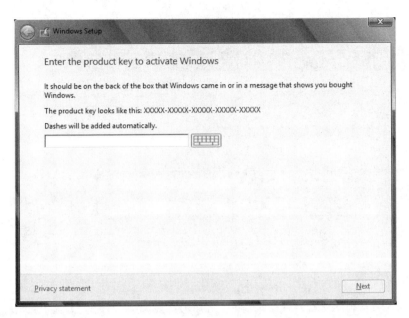

5   Type the product key for your Windows 8 installation and click or tap **Next**.

You are asked to accept the license terms.

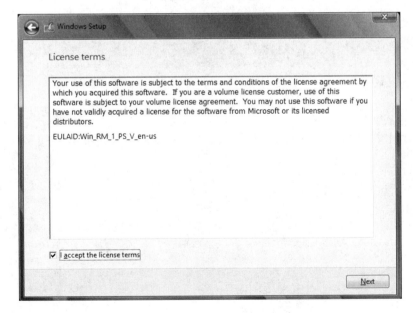

6   Read the license terms and select I **accept the license terms**.

7   Click or tap **Next**.

You are asked to select the type of installation you want to perform.

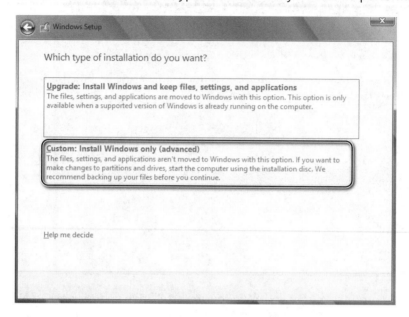

8   Select **Custom: Install Windows only (advanced)**.

You are asked where you want to install Windows.

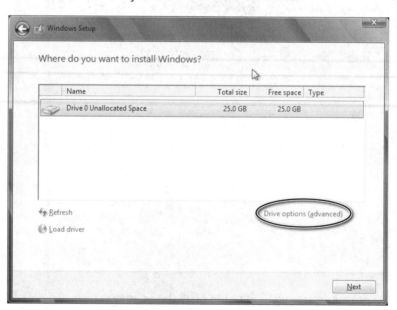

9   Select where you want to install Windows 8.

IMPORTANT If your computer or device has formatted partitions, select the partition on which you want to install Windows 8 and skip to Step 16.

10   Click or tap **Drive options (advanced)** to open a list of options for managing the available disk space.

11   Click or tap **New** and specify the size of the partition that will be created for Windows 8.

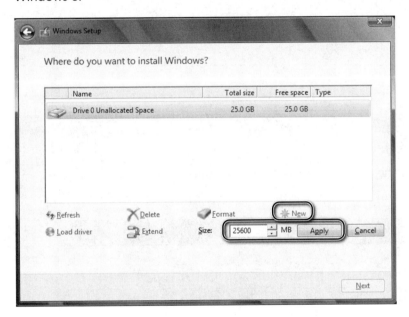

12   Click or tap **Apply**.

You are informed that Windows might create additional partitions for system files.

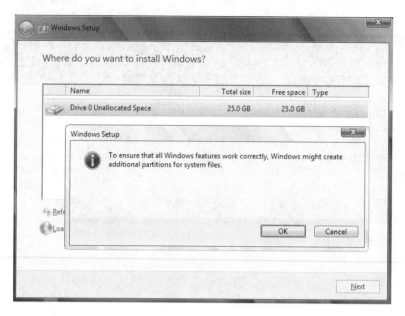

13   Click or tap **OK**.

14   Select the partition you just created and click or tap **Format**.

You are informed that all the data on this partition will be lost.

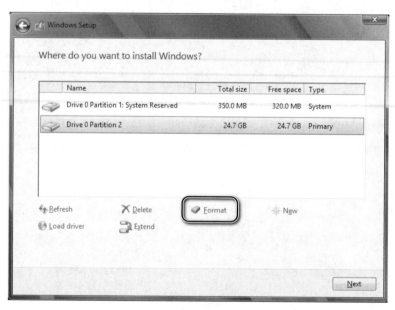

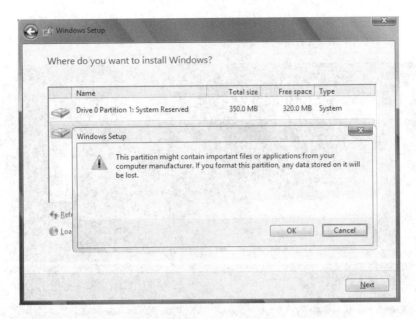

15   Click or tap **OK** to confirm that you want the partition to be formatted.

16   Click or tap **Next** to start the installation process.

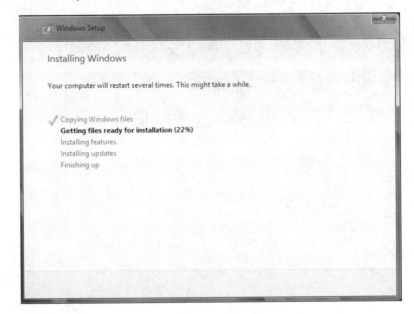

17   Wait for the installation process to finish and for your system to restart.

       The customization process for your Windows 8 installation begins.

18   Select the color you want to use for your Windows 8 installation and type the name
      you want set for the computer or device.

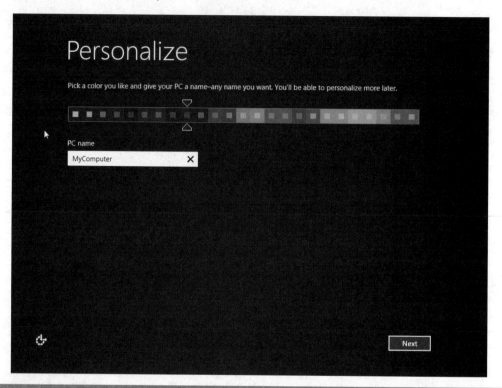

IMPORTANT If you are installing Windows 8 on a laptop or device with a wireless network
card, you are asked to select a wireless network to which to connect and introduce the
appropriate connection details.

19   Click or tap **Next** to start configuring other important settings.

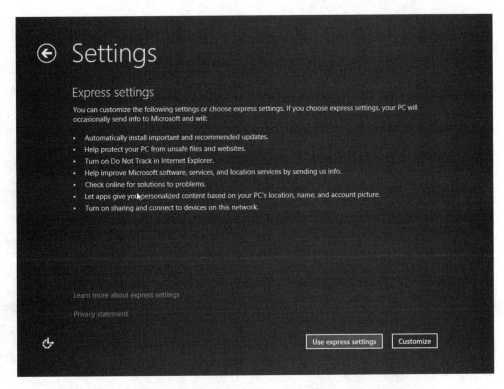

20   Click or tap **Customize** to customize Windows 8 settings in detail.

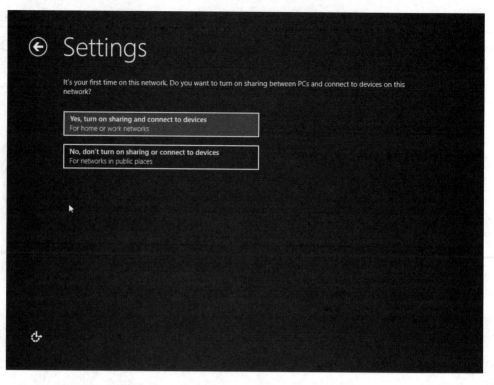

21   Select whether you want file sharing turned on.

22   Select how you want Windows 8 to protect and update your computer or device by turning the switches On or Off.

23   Click or tap **Next**.

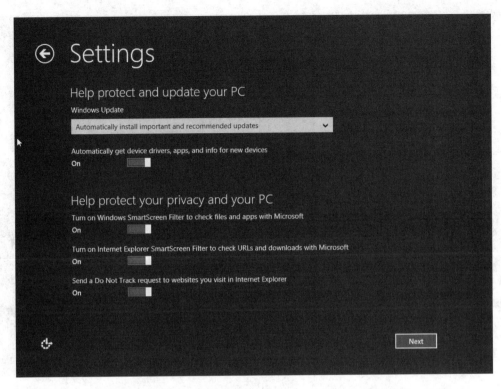

24   Select what kind of information you want to send to Microsoft while using Windows 8 and the apps you install by turning the switches On or Off.

25   Click or tap **Next**.

C

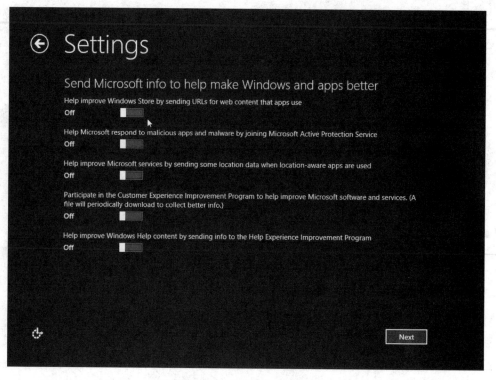

26   Select whether you want Windows 8 to check online for solutions to the problems you might encounter while using it and whether you want to let apps use your name, account picture, or location data. Turn the switches On or Off for each setting according to your preference.

27   Click or tap **Next**.

You are asked for a Microsoft account to sign in.

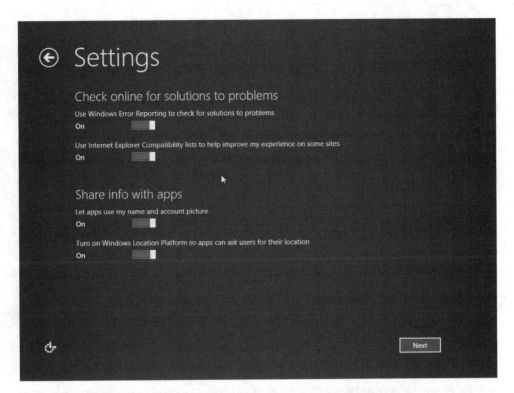

28   Type the email address for your Microsoft account and click or tap **Next**.

You are asked to enter your Microsoft account password.

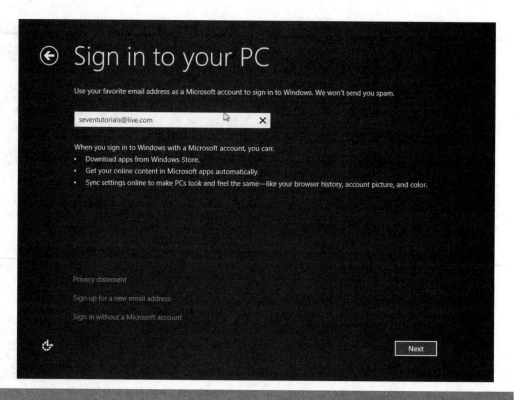

Sign in to your PC

Use your favorite email address as a Microsoft account to sign in to Windows. We won't send you spam.

seventutorials@live.com   ✕

When you sign in to Windows with a Microsoft account, you can:
• Download apps from Windows Store.
• Get your online content in Microsoft apps automatically.
• Sync settings online to make PCs look and feel the same—like your browser history, account picture, and color.

Privacy statement

Sign up for a new email address

Sign in without a Microsoft account

Next

IMPORTANT If Windows 8 doesn't detect an active Internet connection (for example, when it is installed on a laptop not yet connected to a wireless network), it will ask you to connect to the network and then use your Microsoft account to sign in.

29   Type your password in the appropriate field and click or tap **Next**.

You are asked to enter some security verification information that is used if you need to recover your account.

30   Enter the requested details and click or tap **Next**. Windows 8 takes a while to finalize all the required preparations.

31 While you wait for the preparations to complete, watch the tutorial about how to navigate Windows 8.

You are logged on to Windows 8 for the first time.

Move your mouse into any corner

CLEAN UP When you are logged on, don't forget to eject the installation disc and store it safely.

You can now use Windows 8 and all the available features. You will also receive an email or SMS message asking you to confirm this computer or device as a trusted PC. This is important because without this confirmation you can't use all the synchronization features in Windows 8.

If you have used Windows 8 on another computer or device with the same Microsoft account you used to log on, your settings from the other device are automatically migrated to this installation.

TIP To learn more about synchronizing your Windows 8 settings and how to configure this feature, see Chapter 6, "Using SkyDrive."

After you have installed Windows 8, don't forget to activate it. You won't be able to customize it fully until the activation is performed from PC Settings.

C

Dual-booting Windows 8 and Other Windows Versions

You can create a dual- or multi-boot setup on your computer or device. For example, you can run Windows 8 alongside Windows 7 and switch between operating systems as you see fit.

Installing Windows 8 in a dual-boot configuration is not much different from the procedure for making a clean installation.

You have to have a separate partition just for Windows 8. After you create that, follow the steps detailed in the installation guide from the previous section. At step 9, you select the partition created just for Windows 8 and continue with the installation.

Windows 8 automatically detects the other Windows operating systems you have installed and creates the appropriate boot entries for them. When you start your computer or device, you can select the operating system you want to boot into.

When creating a multi-boot setup with multiple versions of Windows, it is best to install Windows 8 last. Earlier Windows versions cannot set the boot entry for Windows 8 correctly because it is a newer operating system using different technologies. However, Windows 8 can manage the boot entries for earlier versions of Windows correctly.

Upgrading to Windows 8

You can upgrade to Windows 8 from Windows XP, Windows Vista, and Windows 7. The process is similar for these operating systems, but there differences when it comes to the settings, files, and apps that can be migrated to Windows 8. You can upgrade from Windows XP and Windows Vista retail editions to Windows 8 Pro. Also, you can upgrade all retail editions of Windows 7 to Windows 8 Pro and upgrade only Windows 7 Home Basic, Home Premium and Starter to the basic edition of Windows 8.

During the upgrade process, the Windows 8 setup will evaluate your system and ask you to choose what you would like to keep.

- **KEEP WINDOWS SETTINGS, PERSONAL FILES, AND APPS** Available only when upgrading from Windows 7 to Windows 8

- **KEEP WINDOWS SETTINGS AND PERSONAL FILES** Available only when upgrading from Windows Vista to Windows 8

- **KEEP PERSONAL FILES ONLY** Available when upgrading from Windows XP, Windows Vista, and Windows 7 to Windows 8

- **NOTHING** Available when upgrading from Windows XP, Windows Vista, and Windows 7 to Windows 8

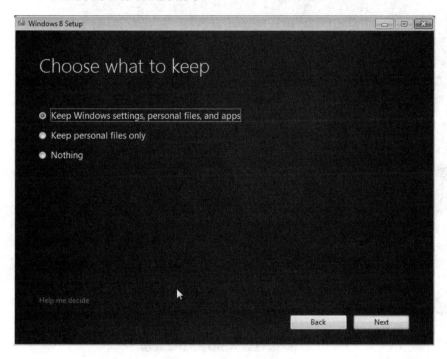

To upgrade from an earlier version of Windows to Windows 8, just insert the Windows 8 installation disc into your DVD or Blu-ray drive and run the setup.exe file. The Windows 8 Setup Wizard starts and guides you through all the steps. The upgrade process involves fewer steps than when installing from scratch, but more requirements must be met. For example, on the partition on which your current operating system is installed, you must have at least 20 GB of free space available for Windows 8 to install itself and preserve the old operating system until the installation is done. The 20 GB are in addition to what the current operating system is using.

A great feature of the Upgrade Wizard is that it automatically checks to see whether all the prerequisites are met for the upgrade to continue. If they are not, you are shown a summary of the problems that were found and you are asked to take action prior to the upgrade procedure.

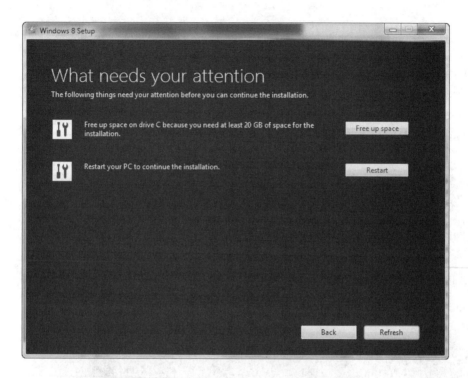

The old operating system is preserved so that if there are any problems with the upgrade you can revert to the previous Windows installation.

> Windows installation was not successful. Your previous version of Windows is being restored.
>
> Do not restart your computer during this time.

The earlier version of Windows is removed only after the upgrade has finished successfully.

IMPORTANT One very important requirement is that you cannot upgrade from a 32-bit version of Windows to a 64-bit version of Windows 8 (or vice versa). If you have purchased a different version, you must perform a clean installation and move your files, settings, and apps manually.

In this exercise, you'll learn how to upgrade from Windows 7 to Windows 8. The process for upgrading from Windows XP or Windows Vista to Windows 8 is similar, and you can follow almost the same steps, although some options might be different.

SET UP Insert the Windows 8 installation disc into your DVD or Blu-ray reader. Open Windows Explorer and run the setup.exe file found on the disc. Make sure you close all active programs before performing the upgrade. Also, make sure you have the Windows 8 product key available.

1 Wait for the setup files to be prepared.

   You are asked whether you want to get the latest updates during the upgrade process.

2 Leave **Go online to install updates now** selected and click or tap **Next**.

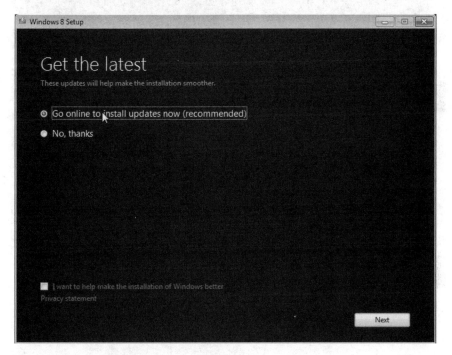

3 Type the Windows 8 product key and click or tap **Next**.

   You are asked to accept the license terms.

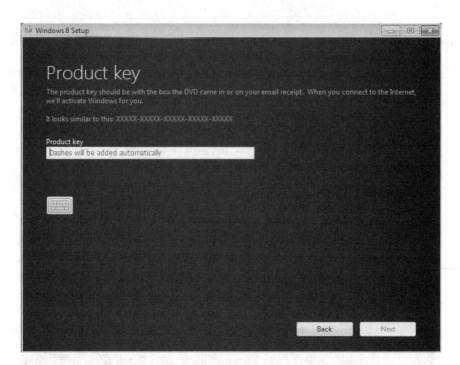

4   Read the license terms and select **I accept the license terms**. Click or tap **Accept**.

5　Choose what you want to keep during the upgrade process and click or tap **Next**. You are shown a summary of what the upgrade process will do.

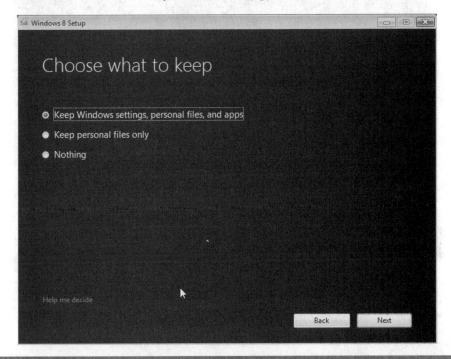

IMPORTANT If any of the prerequisites for the upgrade process are not met, you will be shown a summary of the things that need to be changed at this point. You won't be able to continue the upgrade process until you resolve those issues.

6　If you are ready to go ahead with the upgrade, click **Install**.

C

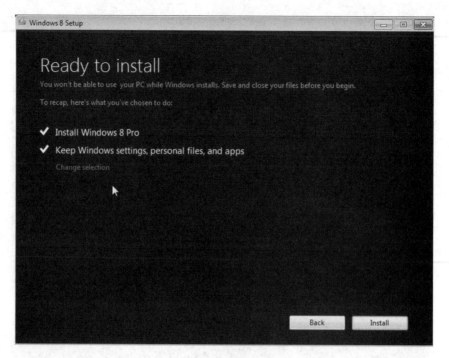

7   Wait for the installation process to finish.

If any problems are encountered, the previous Windows installation will be restored automatically. After several restarts, the personalization process starts.

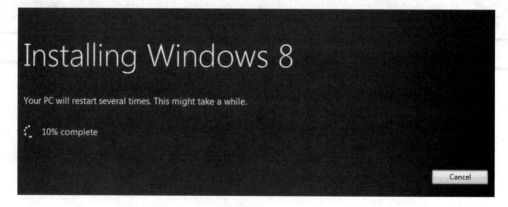

8   Select the color you want to use for your Windows 8 installation.

9   Click or tap **Next** to start configuring other important settings.

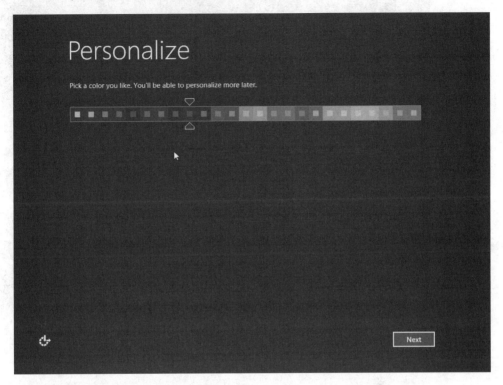

10   Click or tap **Customize** to customize Windows 8 settings in detail.

C

11   Select whether you want file sharing turned on.

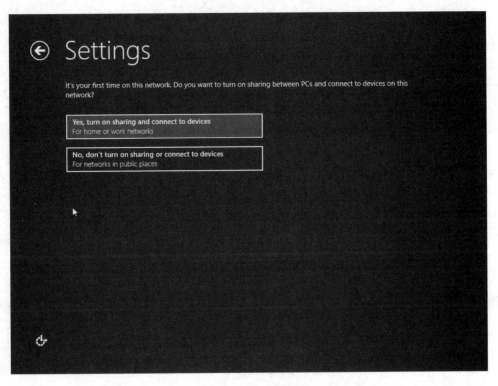

12   Select how you want Windows 8 to protect and update your computer or device by turning the switches On or Off.

13   Click or tap **Next**.

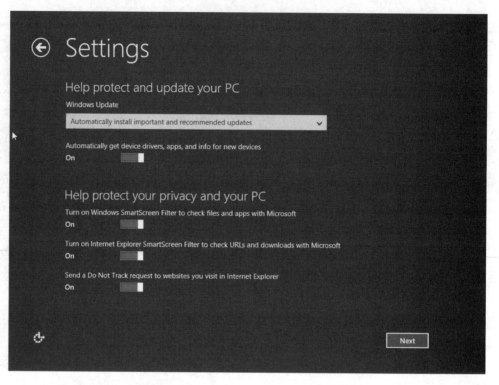

14   Select what kind of information you want to send to Microsoft while using Windows
      8 and the apps you install by turning the switches On or Off.

15   Click or tap **Next**.

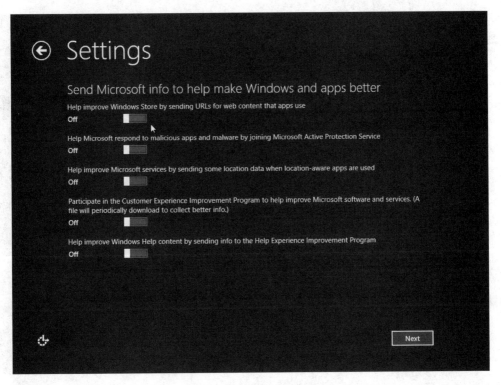

16   Select whether you want Windows 8 to check online for solutions to the problems
      you might encounter while using it and whether you want to let apps use your name,
      account picture, or your location data. Turn the switches On or Off for each setting
      according to your preference.

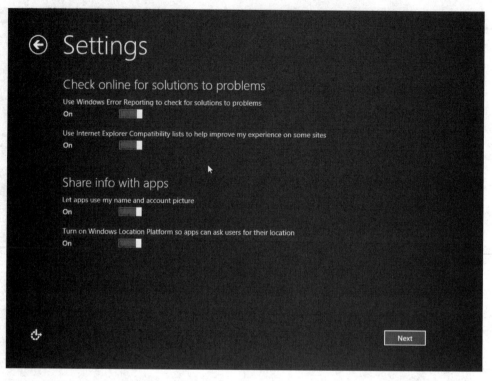

17   Click or tap **Next**.

To sign in, you are asked to enter the password of the user account you used in the previous version of Windows.

18   Type the password and click or tap **Next**.

You are asked to type your Microsoft account address.

Sign in to your PC

To help keep this account secure, we need to confirm your password.

Test

Password ••••

Next

19   Type the email address for your Microsoft account and click or tap **Next**.

You are asked to type your Microsoft account password.

C

Sign in to your PC

Use your favorite email address as a Microsoft account to sign in to Windows. We won't send you spam.

seventutorials@live.com

When you sign in to Windows with a Microsoft account, you can:
- Download apps from Windows Store.
- Get your online content in Microsoft apps automatically.
- Sync settings online to make PCs look and feel the same—like your browser history, account picture, and color.

Privacy statement

Sign up for a new email address

Sign in without a Microsoft account

Next

20   Type your password in the appropriate field and click or tap **Next**.

You are asked to enter some security verification information that is used if you need to recover your account.

21   Enter the requested details and click or tap **Next**. Windows 8 takes a while to finalize
     all the required preparations.

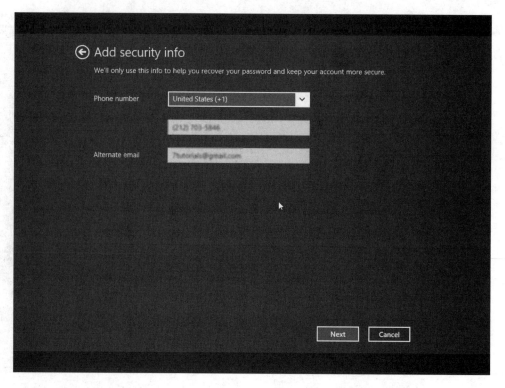

22 While you wait for the preparations to complete, watch the tutorial about how to navigate Windows 8.

You are logged on to Windows 8 for the first time.

Move your mouse into any corner

⊗ CLEAN UP When you are logged on, don't forget to eject the installation disc and store it safely.

The upgrade has been performed, and your files, settings, and apps have been migrated according to your settings.

C

Key Points

- Prior to installing Windows 8, make sure you are aware of its system requirements and that you have a valid product key.

- When creating a dual-boot setup with another version of Windows, install Windows 8 last.

- You can upgrade from Windows XP, Windows Vista, and Windows 7 to Windows 8.

Moving Your Data and Settings to Windows 8

IN THIS APPENDIX, YOU WILL LEARN HOW TO

- Transfer your data and current settings from an old computer to a new computer with Windows 8.

- Use Easy Transfer.

    If you bought a new Windows 8–based computer or device, you might be interested in moving your data and settings from your older computer. If you have used an earlier version of Windows on your previous computer, you can use one of many tools to do this job.

    One of the best available tools is the free Windows Easy Transfer tool Microsoft has provided since Windows XP. You make a backup of your data and settings and then restore that backup on your new Windows 8–based computer or device.

    In this appendix, you'll learn how to use Windows Easy Transfer to restore your backed-up data and settings on your new Windows 8–based computer or device.

    PRACTICE FILES You do not need any practice files for this Appendix. A complete list of practice files is provided in "Using the Practice Files" section at the beginning of this book.

Transferring Your Data to Windows 8 with Windows Easy Transfer

Windows Easy Transfer is a tool that was first introduced with Windows XP; it enables users to switch files and settings between Windows-based computers or devices. You can use this tool to migrate your files and settings to Windows 8 from previous versions of Windows or from other Windows 8 installations.

If you have upgraded to Windows 8 from an earlier version of Windows on the same computer or device, you don't need to use this tool because your data and settings have been migrated.

If you purchased a new computer or device with Windows 8 and you want to transfer files and settings from your old computer to the new one, Windows Easy Transfer is the tool for the job.

The tool can transfer items by using an Easy Transfer cable (a USB-to-USB connection cable), a network connection, or an external hard disk drive or USB flash drive. The external hard disk drive is the most useful device for making such transfers. Not only are external hard disks affordable, but they also have plenty of space and can be used to migrate items between computers that are not in the same network or in the same physical location.

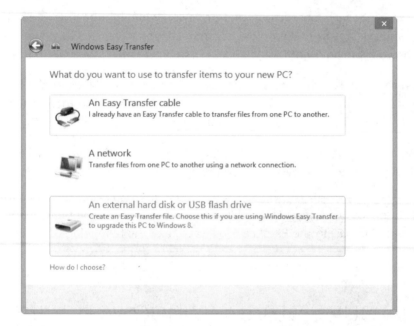

First, back up your data by using Windows Easy Transfer on the old computer or device. This data is stored in a file with the .mig extension (for migration). The file is password protected to make sure unauthorized people cannot use it.

On the computer or device to which you want to transfer your data, select the same file and type the password you have set.

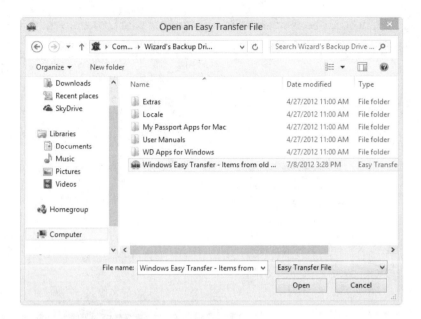

Before transferring your data to the new computer or device, you can customize the items that will be migrated. By default, Windows Easy Transfer will transfer all the data included in the migration file. If you click or tap Customize, you can select the type of items you want transferred. Clicking or tapping Advanced gives you even more precise control over the items to be transferred.

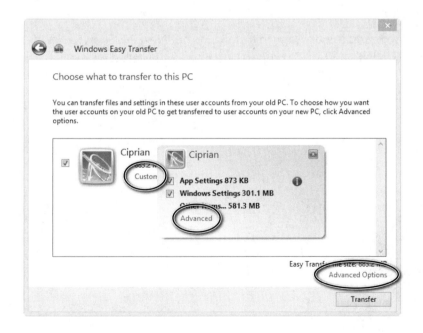

Clicking or tapping Advanced Options opens a new window, in which you can set how you want to map user accounts between computers or how you want to map drives.

At the end of the transfer, you can close the Windows Easy Transfer window, or you can access two reports.

- **See What Was Transferred** Shows a summary of the items that were transferred to the new computer or device.

- **See A List Of Apps You Might Want To Install On Your New PC** Shows a list of applications installed on the old computer that are not installed on the new computer or device. You can use this list as a guide for which apps to install on your new Windows 8–based computer or device.

In this exercise, you'll learn how to migrate your files and settings to Windows 8 by using Windows Easy Transfer. The exercise shows the transfer from an external hard disk drive. Such drives have plenty of space and are one of the most effective media for transferring large sets of data between computers.

SET UP First, back up your data by using Windows Easy Transfer on the old computer. Then, on your new Windows 8–based computer or device, on the Start screen, search for windows transfer. Click or tap the Windows Easy Transfer search result to open Windows Easy Transfer. Plug the external hard disk drive into where the Windows Easy Transfer file is stored.

1   Click or tap **Next.**

You are asked what you want to use to transfer items to your new Windows 8–based computer or device.

2   Click or tap **An external hard disk or USB flash drive**.

You are asked which PC you are using now.

D

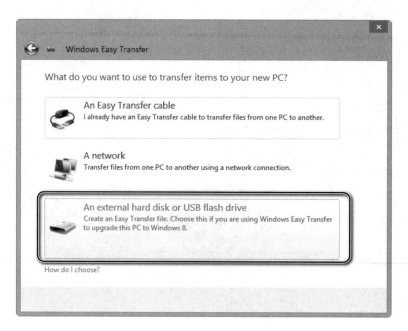

3   Click or tap **This is my new PC.**

You are asked whether Windows Easy Transfer has already saved your files from your old PC to an external hard disk drive or USB flash drive.

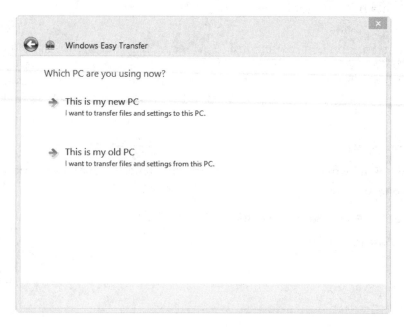

4   Click or tap **Yes**.

You are asked to browse and select the Windows Easy Transfer file in which the data from the old computer is stored.

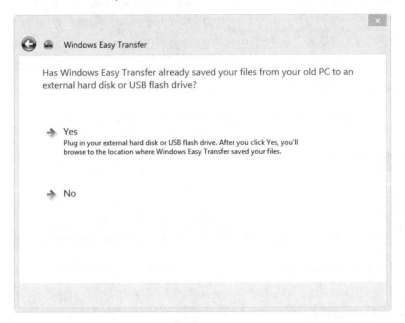

5   Select the appropriate transfer file (with the .mig file extension).

You are asked to enter the password you used to protect the transfer file.

6   Type the password and click or tap **Next**.

You are asked to choose what to transfer to the new PC.

D

7   Click or tap **Customize** and clear the items you do not want transferred, if any.

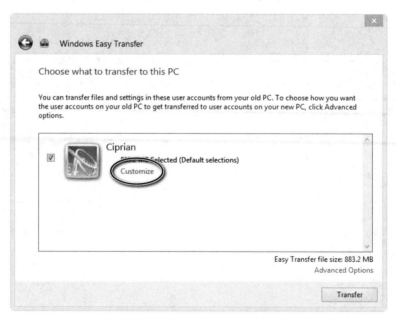

8   Click or tap **Transfer** and wait for the transfer to finish.

You are informed that your transfer is complete.

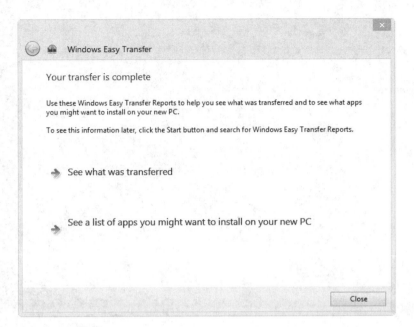

9   Click or tap **Close**.

❌ CLEAN UP Eject and then unplug the external hard disk drive in which the Windows Easy Transfer data is stored.

The selected data and settings have been transferred to your new Windows 8 computer or device.

Key Points

- You can use Windows Easy Transfer to transfer settings and apps from an older Windows-based computer to your new Windows 8–based computer or device.

- Before making the transfer, back up your data and settings.

- For large transfers, it is best to use an external hard disk drive.

D

Glossary

Action Center A feature in Windows 8 by which to view and fix problems and run automated trouble-shooters, among other things.

Activation The process you must complete to verify that you have a valid copy of Windows 8, which includes a Product ID. You usually activate Windows 8 online the first time you turn on your computer or device, but there are other activation options. Activation is mandatory.

Active window The window that is in the foreground and currently in use.

ActiveX control A reusable software component that performs a specific function or set of functions in the Windows operating system, in a program that runs on Windows, or in the Internet Explorer environment.

Address bar In Internet Explorer or any web browser, the area in which you type Internet addresses, also known as URLs (uniform resource locators). Often, an Internet address takes the form of *http://www.companyname.com*.

Administrator account A type of Windows user account with access to all system files and settings and with permission to perform all operations. Every computer must have at least one administrator account. This account type is not recommended for daily use. See also ***standard user account***.

App An application available from the Start screen (and the Store) that is created to use the entire screen and is tailored to work well on desktop computers, laptops, tablets, and Windows Phones. Some apps have desktop counterparts, including Internet Explorer 10. The app has fewer features than its desktop counterpart but is more streamlined and often easier to use.

App bar A toolbar (available in almost all apps) that is typically hidden until needed. The App bar holds commands that might enable the user to configure the app, input a location, add an event, delete an item, view properties, and more.

Application Software that you or the computer's manufacturer install or have installed on your computer or device other than the operating system (Windows 8). Some applications come preinstalled on Windows 8, such as Paint, Notepad, Snipping Tool, and Windows Defender, whereas others can be third-party applications or software you purchase separately and install yourself, such as Adobe Photoshop. Applications differ from apps in several ways; most notably, they run on the desktop and in a window, as traditional programs have always run, and not in full-screen mode as the new apps do.

Attachment Data you add to an email such as a photograph, a short video, a sound recording, a document, or other data. Attachments can be dangerous to open because they can contain viruses.

Autorun file A file that automatically starts an installation program when you insert a disc in a drive or browse to the autorun file in a folder.

Bandwidth The transmission capacity of an electronic communications device or its rate of data transfer, usually expressed in bits per second.

BCC If you want to send an email to someone and you don't want other recipients to know you included that person in the email, add them to the Bcc line. Bcc stands for *blind carbon copy* and is a secret copy.

BitLocker Drive Encryption BitLocker combines drive encryption and integrity checking to keep the hard disk from becoming accessible by thieves. Even if a thief steals the hard disk out of a computer and installs it in another computer, its data cannot be accessed.

Bitmap (.bmp) A patent-free digital image file format. A bitmap image consists of pixels in a grid. Each pixel is a specific color; the colors within the color palette are governed by the specific bitmap format. Common formats include monochrome bitmap, 16-color bitmap, 256-color bitmap, and 24-bit bitmap. The bitmap file format does not support transparency.

Blog Short for *weblog*. An online journal or news/opinion column. Contributors post entries consisting of text, graphics, or video clips. When permitted by the blog owner, readers can post comments responding to the entries or to other people's comments. Blogs are often used to publish personal or company information in an informal way.

Browse Browsing for a file, folder, picture, video, song, or program (among other things) is the process of navigating into the operating system's folder structure to locate the desired item. *Browse* can also describe the act of surfing the Internet.

Burn A term that describes the process of copying music from a computer to a CD or DVD. The term originated because data is actually burned onto this media with a laser. In many cases, music is burned to CDs because CDs can be played in cars and generic DVD players, and videos are burned to DVDs because videos require much more space and DVDs can be played on DVD players.

Byte A unit of measurement for data; a byte typically holds a single character, such as a letter, digit, or punctuation mark. Some single characters can take up more than one byte.

Central processing unit (CPU) The main circuit chip in a computer. It performs most of the calculations necessary to run the computer. Also called a *processor*.

CC If you want to send an email to someone and you don't need that person to respond, you can put that person in the CC line. CC stands for *carbon copy*. (BCC is a blind carbon copy; other recipients cannot see the BCC field address.)

Charm The default charms are a set of five icons that appear when you swipe from the right side of the screen to the left. These icons are Search, Share, Start, Devices, and Settings. Apps have their own charms, generally available from the app bar found there.

Click To point to an interface element and then press the primary mouse button one time, usually for the purpose of selecting an item or positioning a cursor.

Command An instruction you give to a computer program.

Command bar In Internet Explorer, a toolbar located above the Content pane that provides buttons for common tasks associated with the home page, Web Slices and RSS feeds, printing, web content display, and safety, as well as tools for managing Internet Explorer.

Compatibility view An Internet Explorer feature that displays a website as though you were using an earlier version of the web browser. Compatibility view was first introduced with Internet Explorer 8.

Compress To reduce the size of a set of data, such as a file or group of files, inside a compressed folder that can be stored in less space or transmitted with less bandwidth.

Compressed folder A folder containing a file or files whose contents have been compressed.

Computer (Windows System) Computer, in this sense, is the computer window that offers access to installed hard disk drives, CD and DVD drives, connected external drives, network locations (drives), network media servers, and similar connected media and locations.

Connected Standby A new power management mode for ARM–based versions of Windows 8 (often installed on high-end tablet devices) that allows the device to sleep or hibernate efficiently for long periods of time. This enables tablets and similar devices to remain turned on when not in use without draining the battery quickly.

Content pane In File Explorer, the pane that displays files and folders stored in the currently selected folder or storage device.

Control Panel The window from which you can change computer settings related to system and maintenance, networks, and the Internet; user accounts; appearance; security; hardware; and sounds, among others. Control Panel opens on the desktop and is not an app.

Cookies Small text files that include data that identify your preferences when you visit particular websites. Cookies are generally harmless and enable websites such as Amazon.com to greet you by name when you navigate there.

Copy Copies data to a virtual clipboard, which is a temporary holding area for data. You generally copy data so that you can paste it somewhere else.

Credentials Information that provides proof of identification that is used to gain access to local and network resources. Examples of credentials are user names and passwords, smart cards, and certificates.

Cursor The point at which text or graphics will be inserted. The cursor usually appears on screen as a blinking vertical line.

Cut To remove the selected text, picture, or object and place it on the Clipboard. After it's pasted, the item is deleted from its original location.

Desktop Where programs and applications run; where windows open; where you browse File Explorer; and where you work with desktop programs to write letters, create spreadsheets, manage files and folders, install and uninstall programs, and do everything else you're used to doing on Windows 7, Windows Vista, and other earlier operating systems.

Desktop folder Contains icons that represent what's on your desktop. You can access this folder from File Explorer.

Desktop computer A computer designed for use at one location. A typical desktop computer system includes the computer case containing the actual computer components, a monitor, a keyboard, a mouse, and speakers.

Desktop Gadget Gallery A gallery from which you can choose gadgets that display a variety of dynamic information directly on your desktop. The Desktop Gadget Gallery was first introduced in Windows 7 as a replacement for the Windows Sidebar.

Details pane In File Explorer, the pane at the bottom of a folder window that displays details about the folder or selected items.

Dialog box A box from which to make changes to default settings in an application, make decisions when installing programs, set print options for a selected printer, configure sharing options for a file or folder, and perform similar tasks. A dialog box is not a window and does not include minimize and maximize buttons.

Digital signature An electronic signature that is composed of a secret code and a private key. Digital signatures are used to help verify file authenticity. Also called a *digital ID*.

Digital subscriber line (DSL) A type of high-speed Internet connection that uses standard telephone wires.

Disk Cleanup An application included with Windows 8 that offers a safe and effective way to remove unwanted and unnecessary data. You can remove temporary files, downloaded program files, and offline webpages; empty the Recycle Bin; and more, all in a single process.

Disk Defragmenter An application included with Windows 8 that improves performance by analyzing the data stored on your hard disk drive and consolidating files that are not stored together. Disk Defragmenter runs automatically on a schedule, so you should (theoretically) never have to invoke it manually.

Domain In Windows, a logical (rather than physical) group of resources—computers, servers, and other hardware devices—on a network, which is centrally administered through Windows Server. On the Internet, a name used as the base of website addresses and email addresses that identifies the entity owning the address.

Domain Name System (DNS) A technology that translates Internet address names into numerical addresses (IP addresses) so that the address can be found over the Internet. For example, if you type **www.microsoft.com** into a web browser, the name is translated into a numerical address and that address is used to connect you to the server hosting the Microsoft website.

Double-click To point to an interface element and press the primary mouse button two times in rapid succession, usually for the purpose of starting a program or opening a window, folder, or file.

Drag To move an item to another location on the screen by pointing to it, holding down the primary mouse button, and then moving the mouse.

Drafts A folder that holds email messages you've started and saved but not yet completed and sent.

Driver A program that enables Windows to communicate with a software program or hardware device (such as a printer, mouse, or keyboard) that is attached to your computer. Every device needs a driver for it to work. Many drivers, such as the keyboard driver, are built into Windows.

Dynamic Host Configuration Protocol (DHCP) server A server that manages a pool of IP addresses and client confirmation parameters and assigns IP addresses to computers and devices on a network.

dynamic-link library (DLL) An operating system feature that allows executable routines (each generally serving a specific function or set of functions) to be stored separately as files with .dll extensions. These routines are loaded only when needed by the program that calls them.

Early Load Antimalware A new security feature that loads integrated antimalware functionality each time the computer starts. This prevents malware from being loaded into the operating system when the computer is turned on.

EdgeUI UI stands for *user interface*, and EdgeUI stands for the user options you see at the edges of the Windows 8 screen. Charms are part of the EdgeUI, for example.

Ethernet A technology that uses Ethernet cables to connect computers to routers and similar hardware to transmit data and connect multiple computers to form a network.

Executable file A computer file that starts a program, such as a word processor, game, or Windows utility. Executable files can often be identified by the file name extension .exe.

Expansion card A printed circuit board that, when inserted into an expansion slot of a computer, provides additional functionality. There are many types of expansion cards, including audio cards, modems, network cards, security device cards, TV tuner cards, video cards, and video processing expansion cards.

Expansion slot A socket on a computer's motherboard designed to establish the electrical contact between the electronics on an expansion card and on the motherboard. Many form factors (physical dimensions) and standards for expansion slots are available, including AGP, PC Card, PCI, and PCI Express. An expansion slot accepts only expansion cards of the same form factor.

Extensible Markup Language (XML) A text markup language, similar to HTML, used to define the structure of data independently of its formatting so that the data can be used for multiple purposes and by multiple programs.

External peripheral A peripheral device installed by connecting it to a port from outside the computer. Examples are a monitor, keyboard, mouse, and speakers.

Favorite A webpage for which you've created a shortcut in Internet Explorer. You can click a favorite instead of typing the web address to visit a website quickly.

Favorites bar In Internet Explorer, a toolbar located below the Address bar that provides buttons for storing web locations for easy future access, obtaining add-ons, and accessing sites that match your browsing history.

Favorites Center In Internet Explorer, a pane with three tabs: Favorites, on which you can save and organize links to websites and webpages; Feeds, on which you can save and organize RSS feeds; and History, on which you can view your browsing history.

Feed An information stream that contains frequently updated content published by a website. Feeds are often associated with news sites and blogs but are also used for distributing other types of digital content, including photos, music, and video. See also *Really Simple Syndication*.

File A distinct piece of data. A file can be a single Word document, a spreadsheet, a song, a movie, a picture, or even a very large single backup.

File Explorer A window that enables you to browse all the data stored on your computer and your network. You use File Explorer to access your data libraries, personal and public folders, and networked computers.

File name extension Characters appended to the name of a file by the program that created it and separated from the file name by a period. Some file name extensions identify the program that can open the file, such as .xlsx for Microsoft Office Excel 2007 files, and some represent formats that more than one program can work with, such as .jpg graphics files.

File recovery The backup feature included with Windows 8 with which you can perform backups and, in the case of a computer failure, restore the backed-up data.

Filter To display only items that match specified criteria.

FireWire port FireWire is the brand name given to the IEEE 1394 port by Apple, Inc., one of the patent holders of IEEE 1394 technology. See also *IEEE 1394 port*.

Flash drive See *USB flash drive*.

Flick A gesture performed with a single finger by swiping quickly left, right, up, or down.

Flip and Flip 3D A way to move through open windows, open applications, and run apps graphically instead of clicking the item on the desktop or flicking to it. You invoke these with the Alt+Tab and Windows+Tab keys.

Folder A data unit (similar to a folder in a filing cabinet) that holds files and subfolders. You use folders to organize data. Some folders come with Windows 8, including but not limited to My Documents, Public Pictures, My Videos, Downloads, Contacts, Favorites, and Searches.

Form data In Internet Explorer, this is personal data, such as your name and address, that's been saved using the Internet Explorer autocomplete form data functionality. If you don't want forms to be filled out automatically, disable this.

Gadget An icon you can add to the desktop that often contains up-to-date information about the weather, the time, and the news.

Gesture A movement you make with your finger to perform a task. Flick, swipe, tap, double-tap, and others are considered gestures. See also *multi-touch gesture*.

Gigabyte (GB) 1,024 megabytes of data storage; often interpreted as approximately 1 billion bytes.

Glyph An icon that appears on the new Windows 8 Lock screen. You might see information about the network status, power, unread emails, and so on. You can decide which glyphs appear on the Lock screen from PC Settings.

Graphical user interface (GUI) A user interface that incorporates visual elements such as a desktop, icons, and menus, so that you can perform operations by interacting with the visual interface rather than by typing commands.

Graphics Interchange Format (.gif) A digital image file format developed by CompuServe that is used for transmitting raster images on the Internet. An image in this format may contain up to 256 colors, including a transparent color. The size of the file depends on the number of colors used.

Guest account A built-in Windows user account that allows limited use of the computer. When logged on to a computer with the Guest account, a user can't install software or hardware, change settings, or create a password. The Guest account is turned off (unavailable) by default; you can turn it on from the User Accounts window of Control Panel.

Hardware Physical computing devices you connect externally to the computer and the physical items inside it. Common hardware includes printers, external USB drives, network interface cards, CPUs, RAM, and more.

Hibernate A power option by which the computer is still powered on but is using very little power.

History In Internet Explorer, this is the list of websites you've visited or typed in the address bar. Anyone who has access to your computer or device and to your user account can look at your History list to see where you've been, and often it's advisable to clear your History list if you share a computer and do not have separate user accounts.

Homegroup A group of computers running Windows 7 and Windows 8 that have been configured to join the homegroup. Homegroups make sharing easier because the most common sharing settings are already configured. After a homegroup is set up, one only needs the proper operating system, access to the local network, and the homegroup password to join.

Home page The webpage that opens when you open Internet Explorer 10. You can set the home page and configure additional pages to open as well.

Hotspot A Wi-Fi location where you can connect to the Internet without being tethered to an Ethernet cable. Sometimes access to Wi-Fi hotspot service is free, provided you have the required wireless hardware and are at a location with an open connection. You'll find Wi-Fi hotspots in libraries, coffee shops, hotels, bars, and so on.

Hub A device used to connect multiple devices of one type. See also **network hub** and **USB hub**.

Hyperlink A link from a text, graphic, audio, or video element to a target location in the same document, another document, or a webpage.

Hypertext See **hyperlink**.

Hypertext Markup Language (HTML) A text markup language used to create documents for the web. HTML defines the structure and layout of a web document by using a variety of tags and attributes.

Icon A visual representation of a file, folder, or program that you can click or double-click as applicable, and which then opens the item the icon represents. *Icon* is a term generally associated with the desktop and items you find in folders, whereas *tile* is a term generally used to represent the items available from the Start screen.

Information technology (IT) The development, installation, and implementation of computer systems and applications.

InPrivate Browsing A browsing mode that opens a separate Internet Explorer window in which the places you visit are not tracked. The pages and sites do not appear on the History tab, and temporary files and cookies are not saved on your computer.

Input device A piece of hardware that enables you to type, select, open, or otherwise interact with the computer. Common input devices include mice and keyboards. However, your finger can be an input device, and there are several specialty input devices for people with disabilities.

Instant messaging A way to communicate that is similar to email but is instantaneous—the recipient gets the message right after you send it. It is a real-time electronic communication system that you can use to "chat" and interact in other ways with other people by typing in a window on your computer screen. Instant messaging is the term generally reserved for text communications between two or more computers; text messaging is a term generally referring to communication between two cell phones. You can send instant messages with the Messaging app.

Integrated services digital network (ISDN) A high-speed digital technology that uses existing telephone lines to provide Internet access.

Interface What you see on the screen when working in a window. In the WordPad interface, you see the ribbon, tabs, and the page itself, for instance.

Internal peripheral A device installed inside the computer's case, such as an expansion card, a hard disk drive, or a DVD drive. See also *external peripheral* and *peripheral device*.

Internet Explorer 10 The newest version of the Microsoft web browser. It's available as an app and as a traditional desktop version.

Internet Message Access Protocol (IMAP) A method computers use to send and receive email messages. It allows you to access email without downloading it to your computer.

Internet Protocol (IP) address An address that identifies a computer that is connected to the Internet or to a network. There are two types of IP addresses: IP version 4 (IPv4) and IP version 6 (IPv6). An IPv4 address usually consists of four groups of numbers separated by periods, such as 192.200.44.69. An IPv6 address has eight groups of hexadecimal characters (the numbers 0–9 and the letters A–H) separated by colons—for example, 3ffe:ffff:0000:2f3b: 02aa:00ff:fe28:9c5a.

Internet server A computer that stores data offsite, such as one that might store your email before you download it or hold backups you store in the cloud. Through Internet servers, you can access information from any computer that can access the Internet.

Internet service provider (ISP) A company that provides Internet access to individuals or companies. An ISP provides the connection information necessary for users to access the Internet through the ISP's computers. An ISP typically charges a monthly or hourly connection fee.

JPEG (.jpg) file format A digital image file format designed for compressing either full-color or gray-scale still images. It works well on photographs, naturalistic artwork, and similar material. Images saved in this format have .jpg or .jpeg file extensions.

Jump list In the recently opened programs list or pinned items area of the Start menu, an efficient method of accessing the features and files you are most likely to use with a program. Pointing to a right-pointing arrow associated with the program in either location displays a list of tasks and recently opened files.

Kbps Kilobits per second; a unit of data transfer equal to 1,000 bits per second or 125 bytes per second.

Keyword A word or phrase assigned to a file or webpage so that it can be located in searches for that word or phrase.

Kilobyte (KB) 1,024 bytes of data storage. In reference to data transfer rates, 1,000 bytes.

Laptop An outdated term for a portable computer, referring to the fact that portable computers are small enough to set on your lap. See also **netbook**, **notebook**, and **portable computer**.

Library A virtual data unit that offers access to both the related private and public folders. As an example, the Documents library offers access to the My Documents and Public Documents folders, and the data is grouped to appear as a unit. You can separate the data if desired.

Link A shortcut to a webpage. It might be contained in an email, document, or webpage and offers access to a site without actually typing the site's name.

Local area network (LAN) A computer network covering a small physical area, like a home or office, with a central connection point such as a network router and a shared Internet connection.

Local printer A printer that is directly connected to one of the ports on a computer. See also **remote printer**.

Lock To make your Windows computing session unavailable to other people. Locking is most effective when your user account is protected by a password.

Lock screen The Windows 8 welcome screen, which appears when the computer first starts. It features the time, date, and a series of notification glyphs; the screen can be personalized with your own background picture and the glyphs shown.

Log off To stop your computing session without affecting other users' sessions.

Log on To start a computing session.

Magnifier A tool in the Ease of Access suite of applications. You use Magnifier to increase the size of the information shown on the screen; three options are available for doing so. By default, you use your mouse to enlarge what's under it, and you can choose to what degree the material is magnified.

Mail server A computer that your ISP configures to transmit email. It often includes a POP3 incoming mail server and an SMTP outgoing mail server. You'll need to know the names of these servers if you use an ISP to configure Mail. Often, the server names look similar to *pop.yourispnamehere. com* and *smtp.yourispnamehere.com*.

Malware Malicious software. Malware includes viruses, worms, spyware, and so on.

Mbps Megabits per second; a unit of data transfer equal to 1,000 Kbps (kilobits per second).

Media Materials on which data is recorded or stored, such as CDs, DVDs, floppy disks, or USB flash drives.

Megabyte (MB) 1,024 kilobytes or 1,048,576 bytes of data storage; often interpreted as approximately 1 million bytes. In reference to data transfer rates, 1,000 kilobytes.

Menu A title on a menu bar (such as File, Edit, View). Clicking a menu name opens a drop-down list with additional choices (Open, Save, Print). Menus are being phased out by the ribbon in many applications, including those included with Windows 8, such as WordPad and Paint, among others.

Menu bar A toolbar from which you can access menus of commands.

Metadata Descriptive information, including keywords and properties, about a file or webpage. Title, subject, author, and size are examples of a file's metadata.

Modem A device that allows computer information to be transmitted and received over a telephone line or through a broadband service such as cable or DSL.

Multi-monitor A term used when more than one monitor is configured on a Windows 8–based computer. There are multi-monitor capabilities that are new to Windows 8, for both the Start screen and the classic Windows desktop.

Multi-touch gestures Gestures that require two (or more) fingers to perform, such as pinching to zoom in and out of the computer screen.

Narrator A basic screen reader included with Windows 8 and part of the Ease of Access suite of applications. This application will read aloud text that appears on the screen while you navigate using the keyboard and mouse.

Navigate A term used to describe surfing the Internet by browsing webpages. It is the process of moving from one webpage to another or viewing items on a single webpage.

Navigation pane In Windows Explorer, the left pane of a folder window. It displays favorite links, libraries, and an expandable list of drives and folders.

NET Passport See **Windows Live ID**.

Netbook A small, lightweight portable computer designed primarily for web browsing and simple computing. Most netbooks have a 1.6 GHz processor and a screen size of less than 11 inches.

Network A group of computers, printers, and other devices that communicate wirelessly or through wired connections, often for the purpose of sharing both data and physical resources (such as printers). Networks often contain routers, cable modems, hubs, switches, or similar hardware to connect the computers and offer them all access to the Internet.

Network adapter A piece of hardware that connects your computer to a network such as the Internet or a local network. Network adapters can offer wired capabilities, wireless capabilities, or both.

Network and Sharing Center A place in Windows 8 where you can view your basic network information and set up connections. You can also diagnose problems here, change adapter settings, and change advanced sharing settings.

Network discovery A feature that must be enabled so computers can find other computers on the network. When connected to public networks, this feature is disabled by default.

Network domain A network whose security and settings are centrally administered through Windows Server computer and user accounts.

Network drive A shared folder or drive on your network to which you assign a drive letter so that it appears in the Computer window as a named drive.

Network hub A device used to connect computers on a network. The computers are connected to the hub with cables. The hub sends information received from one computer to all other computers on the network.

Network printer A printer that is connected directly to a network through a wired (Ethernet) or wireless network connection or through a print server or printer hub.

Network profile Information about a specific network connection, such as the network name, type, and settings.

Network router A hardware device connecting computers on a network or connecting multiple networks (for example, connecting a LAN to an ISP).

Network share A shared folder on a computer on your network (not your local computer).

Notebook A standard portable computer designed for all types of computing. Notebooks have technical specifications that are comparable to those of desktop computers. Most notebooks have a screen size ranging from 11 to 17 inches.

Notification area The area at the right end of the Windows Taskbar. It contains shortcuts to programs and important status information.

Newsgroup An online forum in which people participate (anonymously or not) to share ideas and opinions, get help, and meet other people with interests similar to theirs.

Notification area The rightmost area of the taskbar. It includes the clock, network status, battery status, and volume icon and holds icons for applications that are running in the background.

Online Connected to a network or to the Internet. Also used to describe time that you will be working on your computer.

On-Screen Keyboard A feature that is available as part of Windows 8 that enables you to input text and interact with the computer by using a virtual keyboard.

Operating system The underlying programs that tell your computer what to do and how to do it. The operating system coordinates interactions among the computer system components, acts as the interface between you and your computer, enables your computer to communicate with other computers and peripheral devices, and interacts with programs installed on your computer.

Option One of a group of mutually exclusive values for a setting, usually in a dialog box.

Option button A standard Windows control that you use to select one from a set of options.

Original equipment manufacturer (OEM) A company that assembles a computer from components, brands the computer, and then sells the computer to the public. The OEM might also preinstall an operating system and other software on the computer.

Parallel port The input/output connector for a parallel interface device. Some types of printers connect to the computer through a parallel port.

Partition A hard drive has a certain amount of space to store data. That can be 120 GB, 500 GB, or 1 or 2 TB. Sometimes people or computer manufacturers separate this space into two or three distinct spaces called partitions (or drives or volumes). The purpose is to separate system files, data files, and application files, among other reasons. Windows 8 creates a small partition at the beginning of the hard disk to hold files needed to repair the computer if something goes wrong.

Password A security feature in which the user is required to input a personal password to access the computer, specific files, websites, and other data.

Password hint An entry you record when you create or change your password to remind you what the password is. Windows displays the password hint if you enter an incorrect password.

Password reset disk A file you create on a flash drive or floppy disk to enable you to reset your password if you forget it.

Path A sequence of names of drives, directories, or folders, separated by backslashes (\), that leads to a specific file or folder.

Paste To place previously copied or cut data in a new location. You can cut, copy, and paste a single word, sentence, paragraph, or page; a file; a folder; a web link; and more.

PC Settings A pared-down Control Panel that offers access to the most-configured settings, including changing the picture on the Lock screen, adding users, viewing installed devices, and configuring Windows Update.

Peek To see what's on the desktop behind open windows and applications. To use Peek, you position your mouse in the bottom-right corner. Peek must be enabled to work.

Peer-to-peer A network, such as a workgroup, where computers and resources are connected directly and are not centrally managed by a server.

Peripheral device A device, such as a disk drive, printer, modem, or joystick, that is connected to a computer and is controlled by the computer's microprocessor but is not necessary to the computer's operation. See also **external peripheral** and **internal peripheral**.

Permissions Rules associated with a shared resource, such as a folder, file, or printer, that define who can use it and what he or she can do after he or she has access to it. You can set permissions to allow a user to print to a printer only during certain hours, for instance.

Personal folder In Windows, a storage folder created by Windows for each user account and containing subfolders and information that is specific to the user profile, such as Documents and Pictures. The personal folder is labeled with the name used to log on to the computer.

Phishing A hacking technique to entice you to divulge personal information such as bank account numbers. Internet Explorer 10 has a phishing filter to warn you of potential phishing websites.

Picture password A new method of logging on to Windows 8. Instead of typing a password or PIN, you can use a series of touch gestures on a particular part of a photo that you select.

PIN password A new method of logging on to Windows 8. The PIN is similar to what you type in an ATM machine and is a four-digit numeric password.

Pinned taskbar button A button representing a program, which appears permanently at the left end of the taskbar. A button that is not pinned appears only when its program is running.

Pinning Attaching a program, folder, or file shortcut to a user interface element such as the taskbar.

Playlist A group of songs that you can save and then listen to as a group. You can also burn a playlist to a CD, copy a playlist to a portable music player, and more.

Plug and play A technology that enables the computer to automatically discover and configure settings for a device connected to the computer through a USB or IEEE 1394 connection.

Podcast An online audio or video broadcast. Podcasts are generally free and can be synced to many types of portable music devices.

Pointer The onscreen image that moves around the screen when you move your mouse. Depending on the current action, the pointer might resemble an arrow, a hand, an I-beam, or another shape.

Pointing device A device such as a mouse that controls a pointer with which you can interact with items displayed on the screen.

POP3 A standard method that computers use to send and receive email messages. POP3 messages are typically held on an email server until you download them to your computer, and then they are deleted from the server. With other email protocols, such as IMAP, email messages are held on the server until you delete them.

POP3 server name The name of the mail server you use to receive your email from your ISP. You must type this server name when configuring email accounts if the email program doesn't know them already.

Pop-up window (pop-up) A small web browser window that opens on top of (or sometimes below) the web browser window when you display a website or click an advertising link.

Port An interface through which data is transferred between a computer and other devices, a network, or a direct connection to another computer.

Portable computer A computer, such as a notebook or netbook, with a built-in monitor, keyboard, and pointing device, designed to be used in multiple locations. See also ***desktop computer***.

Portable Network Graphic (.png) A digital image file format that uses lossless compression (compression that doesn't lose data) and was created as a patent-free alternative to the .gif file format.

Power button The button in the lower-right corner of the Windows Start menu that carries out the default shut-down option. Clicking the Shut-down Options button (the arrow to the right of the

Power button) displays a menu from which you can choose a nondefault shut-down action. See also *shut-down options*.

Power plan A group of settings that denote when and whether to turn off the computer monitor or display and when or whether to put the computer to sleep. You can create your own power plan if desired.

Preview pane In Windows Explorer, a pane used to show a preview of a file selected in the Content pane. See also *Content pane*, *Details pane*, and *Navigation pane*.

Primary display In a multiple-monitor system, the monitor that displays the Welcome screen and task-bar. Most program windows appear on the primary display when they first open. See also *secondary display*.

Product key A unique registration code issued by the manufacturer of a program. The key must be supplied during the setup process to verify that you have a valid license to install and use the program.

Progress ring The new Windows 8 progress indicator that informs the user that a task is in progress.

Public folder Folders from which you can easily share data with other users. Anyone with an account on the computer can access the data here.

Quick Access toolbar The small, thin toolbar that appears across the top of the ribbon in many applications and that enables you to quickly access common commands (such as Save). You can personalize this toolbar by adding your most-used commands and by repositioning it below the ribbon if desired.

RAM Acronym for *random access memory*. It is the hardware inside your computer that temporarily stores data the operating system or programs are using. Theoretically, the more RAM you have, the faster your computer will run. Temporary data can include a document you have written but not saved and have subsequently sent to the printer, or calculations required when resizing or otherwise editing a photo.

ReadyBoost A technology that enables you to improve the performance of your computer by adding additional paging file space. ReadyBoost increases performance in a way that is similar to adding internal RAM, but ReadyBoost is not RAM. Often, you use an external USB flash drive or a secure digital memory card for this.

Really Simple Syndication (RSS) A method of distributing information from a website or blog to subscribers for display in an RSS reader or aggregator.

Recycle Bin The Recycle Bin holds deleted files until you manually empty it. The Recycle Bin is a safeguard and enables you to recover items you've accidentally deleted or items you thought you no longer wanted but later decide you need. Note that after you empty the Recycle Bin, the items in it are gone forever.

Refresh Your PC This is a new service in Windows 8 that, when invoked, automatically backs up all your photos, music, videos, and other personal files, reinstalls your PC with new operating system files, and then puts your data back on it for you. It also backs up and restores your customizations, changes you've made to apps, and more. It enables you to completely reinstall Windows and then easily put your data back on your machine. This process takes only four to five minutes.

Registry A repository for information about the computer's configuration. The registry stores settings related to the hardware and software installed on the computer. Registry settings are typically updated through the proper install and uninstall procedures and programs. You can manually update the registry, but only experienced users should undertake this task because mistakes can be disastrous.

Relative path A path that defines the position of a file or folder in relation to the current location. For example, ..\Images\MyPicture.png defines a path up one level to the parent folder of the current location, down one level into the Images folder, to the MyPicture image. Relative paths are frequently used in website navigational code.

Remote Desktop Connection A program included in Windows 8 by which you can access your computer from somewhere else, such as an office or hotel room.

Remote printer A printer that is not connected directly to your computer.

Reset Your PC A new service in Windows 8 that returns your PC to its factory settings. It does this by wiping all the data from it and reinstalling Windows, after which the computer will appear as it did the first time you turned it on, right out of the box.

Resolution How many pixels are shown on a computer screen. A pixel is a very small square unit of display. Choosing 1280 × 768 pixels means that the desktop is shown to you with 1280 pixels across and 768 pixels down. When you increase the resolution, you increase the number of pixels on the screen, making images sharper and making everything on the screen appear smaller.

Restore point A snapshot of your computer system settings taken by Windows at a scheduled time as well as before any major change, such as installing a program or updating system files. If you experience problems with your system, you can restore it to any saved restore point without undoing changes to your personal files.

Ribbon A feature that appeared in Microsoft Office programs a few years ago and is now part of the Windows 8 graphical user interface. The ribbon contains tabs that, when selected, show a related set of tools and features underneath. The ribbon replaces the older menu bar, menus, and drop-down menu lists.

Right-click To point to an interface element and press the secondary mouse button one time.

Rip A term that describes the process of copying files from a physical CD to your hard drive. Generally, the term is used to describe the process of copying music CDs to the music library on your computer.

Router A piece of equipment that connects two dissimilar networks and sends data from computer to computer on a local area network. A router routes the data to the correct PC and rejects data that is deemed harmful.

Screen resolution The fineness or coarseness of detail attained by a monitor in producing an image, measured in pixels, expressed as the number of pixels wide by the number of pixels high. For example, 1024 × 768. See also *pixel*.

Screen saver A screen saver is a picture or animation that covers your screen and appears after your computer has been idle for a specific amount of time that you set. You can configure your screen saver to require a password on waking up for extra security.

ScreenTip Information that appears when you point to an item.

Scroll bar A scroll bar appears when what is available to show on the screen is more than can be viewed on it. You'll see a scroll bar on the Start screen, on webpages, in long documents, and in other places.

Scroll up and scroll down A process of using the mouse, the arrow keys on a keyboard, or a flick of your finger to scroll when a scroll bar is available.

Search A Windows 8 feature that provides searching capabilities. You can use this feature to search through apps, settings, files, emails, and more. Search is available as a charm, available from the right side of the screen when called on.

Search provider A company that provides a search engine, which you can use to find information on the web.

Search term The term you type in the Search box of the Start menu or any folder window. Windows then filters the contents of the available storage locations or of the folder window's Content pane to include only the items that contain the search term.

Secondary display In a multiple-monitor system, the monitor onto which you can expand programs so that you can increase your work area. See also **primary display**.

Secondary tile A special kind of Start screen tile that is created from inside an app capable of producing one. For example, a contacts app can have its own tile, but you can also create a tile for your favorite contact on the Start screen.

Semantic zoom The technical term for the technology that enables you to pinch with two fingers to zoom in and out of the screen.

Shared component A component, such as a DLL file, that is used by multiple programs. When uninstalling a program that uses a shared component, Windows requests confirmation before removing the component.

Shared drive A drive that has been made available for other people on a network to access.

Shared folder A folder that has been made available for other people on a network to access.

Shared printer A printer connected to a computer and made available from that computer for use by other computers on a network.

Share A charm that is available from the right side of the screen that enables you to share information in one app with another app and, possibly, with other people (by Mail, for instance). This charm can also make local files or resources available to other users of the same computer or other computers on a network.

Shortcut An icon with an arrow on it that offers access to a particular item on the hard disk drive. You can put shortcuts on your desktop, for instance, that, when double-clicked, open programs, files, and folders stored in places other than the desktop.

Shortcut menu A menu displayed when you right-click an object, showing a list of commands relevant to that object.

Shut down To initiate the process that closes all your open programs and files, ends your computing session, closes network connections, stops system processes, stops the hard disk, and turns off the computer.

Shut-down options Ways in which you can disconnect from the current computing session. You can shut down the computer, switch to a different user account, log off from the computer, lock the computer, restart the computer, or put the computer into Sleep mode or Hibernate mode.

Simple Mail Transfer Protocol (SMTP) A protocol for sending messages from one computer to another on a network. This protocol is used on the Internet to route email.

SkyDrive A location in the cloud offered by Microsoft where you can store data, including documents and pictures, among other things. Data you save are saved on Internet servers, enabling you to access the data from an Internet-enabled compatible device.

SMTP server name The name of the computer that you use to send email using your ISP. You will be required to enter this information manually when setting up your email address if Windows can't find the information on its own.

SmartScreen A Windows 8 security technology that prevents malware from infecting your system.

Snap The process by which two apps can be displayed side by side in Windows 8. One app takes up about a third of the screen, and the other takes up the rest. This enables you to work with two apps at one time.

Snipping tool A feature in Windows 8 by which you can drag your cursor around any area on the screen to copy and capture it. You can then save the captured data to edit it or attach it to an email.

Software Programs that you use to do things with hardware.

Software piracy The illegal reproduction and distribution of software applications.

Sound card Hardware that enables audio information and music to be recorded, played back, and heard on a computer.

Sound recorder A tool included with Windows 8 that offers three options: Start Recording, Stop Recording, and Resume Recording. You can save recorded clips for use with other programs.

Spam Unwanted email; junk email.

Speech Recognition A program included with Windows 8 by which you control your computer with your voice. Speech Recognition provides a wizard to help you set up your microphone and use the program.

Spyware Software that can display advertisements (such as pop-up ads), collect information about you, or change settings on your computer, generally without appropriately obtaining your consent.

Standard toolbar A toolbar that is often underneath a menu bar in applications that do not offer a ribbon, which contains icons or pictures of common commands. You might already be famIllar with the graphic icons for Save, Print, Cut, Copy, Paste, Undo, and others. These toolbars are being phased out and are being replaced by the ribbon.

Standard user account A type of Windows user account that allows the user to install software and change system settings that do not affect other users or the security of the computer. This account type is recommended for daily use.

Start screen The new Windows 8 graphical user experience that offers access to apps, desktop programs, the desktop itself, and more. You can type while at the Start screen to locate something on it or elsewhere on your computer.

Status bar A toolbar that often appears at the bottom of an application window (such as the desktop version of Internet Explorer 10) and offers information about what is happening at the moment.

Sticky Keys A setting by which you can configure the keyboard so that you never have to press three keys at once (such as when you must press the Ctrl, Alt, and Delete keys together to access Task Manager).

Store See **Windows Store**.

Subfolder A folder inside another folder. You often create subfolders to further organize data that is stored in folders.

Sync To compare data in one location to the data in another. Syncing is the act of performing the tasks required to match up the data. When data is synced, the data in both places matches.

System cache An area in the computer memory where Windows stores information it might need to access quickly for the duration of the current computing session.

Ssystem disk The hard disk on which the operating system is installed.

System folder A folder created on the system disk that contains files required by the Windows operating system.

System Restore If enabled, this features creates and stores restore points on your computer or device's hard disk drive. If something goes wrong, you can run System Restore and revert to a pre-problem date by selecting the desired point in time. System Restore deals with system data only, so none of your personal data will be changed when you run the program.

Tab In a dialog box, tabs indicate separate pages of settings within the dialog box window; the tab title indicates the nature of the group. You can display the settings by clicking the tab. In Internet Explorer, when tabbed browsing is turned on, tabs indicate separate webpages displayed within one browser window. You can display a page by clicking its tab or display a shortcut menu of options for working with a page by right-clicking its tab.

Tabbed browsing An Internet Explorer feature that enables you to open and view multiple webpages or files by displaying them on different tabs. You can easily switch among pages or files by clicking the tabs.

Tags Metadata included with a file, such as the date a photo was taken or the artist who sang a particular song. You can create your own tags in compatible programs and then sort data by using those tags.

Tap (Touch) A gesture you perform with your finger or a pen or stylus. A tap or touch is often the equivalent of a single left-click with a mouse.

Taskbar The bar that runs horizontally across the bottom of the Windows 8 desktop. It contains icons for running programs, your user folder, and Internet Explorer, and offers the Notification area, among other things. You can access open files, folders, and applications from the taskbar, too.

Taskbar button A button on the taskbar representing an open window, file, or program. See also **pinned taskbar button**.

Task Manager A way to access, manage, stop, or start running applications, processes, and services. You often use Task Manager to close something that has stopped working and is unresponsive, such as a program or process.

Task pane A fixed pane that appears on one side of a program window, which contains options related to the completion of a specific task.

Theme A set of visual elements and sounds that applies a unified look to the computer user interface. A theme can include a desktop background, screen saver, window colors, and sounds. Some themes might also include icons and mouse pointers.

Tiles Graphical user interface elements on the Windows 8 Start screen. Tiles can be small (square) or large (rectangular). Some can offer live information, such as the news headlines or the number of unread emails. Tiles are said to be pinned to the Start screen.

Title bar The horizontal area at the top of a window that displays the title of the program or file displayed in the window and buttons for controlling the display of the window.

Toolbar A horizontal or vertical bar that displays buttons representing commands that can be used with the content of the current window. When more commands are available than can fit on the toolbar, a chevron (>>) appears at the right end of the toolbar; clicking the chevron displays the additional commands.

Transition A segue you can configure to appear when moving from one picture to another in a slide show, such as fading in or out. Transitions can be applied in other places, too, such as in PowerPoint presentations.

Uniform Resource Locator (URL) An address that uniquely identifies the location of a website or webpage. A URL is usually preceded by http://, as in *http://www.microsoft.com*. URLs are used by web browsers to locate Internet resources.

Universal Naming Convention (UNC) A system for identifying the location on a network of shared resources such as computers, drives, and folders. A UNC address is in the form of \\ComputerName\SharedFolder.

Universal Serial Bus (USB) A connection that provides data transfer capabilities and power to a peripheral device. See also **USB hub** and **USB port**.

Upgrade To replace older hardware with newer hardware or an earlier version of a program with the current version.

USB flash drive A portable flash memory card that plugs into a computer's USB port. You can store data on a USB flash drive or, if the USB flash drive supports ReadyBoost, use all or part of the available drive space to increase the operating system speed. See also ***ReadyBoost***.

USB hub A device used to connect multiple USB devices to a single USB port or to connect one or more USB devices to USB ports on multiple computers. The latter type of USB hub, called a sharing hub, operates as a switch box to give control of the hub-connected devices to one computer at a time.

USB port A connection that provides both power and data transfer capabilities to a hardware device.

User account On a Windows computer, a uniquely named account that allows an individual to gain access to the system and to specific resources and settings. Each user account includes a collection of information that describes the way the computer environment looks and operates for that particular user, as well as a private folder not accessible by other people using the computer, in which personal documents, pictures, media, and other files can be stored. See also ***administrator account*** and ***standard user account***.

User Account Control (UAC) A Windows security feature that allows or restricts actions by the user and the system to prevent malicious programs from damaging the computer.

User account name A unique name identifying a user account to Windows.

User account picture An image representing a user account. User account pictures are available only for computer-specific user accounts and not on computers that are members of a network domain.

User interface (UI) The portion of a program with which a user interacts. Types of user interfaces include command-line interfaces, menu-driven interfaces, and graphical user interfaces.

Video projector A device that projects a video signal from a computer onto a projection screen by using a lens system.

Virtual A software system that acts as if it were a hardware system. Examples are virtual folders (called libraries) and virtual printers.

Virtual printer A program that "prints" content to a file rather than on paper. When viewed in the file, the content looks as it would if it were printed.

Virus A self-replicating program that infects computers with intent to do harm. Viruses can come as an attachment in an email, from a USB stick, from a macro in a Microsoft Office program, through a network connection, and even in instant messages.

Visualizations Designs produced by Windows Media Player that are graphical representations of the music you play.

Wallpaper The picture that appears on the desktop. Windows 8 comes with several options, but you can use your own picture(s) or graphics if desired.

Web An abbreviation of *World Wide Web*. A worldwide network consisting of millions of smaller networks that exchange data.

Web browser A software program that displays webpage content and enables you to interact with webpage content and navigate the Internet. Internet Explorer is a web browser.

Webcam A camera that can send live images over the Internet. Windows 8 comes with a camera app that should be able to find and use your camera without any setup.

Website A webpage or a group of webpages that contain related information. The Microsoft website contains information about Microsoft products, for instance.

Window Programs, documents, pictures, videos, folders, and so on open a window of their own. Window, as it is used here, has nothing to do with the name of the operating system Windows 8; it is a generic term. Windows have minimize, restore, and maximize buttons so you can resize them.

Windows Defender A built-in tool that provides antivirus and antimalware functionality.

Windows Experience Index A Windows utility that assesses a computer system and assigns a base score that reflects the lowest of a set of subscores for the processor, memory, graphics card, and hard disk.

Windows Live ID An email address, registered with the Windows Live ID authentication service, that identifies you to sites and services that use Windows Live ID authentication.

Windows Firewall If enabled, the firewall should lessen the ability of unauthorized users to access your computer or device and its data. The firewall blocks the programs that can be a threat. You can allow programs through the firewall or create exceptions if the need arises.

Windows Media Center A full-fledged media and media management application. You can view and manage photos, music, videos, and even television here. This is not included with Windows 8 by default; it is an add-on.

Windows Store The Microsoft online store for Windows 8 apps. You can also shop for music, videos, and more.

Windows To Go A way to run Windows 8 from a USB key (or something similar) rather than from a traditional hard disk drive. This enables you to take Windows anywhere.

Windows Update When set to use the recommended settings, Windows 8 checks for security updates automatically and installs them. You can choose which optional updates to install.

Wizard A tool that walks you through the steps necessary to accomplish a particular task.

Workgroup A peer-to-peer computer network through which computers can share resources, such as files, printers, and Internet connections.

XML Paper Specification (XPS) A digital file format for saving documents. XPS is based on XML, preserves document formatting, and enables file sharing. XPS was developed by Microsoft but is platform-independent and royalty-free.

Index

contextual menu. *See also* right-click
    for SkyDrive, 182
contiguous files, selecting, 132
Continue option, for restart, 604
Control Panel, , 35–42
    adding shortcut to Start screen, 554–555
    Appearance and Personalization, 68–69
    changing defaults for programs, file types and
        AutoPlay, 595
    Ease Of Access, 488, 490
    Hardware and Sound
        View devices and printers, 379
        Windows Mobility Center, 511
    Hardware And Sound, 544
    Network and Internet, Network and Sharing
        Center, 282
    Power Options, 70–71
    Programs
        Programs and Features, 568
    Settings charm to access, 14
    System and Security
        File History, 436
        System, 271, 441
        Windows Update, 424, 425
    User Accounts and Family Safety, , 309, 3
conversation, starting in Messaging app, 223–226
copy and paste operation, in File Explorer, 128
cost of apps, 239
CPU
    Task Manager information on usage, 620
    usage in idle computer, 619
Create A Picture Password Wizard, 326
Create A PIN Wizard, 332
Create Playlist command in Windows Media Player,
    252
Ctrl+Alt+Del, for Task Manager, 589, 617
Ctrl key, for selecting noncontiguous files, 132
Ctrl+Shift+Esc, to launch Task Manager, 589
Curfew window, 463
currency format, for Windows 8 install, 651
Current Profile statement, 351
Cursor Thickness option, 487
Customize your lock screen and notifications option,
    37

customizing
    Advanced settings, 68–69
    desktop, 60–62
    libraries, 142–147
    Lock screen, 52–55
    Start screen, 48–51
        with live tiles, 10–12
    user account settings, 57–59
cut operation, in File Explorer, 128
cycling through open apps, 628

D

Date And Time window, 559
decrypting drive encrypted with BitLocker, 530–531
default libraries, viewing personal folders in, 125
default logon user, 565
default network sharing settings, 350–355
default power scheme, 43
default save location, 147
default settings
    changing for programs, file extensions, and
        autoplay dialog boxes, 595–599
    restoring Windows Firewall to, 409–410
Default sound scheme, 67
default user account, 305
default version of Internet Explorer, setting, 170–173
defragmenting
    disk drives, 573–575
Delete Account window, 343
deleted files, and Recycle Bin, 147–149
deleting
    active messaging thread, 222
    Calendar event, 216
    contacts in People app, 214
    email message, 197
    file in File Explorer, 130
    files with Disk Cleanup, 577
    items from SkyDrive, 182
    libraries, 146
    picture, 81
    shortcuts, 553
    user accounts, 342–346

About the Authors

CIPRIAN ADRIAN RUSEN is a technology aficionado and former IT project manager for a major consumer goods corporation. In his spare time, he likes to experiment with the latest technologies, learning how to use them and sharing his knowledge with others. He coordinates the team of bloggers at 7 Tutorials, writing tutorials for Windows users and helping them achieve the best possible computing experience. He is also the author of *Network Your Computers and Devices Step by Step* from Microsoft Press.

JOLI BALLEW is a Microsoft MVP for Windows and holds many Microsoft certifications, including MCSE, MCTS, MCDST, and MCT. She is an award-winning, best-selling technical author of almost 50 books. Joli has been working with computers, gadgets, and all things media since her freshman year in college in 1982, where, even then, she was aware of her interests and strengths and majored in computer science and systems analysis. Joli is the Microsoft IT Academic Coordinator at Brookhaven College in Dallas, Texas, where she also teaches. Among the many titles Joli has written for Microsoft Press, she is the co-author of *MCTS Self-Paced Training Kit (Exam 70-632): Managing Projects with Microsoft Office Project 2007.*

How To Download Your eBook

Thank you for purchasing this Microsoft Press® title. Your companion PDF eBook is ready to download from O'Reilly Media, official distributor of Microsoft Press titles.

To download your eBook, go to

http://go.microsoft.com/FWLink/?Linkid=224345

and follow the instructions.

Please note: You will be asked to create a free online account and enter the access code below.

Your access code:

JDXMBDG

Windows® 8 Step by Step

Your PDF eBook allows you to:

- Search the full text
- Print
- Copy and paste

Best yet, you will be notified about free updates to your eBook.

If you ever lose your eBook file, you can download it again just by logging in to your account.

Need help? Please contact:
mspbooksupport@oreilly.com
or call 800-889-8969.

WITHDRAWN

What do you think of this book?

We want to hear from you!
To participate in a brief online survey, please visit:

29.99   2/18/13.

Tell us h   ly, and what we can
do bette   s and learning
resource

Thank y

Microsoft®
Press